DATE DUE

THE MYTH OF
THE MADDING CROWD

SOCIAL INSTITUTIONS AND SOCIAL CHANGE

An Aldine de Gruyter Series of Texts and Monographs

Edited By

Michael Useem • James D. Wright

THE MYTH OF
THE MADDING CROWD

Clark McPhail

ALDINE DE GRUYTER
New York

About the Author

Clark McPhail is Associate Professor of Sociology, University of Illinois at Urbana-Champaign. His studies on social psychology, on individual and collective actions in prosaic, religious, sport, and political gatherings, and his work on the peer review of and editorial decision on scholarly manuscripts have been widely published.

ALDINE DE GRUYTER
A division of Walter de Gruyter, Inc.
200 Saw Mill River Road
Hawthorne, New York 10532

The paper used in this publication meets the minimum requirements of American National Standard for Information Sciences—Permanence of Paper for Printed Library Materials, ANSI Z39.48-1984.

Library of Congress Cataloging-in-Publication Data
McPhail, Clark, 1936–
 The myth of the madding crowd/Clark McPhail.
  p.cm. — (Social institutions and social change)
 Includes bibliographical references and index.
 ISBN 0-202-30424-8 (cloth). — ISBN 0-202-30375-6 (pbk.)
 1. Collective behavior. 2. Crowds. I. Title. II. Series.
HM281.M39 1991
302.3'3—dc20   90-42787
                CIP

Manufactured in the United States of America

10 9 8 7 6 5 4 3 2 1

to Robert L. Stewart
mentor! colleague! critic!

Contents

Acknowledgments

I am grateful to the professors who introduced me to sociology (Charles J. Browning and Jack Dodson), to social psychology (Muzafer Sherif, Frederick Waisanen, Robert L. Stewart, and Arch Haller), to field work (Norman Jackman and John Useem), and to the study of collective behavior (Norman Jackman and Carl Couch).

I particularly thank Robert L. Stewart, with whom Charles Tucker and I began discussing assembling processes, violent and nonviolent collective action within gatherings, and dispersing processes following the 1968 Orangeburg Massacre.

I thank those colleagues who joined me in the early fieldwork in Orangeburg and Columbia (Bob Stewart and Charles Tucker), later in Charleston and Atlanta (Tom Burns, Edith Cobb, David Miller, Bob Pickens, Dick Smith, Bill Westbrook, and David Wyatt), and subsequently in Chicago and Urbana-Champaign (David Miller, Bob Pickens, Ernest Rigney, Dick Smith, and Ron Wohlstein).

I thank those doctoral students (David Miller, Dick Smith, Bob Pickens, Ernest Rigney and Ron Wohlstein) with and from whom I learned a great deal about human beings acting together.

Special thanks to John McCarthy and Ann McPhail for assistance and support during the fieldwork and archival data collection in Washington, DC.

The contributions of my companion and closest friend Ann McPhail are too longstanding and numerous to detail. But it is with enormous gratitude that I acknowledge her patience, constructive criticisms, and encouragement, all so essential to the continuation of this project, indeed to life itself.

I thank those colleagues who have read and commented on one or more unpublished papers, a few published papers, and undoubtedly too few drafts of the chapters that compose this book: Benigno Aguirre; Von Bakanic; Harvey Choldin; Carl Couch; William Feinberg; Peter Hall; Norris Johnson; Jerry Lewis; John Lofland; Lyn Lofland; Gary Marx; George McCall; Jim McKee; John McCarthy; Dan E. Miller; David L. Miller; David Snow;

Worth Summers; Merlin Taber. In particular, I thank Charles Tucker and Ron Wohlstein who read the entire manuscript in at least two drafts. Although I disagreed with some of their criticisms and did not follow all their suggestions, our discussions of the disputed issues made the manuscript a better one, despite the flaws that undoubtedly remain. I also thank Trev Leger, then Aldine de Gruyter's executive editor, for making the book a possibility, and managing editor Arlene Perazzini for making it a reality.

Portions of Chapter 1 were reprinted from "Blumer's Theory of Collective Behavior: The Development of Non-Symbolic Interaction Explanation." *The Sociological Quarterly* 30(3):401–423. Copyright © 1989, JAI Press. Reprinted with permission. This book also contains portions of "Purposive Collective Action." *American Behavioral Scientist* 34:81–94. Copyright © 1989. Reprinted with permission of Sage Publications.

Finally, I acknowledge again the continuing intellectual challenges and contributions of Robert L. Stewart. He directed my attention to the central problems which the book addresses; he has persistently but patiently reminded me to keep my eye on the ball; and he has set the highest standards, pragmatic ones, against which to measure progress. I am grateful for those reminders, and for the knowledge that we share the same problems. This book offers no solutions; it reports some steps in that direction.

Foreword

A most peculiar thing has happened. A few scholars of crowd behavior actually have begun to observe and describe systematically the empirical features of crowds. Disconcertingly, this represents a radical development in the annals of crowd analysis. Clark McPhail is the intellectual leader without peer in chronicling and categorizing temporary gatherings before trying to explain them. As a result, his accounts of their variable features have virtually no counterpart.[1]

The Myth of the Madding Crowd is McPhail's prolegomenon to his own, unfolding research agenda. In it he carefully evaluates the work of the most widely revered past theorists of the crowd. With charitable but relentless incisiveness, he reveals that most of those theorists made almost no attempt to observe crowds systematically, to isolate their main internal elements, nor to enumerate the central features that distinguish them from other human institutions. His critique culminates in an elaborate taxonomy of crowd dimensions that is derived—in an ongoing dialectic between evidence and category—from his own extensive efforts to observe a broad sample of crowds. It is precisely that taxonomy and the empirical detail on which it rests that provide him the critical perspective for evaluating the dominant theoretical accounts of crowd behavior.

McPhail's elegant critical labors raise an intriguing puzzle: How it is possible that earlier ideas about crowds have been so uncoupled from empirical detail about their nature? Its solution hinges, I think, on the crucial, if chronically disputed, issues of (1) the appropriate criteria for theoretical persuasiveness and (2) the pretheoretical categories of apprehension—questions to which McPhail has given much thought here and elsewhere. I will return to them after I nest the underlying assumptions of his analyses in the broader theoretical streams of the recent period, and position his research in the context of ongoing research communities, as I touch upon the main lines of his critique.

A Broad Theoretical Shift

The academic study of collective behavior, centering mostly on crowds, and the study of organized efforts to bring about social change, social movements, have been inextricably linked for American sociologists by the work of successive generations of successful "Chicago school" textbook writers. Beginning with Robert Park and Ernest Burgess' chapter in their several editions of *Introduction to the Science of Sociology,* followed by Herbert Blumer's often reprinted chapter on collective behavior and social movements, and carried into the modern period through three editions of Ralph Turner and Lewis Killian's *Collective Behavior,* scholars in this tradition have insisted on wedding the study of crowds and social movements. A distinctively American marriage, it was one not consummated in Europe, where theorists of the mob and those of social movements as historical actors spoke separate conceptual languages from different podiums.[2] It has, nevertheless, survived the major theoretical realignment that has occurred among researchers of social movements.[3]

It is now widely recognized that a fundamental shift in perspective occurred among scholars of social movements in the last several decades in the United States (Morris and Herring 1984). While debates remain about its substantive details, two central tenets of the newer approaches are the assumption of the normality of social movement phenomena, and its corollary, that the behavior of those participating in social movements can be accounted for conceptually as can any other behavior. Embracing these tenets allowed analysts of social movements access to the range of explanatory schemes available across other substantive sociological specialties. The ascendant resource mobilization perspectives, as these approaches came to be known (Jenkins 1983), generally relied on assumptions of means/ends rationality in analyzing the goal-seeking activity of social movements through series of planned strategic steps.[4] Observing social movements through such a lens leads to seeing many manifestations of crowd behavior as similarly calculated: marches, demonstrations, rallies, sit-ins, and the like are seen as rationally calculated attempts to achieve goals by other than orthodox political means (Tilly 1978).

Not surprisingly, the assumptions of the newer social-movement theorists are also reflected in recent research focusing primarily on crowds. For instance, both Benigno Aguirre's (1984) own work analyzing the elaborate social production necessary for creating massive crowds for Cuban revolutionary celebrations as well as his work with colleagues illustrating the group planning typically preceding streaking incidents and the socially structured pattern of dissemination of the fad across college and university campuses (Aguirre, Quarantelli, and Mendoza, 1988) portray behavior in temporary gatherings as to some extent structured, organized, and planned. So, too, McPhail's theoretical framework for understanding individual behavior in public settings, elaborated in Chapter 6, bears a strong resemblance to the means/ends rationality embedded in the resource mobilization formulations. He presents an orienting set of assumptions about how individual actors in interaction with others (friends, acquaintances, leaders, crowd organizers) in temporary gatherings make decisions about how to act. His perspective conceives actors as responsive to short-term purposive calculations about what to do next in such public settings. It is a theory of purposive self-control in temporary gatherings. The formulation stands in stark contrast to earlier formulations of individual behavior in crowds that saw it as controlled by crowd minds, predispositions to behave, or emergent norms.

McPhail views individual actors in temporary gatherings as cognitively capable of setting the terms of their own cooperation with attempts by others to direct them in concerted lines of action. To the extent that actors are amenable to such direction, highly complex forms of collective action are possible in temporary gatherings. So the intersection of rational means/ends calculations by both individual and corporate actors in temporary gatherings may account for many of the variable features of these events. His framework, as should be obvious, is far more compatible theoretically with recent social-movement scholarship than are other reformulations of crowd theory that continue to rely heavily on spontaneous, emotional images of crowds (e.g., Lofland 1981; Marx 1980).

Crowd Research

It is no exaggeration to assert that comparatively little original empirical work on crowds has been completed since 1945, that the bulk of it has been done in the last 15 years, and that very little of it has involved actual observation of what people do in public gatherings. And McPhail has done most of that work!

A "critical mass" of scholars and researchers necessary to the development of both the study of collective behavior and social movements was lacking until quite recently (Quarantelli and Weller 1974). A vigorous network of researchers has emerged around the study of social movements, but has in large part failed to materialize around the study of public gatherings. While collective-behavior scholarship has been plagued by conceptual confusion (Aguirre and Quarantelli 1983), research communities do not emerge and thrive simply as a result of the weight of their ideas. Success also depends importantly upon networks of scholars who are able to communicate with one another, their collective control of institutional research and training locations, and a steady flow of material support for their research (Mullins 1973; Shils 1980). It is in all of these that we can find the elements of an account of where crowd research has been accomplished as well its constant and continuing dearth.

The few bursts of earlier crowd research were fueled by public attention to cycles of lynchings and to several cycles of what came to be known as "civil disorders." For example, a brief increase in scholarly attention followed the public concern over the civil disturbances of the 1960s. Official interest provided some financial support, enabling researchers to gather systematic empirical evidence about who did what under what circumstances during the widespread looting and property destruction in many American cities (e.g., Berk and Aldrich 1972). Some of that work began to challenge the earlier conceptions of behavior in temporary gatherings that McPhail evaluates here. But the interest in these questions quickly subsided, as did the resources to support ongoing research. Nevertheless, this burst of work left many conceptual and methodological traces that were important to later developments. While a few scholars established careers in this arena, a critical mass of scholars communicating with one another around the issues raised by those events did not emerge.

However, two relatively coherent communities that have contributed important research on crowds did emerge. These are the disaster researchers and the protest event researchers. Each group established some continuous support and a few research training sites, but neither group made the direct observation of a *wide range* of temporary gatherings the center of its efforts. As a result, both groups contributed sporadically but importantly to the questions that are central to McPhail's agenda.

Major financial support for research on a very rare, but important, form of collective behavior has been available for the study of human behavior and social structure during natural disasters such as earthquakes and floods. A division of the National Science Foundation supports ongoing research centers devoted to these questions. Early centers at UCLA and Ohio State University, and more recently those at the University of Delaware and Texas A&M University have provided resources and training for disaster research. In fact, many of the few sociologists who have contributed to crowd research lately have been associated with one or another of these centers (e.g., Henry Quarantelli, Russell Dynes, Benigno Aguirre, Ralph Turner, Dennis Wenger, and their students). While these groups have widened our understanding of collective behavior during disasters, their scholarship of crowds has been typically incidental to their narrower, practical efforts.

The other emergent research community that has contributed to our understanding of behavior in temporary gatherings links the sociologists and social historians who utilize newspaper records to describe the extent and nature of public protest (Olzak 1989; Tarrow 1989). Charles Tilly (1981) has been an important intellectual leader of this community, and its opus has established many important insights about the social and spatial location, timing, social composition, and changing tactical repertoires of protest gatherings. This pioneering methodology has been widely adopted (Franzoni 1987), I believe, because it is far less expensive than direct observation of large numbers of protest events.

Since these researchers rely primarily on newspaper records of protest events, they are limited in their ability directly to address the character of individual and interactional behavior in protests that is open to systematic observation but is unremarked by journalists. The exclusive focus upon protest events also severely restricts the range of temporary gatherings that are the focus of research attention. As a result the work of this community treats only a small part of the range of temporary gatherings that are the focus of McPhail's agenda. Segments of this community have had access, for a time, to institutional training sites at SUNY Stony Brook and the University of Michigan, and more recently at the University of Arizona and Cornell University. Many of the younger researchers of protest events have been associated with one or another of these training centers (e.g., Doug McAdam and Craig Jenkins).

There are also many researchers of temporary gatherings who labor in isolation without the benefit of local networks of scholars to sustain their efforts.[5] Because the research community is small, the two main branches that sustain such work focus on only a small subset of such gatherings, and observation of large samples of temporary gatherings is incredibly labor intensive, the advancement of crowd studies has been hindered. But they have also been slowed by theoretical and conceptual deficiencies.

Armchair Theory

McPhail's review of the previously dominant accounts of crowd behavior makes painfully obvious that, at best, they are rooted in biased fragments of evidence and narrow samples of temporary gatherings. Rarely has an approximation of systematically derived samples of evidence of these events been offered to back up the broad generalizations that have been drawn about crowd behavior. Argument by strategically chosen example has typically represented the most sophisticated methodology. This long-held penchant for expostulating about crowds with little anchor in evidence of their form and variety has had two disastrous consequences for the advancement of our understanding of them.

First, theories of crowds have been found acceptable primarily for their qualities of "resonance." Alvin Gouldner (1970) persuasively reminded us that a theory has stronger appeal if it seems plausible—that is, if its central assumptions mesh with our most deeply held sentiments. Of course, our methodological norms counsel us to try to evaluate theories in concert with observations about social life. However, when we lack systematic evidence, plausibility must depend more on ideological and emotional resonance (which varies across time, place, and social group). It is not news that LeBon's ideas—embodying images of the "manipulated mob"—appealed to counterrevolutionary ideological sentiments, but it is also the case that Miller and Dollard's analysis of lynch mobs was widely admired because of its strong ideological appeal. Liberal social scientists found it attractive since the behavior of lynch mobs was characterized as irrational. The ideas resonated even though, as McPhail demonstrates, they were no more veridical in the face of records of observed lynch mob behavior than Lebon's ideas had been with regard to records of the crowds whose behavior he purported to explain.

Both scholars' personal experience in temporary gatherings during the 1960s and small increments of systematic research began to overcome some of the theoretical difficulties stemming from the previous lack of rootedness in evidence. Ralph Turner's insistence on the unanimity of crowd behavior constituting an "illusion," Carl Couch's devastating comparison of previous theoretical images of crowds with empirical accounts of them, Richard Berk's description and analysis of a number of contemporary crowd sequences, as well as the later analyses of systematic traces of crowd behavior by Charles Tilly and John Lofland were all important in setting the stage for a concerted collective move out of the armchair into the field. But McPhail tells this story in Chapters 3 and 4 far better than I can.

The earlier armchair theorizing also meant that the simplest, if possibly the most difficult, work of taxonomy of crowds and crowd behavior was for a long time seriously neglected and has only now just begun. McPhail strongly believes that explaining temporary gatherings before elucidating their form and variability is putting the cart before the horse. While the point—Robert Merton phrases it "naming the thing to be explained before trying to explain it"—may seem obvious to modern social scientists, the simple lesson has even yet to take wide hold among theorists of crowds.[6] Chapter 5 of *The Myth of the Madding Crowd* develops several classification schemes of crowd elements and, in various aggregate combinations, crowd types. McPhail has been busy at this project for some time now and, in my view, has made substantial progress. The results of his efforts have provided him the tools to accomplish many of the substantive contributions that are recorded in *Acting Together: The Organization of Crowds*.

Developing taxonomies of social elements is unsung labor in sociology as it is in other disciplines. Steven Jay Gould remarks that it "occupies a low status among the sciences because most people view the activity as a kind of glorified bookkeeping dedicated to pasting objects into preassigned spaces in nature's stamp album [But] "classifications are . . . theories of order, not simple records of nature. . . . [They] are actively imposed, not passively imbibed, they shape our thoughts and deeds in ways that we scarcely perceive because we view our categories as 'obvious' and 'natural'" (1990:73). Since most of us have very narrow personal experiences of temporary gatherings, our knowledge of them is heavily mediated. Creating categories of crowd elements and crowds is therefore crucial for beginning to understanding them. Clark McPhail has provided us with new categories for perceiving temporary gatherings. Debates about the adequacy of his classification schemes (their inclusiveness, elegance, appropriateness, hidden biases, etc.) await other researchers who are willing to sample the variety of crowds that he has and try their own hand at taxonomies to contain it. I do not know of another scholar who is now prepared to do so.

Bringing the Crowd Back In

Serious scholars of crowd behavior have recently pleaded for a reinvigoration of crowd studies in order to reemphasize the centrality of temporary gatherings to analyses of social-movement phenomena (Oliver 1989; Aguirre and Quarantelli 1990). These calls suggest that contemporary researchers of social movements have been inattentive to temporary gatherings, primarily because their theoretical perspectives blind them to the whole range of less routine behavior and social organizational forms that make up ongoing movements, and because the contributions of past scholars have been unfairly stigmatized. Instead, I think it is the lack of categorical tools to contain these forms of social life and the consequent inability to speak about their variation that has hampered the efforts of some of the most insightful scholars to "bring the crowd back in."

McPhail has created, inductively, a set of categories of collective behavior in-common (and in-concert) that allow him systematically to describe ever more complex temporary gatherings and to compare them with one another, categories that ultimately give him the tools to analyze the links between temporary gatherings and other forms of social-movement behavior. Temporary gatherings are preceded by assembling phases and followed by disassembling phases. Collective behavior in-common can include clustering, vigiling, booing, chanting, kneeling, and marching. As he puts it in Chapter 5, "Gatherings merely provide opportunities for various sequences of collective behavior to occur." Gatherings may be characterized by the aggregate substantive forms and sequences of collective behavior in gathering types such as rallies, marches, and pickets and ultimately into ever more complex demonstration events such as a combination march and rally. Aggregating these units of analysis over time and geographical scope allows the bounding and characterizing of campaigns and waves of collective behavior. It is difficult to overstate the comparative promise of these categories for helping to understand temporary gatherings. McPhail's use of them, displayed in his (1985) paper "The social organization of demonstrations," provides an opening glimpse of their great potential.

Clark McPhail has labored long and hard at overcoming the epistemological deficiencies of earlier crowd analyses, often without recognition of the cumulating impact of his efforts. *The Myth of the Madding Crowd* and *Acting Together: The Organization of Crowds* will firmly establish his pre-eminent place in thinking about and researching temporary gatherings. And I hope that, together, they will create a new enthusiasm for studying public assemblies among students of social behavior. If that excitement can be translated into structural and material support for an expansion of systematic research, then a new generation of crowd researchers may emerge. Following McPhail's lead, since he has provided us the tools, I trust that they will continue the vast project of chronicling what is going on in temporary gatherings—the mundane details as well as the dramatic moments—that he has begun. If enough scholars choose to follow McPhail's lead, the prevailing barrenness of the marriage between collective behavior and social movement studies may be finally overcome.

John D. McCarthy
Catholic University of America

Notes

1.   These are presented in intriguing, and many times counterintuitive, detail in his companion volume, *Acting Together: The Organization of Crowds.*

2.   Alberto Melucci (1990), an Italian theorist of the "new social movements," develops a perspective very much along the lines of the Chicago school of collective behavior. In it he transcends the traditional European disjunction between collective behavior and more routinized social movement phenomena.

3.   The connection is institutionalized in the Section on Collective Behavior and Social Movements of the American Sociological Association. Its many activities provide a mechanism for scholars who study both collective behavior and social movements to come together regularly to discuss their work.

4.   Means/ends rationality should be clearly distinguished from the rationality attributed to actors who calculate the potential costs and rewards of particular behaviors and lines of action. The strategic rationality of collective actors aims at best deciding how to achieve, with limited information, group ends. Such calculations may be based on diverse logics, including but not limited to individual actors' calculations of potential costs and rewards. The appropriateness of the latter form of rationality for understanding social movements remains the subject of continuing debate. The usefulness of the former has been rarely challenged.

5.   These include Norris Johnson and William Feinberg at the University of Cincinnati, who have creatively used computers to simulate temporary gatherings; Jerry Lewis at Kent State University, a close observer of sports gatherings; John Lofland at the University of California at Davis, who has observed large numbers of demonstrations and gatherings at the California state capitol and chronicled cycles of citizen surges; and, of course, Clark McPhail.

6.   The work of Canetti (1960) and Moscovici (1985) illustrate this continuing problem. Each of these theorists has much to say about the behavior of crowds without specifying in any coherent fashion the referent of their theoretical labors.

Prologue

Far from the madding crowd's ignoble strife,
Their sober wishes never learned to stray;
Along the cool sequestered vale of life
They kept the noiseless tenour of their way.
("Elegy Written in a Country Churchyard," Thomas Gray 1750)

The first lines of Gray's elegy have provided an enduring epithet for the crowd. On the one hand he celebrated the sobriety of country folk, implying that their separation from others enabled them to control their behavior on a steady course. On the other hand, crowd membership drove folks mad and—by implication—out of control, and therefore rendered them capable of disgraceful if not violent behavior. One century after Gray's elegy, Charles Mackay (1852) published his treatise *Extraordinary Popular Delusions and the Madness of Crowds.* "Men, it has been well said, think in herds; it will be seen that they go mad in herds, while they only recover their senses slowly, and one by one." That Mackay's book remains in print today is testimony to a continuing fascination with the idea of the madness of crowds.

In this century, Festinger, Pepitone, and Newcomb (1952) offered "deindividuation theory," the most recent version of the idea that crowds cripple individual cognition and transform behavior. They argued that crowds render individuals "more free from restraints, less inhibited, and able to indulge in forms of behavior in which, when alone, they would not indulge" (1952:382). The same argument has resurfaced with regularity (Zimbardo 1969; Diener 1977, 1980; Moscovicci 1985) as we approach the end of the twentieth century.

The principal contributor to the development of the idea of the madding crowd, however, was none of the above. It was unquestionably Gustav LeBon, whose (1895) *Psychologie des Foules* remains the classic statement of late nineteenth-century collective psychology. LeBon's book has since been translated into 16 languages, and is now (ca. 1990) in its forty-seventh French edition. Some believe (e.g., Gordon Allport 1954) it may have been the most influential book on social psychology during the first half of the twentieth century. The central thesis is that individuals are transformed by the crowd:

> Whoever be the individuals that compose it, however like or unlike be their mode of life, their occupations, their character, or their intelligence, the fact that they have been transformed into a crowd puts them in possession of a sort of collective mind which makes them feel, think, and act in a manner quite different from that in which each individual of them would feel, think, and act were he in a state of isolation. (LeBon 1895:57)

These ideas were kept alive by a variety of psychologists (McDougall 1908; Martin 1920; Freud 1921) and sociologists, among whom the principal proponents were Park (1904, 1930; Park and Burgess 1921), his student Blumer (1939, 1957), and Blumer's students (e.g., Lang and Lang 1961; Klapp 1972).

LeBon was not without his critics. First and foremost was Floyd Allport (1924), who dismissed the significance of groups and institutions and vehemently rejected any notion of "crowd mind" or transformation of the individual. He maintained that "the individual in the crowd behaves just as he would behave alone, only more so" (1924:295). But Allport's emphatic individualism did not dispense with the myth of the madness of crowds; instead, he merely offered a different explanation for crowds that kept a variation of the myth alive. He argued that individual behavior inside and outside the crowd was controlled by innate and learned tendencies that predisposed the individual to behave. Thus, crowds formed because individuals with similar predispositions were compelled to converge on a common location—"birds of a feather flock together." Once assembled, any further collective action was also the result of their shared tendencies to behave. This required only that one of them act, thereby triggering or encouraging the remainder to follow suit. For Allport the keynoters were lessers among equals: "the more suggestible, . . . uninhibited, . . . ignorant and impulsive" (1924:300). This list of "lesser types" was readily expandable by nonacademics who looked askance at crowd action: they attributed extraordinary collective acts to the extraordinary predispositions of the actors who allegedly performed them, e.g., the riffraff, the criminal element, the mentally ill, or various and sundry political and religious fanatics.

Allport's explanation was readily embraced by most politicians and police officials, and by many professors as well. It fit the developing explanation of human behavior that would become predominant in the first half of the twentieth century. Individuals do what they do because of the types of predispositions or tendencies to behave they "carry within them from place to place" (Melbin 1969:664), predispositions that compel them to behave. The labels given those predispositions ranged from drives, needs, or motivations, to character, personality, or self, to values, beliefs, or attitudes. Thus, just as the dancing manias of the middle ages had been attributed to devil possession, and participation in the crusades had been attributed to religious fanaticism, participation in lynch mobs, race riots, and urban riots was now attributed to deprivation and frustration, to racial bigotry, or to the criminal element, and participation in campus political demonstrations was attributed to youthful idealism, adolescent irresponsibility, and the like.

In this manner, the formation of crowds and their collective action were attributed to some form of madness-in-common already shared by those who converged on a location where their similar predispositions allegedly compelled them to act alike if not together. Instead of being controlled by the crowd, the individuals were controlled by their shared predispositions. Although Allport did not provide a very detailed explanation of how those predispositions were learned or of how they were turned into complementary collective action, that gap was soon filled by other scholars. Psychologist Neil Miller and sociologist John Dollard (1941) combined elements of classical learning theory and psychoanalytic theory to develop an explanation for how tendencies or predispositions to behave were learned by means of reward, how the deprivation of opportunities to respond or to receive rewards for responses resulted in frustration, and how that frustration eventually led to aggression to eliminate or punish the sources of deprivation.

It was with this deprivation-frustration-aggression hypothesis that social and behavioral scientists approached the task of explaining participation in the U.S. urban riots of the 1960s and 1970s. Their explanation was that rioters were compelled by a shared frustration and anger—yet another form of madness—at the absolute or relative deprivation they had experienced at the hands of society. To the surprise and dismay of the social and behavioral scientists, this hypothesis was consistently rejected by systematic statistical comparisons of riot and nonriot cities (Lieberson and Silverman 1965; Snyder and Tilly 1972; Spilerman, 1976), and of riot participants and nonparticipants (McPhail 1971; Abudu et al. 1972; Miller et al. 1977), not to mention numerous experimental studies of aggressors and nonaggressors (Berkowitz 1965a,b, 1969; Geen and Berkowitz 1967; Geen and Quanty 1977).

The urban riot research demonstrated that participants could not be distinguished from nonparticipants on the basis of deprivations or frustrations shared in common, nor could they be distinguished on the basis of a large variety of other demographic, sociological, and psychological attributes. That research complemented the growing body of evidence against the hypothesis that knowledge of an individual's attributes or attitudes (and inferred predispositions) in one situation at time one is a useful predictor of behavior in another situation at time two. These results led to calls for more attention to and analyses of *interaction* between people in developing crowd situations.

Those postriot calls for attention to situated social interaction were not the first. Whereas transformation and predisposition explanations of the crowd were primarily concerned with the consequences of the crowd for the individual, Muzafer Sherif (1936), and later Turner and Killian (1957), had already called attention to what two or more persons do in relation to one another and what they do together in crowds. Since interaction and collective action are sociological phenomena, an attempt was made to develop a sociological explanation for those phenomena. Sherif reasoned that since norms were thought by sociologists to be of consequence for what two or more persons do together in routine situations, it would be worthwhile to examine how people develop new or emergent norms in nonroutine situations. Turner and Killian (1957, 1972, 1987) placed Sherif's ideas in a sociological framework of emergent problems in the community, of ecological, political, and attitudinal conditions within which and communication processes by which crowds might develop. They also attempted to translate the interaction processes Sherif and Harvey (1952) had studied in the laboratory into the milling crowd's interaction that develops emergent norms that lead to collective behavior.

The United States' most recent decade of urban riots (ca. 1963–1972) was preceded and followed by thousands of civil rights and antiwar demonstrations in communities and on college campuses throughout the country. These demonstrations were contemporaneous with an unprecedented number of students and faculty in the social and behavioral sciences. From their ranks emerged both participant and nonparticipant observers of the crowd. Some of those observers were outraged by the discrepancies between what they saw and heard taking place around them and the commonsense/social science stereotypes of crowd participants and behaviors. No small number of ideological and conceptual challenges were hurled against the stereotypical traditional wisdoms, and a sizable amount of research was launched to examine systematically some of the pertinent claims and counterclaims (e.g., Pinard et al. 1969; Eisinger 1973; Fisher 1972; McPhail 1972; MacCannell 1973; Berk 1972b, 1974a; Wright 1978).

After conducting some of that research (McPhail 1969, 1972) and reviewing others' research on behavior in urban and campus crowds, demonstrations, and riots (McPhail 1971; McPhail and Wohlstein 1983), three conclusions seemed increasingly clear. First, individuals are not driven mad by crowds; they do not lose cognitive control! Second, individuals are not compelled to participate by some madness-in-common, or any other sovereign psychological attribute, cognitive style, or predisposition that distinguishes them from nonparticipants. Third, the majority of behaviors in which members of those crowds engaged are neither mutually inclusive nor extraordinary, let alone mad, and are therefore not even addressed by traditional theories. The first two points have been made in various forms by other contemporary students of the crowd (e.g., Bramson 1961; Turner 1964a,b;

Couch 1968; Milgram and Toch 1969; Fisher 1972; Berk 1972a; Wright 1978). However, few have given attention to the third point.

Students of the crowd, like social and behavioral scientists in general (Merton 1987), have devoted far more time and effort to criticizing, debating, and offering alternative explanations than they have to specifying and describing the phenomena to be explained (exceptions are Milgram and Toch 1969; Fisher 1972; Wright 1978; Lofland 1985). In my judgment this places the cart before the horse. It is misguided to debate the pros and cons of competing explanations before the phenomena to be explained have first been examined, specified, and described. After 20 years of observing hundreds of crowds, I do not claim that extraordinary behaviors never take place; occasionally they do. But my own experiences, and the reports of colleagues who have done their fieldwork, suggest that such behaviors are infrequent and virtually never involve more than a few crowd members. Theories of the crowd and crowd behavior should not be theories of rare events (cf. Turner 1964a). They should be developed to describe and explain the full range of crowds and crowd behavior, the ordinary as well as the extraordinary.

Why then even bother with a review of the older theories? Why not proceed directly from a discussion of what I want to explain, to a discussion of the kinds of explanation that are required, and then to the evidence that is available or must be generated to demonstrate that explanation? There are at least three reasons!

First, some of the problems with which earlier students of the crowd struggled were important problems, then as now, even if all the solutions they proposed were not very useful. For example, Park and Blumer called attention to the importance of communication within the crowd despite their failure to observe it, or to specify it in a way that would permit their students and others to proceed with a more systematic examination of that phenomenon. A second example is the necessity of a general theory of human behavior to explain the alternating and varied sequences of individual behavior and collective behavior that make up the temporary gathering. Miller and Dollard addressed this problem even if their solution has proven quite unsatisfactory. A third example is provided by Turner and Killian's attention to the demographic, social, and legal conditions that lend themselves to the communication processes that are so central to the formation of temporary gatherings. This is a very significant problem; unfortunately it is not one they pursued or resolved. Thus, my review of the earlier theories and their critics should not be viewed as a gratuitous gesture.

Second, while there have been some reviews of the research of the last two decades (e.g., Lofland 1981; McPhail and Wohlstein 1983) and some limited reviews of specific crowd theories as well (e.g., Tierney 1980; Moscovici 1985; Graumann and Moscovici 1986), there have been no comprehensive reviews of the chronological development of transformation, predisposition, and emergent norm theories of the crowd, no assessment of their ontological, epistemological, and conceptual strengths and weaknesses, and no judgment of how they fare against the accumulated evidence. I have attempted to provide a comprehensive and even-handed review. I hope the weaknesses I have identified will caution others against repeating the same mistakes, and that my attention to the strengths may provide some stepping stones on which others may proceed. I believe the historian's adage: unless reminded of past mistakes, we run the risk of repeating them. For those who take exception to the criticisms I set forth, I hope that I have stated my case simply and clearly so that we have some basis upon which to pursue the debate and, better yet, to move the issue from the debating stand to some form of empirical if not pragmatic test.

There is a third important reason for reviewing the classic theories and their critics. Students and studies of the crowd reflect a basic division in social psychology. From the beginning there have been at least two social psychologies: psychological social psychology has been concerned with the influence of others' presence and behaviors on individual cognition, behavior, and emotion; sociologial social psychology has been concerned with the origins, development, and consequences of what two or more persons do together. The pioneer students of the crowd and their principal critics, e.g., LeBon and Allport (and their respective intellectual offspring), were primarily concerned with the influence of the crowd upon the individual. To a very great extent, that remains the case today in psychological social psychology. On the other hand, and despite some early but short-lived sociological interests in the crowd, it was not until much later that social behavior in the crowd, and crowds as social systems, became focal concerns of sociology and sociological social psychology.

My primary interests are the description and explanation of what two or more persons do together: cooperation, competition, and conflict.[1] Despite my preoccupation with these forms of social behaviors, my fieldwork has convinced me that the most characteristic feature of most crowds is alternation and variation: alternation between sequences of individual behavior and sequences of social behavior, and variation in the form, content, complexity, and duration of the sequences of social behavior as well as the proportion of the crowd participating in any sequence. Thus, to explain the behavior in and by crowds requires attention to the problems of psychological *and* sociological social psychology. It requires attention to the organization of individual behavior and to the merger of the behaviors of two or more individuals into social behavior.

I have not arrived at my concerns with variations in social behavior, nor the type of explanation I believe such behaviors require, without considerable intellectual provocation, numerous suggestions, and a variety of exemplars in the work of other sociologists. Carl Couch, Richard Berk, Charles Tilly, and John Lofland, among others, have seen many of the same problems I have seen in the work of our predecessors. Often my colleagues have sought to resolve those problems at different levels of analysis, or by working on different units of analysis, and therefore have developed different levels and units of explanation (and corresponding methodological strategies) appropriate to their concerns.

I have also drawn extensively upon the ideas of George Herbert Mead and William T. Powers for elements of an explanation of individual and social behavior. Too often sociologists and social psychologists think only of Mead's analysis of the genesis of self, and fail to appreciate his analyses of individual acts and social acts, and the extension of those analyses to the problem of collective action. Mead's analysis of the act was a precursor to many of the basic features of the cybernetic models of human behavior that are now at the cutting edge of cognitive science. One of those models, developed by William T. Powers, will be detailed here. When combined with Mead's equally powerful analysis of the role of language in fitting together the behaviors of two or more persons, we have the elements of a sociocybernetic model of collective action.[2] This allows the development of an explanation, with the same basic principles, for the varied and alternating sequences of individual and collective behavior that take place in temporary gatherings.

Cybernetic means self-governing. The basic idea is that human beings are purposive actors and that, unless physically constrained (a phenomenon that sometimes occurs in very dense crowds), they control their own behavior by means of self-instructions regarding the achievement of their goals and objectives. Individual behavior is not controlled by crowd minds or crowds; it is not controlled by predispositions or tendencies to behave; it is not controlled by norms or social relationships. Individuals control their behavior by self-instructions, often by telling themselves to do what is proposed or required by the small groups of family, friends, or acquaintances with whom they assemble, and sometimes by telling themselves to do what is proposed by larger political, sports, and religious groups who have organized the gathering or who are attempting to organize sequences of action within the gathering.

Simple sequences of collective action, even those involving large numbers of participants, can be independently generated by participants who are already controlling for similar objectives, e.g., the cheers or applause of political, religious, or sports partisans.

More complex sequences of collective action are often interdependently generated through the interaction of the individual with his or her companions that establishes an objective-in-common, e.g., to move closer for a better look or listen to, or maintain a comfortable distance from, an argument, fight, or arrest within a gathering. But there are limits to the number

of persons, perhaps a half-dozen, who can participate in the mutually inclusive face-to-face interaction that interdependently generates the objec-
tives-in-common that yield collective action.

Larger numbers of participants in complex and/or sustained sequences of
collective action ordinarily adopt objectives and directions from third parties, who in turn have often planned, rehearsed, and made preparations to
ensure that their directions will be disseminated and can be carried out.

The common denominator across these three categories of social behavior
is that two or more individuals are giving themselves, are controlling or
governing their behavior in terms of, common goals or objectives—hence, a
sociocybernetic theory of social behavior or collective action. I will attempt
to illustrate some of these analyses in the final chapter of this book. Before
doing so, some comments are in order regarding the intervening chapters.

In Chapter 1, I trace the development of the transformation explanation of
collective behavior from LeBon's theory of crowd mind, through Park's dissertation on rational and critical discussion in publics vs. psychic reciprocity
in crowds, to Blumer's distinction between symbolic interaction in routine
social life and circular reaction in collective behavior. I then review the
accumulated criticisms and empirical evidence against the transformation
hypothesis, and note some theoretical and methodological paradoxes in
Blumer's adoption of his mentor Park's, rather than his mentor Mead's,
explanation for human behavior in problematic situations.[3]

In Chapter 2, I review Allport's, and Miller and Dollard's predisposition
explanations of the crowd. Drawing upon a wide range of empirical evidence, I then offer a critique of those explanatory perspectives. In the course
of that critique, I offer some evidence for an alternative explanation of individual and collective violence in lieu of the discredited deprivation-frustration-aggression hypothesis.

In Chapter 3, I describe Sherif's (1936) classic autokinetic experiments and
his subsequent work with O. J. Harvey (Sherif and Harvey 1952) on the
development of emergent norms in situations of varying uncertainty. Turner
and Killian (1957, 1972, 1987) placed those ideas in a macrosociological
framework of emergent problems in the community, of ecological, political,
and attitudinal conditions within which crowds might develop, and of communication processes by which that development might occur. They further
attempt to translate the interaction processes Sherif and Harvey studied in
the laboratory into the interaction that takes place in a milling crowd, as well
as the development of an emergent norm that allows the crowd to engage in
collective behavior. Most contemporary students of the crowd and collective
behavior agree that we owe an enormous debt to Turner and Killian's pioneering sociological analysis, this despite the problems I note in Chapter 3:
e.g., their failure to provide an operational definition of collective behavior
or to acknowledge the range of collective behavior to be explained; their too

frequent dependence on a predisposition model of individual actors in the interaction process; their lack of analysis of interaction processes per se; their apparent inference of the emergent norm from the collective behavior it is supposed to explain.

In Chapter 4, I review some additional criticisms of the transformation, predisposition, and emergent-norm explanations of the crowd advanced by four sociologists who have been keen observers of contemporary demonstrations and riots in the United States (Carl J. Couch, Richard Berk, and John Lofland) and in other countries and centuries as well (Charles Tilly). These sociologists offer important and diverse, alternative characterizations and explanations that must be considered by any serious student of crowds and collective behavior. Couch's masterful critique of sterotypical characterizations and explanations of the crowd is surpassed only by his radical proposal to view crowds as elementary social systems, and his analyses of what two or more persons must do to merge their behaviors into sequences of collective actions that differ from those taken by other social systems in degree more than in kind. Berk has observed and described a variety of sequences of collective action within crowds and offers an explanation for the rational organization of the behaviors composing those sequences. Tilly also treats collective action as the rational efforts of human beings to promote or resist change. He has identified, documented, and described a wide range of repertoires of collective action forms in nineteenth- and twentieth-century France, Italy, Germany, England, and the United States. Last but not least, John Lofland has persistently reminded us that rational, collective actions also have an emotional dimension that cannot be ignored, and, more importantly, that students of collective action often work with different units and at different levels of analysis, all of which should be considered if we are fully to understand the context, the development, the organization, and the individual and social consequences of collective action.

In Chapter 5, I offer some criteria and a taxonomic scheme for the study of collective behavior in temporary gatherings. The concepts of crowd and collective behavior have been used interchangeably in the sociological literature for more than a half-century. Neither has proven fruitful. The traditional concept of crowd has been useless because it connotes too much. Traditional conceptions of collective behavior have been equally useless because they denoted too little, more frequently implying an explanatory perspective than specifying, describing, and classifying a class of social phenomena to be explained.

The common denominator in most dictionary definitions of *crowd* is a compact gathering or collection of people. Unfortunately the additional suggestion or connotation ordinarily conveyed is one of the homogeneity of that collection of people or the unanimity of their behavior, or both. Neither popular nor scholarly usage has allowed for variation in behavior across the collection of people at any one point in time, let alone variation across successive points in time. In short, the concept of crowd has prevented recognition of alternation between and variation among collections of people behaving individually and collectively. In failing to recognize this variation and alternation, students of the crowd (and of collective behavior) have proceeded to develop explanations for unanimous and homogeneous behavior, for phenomena that rarely occur and are short-lived, if and when they do occur.

People do behave collectively, but what they do together varies greatly in complexity, in duration, and in the proportion of the gathering that actually participates. In one sense, recognition of this variation would appear to make more difficult the task of the student of crowds and collective behavior. But in fact, the task is made more manageable and is therefore a simpler one. Attempts to describe and explain the crowd have been an impossibly large task to date. By breaking that task into smaller components, the problem is reduced to several tasks, each of more manageable proportions.

First, in lieu of crowd, I propose the alternative concept of *gathering*, i.e., two or more persons in a common space and time frame who may behave collectively, although not necessarily so. I further argue that just as behaviors within gatherings vary across space and time, so do the gatherings themselves. I therefore propose recasting gatherings into a simple three-phase life cycle: the assembling or formation process, itself a form of people behaving collectively; the assembled gathering of people, within which a variety of sequences of individual and collective behavior may occur; and the dispersing process.

Second, I offer a working definition of collective behavior, of collective behavior-in-common, and of collective behavior-in-concert. I specify and briefly describe more than three dozen elementary forms of the former and a half-dozen forms of the latter, illustrated by the work of sociologists and social psychologists who have systematically examined what people do collectively within temporary gatherings. I also discuss variation in the duration and complexity of these forms of elementary collective behavior, and in the proportion of the gathering participating.

If comparatively few sociologists have given attention to what people do collectively within gatherings, an increasing number have given attention to larger units of analysis, at more macro levels of analysis, e.g., gatherings, events, campaigns, and waves. The relationships between what people do collectively at micro and macro levels of analysis are too important to ignore. They must be considered in relation to rather than at odds with one another.

Third, to demonstrate some of those relationships, I first suggest a way of characterizing gatherings by scaling variation in their collective behavioral complexity. Thus, by establishing the phenomena to be explained—in effect, by decomposing or disaggregating the crowd into the varied and alternating elementary forms of collective behavior that occur within gatherings—I provide a way of specifying our ignorance about the composition of and variation across gatherings. I hope this will contribute to the systematic recharacterization and comparison of gatherings in terms of some set of forms of collective behavior, perhaps like those I have proposed.

Finally, I report my own research aggregating various sequences of protest demonstration forms into political events. I note the relationships between these units of analysis and the campaigns and waves investigated by other sociological colleagues. This chapter is one small step toward examining the relationships between the various units and levels of analysis of what human beings do collectively, ranging from sequences of behavior, to gatherings, to events, to campaigns, and to waves of and trends in those units of analysis. My objective is to indicate the range of behaviors in which human beings collectively engage within and across temporary gatherings, and therefore the range of collective phenomena for which I believe explanations must be developed.

In Chapter 6, I offer the elements of an explanation for many of the collective phenomena I have identified and described in the preceding chapter.[4] I first summarize Mead's theories of self and of the individual act. I then summarize Powers' cybernetic theory of purposive individual behavior. I review Mead's "principle of organization"—the role of significant symbols in coordinating the behaviors of two or more purposive individuals. I recast Mead's analysis of social behavior in terms of Powers' cybernetic model and suggest three ways by which two or more purposive actors can generate a sequence of collective action. I present illustrative evidence for those arguments and discuss, all too briefly, the relationship between cooperation, competition, and conflict. I conclude with a brief discussion of how this sociocybernetic model of human behavior can be extended to the macro levels and units of analysis for gatherings, events, and campaigns.

Notes

1. I give far more attention here to cooperation than to competition and conflict. At first glance this may seem odd in a book concerned with crowds. But of the three forms of social behavior with which sociologists and social psychologists are usually concerned—cooperation, competition, and conflict—cooperation is without question the most frequent social behavior in crowds and elsewhere. Further, the violence associated with competition and conflict is extremely rare in prosaic (Edgerton 1979), political (Eisinger 1973; MacCannell 1973; Tilly 1978; McPhail 1985), and sports (Smith 1983; Lewis 1982) crowds. Collective violence is rarer yet. Tilly argues (1978) that collective violence develops out of actions that are initially nonviolent, and that we cannot understand that development without understanding the routine and nonviolent actions as well. Moreover, when collective violence is at issue, it is imperative to understand how two or members of a gathering fit their behaviors

together cooperatively to compete collectively against their opponents, to aggress collectively against their targets, or to resist collectively against their antagonists.

2.   The concept *sociocybernetic* has been used earlier (Geyer and van der Zouwen 1978) to refer to the applications of "the new cybernetics" to social systems. I will use the concept sociocybernetic here to refer to related purposive control systems that are organizing and directing their collective actions in terms of similar or related goals, objectives, or reference signals. I outline this explanatory formulation in Chapter 6, drawing upon the ideas of Mead (1924, 1936, 1938) and Powers (1973a,b, 1988).

3.   An earlier version of portions of Chapter 1 was published in McPhail (1989b).

4.   An earlier and much abbreviated version of Chapter 6 was published in McPhail and Tucker (1990).

1

Creating the Myth:
LeBon; Park; Blumer

Introduction

The idea of the madding crowd was born of social, economic, and political challenges to the status quo in Europe during the eighteenth and nineteenth centuries. These challenges were accelerated in France during the middle third of the nineteenth century and gave rise to the development of a school of "collective psychology," which offered an explanation for the madding crowd, the transformation of individual participants, and their extraordinary behavior that was believed to result from that transformation. The principal though not necessarily the first architect of those ideas was Gustave LeBon. His views of the crowd were transported to the United States by students pursuing advanced degrees in Europe and then returning to the professoriat at American universities. Foremost among these was Robert E. Park, who perpetuated the idea of the madding crowd at the University of Chicago for more than two decades. One of his students, Herbert Blumer, systematically elaborated those ideas and extended their longevity well beyond mid-century.

In this chapter I trace the development of a transformation explanation of collective behavior from LeBon's theory of crowd mind, through Park's dissertation on rational critical discussion in publics vs. psychic reciprocity in crowds, to Blumer's distinction between symbolic interaction in routine social life and circular reaction in collective behavior. The LeBon-Park-Blumer hypothesis holds that crowds transform individuals, diminishing or eliminating their ability to control their behavior rationally. I close with a review of the accumulated logical arguments and empirical evidence against the transformation hypothesis, and note some theoretical and methodological paradoxes in Blumer's adoption of Park's rather than George Herbert Mead's explanation for human behavior in problematic situation.

1

Gustave LeBon (1841–1931)

European Origins of
Collective Psychology

The social, economic, and political turmoil of urban Europe throughout the last half of the nineteenth century made crowds a formidable problem for the stability of the political status quo, not to mention social order in public places. Various explanations were advanced (Moscovici 1985). One held that crowd members were mad or insane, akin to folklore explanations for the dancing frenzies of the middle ages (cf. Rosen 1968). Anyone engaging in extraordinary collective activity was thought demon possessed or mentally deranged.

A second explanation was that status quo–challenging crowds were composed of the riffraff of society, "an accumulation of disintegrated social elements, human waste swept out of society and hence hostile to it" (Moscovici 1985:71). Thus, crowds were viewed as by-products, not the producers of social change.

A third explanation argued that crowd members were criminals. Lombroso believed some individuals were born with criminal tendencies, that crowds violating person or property were composed or led by criminals. Lombroso and colleagues developed the Italian school of "collective psychology."[1] Scipio Sighele's book *The Criminal Crowd* (1894) set forth many of the arguments later stated in Gustav LeBon's (1895) *The Psychology of the Crowd*.[2]

It may have been LeBon's "stroke of genius" (Moscovici 1985:74) to dismiss all three of these explanations for the crowd. He argued, to the contrary, that crowds were composed of normal folks who, by virtue of their participation, were *transformed* by some unique, collective psychological processes in the crowd. Before reviewing LeBon's analysis, I briefly outline a sequence of events that may have contributed to its development.

LeBon, the son of a middle-class Burgundy bureaucrat, arrived in Paris in 1860 to study medicine. Six years later he completed his internship and was licensed to practice. He decided against a medical career, electing to pursue broader interests by writing popular accounts of others' scientific work. LeBon spent most of the next 50 years in Paris, writing and publishing prolifically.

Between 1869 and 1871 there were massive violent strikes throughout France, but particularly in Paris, ending with the violent suppression of the Paris Commune in 1871. The latter events were few in number but involved many participants and consisted of "day after day of violent encounters instead of the intense but more scattered conflicts of 1848 or 1934" (Tilly, Tilly, and Tilly 1975:60).

LeBon witnessed many of these disorderly gatherings between 1869 and 1871, particularly those involving the Paris Commune and their subsequent repression by national forces. LeBon was alarmed and disturbed by what he saw and heard. He feared the crowd; he feared the impact of a popularly based democracy on the future of France. Given these considerations, LeBon believed it essential to develop and apply scientific knowledge of collective psychology so that politicians could be taught how better to lead crowds and governments how better to control them. "LeBon's burning ambition for his new science was that it would provide a method and a solution for the problem of governing mass societies" (Moscovici 1985:80).

LeBon was but one of many scholars and writers attempting to make sense of the crowds of the time. The sociologist Gabriel Tarde, LeBon's close friend, had already published *The Laws of Imitation* (1890), and had written two important papers on the crowd (1892, 1893).[3] I noted the work by Italian criminologists on the collective psychology of crowds. Nye (1975) suggests LeBon's talents were those of synthesis and popularization rather than creativity and systematization. Sighele, of course, thought those talents better described as plagiarism. Whether synthesis or plagiarism, LeBon's (1895) statement of nineteenth-century collective psychology—*Psychologie des Foules*—was both enduring and influential. It is now in its forty-seventh French edition and has been translated into at least 16 languages (Nye 1975). Freud (1921) devoted more than one-third of his *Group Psychology and Analysis of the Ego* to an enthusiastic synopsis, analysis, and elaboration of LeBon's book. Gordon Allport (1954) proclaimed LeBon's book the most influential work in the first half-century of social psychology.

LeBon's basic argument is summarized in the following:

> Whoever be the individuals that compose it, however like or unlike be their mode of life, their occupations, their character, or their intelligence, the fact that they have been *transformed* into a crowd puts them in possession of a sort of collective mind which makes them feel, think and act in a manner quite different from that in which each individual of them would feel think and act were he in a state of isolation. (1895:27; emphasis added)

The transformation was said to develop under specific conditions and in several steps.[4] Those conditions were the crowd's *anonymity,* the resulting belief of individual *unaccountability* for behavior within the crowd, and a cumulative sense of *invincibility* on the part of the crowd. LeBon believed these conditions gave rise to the "disappearance of the conscious personality." By this LeBon referred to the individual's capacity for critical reasoning, plus all innate and acquired traits, habits, beliefs, and "phenotypic characteristics" that would normally differentiate one person from another. LeBon believed the "unconscious personality emerged" into this vacuum, dominated by "genotypic characteristics"—instincts, traits, primitive beliefs—shared by all individuals, by all members of a nation or a race.[5] He wrote:

> Our savage, destructive instincts are the inheritance left dormant in all of us from the primitive ages. In the life of the isolated individual it would be dangerous for him to gratify these instincts, while his absorption in an irresponsible crowd, in which in consequence he is assured of impunity, gives him entire liberty to follow them. (1895:57)

LeBon called this state of affairs "the collective mind," more specifically, "the law of mental unity." He never defined this law, but it was central to his entire argument since he believed its most direct consequence to be *increased suggestibility*. He characterized this as:

> impulsiveness, irritability, incapacity to reason, the absence of judgments and of the critical spirit, the exaggeration of the sentiments, and others besides— which are almost always observed in beings belonging to inferior forms of evolution—in women, savages, and in children, for instance. (1895:36)

It is important to recognize that LeBon's explanation for crowds was developed at a time when hypnosis had only recently been introduced to treat psychiatric patients. Moscovici (1985:94) suggests LeBon merely applied to crowds conclusions drawn from observing individuals undergo hypnosis in hospitals.[6] LeBon wrote:

> An individual immersed for some length of time in a crowd in action soon finds himself—either in consequence of the magnetic influence given out by the crowd, or from some other cause of which we are ignorant—in a special state which much resembles the state of fascination in which the hypnotised individual finds himself in the hands of the hypnotiser. (1895:31)

LeBon further believed that, just as patients would not do everything suggested by a hypnotist, crowds would not do everything suggested by a leader. He argued that suggestions would more likely be carried out if consistent with the "genotypic primitive beliefs" shared by the leader and the crowd.[7] Even so, LeBon did not overlook some Aristotelian rhetorical principles practiced by successful orators of his day and in our own: suggestions are more effective if stated simply, positively, and repeatedly.

LeBon characterized the next stage of crowd development as *contagion*, a condition he believed was "neither more nor less than the effect of suggestibility" (1895:31). He defined contagion as a form of collective hypnosis. He argued that contagion yielded uncritical and immediate implementation of the leader's suggestions by crowd members. He wrote:

> We see, then, that the disappearance of the conscious personality, the predominance of the unconscious personality, the turning by means of suggestion

and contagion of feelings and ideas in an identical direction, the tendency to immediately transform the suggested ideas into acts; *these*, we see, *are the principal characteristics of the individual forming part of a crowd.* He is no longer himself but has become an automaton who has ceased to be guided by his will. (1895:32; emphasis added)

The consequence of the preceding developments, according to LeBon, is "extraordinary behavior" by crowd members (1895:27).

The fact that *they have been transformed* into a crowd puts them in possession of *a sort of collective mind* which *makes them feel, think, and act in a manner quite different from that in which each individual of them would feel, think and act were he in a state of isolation.* (1895:27; emphasis added)

LeBon may have rejected the explanation that crowds are composed of persons who were mad, but his own theory set forth an explanation for how the crowd seized control of, transformed, and made the individual behave in extraordinary ways.

LeBon's (1895) explanation for the crowd was widely circulated, widely read, and widely accepted in lay circles, and it was featured in the first social psychology textbooks published in England (McDougall 1908) and in the United States (Ross 1908).[8] But perhaps the most consequential means by which LeBon's ideas were carried to and spread in the United States were the writings and lectures of Robert E. Park at the University of Chicago from 1916 until 1933.

Robert Ezra Park (1864–1944)

Crowd; Public;
Collective Behavior

Park studied philosophy with John Dewey at the University of Michigan (B.A., 1887), briefly taught school in Minnesota, then worked as a newspaper reporter in Minneapolis, Detroit, Denver, and New York. He entered graduate school at Harvard in 1898 to investigate the impact of the newspaper on its readers and society. After studying philosophy with James and Royce, and psychology with Munsterberg, Park received a master's degree in 1899. He went to Germany, attended Simmel's lectures in Berlin in 1899, and enrolled at Strassburg in 1900 to study philosophy with Windelband. In 1903 he followed Windelband to Heidelberg and began work on a dissertation, *The Crowd and The Public (Masse und Publikum)*, which was completed and published in 1904. He returned to the United States to teach at Harvard and then to work in 1906 as secretary to Booker T. Washington at the Tuskegee Institute, enabling him to study the American Negro in the

South for the next seven years. He joined the University of Chicago faculty in 1916 and taught there until retirement in 1933 (Turner 1967; Faris 1972; Elsner 1972).

Although Park was better known for his scholarship on race relations and on urban life, he retained an interest in his dissertation topic, frequently teaching his course, "The Crowd and the Public." In his dissertation, and in all his subsequent writings on the crowd, Park addressed three themes. First, sociology is concerned with all collective and group life, and "every significant advance in sociology must, in the last analysis, proceed with research like that begun in the field of crowd psychology, that is, the description and explanation of the activities of human groups" (Park 1904:6). He also expressed intrigue with Rossi's (1904) analysis of "progressive social differentiation and increasingly stable forms of social life." Later, in their classic textbook, *Introduction to the Science of Society,* Park and Ernest W. Burgess defined sociology as "the science of collective behavior" (1921:42) and subsequently referred to collective behavior as a continuum along which a variety of increasingly complex forms of social life could be placed: social unrest, the crowd, the gang, the public, the political party, the social movement, and the state, respectively (1921:193).[9]

A second theme in Park's work referred to collective behavior as the formation, breakdown, and re-formation of society (cf. Turner 1967:xiii). This appears in his early reference (Park 1904:14) to Spencer's principle of social evolution; and his subsequent reference to collective behavior as

> those phenomena which exhibit in the most obvious and elementary way the processes by which societies are disintegrated into their constituent elements and the process by which those elements are brought together again into new relations to form new organizations and new societies. (Park and Burgess 1921:441)

Indeed, it was in the context of social unrest that Park introduced the mechanism of "circular reaction" with which he explained collective behavior:

> The most elementary form of collective behavior seems to be what is ordinarily referred to as "social unrest" . . . [which] is transmitted from one individual to another . . . so that the manifestations of discontent in A communicated to B, and from B reflected back to A, produce the circular reaction described in the preceding chapter [on Social Control]. (Park and Burgess 1921:382)

It is the third theme, however, for which Park's work on the crowd and collective behavior is probably best remembered, viz., the distinction he drew between the rational and prudent processes of discussion in the public, and the uncritical, impulsive, and anarchical processes in the crowd. Here collective behavior was defined quite differently as:

the behavior of individuals under the influence of an impulse that is common and collective, an impulse, in other words, that is the product of social interaction. (1921:381)

But *not* ordinary social interaction! Park referred instead to a form of social interaction he initially termed "psychic reciprocity" (1904:18) and later came to call "circular reaction" (Park and Burgess 1921:382).[10]

By today's standards, Park's first theme states an eminently fundamental sociological perspective. Even the second is plausible, stripped of reactionary social evolutionary implications. But the third is difficult to understand, let alone accept, unless viewed in the context of the problem that launched Park's graduate study in sociology.

Park was concerned with the impact of the newspaper on modern society. The French sociologist Gabriel Tarde published a paper in 1898, the year Park entered graduate school, entitled "The Public and the Crowd." Tarde argued that while the crowd was one of the oldest forms of human association, the public was a product of modern technological developments. Crowd members are copresent; publics are physically dispersed, given cohesion only by participants' awareness they share some idea. Since that awareness could not be attributed to proximate social interaction, another source was required. Tarde suggested one such source was the newspaper, itself the nineteenth-century product of the printing press, the railroad, and the telegraph. Thus, the form of social life Tarde called "the public" simply did not exist prior to the nineteenth century.[11]

Tarde further argued that whereas individuals could simultaneously be part of several publics, they could participate in but one crowd at a time. Since crowds are comparatively limited in size, their influence may not extend beyond what participants and onlookers can see and hear. By comparison, publics are virtually unlimited in size and perhaps in the scope of their influence. But Tarde argued that the fundamental distinction between the crowd and the public was that interaction in the latter took the form of critical discussion. The result, Tarde suggested, is that publics yielded heterogeneity whereas crowds tended toward homogeneity.

Unfortunately Park did not adopt Tarde's complete analysis of variations in crowds, a critical point to which I shall return. Instead, Park pursued and elaborated Tarde's arguments concerning heterogenous and critical publics vs. homogeneous and uncritical crowds. In the heterogeneous public, "issues are raised . . . opinions clash and thus modify and moderate one another" (Park and Burgess 1921:385).[12] By implication, the homogeneous crowd has nothing to argue about and whatever is expressed there can only amplify or reinforce what is already present. Park wrote:

When the public ceases to be critical, it dissolves or is transformed into a crowd. This provides the essential characteristic differentiating the crowd from the public. The crowd submits to the influence of a collective drive which it obeys without criticism. The public, in contrast—precisely because it is composed of individuals with different opinions—is guided by prudence and rational reflection. (Park 1904:80)

If Park drew heavily upon Tarde's work for his views of the public, there was much less to draw upon for his analysis of the crowd. Terry Clark (1969) suggests Tarde thought *most* crowds were neither very interesting nor very important, and therefore directed the majority of his attention to the more consequential phenomenon of the public, leaving crowds to popular writers such as LeBon.

Thus it was to LeBon, to Sighelle, and to Rossi that Park turned for an explanation of what he believed was a unique form of social interaction. He embraced LeBon's contention that "all individual and particular self-consciousness" disappears in the crowd; that "the feelings and thoughts of all the crowd members move in the same direction" (Park 1904:12); that suggestibility is increased; and, that the defining characteristic of the crowd is not physical proximity but that crowd members "mutually infect each other with their thoughts and feelings" (1904:18). Park believed the mechanism for this was "psychic reciprocity" or, later, "circular reaction."

Park embraced LeBon's analysis for the remainder of his career. Shortly before his retirement in 1933, Park wrote:

The general characteristics of crowds have been well explored and may be rapidly summarized. . . . Social and personal distinction disappear. . . . Only those attitudes, passions and sentiments which are the common heritage of mankind remain. With the evolution of what LeBon calls "the crowd consciousness" there is a corresponding loss of personality by the individual; the individual tends to act impersonally and to feel something less than the ordinary responsibility for his actions. (1930:631–632)

Park also maintained Tarde's distinction between crowd and public, arguing that if crowds behave collectively they must do so under the influence of a common mood or impulse that results from circular reaction.

The fundamental distinction between the crowd and the public, however, is not to be measured by numbers nor by means of communication, but by the form and effects of the interactions. In the public, interaction takes the form of discussion. Individuals tend to act upon one another critically; issues are raised and parties form. Opinions clash and thus modify and moderate one another. The crowd does not discuss and hence it does not reflect. It simply "mills." Out of this milling process a collective impulse is formed which dominates all members of the crowd. (Park and Burgess 1921:385)

He attributed the collective impulse and the collective actions of the crowd to a "circular form of interaction" (1921:370), which, as I have already noted, he called "circular reaction" (1921:382) and which he believed (1921:369) to be the most elementary form of social control in human society.

Park's elaborations of LeBon's collective psychology and Tarde's distinction between crowd and public were presented for more than two decades at the University of Chicago in his course, "The Crowd and The Public," in his (1921) textbook (with Ernest Burgess), *Sociology: Introduction to the Science of Society,* and in his (1930) article, "Collective Behavior," in the *Encyclopedia of the Social Sciences.* But the LeBon-Park transformation perspective received its definitive elaboration, systematization, and perpetuation from one of Park's students at the University of Chicago: Herbert Blumer.

Herbert George Blumer (1900–1987)

Systematizing the Transformation Explanation

In his history of the Department of Sociology at the University of Chicago between 1920 and 1940, Robert E. L. Faris wrote that "in 1939 Herbert Blumer published a concise outline of the Park materials on collective behavior" (1972:106). In my judgment Blumer made three significant contributions in that statement. First, he elaborated Park's (Park and Burgess 1921) notions of the role of social unrest as a context within which crowds formed and collective behavior developed. Second, in an apparent attempt to explain the problem of psychic reciprocity with which Park had struggled, Blumer introduced his own distinction between "interpretative or symbolic interaction" underlying routine social behavior and "circular reaction" underlying collective behavior. Third, Blumer's concise statement of the LeBon-Park perspective was a very systematic and developmental explication of the transformation analysis of crowds and collective behavior. Blumer's version came to be and remains widely circulated in sociological textbooks, military and police crowd control manuals, and popular thought. The idea that human beings are transformed by the crowd became the definitive sociological explanation for such phenomena for the next quarter-century.

Blumer, like Park, conceded that in one sense "practically all group activity can be thought of as collective behavior" since "individuals are acting together in some fashion" (1939:137). But he distinguished between routine collective behavior, for example, by teachers and pupils in a classroom, and elementary collective behavior, for example, by members of a crowd, in terms of the bases upon and the mechanisms by which he thought the two social phenomena developed.[13]

The great majority of routine collective behavior occurs, according to Blumer, because "people have common understandings and expectations" (1939:168). Those understandings provide the substance and the basis for participants' *interpretative interaction* with one another.[14] Each responds to his or her interpretation of the other's behavior rather than directly to that behavior. This results in individuals responding differently to one another but enables them to fit their different behaviors into some line of collective conduct.

According to Blumer, the disruption of routine activities thwarts the satisfaction of routine individual impulses and dispositions to act; or individuals may develop new impulses or dispositions that the existing social order cannot accommodate. In either circumstance, individuals are said to experience unrest. Their behavior becomes erratic, random, and uncoordinated. Blumer termed this "restlessness," and argued that it had a "reciprocal character," i.e., when some individuals engaged in this behavior, there was a tendency for onlookers to do the same. He called this reciprocal process *circular reaction*, that is,

> a type of interstimulation wherein the response of one individual reproduces the stimulation that has come from another individual and in being reflected back to this individual reinforces the stimulation. (1939:170–1)

Circular reaction results in people behaving alike and is "the natural mechanism" underlying all elementary collective behavior (1939:171). When the restlessness of individuals is stirred by circular reaction, the result is *social unrest*.[15] This is more likely among people who have undergone together the experience of a disrupted living routine or have otherwise been sensitized to one another.[16]

Blumer argued that people in a condition of social unrest are seeking something but do not know what it is. They are aimless, engage in random and erratic behavior, are apprehensive about the future, are vaguely excited, and are particularly vulnerable to rumors. Finally, Blumer argued that as a result of their disrupted routine and "blocked impulses," people are irritable, have unstable attention spans, and are highly suggestible. Thus, social unrest both represents a disruption of routine behavior and provides the context in which new forms of collective behavior may develop (1939:173). This is illustrated in Figure 1.1 along with the major stages and mechanisms by which Blumer argued that such developments proceed.

Collective behavior by an *acting crowd* is said to develop in five steps.[17] First, an *exciting event* (presumably related to the social unrest) catches the attention of a number of people. To the extent those individuals are preoccupied with the exciting event, Blumer argues, they cede control over their behavior to that event (1939:175) and the potential for the future development of an acting crowd is under way.

SOCIAL UNREST

Steps in the
Development
of the Acting Crowd

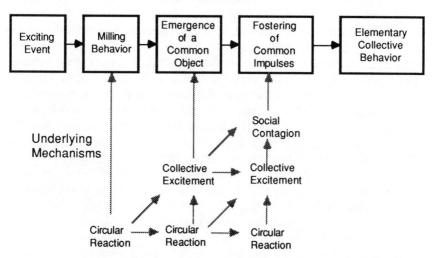

Figure 1.1. The steps and underlying mechanisms in Blumer's explanation of elementary collective behavior.

The mechanisms underlying the development of the next three stages—milling, common object, and common impulse—are circular reaction and its two advanced forms: collective excitement and social contagion. Blumer contends these mechanisms "are present, in varying degree, in all instances of spontaneous group behavior" (1939:176). I have construed these as an ordinal scale pattern in the lower half of Figure 1.1, underlying and driving the development of each successive stage in Blumer's explanation for the development of collective behavior in the acting crowd.

Second, *milling* involves people standing or walking around, even talking about the exciting event. Blumer construed milling as virtually pure *circular reaction* in which people respond directly to and reproduce one another's behavior. He wrote:

> The primary effect of milling is to make the individuals more sensitive and responsive to one another, so that they become increasingly preoccupied with one another and decreasingly responsive to ordinary objects of stimulation. (1939:174)

Blumer compared this preoccupation to hypnosis, and suggested that participants were "inclined to respond to one another quickly, directly, and unwittingly" (1939:197). This, in turn, feeds the development of the common mood.

Blumer's third stage of development is *the emergence of a common object* of attention, presumably one established during the milling of people regarding the exciting event. Its importance is twofold. First, "it gives a common orientation to the people and so provides a common objective to their activity" (1939:179–180). Second, if my interpretation of his reasoning is correct, Blumer argued that people are excited about the common object to which they are giving attention, emphasizing "the power of excited behavior in catching and riveting the attention of observers" (1939:175) who thereby come under the control of that excited behavior. These developments correspond to the underlying mechanism of *collective excitement*, which Blumer characterized "as a more intensive form of milling" (1939:174–175), the phenomenon he has previously defined as "pure circular reaction" (1939:174). This eliminates the individual's normal capacity to use language or imagery to formulate alternative images to whatever is the object of attention (1939:175). Thus, the individual is said to be increasingly aroused, unstable, irresponsible, and likely to "embark on lines of conduct which [he or she] previously would not likely have thought of, much less dared to undertake" (1939:175). The transformation of the individual is at hand!

Recall that, for Blumer, individuals operating in a context of social unrest share thwarted or unsatisfied impulses and dispositions to behave. Thus, the fourth and penultimate stage in the development of the acting crowd is *"the stimulation and fostering of [these common] impulses* that correspond to the crowd objective" (1939:179, emphasis added). Blumer argued that this occurs

> as a result of images that are aroused through the process of suggestion and imitation and reinforced through mutual acceptance. When the members of a crowd have a common impulse oriented toward a fixed image and supported by an intense collective feeling, they are ready to act in the aggressive fashion typical of the acting crowd. (1939:180)

The underlying mechanism for this stage is *social contagion*, which is "an intense form of milling and collective excitement" (1939:176) and therefore an advanced form of circular reaction. Caught up in the excitement, suffering from reduced self-consciousness and the ability to interpret, and preoccupied with a common object and behavior regarding that object, people "are more likely to be subject to the impulses awakened in them." Given that:

> people already have a common disposition to act in a certain way, such as to seek gain, to flee from danger, or to express hatred, the display of such behav-

ior under the conditions of collective excitement easily releases the corresponding impulses on their part. Under such conditions the given kind of behavior will spread like wildfire. (1939:176)

Blumer extended these effects to persons who initially may have been merely interested onlookers and passersby. By the same reasoning noted above, he argued they were "attracted and infected" by the excited behavior they observed. Blumer referred to this (1939:176) as a spectacular feature of social contagion.

Since Blumer believed the acting crowd to be spontaneous, lacking in the traditions, rules, established social organization, division of labor, roles, norms, "we-consciousness," or recognized leadership found in routine social groups, the only basis on which circular reaction could work was the aroused common impulse. He wrote:

That many of these impulses should have an atavistic character is not strange nor, consequently, is it surprising that much of the actual behavior should be violent, cruel, destructive. (1939:181)

The result is that Blumer's "genuine" acting crowds engage in *collective behavior* that is "queer, vehement, and surprising" (1939:181), "strange, forbidding, and sometimes attrocious" (1939:180). Without the faculties of interpretation and self-consciousness, and caught up in the circular reaction of collective excitement and social contagion, crowd members are vulnerable to whatever suggestions complement their surging common impulses and dispositions to act. Blumer wrote:

An individual loses ordinary critical understanding and self control as he enters into rapport with other crowd members and becomes infused by the collective excitement that dominates them. He responds immediately and directly to the remarks and actions of others instead of interpreting these gestures, as he would do in ordinary conduct. (1939:180)

Thus, by Blumer's account as by the preceding accounts of LeBon and Park, the individual has been transformed by the crowd.[18]

The Transformation Hypothesis: An Assessment

The transformation explanation has been widely accepted by laypersons and, until recently, by academics as well.[19] It is frequently used to explain behavior that is unacceptable to the person using the explanation. This dubious tradition dates at least to LeBon, who disapproved of virtually any form of crowd behavior. On the one hand, it is easy to dismiss LeBon's viewpoint as that of a threatened member of the upper classes, fearful of revolutionary street crowds' assault on public order and the stability of the

French Republic. But, on the other hand, LeBon and Park and Blumer did address a fundamental theoretical problem. If conscious and rational individuals are in control of their own behavior most of the time, pursuing their diverse interests and engaging in a diversity of behaviors, when and how and why do they begin to act in common or in concert? Transformation theorists argued that it was necessary to eliminate individual consciousness and rationality for a number of people to act in common or concert. Their argument was and is, upon careful scrutiny, without logical or empirical foundation.

Anonymity, Accountability, and Invincibility

Research on participation in a variety of prosaic gatherings (McPhail 1987), in political (McPhail 1985), religious (Wimberly, Hood, Lipsey, Clelland, and Hay 1975), and sports (Aveni 1977) demonstrations, and probably in riots (cf. Quarantelli and Dynes 1968; Singer 1970; Berk and Aldrich 1972), establishes that most participants are neither alone nor anonymous; rather, they assemble with or soon encounter family members, friends, or acquaintances. Further, the individual's alleged perception that she or he can not be held accountable for her/his own behavior because of the "safety in numbers,"[20] and crowd members' alleged perceptions of their invincibility due to their superior numbers (strength, organization, etc.) over the police, provide evidence of the presence of individual consciousness and reasoning within the crowd, not their absence.

Social Unrest and Self-Control

Blumer argued that the introduction of social unrest, and the widespread disruption of routine behaviors and social relationships, contributed to the loss of critical thought and self-control. A substantial body of evidence now challenges this line of reasoning. Three decades of research establish that human beings confronted with a wide range of problematic situations in hurricanes, floods, tornadoes, explosions, fires, and other disasters remain in control of their wits and their behaviors (e.g., Quarantelli 1954, 1957, 1960, 1981; Smith 1976; Keating 1982; Drabeck 1986; Johnson 1987a,b). In such situations problems are incessant and fear is not uncommon; but incapacitating fear, diminished cognitive ability, and observable loss of control are rare events. Contrary to Blumer's claims, it is characteristic of such problematic situations that individuals' critical thinking and purposive control of behavior are enhanced rather than diminished.[21] Paradoxically, this was a central argument of George Herbert Mead, Blumer's purported mentor. Mead's (1938) "theory of the act," a precursor of today's cybernetic models of cognition and behavior, argued that consciousness, intelligence, and purposive control emerge in relation to problems as individuals formulate, modify, implement, and further modify solutions to those problems. It is puzzling that Blumer did not adopt and apply his mentor's argument.

Contagion, Circular Reaction, and Circular Reasoning

LeBon argued that "the psychological law of mental unity" led to suggestibility, which in turn led to contagion, which in turn led to extraordinary crowd behavior. But the only evidence for any of those underlying mechanisms is the behavior they are supposed to explain. The same flawed reasoning provides the sole evidence for Park's mechanisms of "psychic reciprocity" or "circular reaction," and for Blumer's mechanisms of "circular reaction," "collective excitement," and "social contagion." The fact that people behave collectively is attributed to those underlying mechanisms; but those mechanisms are inferred from the very behaviors they are supposed to produce. This is particularly problematic for Blumer's formulation since, as we have seen, the entire structure of his explanation is based on circular reaction or one of its advanced forms. Thus, the foundation of Blumer's argument is a tautology.

Suggestibility, Suggestion, and Social Psychology

Another unfortunate tautology in the transformation explanation is suggestibility, a mental state that LeBon inferred from the observed compliance of some crowd members with the suggestion(s) addressed to them by another crowd member. In fact, suggestibility is nothing more or less than verbal magic, one more instance of inferring an underlying causal mechanism from the phenomenon that mechanism is alleged to explain. Such circular reasoning is all too common in many social science explanations of crowd behavior.

We must not lose sight, however, of the important, recurring, and falsifiable relationship between explicit or implicit suggestions (at time one) for alterations in behavior and the presence or absence of corresponding alterations in behavior (at time two). That relationship was a central focus of the new discipline of social psychology emerging in Europe and the United States at the turn of the twentieth century. It was examined in the early experiments of Triplett (1898) and F. Allport (1920a) on the impact of others' presence or behaviors on the individual's behavior. The classic experimental studies by Sherif (1936), Asch (1951), and Milgram (1961) examined the impact of others' judgments on the individual's perceptions of the physical world. Dozens of subsequent experimental studies examined the impact of others' presence and behaviors on many additional aspects of individual perception, opinion, and behavior. A half-century of social psychological research has now rendered suggestion a viable and important piece of the much larger and well-documented phenomenon called social influence. The individual may behave differently in the presence of others than when alone. But others' presence and behaviors are of consequence for the individual's behavior in a wide range of social situations, not primarily, let alone uniquely, in the crowd as proposed by LeBon, Park, and Blumer (cf. Rigney 1972).

I do not argue that the individual unwittingly absorbs others' suggestions or that those suggestions somehow take control of the individual's behavior without his or her active participation. The individual must tell himself/herself to do what is suggested, or some approximation thereof, if the suggestion is to have an impact. Nowhere is this more clearly illustrated than in hypnosis, the phenomenon frequently offered as the ultimate evidence of suggestibility.

Hypnosis

Virtually all the transformation theorists have linked heightened suggestibility to a hypnotic state in the crowd. Under the influence of collective hypnosis individuals are alleged unwittingly and uncritically to enact suggestions directed to them by crowd leaders or other authority figures. I am unable to locate any published research on collective hypnosis.[22] However, since 1955 there have been hundreds of experimental studies of hypnosis, and of its behavioral, phenomenological, and neurophysiological effects on individuals. That research bears directly on the present discussion.

For several centuries hypnosis has been thought to be a unique state of consciousness—the hypnotic trance state—fundamentally different from that of the fully waking state, and brought about by the now-standardized trance induction procedures, e.g., "Relax. You are getting very relaxed. You are now very drowsy. You are falling into a deep, deep, peaceful sleep." The alleged consequences of the hypnotic trance state include subjects carrying out the suggestions for extraordinary nonverbal and verbal behaviors (e.g., the plank posture, arm levitation, locked clasped hands, verbal inhibition, posthypnotic response, selective amnesia, selective analgesia and anesthesia).

Carefully controlled experimental studies have demonstrated that subjects perform those standardized nonverbal and verbal behaviors as well or better in a positive suggestion condition as in the traditional trance induction condition (Barber 1969; plus more than 100 experimental papers summarized in Barber 1972, 1973; see also Spanos, Ham, and Barber 1973; Spanos and Barber 1974; Spanos 1982; Sarbin 1950).

Subjects who comply with suggestions do have different experiences than those who do not. This occurs, however, "not because they are in different 'states' but because they are receiving different communications" from others and are giving those communications to themselves (Barber 1972:120).[23] The trancelike characteristics of subjects "appear to be artifacts that the experimenter can put into the suggestive situation and can also take out of the situation, and they certainly are not necessary (and may be extraneous) for high response to [i.e., compliance with] test suggestions" (Barber 1972:149–150).

Finally, repeated efforts have failed to establish any physiological differences in the alleged trance state of compliant vs. noncompliant subjects.

> Physiological variables vary in hypnotic subjects in the same way as in normal individuals, that is, in accordance with whatever activity they are engaged in.
> . . .
> In the same way as any other normal individual, the subject who is highly responsive to test suggestions (and said to be in a hypnotic trance) shows a high level of skin conductance, basal metabolic rate, heart rate, and so forth, when he is given suggestions leading to activity or arousal, and a lower level when he is given suggestions that lead to quietude or relaxation. (Barber 1972:159)

Until there is systematic evidence to the contrary, we can reasonably reject claims of collective hypnotic states and related explanations for people in crowds mindlessly doing what is suggested by others. Unless physically or chemically constrained, the individual in the crowd, as elsewhere, controls his or her behavior by means of self-instructions for behavioral adjustments in relation to the goals or objectives he or she is pursuing (Mead 1938; Powers 1973a). The fact that, in the crowd as elsewhere, individuals frequently tell themselves to pursue goals or objectives suggested by others does not alter the fact that those individuals remain in control of their own behavior. They are simply doing so with information or proposals provided by others.

Routine Social Behavior vs. Crowd Behavior

Tarde (1901) made two elementary distinctions among crowds. One was fundamentally erroneous; the other was fundamentally sound but was never developed. Unfortunately, the erroneous distinction was seized upon by Park and perpetuated by Blumer. I refer here to the distinction Tarde advanced between "rational discussion" within publics and its absence within crowds.

We now know that most contemporary gatherings, and I suspect also those in the time of Tarde, Lebon, Park, and Blumer, are composed not of isolated individuals but of small groups of family, friends, or acquaintances. Only cursory investigation might have established this fundamental fact for Park and Blumer, both renowned advocates of field research. Further field research would have established for Park and Blumer that members of most crowds, or temporary gatherings engage in individual sequences of behavior and occasionally in sequences of behavior in common or in concert with other members of the gathering.[24] But the form of social behavior in which they most frequently engage is some form of interaction, including conversations, within their small groups of family, friends, or acquaintances. While the content of those conversations among companions varies, sometimes (but not always) dealing with the substantive focus of the gathering, and the criteria for judging a conversation rational may be arguable, my own observations and those of many others suggest these conversations within crowds are just as rational as those taking place in living rooms, bars, classrooms, and churches (cf. Couch 1968; Berk 1972b, 1974a).

Of course, as the number of individuals in any gathering increases, the possibility diminishes for every individual to engage in conversation with every other individual in that gathering. But this is as true of any public as it is of any crowd, and perhaps more so because of the physical separation of members of the former and the physical proximity of members of the latter. Unfortunately, Park and Blumer seem not to have done their fieldwork. Instead, they proceeded to develop general explanations for phenomena that are rare events if they ever occur at all.

Tarde's (1901) valid and important distinction among crowds was overlooked by Park, and therefore by Blumer. Although Tarde accepted LeBon's characterization and explanation of the proletarian street crowds, he noted that these hardly exhausted all the possibilities. He considered such crowds "rudimentary, transitory and amorphous aggregate[s]" (1901:168, cited in Moscovici 1985:164). He contrasted these with the "organized, hierarchical, durable and regular crowd[s]" (1901:168) observed in the collective actions of strikers, in demonstrations, and in processions. Tarde regrettably termed the former "natural" and the latter "artificial" crowds, but he usefully distinguished between the capabilities and potentials of the two, viz., the improvisations of the former vs. the planning and organizing of the latter (cf. Moscovici 1985:160–69).[25] Had Park and Blumer analyzed crowds on the basis of variations in their social organization and their capacity for planning, organizing, and coordinating social behavior, rather than on the basis of alleged variations in underlying psychological mechanisms, the history of collective psychology would have been dramatically different. It might have been what it surely must become, viz., a collective sociology, the study of people behaving with and in relation to one another within temporary gatherings.

One problem with Tarde's analysis, of course, is that gatherings should not be dichotomized. They are more accurately and usefully construed along continua, e.g., one registering variations in the complexity of the collective behaviors in which members of the gathering engage, and another registering variations in the social relationships, the organizing and coordinating behaviors taken by those people to produce the collective behaviors that occur.[26] The more social relationships among participants and the more organizing behaviors taken by them, the more likely their collective behaviors will be both complex and sustained (cf. McPhail and Wohlstein 1986). Those relationships and organizing behaviors are not limited to political, religious, or sports demonstrations and ceremonial gatherings; elementary forms are found in even the most prosaic temporary gatherings of human beings on beaches and campus quadrangles, in parks and plazas, and in other public places (McPhail 1987).

There are two remaining, and in my judgment quite serious, problems with transformation explanations of collective behavior and the crowd. The first was noted by Turner (1964a:386) but bears repeating here. Transformation explanations, almost by definition, are limited to extraordinary sequences of behavior within the crowd, to "the extreme and rare instances of behavior" seldom observed by field-workers (cf. Wright 1978; Snow, Zurcher, and Peters 1981; McPhail 1988). Turner properly reminds us that "it would be unwise to adopt the exceptional abberation as the model for collective behavior as a whole" (1964a:386). Moreover, Tilly (1978) argues, it is from the routine and the ordinary that the extraordinary develops; we must therefore understand the former if we ever hope to understand the latter.

The second and I believe even more important point, concerns a flaw that LeBon, Park, and Blumer share with virtually all other traditional and contemporary theorists of the crowd and collective behavior. They failed to specify and define, let alone carefully describe, the behaviors they claimed to explain. As Merton (1987) has recently argued so persuasively, we must first establish the phenomenon to be explained before we proceed to develop explanations for that phenomenon.

It is perhaps in this respect that Blumer's theory of collective behavior provides the most puzzling paradox of all. Throughout his career Blumer advocated a methodology of exploring and inspecting the phenomena to be explained, enabling the scholar to

> talk from fact and not from speculation . . . so that he knows that the questions he asks of the empirical area are meaningful and relevant to it, that the problem he poses is not artificial, that the kinds of data he seeks are significant in terms of the empirical world . . . (1969:42)

There is little evidence that Blumer pursued those steps either in his initial development and systematization of the LeBon-Park analysis of collective behavior, nor at any point in the next four decades across which he clung to that analysis (Blumer 1978).

A number of sociologists (e.g., Quarantelli and Hundley 1969; Berk 1972b, 1974a; Wright 1978; Snow et al. 1981; Lofland 1982a; Lofland and Fink 1982; McPhail 1988; McPhail and Wohlstein 1986) have pursued one version or another of Blumer's call for field research, for detailed observations and careful analyses of crowds and collective behavior. Most reach similar conclusions, viz., the range and variation of individual and social behaviors in which people engage in temporary gatherings, and the ongoing alternation between these different forms of behavior, requires a full measure of conscious, purposive, and intelligent effort by participants. Not only is circular reaction or nonsymbolic interaction a tautological explanation, it simply will not bear the weight of the range of phenomena to be explained. There is a lesson here for students of Herbert Blumer and for students of the range of social behaviors Blumer urged us to investigate even if he failed to do so himself.

Notes

1.   According to Becker and Barnes (1961:1008), the criminologists were not the first. As early as 1833, Gioia gave considerable attention to the relationship between the number of people in the crowd and the intensity of imitation and suggestion. Cattaneo, in 1859, outlined "a system of collective psychology."

2.   Sighele's claim that LeBon (1895) plagiarized his ideas probably had some validity. Park's (1904) doctoral dissertation reviewed the literature of the collective psychologists and began with Sighele's (1891) work before turning to LeBon (1895). The latter's basic arguments were very similar to Sighele's ideas, many of which he, in turn, attributed to his mentor Ferri (Becker and Barnes 1961:1008).

3.   Terry Clark (1969) reports Tarde's basic ideas on the crowd were first set down in a (1892) paper, "The crimes of crowds." Tarde published another (1893) paper on "Crowds and sects from the Point of View of the Criminal." Tarde's distinctions between publics and crowds, and among crowds, were outlined in his (1898) paper on "The Public and the Crowd," and his (1901) book on *Opinion and the Crowd*.

4.   LeBon's emphasis on the *transformation* of the individual within or by the crowd is maintained by Park and by Blumer. Thus I label their approaches as transformation rather than contagion explanations, as they are sometimes called (cf. Turner 1964a). Contagion is an equivocal and confusion concept. On the one hand it is occasionally used to describe the spread of a behavior across a number of people. More frequently it is used improperly to refer to some psychological state of those people or some attribute of the behavior (e.g., contagious) that is alleged responsible the spread of the behavior but that, in practice, is inferred from the very behavior it is supposed to produce.

5.   This feature of LeBon's argument, of course, drew praise and elaboration from Freud (1921); e.g., the crowd strips away the individual's superego, allowing the id to emerge and to control the individual's behavior.

6.   LeBon's extrapolation from the hypnotist and patient in the hospital to the

leader and the crowd may not be as crude as one might first suspect. Moscovici reports Freud's observations of hypnosis in group settings in hospitals: "Every patient who is making his first acquaintance with hypnosis watches for a while how older patients fall asleep, how they are obedient during hypnosis and how, after waking up, they admit that their symptoms have disappeared. This brings [the observing patient] into a condition of psychical preparedness, which causes him, for his part, to fall into deep hypnosis as soon as his turn comes" (1985:83).

7.   LeBon believed leaders were more likely to do this anyway because they were presumed to be under greater influence, than mere rank-and-file crowd members, of "the psychological law of mental unity" and the effects of "genotypic similarity."

8.   The general French academic community remained skeptical of LeBon's ideas for many years (Nye 1975; and Moscovici 1985).

9.   Park coined the concept "collective behavior" and he offered some interesting proposals for its analytic use; regrettably he did not provide an operational definition of the concept enabling the investigation of those proposals.

10.   A reviewer argues that while "the main thrust of Park's analysis is as you say . . . Park was never so precise and internally consistent about anything as you paint him" including his treatment of circular reaction and collective behavior. "Park did introduce the term "circular reaction" but as a sensitizing concept rather than a precise term, and he left the dynamics quite vague" (Annoymous 1988). The same reviewer contends it was "Blumer's nature to try to make things precise" and that it was Blumer, not Park, who placed the nonsymbolic interpretation upon "circular reaction." This may be, but it was Park not Blumer who contrasted the public with the crowd: "In the public, interaction takes the form of discussion. . . . The crowd does not discuss and hence it does not reflect" (Park and Burgess 1921:385). Blumer could have construed Park differently of course, but he did not do so.

11.   I draw here on Clark's (1969) excellent introduction to his edited collection of Tarde's work, including a translation of selections from Tarde's (1901) book, *Opinion and the Crowd*.

12.   Park does not mention Tarde's (1898) paper but repeatedly cites Tarde's (1901) *Opinion and the Crowd*, in which, according to Park and Burgess' (1921:385) discussion, "The Public and the Crowd" was reprinted.

13.   For a critical examination of Blumer's analysis of collective behavior applied to a classroom, see McPhail (1969).

14.   Blumer used the concepts of interpretative interaction and symbolic interaction interchangeably and distinguished them from nonsymbolic interaction in two earlier publications (1936, 1937).

15.   Blumer followed Park's analysis of social unrest and circular reaction although the chronological and causal relationships between the two phenomena were neither clearly nor consistently presented.

16.   Blumer (1978) developed a more extensive analysis of social unrest based in part on his observations of gatherings associated with various movements on the campus of the University of California at Berkeley during the 1960s and early 1970s. I do not draw from that analysis here because therein (a) Blumer maintains his initial (1939) distinction between circular reaction and interpretative interaction; (b) Blumer maintains his earlier (1939) analysis of the crowd and collective behavior; and (c) Blumer's primary focus in the later (1978) article is on the origins, characteristics, and consequences of social unrest rather than on the dynamics of collective behavior in the crowd.

17.   According to Blumer (1939) the acting crowd (e.g., a lynch mob) has a longer duration than the casual crowd around an accident, engages in more nonroutine

behavior than the conventionalized crowd at a spectator sports event, and has an external objective unlike the expressive crowd at an evangelical religious revival.

18.   Blumer, like LeBon, believed crowd members acquire a "sense of power, of ego-expansion, . . . of rectitude," and, "a sense of invincibility and conviction in [their] actions" (Blumer 1939:181).

19.   The first critiques of the transformation explanation were advanced by pre-disposition theorists (e.g., Allport 1924; Miller and Dollard 1941), who argued that the individual behaves no differently in the crowd than when alone; instead, the presence of others with similar predispositions as the individual provide "social facilitation" for the individual's predispositions and corresponding behaviors. The predisposition argument is logically flawed and without empirical support (cf. McPhail 1971; Miller, Bolce, and Halligan 1977).

Early sociological critiques of the transformation explanation were set forth by Bramson (1961), Turner (1964a), Couch (1968), McPhail (1969), and Berk (1974b). I have incorporated many of those criticisms here.

Psychologists have perpetuated the transformation hypothesis under the rubric of deindividuation theory (cf. Festinger et al. 1952; Zimbardo 1969; Diener 1980) and claim empirical evidence for altered cognitive states. I believe that theory and evidence as flawed as the claims of transformation theory, but a separate essay will be required to give deindividuation theory the careful examination it warrants.

20.   Crowd members occasionally observe the police extricate individual offenders from the crowd and hold them specifically accountable for their illegal behavior. On other occasions the police may respond to an entire gathering, holding everyone categorically responsible and accountable for the illegal actions of a few. The relationship between safety in numbers and accountability makes more sense on paper than it does in the streets.

21.   It is ironic that one of Blumer's graduate students, E. L. Quarantelli (1954, 1957, 1960), was one of the pioneer investigators of individual and group behavior in disasters, documenting the rational vis-à-vis irrational and organized vis-à-vis disorganized nature of human behavior in problematic situations.

22.   Stage hypnosis exhibitions involving several subjects at once, e.g., at state fairs, in shopping malls, or at conventions, have been the subject of investigation and analysis by Meeker and Barber (1971). Those exhibits involve the very careful selection of "highly cooperative" subjects by the hypnotist, and extensive *sotto voce* coaching of the former by the latter, e.g., "Let's put on a real good show for these folks now." In short, what the audience observes in stage hypnosis, magic shows, and healing demonstrations is a carefully contrived performance by a skilled conjurer and very cooperative, often quite earnest, subjects.

23.   For a sociological analysis of the interaction and communication between hypnotist and subject in the construction of varying levels of hypnosis, see Dan Miller (1986).

24.   Turner (1964a:387) was the first critic to note that transformation (or contagion) theories cannot explain the shifts that occur in crowd behavior.

25.   Moscovici's *L'age des foules* was originally published in French (1981) and includes quotations and pages from a (1910) second edition of Tarde's (1901) *L'opinion et le foule*. I have quoted from J. C. Whitehouse's (1985) English translation of Moscovici's book, *The Age of Crowds*.

26.   In fact, Tarde sketches such a continuum. "From that rudimentary, transitory and amorphous [natural] aggregate, a series of intermediate stages lead up to the kind of [artificial] organized, hierarchical, durable and regular crowd that can be called a corporation, in the widest sense of the word. The most intense form of a religious

corporation is a monastery, the most intense form of a secular one is a regiment or a workshop. The largest forms of them are respectively church and state (1901:168, cited in Moscovici 1985:164). Regretably Tarde did not pursue this analysis of variations in the organization of crowds.

A similar continuum was implied but never developed in Park's work (1904; 1930; Park and Burgess, 1921). Park unfortunately opted for a psychological rather than an organizational analysis of collective behavior.

2

Perpetuating the Myth: Allport; Miller and Dollard

Introduction

LeBon's characterization and explanation of the crowd gained widespread acceptance in nonacademic circles at home and abroad. Among sociologists and psychologists, the reception was mixed. I have noted that his ideas were accepted by some French (e.g., Tarde 1901) and some American (e.g., Park 1904; Park and Burgess 1921) sociologists. Sigmund Freud devoted more than a third of his *Group Psychology and Analysis of the Ego* (1921) to an enthusiastic analysis and elaboration of LeBon's views of the crowd. But LeBon's ideas remained suspect for many French academic psychologists, and they were vigorously attacked by the American social psychologist Floyd Allport (1920b). Allport offered an alternative theoretical explanation of individual behavior in the crowd that turned on (1924) innate drives, learned responses to those drives, and the social facilitation of those individual predispositions. American psychologist Neal Miller and sociologist John Dollard (1941) ignored LeBon and the transformation theorists, and offered a learning theory of crowd behavior based on rewarded responses to innate drives and learned cues, the aggressive consequences of depriving learned responses or frustrating their reward, and the crowd's intensification of learned responses.

In this chapter I review and critique Allport's and Miller and Dollard's explanations of crowd behavior. Their arguments were among the most influential in the mid–twentieth century and warrant careful review for at least three reasons. Allport offered the first sustained critique of the transformation perspective while, at the same time, providing some experimental evidence for his alternative theory of the social facilitation of individual responses. Miller and Dollard were the first to offer a systematic, cumulative theory of individual and crowd behavior, including their deprivation-frustration-aggression hypothesis, which was widely adopted to explain the incidence of and participation in violent crowds. Beyond this, Allport's and Miller and Dollard's explanations were influential because they were reflections of and contributions to a view of human behavior that came to be dominant in the twentieth century, viz., that behavior is a function of innate or acquired predispositions to behave that individuals carry within them from place to place, and require only a situational stimulus to trigger the predisposed response. The crowd, in turn, is simply a collection of individuals brought together by, and behaving alike within the crowd because of, their similar predispositions.

Floyd H. Allport (1890–1978)

LeBon failed to realize that . . . it was not the "collective mind" or the "crowd impulse" which stormed the Bastille and guillotined scores of aristocrats. It was the individual citizen who did this. . . . It is the individual who is the raison d'être of the crowd. His response both provides the motive for the collective behavior and limits its direction. Action is facilitated and intensified through the presence of the crowd; but it originates in the drives of the individual. (F. Allport 1924:295–96)

Allport's rejection of the transformation explanation was based on his rejection (1920b, 1924, 1927a,b) of what he called "the group fallacy" advanced by LeBon and other collective psychologists (e.g., McDougall 1908), and sociologists. By group fallacy Allport referred to "the error of substituting the group as a whole as a principle of explanation" (1920b:62). He argued that error took two forms. The first alleged a group psychology, e.g., LeBon's psychological law of mental unity or McDougall's group mind. Allport considered this fallacious because only individuals have minds. He believed the second fallacy was any attempt to explain collective or individual behavior in terms of groups, societies, or cultures without regard to their underlying causes. Allport argued (1920b:69–70) that collective phenomena could only be explained in terms of their underlying individual psychological processes, which could only be explained in terms of their underlying physiological processes, which in turn could only be explained in terms of their underlying physical and chemical processes. Thus, for Allport, sociologists were limited to the description of social or collective phenomena, which for him, at the time, referred to two or more individuals simultaneously engaging in the same behavior.[1]

For an explanation of social or collective phenomena, Allport claimed sociologists must rely on the underlying social psychology of the individual, which he defined as "the behavior of the individual which stimulates other individuals or is a response to such stimulation from others" (1920b:73).

Allport subsequently developed the argument (1924) that all individual behavior, inside or outside the crowd, is predisposed by innate or acquired responses to satisfy basic drives or overcome interference with their satisfaction. Allport's formulation exemplifies what I will call *the predisposition explanation* for the crowd and collective behavior.[2]

Allport viewed all human behavior as learned modifications of two types of innate human response: the avoidance response, such as the infant's withdrawal from or struggle against noxious stimuli; and the approach response, such as the movement of a hungry person toward a food source or the movement of a sexually aroused person to maintain excitation of erogenous zones:

> These reflexes are prepotent. They are of highest importance for the welfare of both the individual and the species. The intracies of human conduct arise from modifications of these simple prepotent responses. (1924:79)

Allport viewed the family and the work group as routine struggle groups. Crowds were another matter. He wrote:

> Crowds . . . are struggle groups of an elementary and violent character. With the exception of a few varieties, such as panics and religious revivals, the reactions of struggling fighting, and destroying are their universal phenomena. (1924:294)

Allport made an additional distinction between routine group action and crowd action that is unique. Rarely did any early theorists of crowds offer a definition of the phenomenon to be explained. Allport's characterization provides a rough image of one kind of crowd phenomena:

> A crowd is a collection of individuals who are [arranged more or less side by side and face to back, and are] all attending and reacting to some common object, their reactions being of a simple prepotent sort and accompanied by strong emotional responses. (1924:292)

Allport contrasted this with routine coacting groups in which individual members either take actions toward one another face-to-face, or they take actions regarding the separate objects that compose their collective task. Allport also contrasted the complex and nonemotional actions of routine groups with the simple and emotional actions of the crowd.

Whereas transformation theorists offered no explanation for the origins or formation of the crowd, this problem was central to Allport's formulation. He argued that two or more people are brought together by their common interest in overcoming interference with some response they have learned in order to satisfy their drives. He wrote:

The menacing of the drives of a large number of individuals simultaneously both draws them together and incites them to common action. The struggle and anger may take a middle form such as rivalry for supremacy in a football match; or it may be as violent as that of the lynching party. But it is always a struggle of some sort against limitation, oppression, and oppositions to the free satisfaction of original or derived drives. (1924:294)

Allport believed (1924:294) the common predispositions that brought people together could be further prepared to be more readily released in one or both of two ways: by a leader commanding or suggesting a course of collective action, or by other crowd members modeling a course of action. Allport (1924:245) treated suggestions as conditioned stimuli that controlled behavior (1) by preparing the individual to respond once a signal was given, (2) by signaling the individual to respond, or (3) by augmenting a response that was already underway. Allport noted that a leader might ask people to stand and sing a song, or to pledge allegiance to the flag; or the leader might tell jokes to evoke laughter, or ask rhetorical questions to evoke answers. In each instance, similar responses by those people would make them aware of one another, and of their actions in common.

Allport argued that suggestions have no compelling consequences in and of themselves:

Crowd members are suggestible in the hands of a leader; but the suggestion must always be in the direction of some compelling response of the individuals. . . . Action is facilitated and intensified through the presence of the crowd; but it originates in the drives of the individual. (1924:195–196)

The first crowd members to comply with those suggestions, according to Allport's analysis, constituted models for those who had not yet acted. But who might be the first to comply? Where might such persons be found? Allport wrote:

The first to act or express their feelings are the most suggestible and unin-hibited persons. Ignorant and impulsive individuals may thus precipitate an avalanche of social stimulation which finally overwhelms the more intelligent and self-controlled. The vast power of crowd facilitation may thus be at the disposal of the least competent. This is one of the serious charges brought against the crowd as a factor in modern social life. . . . The initial movements which release and augment the activity of the crowd members usually begin at some center, and spread in widening circles to the periphery of the crowd. The process is swift and complete.[3] (1924:310)

Allport used an example of striking mine workers confronting scab la-borers hired by the owners to cross the picket lines. He described a hypo-thetical striker with conflicting tendencies to behave. On the one hand, the individual's prepotent drives for food and for protecting his family had been thwarted by the labor dispute. His learned tendency to respond was to attack the scab intruders, "to drive them out, or if necessary destroy them" (1941:310); but, on the other hand, Allport reasoned the same individual had also learned to refrain from attacking others, particularly when such attacks could be observed, disapproved, and punished by authorities. The resolution of these competing tendencies to respond, according to Allport, might be influenced by the less inhibited, more impulsive striker who fired the first shot or struck the first blow against the scabs:

> The individual sees with his own eyes that others are delivering the blow he longs to deliver, and are thereby expressing, not disapproval of acts of violence, but the strongest kind of approval. (1924:300)

Assuming the individual joins in, the result is more inclusive collective action; and "the sights and sounds of others' reactions facilitate and increase further the responses of each" (1924:292). Allport called this "social facilitation."[4]

It bears repeating that Allport did not construe others' suggestions for or modeling of behavior as creating or instigating anything the individual would not or could not have done anyway. Allport wrote:

> Since individual preparation for response underlies [all] crowd phenomena, it follows that *the course of action is fairly determined from the start*. . . . As long as it remains a crowd it must cling to the fundamental reactions upon which the individuals have been launched. (1924:295; emphasis added)

Allport continued:

> Nothing new or different is added by the crowd situation except an intensification of the feeling [and responses] already present and the possibility of concerted action. The individual in the crowd behaves just as he would behave alone, only more so. (1924:295)

Allport's own experimental work (1920a), and earlier experiments by Triplett (1898) and Mayer (1903), led him to conclude that "the social stimulations present in the co-acting group brought about an increase in the speed and quantity of work produced by individuals" (1924:284). He reported that this "social increment effect" was more pronounced in overt, physical efforts than in purely intellectual tasks; more pronounced in younger than older persons; and more pronounced in less competent than in more competent workers.[5]

Allport construed social facilitation as a reciprocal phenomenon. Individuals seeing others perform the acts they are prepared to perform are more likely to proceed accordingly. In turn, they "see or hear the intensified response which their behavior . . . produced in [their neighbors] and are in turn restimulated to a higher level of activity" (1924:301). Allport called this "circular reverberation" and illustrated it with the exchange and escalation of the exhortations of fundamentalist preachers and the *amens* of their congregations.

Allport recognized the potential contribution of crowd ecology and suggested that the physical juxtaposition of individuals to one another further prepared their predispositions and their recognition that surrounding others were behaving the same:

> In a crowd . . . the irregular grouping of persons makes it possible for each to be affected from all sides, and to receive stimuli, not from merely one or two, but from a large number of individuals. . . . [T]he strength of social facilitation is multiplied manyfold by this [spatial] arrangement; [and] the individual is overwhelmed with greater submissiveness in the observed presence of large numbers. (1924:301)

Allport made repeated references to the individual's learned "attitude of submission to large numbers" and argued that most humans were conditioned to submit to the will of the majority. He speculated that the consequence of large numbers was "probably based on the primitive ascendance of direct physical power" (1924:301); that is, larger numbers of others can physically overwhelm and thereby secure the submission of any individual. Allport also suggested that "the strength of [crowd] excitement increases in geometrical proportion to the number of individuals present."

Allport's differences with transformation theorists extended to his explicit treatment of the individual's recognition of the presence and actions of others in relation to the individual's own actions. Allport's model of crowd development turns on the individual hearing and reacting to a speaker's utterances or a model's actions, seeing and hearing immediate neighbors responding in kind, and comparing those responses to the individual's own inclinations. Allport conjectured the individual might then conclude that "my meaning is their meaning" and even perhaps that "our meaning is the meaning of all persons throughout the crowd, both near and far" (1924:306–7). Thus, Allport viewed the individual as projecting from his or her own responses and those in the immediate surround to those out of sight and perhaps out of earshot as well.

Allport called this the "impression of universality" but conceded (1924:307) it was more likely an illusion of universality (cf. Turner and Killian 1972). Illusion or not, Allport believed the individual used such impressions of "the entire throng" to justify engaging in extraordinary action: "All doubt or worry as to one's own course of action disappears when one finds one is acting with the other members of the crowd" (1924:312). The individual might therefore justify mob violence as follows:

> (1) I could do this thing which I want to do as a member of a crowd because no one would observe me, and I would therefore escape punishment. (2) Even if I should be detected, no one could punish me without punishing all the others. But to punish all would be a physical impossibility. And (3) more than that, it doesn't seem possible to punish a crowd because that would be making a large number of people suffer. And that is unjust; it is the interest of the many which must always be safeguarded. Hence (4) since the whole crowd show by their acts that they wish the deed to be done, it must be right after all. So large a number of people could not be in the wrong. And finally (5) since so many people will benefit by this act, to perform it is a public duty and a righteous deed. (1924:312–13)

But, according to Allport, the preceding is not merely a spurious line of reasoning. It is rationalization. *"The deeds of crowd members are not rationally controlled,* because the thought process in crowds is used only to serve the prepotent interests, and not to direct them" (1924:317; my emphasis). Instead, the individual is controlled by predispositions; and the resulting crowd behaviors are characterized by Allport as unsocialized, primitive, and nonrational responses to thwarted drives. Thus, Allport's crowd did not drive individuals mad; it was driven by people sharing some "madness" in common.

Over the next 15 years, theories of individual learning and personality dynamics grew to new heights and strengths in academic psychology, supplanting Allport's comparatively elementary explanation. Miller and Dollard capitalized on those developments by proposing a learning theory explanation for crowd behavior that drew from and extended Allport's predisposition and social facilitation approach.

Neil E. Miller (b. 1909) and John Dollard (1900–1981)

> Several generations of sociologists and psychologists have examined [crowd behavior] and have made available a body of facts and principles. The most obvious and certain of these conclusions will be analyzed here. (Miller and Dollard 1941:218)

> Crowds are most likely to react . . . with common mass responses which have been learned individually by everyone . . . running, striking, pursuing, fleeing, jeering, and copying. (229)

> Crowd behavior is often surprising because we have such a poor idea of how individuals can act when they are alone. (230)

> Men act in crowds the same as they do when alone, but under some circumstances, more so. (230)

The Learning Formulation

The psychologist Neal Miller and the sociologist John Dollard argued that all human behavior is a function of drives, cues, responses, and rewards:

> In order to learn one must want something [drive], notice something [cue], do something [response], and get something [reward]. (1941:2)

Figure 2.1 is my representation of the relationships between these basic building blocks in Miller and Dollard's theory of individual behavior. They defined *drive* as "any strong stimulus which impels action" (1941:8), e.g., innate or primary drives (pain, thirst, hunger, fatigue, cold, sex). Miller and Dollard argued that individuals behave to reduce the strength or intensity of the pain, thirst, or hunger drives, and that social organization developed to satisfy those drives and to keep them under control (cf. Freud 1921). They claimed secondary drives were acquired on the basis of primary drives, and included anxiety (based on pain), appetites (based on food, sex, thirst), money, approval, and ambition (based on various combinations of primary drives) (1941:18–19).

Cues were construed as stimuli determining when and where the indi-

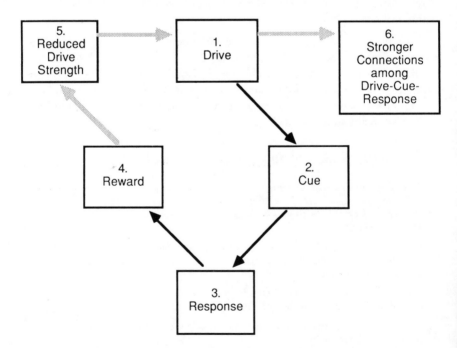

Figure 2.1.   The learning formulation. (after Miller and Dollard 1941)

vidual should make what responses; e.g., an individual's statements or movements, a traffic light, the date on a calendar, a factory whistle, or hands on a clock. Miller and Dollard distinguished (1941:21) drive stimuli from cue stimuli on the basis of the strength of the former and the distinctiveness of the latter.

Response was construed as any individual behavior, sound, or movement. Miller and Dollard believed that all individuals have hierarchies of response, ranging from the most dominant and frequent to the weakest and least frequent responses to particular combinations of drives and cues. Each response was said to be learned in combination with a particular cue; the hierarchy of responses could therefore be changed through learning. Lengthy sequences of varied but related responses could be elicited by the presentation of a single cue, e.g., the statement "Back the car out of the driveway." New responses were merely a matter of learning a new sequence or combination of old responses, or pairing them with new or different eliciting cues.

Miller and Dollard defined *reward* (1941:29) as any event that strengthens a stimulus-response connection. "Without reward, people fail to learn" (1941:32). Primary rewards include comfort, water, food, and sex. Secondary rewards include money, social approval, and high status, but secondary rewards lose their value unless occasionally paired with innate primary rewards (1941:30). Rewards have their effect because they reduce drive strength (1941:36). Responses that reduce drive strength are rewarded. Responses that do not reduce drive strength are not rewarded.

Miller and Dollard claimed that when "some one response is followed by a reward, the connection between the [drive-cue] stimulus pattern and this response is strengthened [in the hierarchy], so that the next time the same drive and other cues are present, this response is more likely to occur" (1941:20). Miller and Dollard believed that the majority of human behaviors were learned in this manner, including language (which they acknowledged accelerated and expanded the range of learning), imitative behaviors (by observing others engage in rewarded responses related to the observer's drives), and aggressive responses (e.g., striking and pursuing, which were said to be learned upon the frustration of a routine drive-cue-response-reward sequence).

The Frustration-Aggression
Formulation

The idea that "aggressive behavior always presupposes frustration," and is therefore an innate response, was initially stated by Dollard, Doob, Miller, Mowrer, and Sears (1939). Miller and Dollard (1941:63) subsequently took the revised position that aggression was but one response to frustration and that the likelihood of frustration producing aggression was "largely a product of learning." I have diagrammed their deprivation-frustration-aggression (DFA) formulation in Figure 2.2. They construed *frustration* as some type of disruption of a previously learned sequence of relationships among (1) drive, (2) cue, (3) response, or (7) reward. They believed that, typically, (4) frustration involved an interference with the completion of a response leading to a reward (1941:63), or the presentation of a reward ordinarily following a particular drive-cue-response sequence (1941:63), or the threat of interference or prevention of response and reward (1941:238, 240–1). The original hypothesis (Dollard et al. 1939) that frustration always led to aggression was subsequently modified to assert that aggression was but one form of learned response to frustration. The individual was thought to learn, by direct experience or observation, that when another person intervened or blocked a reward, "responses of aggression are likely to cause the other individual to get out of the way and to allow the reward to be secured" (Miller and Dollard 1941:63).[6]

Thus, for Miller and Dollard "reward is the selective agent in the learning [process] which produces the adult habits of aggression" (1941:63). More-

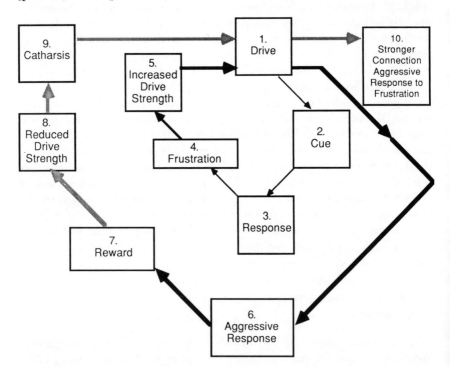

Figure 2.2. The deprivation–frustration and aggression formulation (DFA) (after Miller and Dollard 1941).

over, if an individual's repeated nonaggressive responses were also frustrated, the probability increased that some form of aggressive response would occur. Miller and Dollard further assumed that threat or actual interference with a response or its reward would (5) increase drive strength until the person's response repertoire yielded (6) an aggressive response to overcome (4) the frustration, and result in (7) a reward.

Consistent with their learning formulation, rewards were said (1941:36) to (8) reduce drive strengths, which in turn was said to have two consequences (1941:63): (9) a "catharsis" of frustration thereby relaxing the individual, and (10) a strengthening of connections in the individual's response hierarchy between frustrations of the drive-cue-response-reward sequence and aggressive responses to that frustration.

In this manner the individual was said to learn the consequences of aggressive responses by direct experience as well as through observing the consequences of others' responses. Although most individuals learned that aggression was frequently punished, Miller and Dollard believed individuals also learned that "aggressive responses are most rewarded when performed in concert" (1941:249). Thus, they extended their explanation of learned aggression to crowd behavior.

The Crowd Behavior
Formulation

Miller and Dollard's explanation of the crowd included much of the litany that appeared in both earlier and in later analyses of the crowd. For example, they believed crowd *anonymity* contributed to the individual's willingness to join in because it reduced the individual's sense of responsibility for actions taken. Miller and Dollard treated *leaders as authority figures* that most individuals were already conditioned to obey, or as superordinates in a position to reward or punish subordinate crowd members for compliance or noncompliance with the leaders' suggestions. They also believed suggestions were more likely to be successful if they were agreeable to crowd members and if stated repeatedly and rhythmically. Miller and Dollard also believed that if an individual saw that he or she was not engaging in the same actions as the majority of others, the individual would become anxious because of appearing different, would carefully observe what others were doing, copy it, and thereby reduce the anxiety. (Other emotions were construed as learned responses to basic drives.)

These similarities to other crowd theories aside, most of Miller and Dollard's explanation derived from their theory of learning and their DFA hypothesis, plus what they termed "crowd intensification." They argued that the majority of crowd behavior was simply "common mass responses which have [already] been learned individually by everyone . . . [e.g.,] running,

striking, pursuing, fleeing, jeering and copying" (1941:229). The basic difference between individual and crowd behavior was merely a matter of the
intensity of responses. To explain that intensification they added a crowd
stimulus to the same drive-cue-response-reward formulation with which
they explained individual behavior.

Although Miller and Dollard believed that all behavior was mobilized by a
drive stimulus, they conceded the crowd could make a difference; thus, they
posited an interaction between the response produced by any drive stimulus
and the crowd's intensification of that response. If the drive stimulus was
weak, the initial response would also be weak and no amount of crowd
stimulation could increase the intensity of the response. Conversely, if the
drive stimulus was strong, the initial response would be strong and the
crowd stimulus would increase the effects of the drive stimulus and result in
a more intense response.[7]

Miller and Dollard referred to the various sensory modalities as "avenues
of crowd stimulation . . . the nudges, pushes, cries and the sight of the
gestures of others" (1941:222). The greater the proximity of people to one
another, the more sensory modalities stimulated, the greater the effect of the
crowd stimuli, and, in turn, the more intense their responses should be to
those stimuli. Miller and Dollard used the concept of circular reaction to
designate the mechanism by which they believed crowd stimuli increased
the intensity of individual responses.[8] I have diagrammed their analysis in
Figure 2.3 and summarize it below in their words:

> Two members of a crowd begin by responding [3] to the drive stimulus [1 plus
> cue stimulus 2] with a certain level of intensity, depending on the strength of
> [these stimuli]. At this point the crowd variable [4] may set in. The first
> individual notices the response of the second, and the stimuli given off by this
> response operate to intensify his own response. The first person is now respond-
> ing more vigorously than he would to the drive stimulus alone. The second
> person, in his turn, is stimulated by the intensified response of the first, and
> increases the vigor of his own response. This [circular reaction] process con-
> tinues, following the particular situation of crowd excitation, until it is termi-
> nated by some [intensified] goal response [5] which is rewarding [6], and
> reduces [drive] stimulation [7]. The reciprocal exposure to stimuli activates
> summatively the behavior of each person. Whispering becomes more intensive
> and widespread . . . talking turns to shouting or booing, walking becomes
> running, striking or batting becomes tearing, cleaving, or smashing. (1941:227–
> 8)

Although the crowd's circular reaction might increase individual response
intensity, Miller and Dollard argued that the particular drive-cue-response-
reward sequence within the crowd depended upon the learning histories
individual crowd members brought with them. They assumed three points.
First, most "adults have learned it is not always expedient to make the first

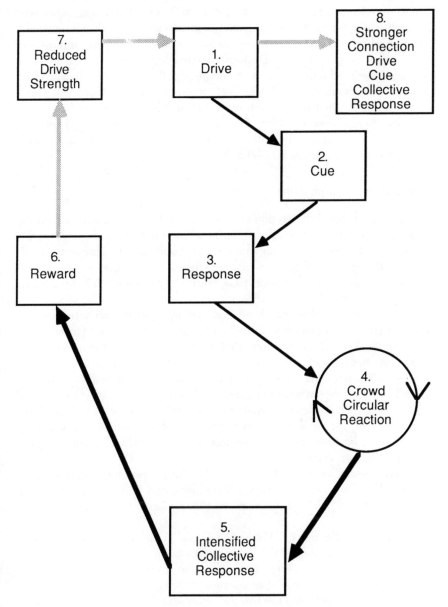

Figure 2.3. The crowd intensification model (after Miller and Dollard, 1941).

response that occurs to them" (1941:233). Instead, they have learned to check impulsive action because of the punishment that might otherwise follow. Second, when others are making similar responses, the individual has less to fear for acting out his or her similar impulses, and crowd intensification is more likely. Third, when others are engaging in diverse responses and thus confronting the individual with competing stimuli, there is no apparent safe option—the individual is less likely to pursue any one response. Thus, "when an individual is . . . battered by stimuli suggesting conflicting responses, there is less possibility for accumulative pressure to carry out one line only. . . . Circular stimulation never gets going to intensify the stimuli to a given line of response" (1941:233).

Analysis of a Lynch Mob

The most detailed illustration or evidence Miller and Dollard offered for their crowd formulation was derived from a case study of a lynch mob. In the decade (1931–1940) preceding their (1941) book, 114 lynchings were recorded; 90 percent of the victims were black.[9] Lynchings were and are horribly violent actions (Raper 1933; Huie 1965; Mars 1977; McGovern 1982; Smead 1986; Whitfield 1988).

Lynching by hanging may have first appeared on the western frontier, where a rider's loss of a horse in that harsh environment was a virtual death sentence and where, after about 1830, the common punishment for horse theft came to be hanging. [Cattle thieves were also hanged, cf. Clark (1940).] In the 1850s, lynchings were used against southern abolitionists. After the Civil War, lynchings were used against blacks during Reconstruction. For the first years that records are available (1882–1885), more whites than blacks were lynched; for the subsequent years (1886–1964), far more blacks than whites were lynched, although the frequency of lynchings fortunately declined (Williams 1970).[10]

Miller and Dollard's explanation for lynchings combined their learning theory, their frustration-aggression hypothesis, and their crowd intensification formulation.[11] I have diagrammed that explanation in Figure 2.4.

1. The Drive Stimulus. The year was 1933. The place was a farm in a southern state. The alleged crime was murder; the victim was a young white female, the suspect a young black male who lived on the farm across the road. They had known one another since childhood. Members of the local black community believed the two had been sexually intimate for some time and that when she attempted to terminate the relationship, he refused. After she threatened to "tell some white men" of their relationship, the unhappy and frightened young man allegedly killed her and hid the body. When the body was discovered the following day, the young man was arrested and

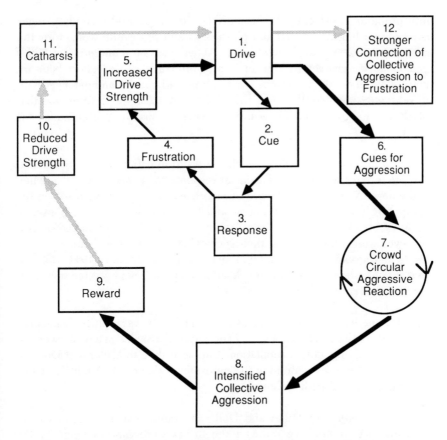

Figure 2.4. The lynch crowd model (after Miller and Dollard 1941).

charged with rape and murder. The accused subsequently "confessed" although Miller and Dollard believed this was probably coerced by the police. (Other accounts report medical examiners found no evidence of rape; they also report reasonable doubt that the accused young man committed the murder.)

Accounts of the murder, arrest, and confession spread rapidly and, according to Miller and Dollard, triggered several primary fear drive stimuli: physical, sexual, but primarily economic.[12] Outnumbered whites feared physical attacks by blacks on whites in general, and sexual attacks by black males on white females in particular. In the depression of the 1930s, blacks were hired for less money than whites, and economically deprived lower-class whites were allegedly frustrated by and fearful of continued economic competition with blacks. But the loss of work or income to a black could not by itself condone a white murdering a black competitor. By Miller and Dollard's interpretation (1941:241), this primary fear drive aroused secondary anger drives regarding the sexual and physical assault of a white woman (or the social assault of "sassing" a white man). What follows is *a quotation of Miller and Dollard's* characterization of local sentiments: "The niggers [sic] are getting out of hand. . . . If one . . . can rape and murder and get away with it, others . . . will try the same thing" (1941:240). The implication was that blacks had to be taught a lesson and that lynching was the appropriate means for doing so.

2. *Cue Stimuli.*   In Miller and Dollard's formulation, drives compelled responses; cues selected the particular response to be made, as well as when and where. Newspaper and word-of-mouth accounts may have resolved the competing drives of fear vs. anger, and their complimentary responses of flight vs. attack. The victim's father reported the victim was "choked so hard her eyes were coming out of their sockets" (1941:239). Her sister reported her head was violently "bashed in, [her] arms [were] broken" (1941:239), and that anyone who saw the body would agree no punishment was too severe for the murderer.

3. *Competing Responses.*   The white community was reportedly angered by reports of the black man's sexual and physical assaults on a white woman, offenses justifying violent retaliation. But, according to Miller and Dollard, individual whites were afraid of the punishment that could result if any one of them retaliated with violence.

4. *Frustration.*   In Miller and Dollard's formulation, the aggressive responses that would have reduced the drives were cancelled out by the individual's fear of punishment for such aggression. The result was increased frustration.

5. *Increased Drive Strength.*   Blocked responses thwart reward and this should result in increased drive strength. But which drive should be increased: the anger leading to aggression or the fear leading to avoidance? According to Miller and Dollard the more often that "successive responses of non-aggression are extinguished by continued frustration, the greater the probability that the instigation to aggression eventually will become dominant so that the response of aggression will occur" (1941:239). They qualified this escalated frustration-aggression argument by assuming that the anger drive strengths of some community members—presumably those more deprived and therefore more frustrated—would be greater than their fear drive strengths, and that these individuals would be the first to engage in some form of aggression, which in turn provided cues for aggression by others.

6. *Cues for Aggression.* Word spread that friends promised the father of the murdered woman the opportunity of first retaliation as soon as the accused black male could be seized from authorities. The local sheriff had already transferred the accused from one jail to another, supposedly for safekeeping. But each transfer away from the community probably provided less secure holding places. A prominent local businessman arranged for friends in distant communities to notify him if the accused was transferred to their jails. A local deputy sheriff was quoted in the paper on the morning of the lynching as saying that "the mob will not be bothered before or after the lynching" (1941:237). A local radio station announced "a lynching party to which all white people are invited" (1941:244). All these statements and actions were construed by Miller and Dollard as cues for aggression.

7a–8a. Crowd Intensification/Collective Aggression: The Raid. Nine days after the discovery of the woman's body, approximately "one hundred grim, determined, silent and efficient" (1941:245) men drove 200 miles to the jail where the accused was held. This "nuclear mob" (Miller and Dollard 1941:245) seized the accused from his jailers and returned to a location several miles from the farm site where the woman's body had been discovered. An estimated 3,000–7,000 people then converged on the farm site. Miller and Dollard believed (1941:245) the smaller group avoided returning to the murder site for fear the larger crowd would kill the accused too quickly, or that things might "get out of hand" and that innocent people might be hurt.

7b–8b. Crowd Intensification/Collective Aggression: Torture and Lynching. According to Miller and Dollard, "the nuclear mob" reportedly tortured the accused for nearly ten hours:

> To make the punishment fit the crime, [the accused] was castrated, and, to add horror, he was compelled to eat his own genitals. Red hot irons were plunged into his body at various points. To make his suffering more intense, he was several times promised a swift death; each time he was given a simulated hanging in which life was almost choked out of him, but he was then cut down and tortured more. His belly and sides were sliced with knives, and fingers and toes were cut off. Finally, he was "just killed." His body was tied behind a car and dragged to the . . . farm, where the larger mob was waiting. (1941:246)

Miller and Dollard acknowledged that many persons were capable of imagining such atrocities but claimed that only "the rare and sadistic individual" could actually perform them as a function of individual anger drives. But they conceded this was augmented by "crowd stimulation" and speculated that "crowd permissiveness released aggression and that crowd excitation increased it" (1941:246).

7c–8c. Crowd Intensification/Collective Aggression: Further Mutilation.
Miller and Dollard's (1941:248) informant reported the larger gathering of
people roared approval when the car dragging the dead body stopped in
front of them and the body was cut loose from the car. The larger gathering
had been waiting for many hours and Miller and Dollard believed (1941:240)
this probably increased their frustration, which increased their drive
strength.

When members of the larger gathering observed the mutilated body, they
were provided with evidence of aggression that had gone unpunished. According to Miller and Dollard, this cued yet another cycle of crowd intensification of aggression. They report that:

> The crowd saw a woman come out of the [murdered woman's] house and drive
> a butcher knife into [the accused's] heart. Members of the crowd [then] rushed
> toward the body. Some kicked it; others drove their cars over it. Children came
> and drove sharpened sticks into the body. Thereupon the larger crowd went on
> a rampage. One of its first acts was to burn down the house of [the accused's]
> mother, which stood across the road from the [dead woman's] home. [The
> accused's] body was then dragged into [town] at the back of a car and hung to
> the limb of a tree. After these aggressive acts, the mob subsided for the night.
> (1941:247)

7d–8d. Crowd Intensification/Collective Aggression: The Riot. The
body was cut down from the tree around 8:00 A.M. the following (Saturday)
morning. Whites roamed the streets. Most blacks, terrorized by what had
occurred, stayed away from town. Those who had to travel through town to
go to work avoided whites. About noon a white man struck a black man.
When the black man defended himself, "a crowd gathered rapidly and flew
into a frenzy" (1941:247). The black man ran to the courthouse and was
protected by some armed deputies. The crowd of whites, headed by a local
and highly respected young man, began roving the community, attacking
black people and driving them from town. Many white citizens came to the
aid of their black employees; the outnumbered police did very little to
intervene.

*9–12. Reward, Drive Reduction, Catharsis, and Stronger Frustration:
Collective Aggression Connections.* The riot continued in the community
until the National Guard arrived late in the afternoon (1941:244). "The riot-
ing of the mob ended only when crucial punishment symbols were again
restored" (1941:244). Thus, collective aggression was terminated not as a
function of catharsis, but because of the appearance of the armed National
Guard, which reintroduced and elevated (1941:250) the fear of punishment
for further aggression.

Summary. Miller and Dollard did not critique the ideas of LeBon and other transformation theorists so much as they ignored them. While their learning theory's individualistic emphasis rejected many ideas of collective psychology, Miller and Dollard managed to perpetuate the idea of the madness of crowds if not the madding crowd. They wrote:

> *Crowds and crowd mindedness constitute a continual danger to an orderly social life, since they tend to suppress that rational canvass of alternative responses which makes possible an intelligent social policy.* Even if *crowds* are occasionally useful in the survival of a society—as in fund raising rallies or war emergencies—they *are* as *patently dangerous* a great part of the time—as in revolutions, riots, and lynching mobs." (1941:218; emphasis added)

The Predisposition Hypothesis: An Assessment

The *first and foremost problem* with predisposition explanations is one shared with transformation explanations and virtually all subsequent theories of the crowd and crowd behavior. Most of these theorists failed to first observe, describe, and specify the behaviors they sought to explain. Consequently, they developed their explanations without much familiarity with what they claimed to explain. Miller and Dollard's statement, repeated here, exemplifies the problem:

> The data used in [our] examination of the mechanisms of crowd behavior are not, and need not be, original. Several generations of sociologists and psychologists have examined the problem and have made available a body of facts and principles. The most obvious and certain of these conclusions will be analyzed here (Bernard, 1926, 438–451; 1931, 612–613; Ogburn and Nimkoff, 1940, 272–303; Young, 1927, 627–690; cited in Miller and Dollard 1941:218).

My examination of the cited work of Bernard, Ogburn and Nimkoff, and Young readily established that, in fact, those sociologists had made no more observations of crowds than Miller and Dollard; instead, those sociologists cited or quoted earlier writers who had done their fieldwork in the same armchair manner.[13] Recall Miller and Dollard's claim (1941:230) that crowd behavior is often surprising because of poor impressions of how individuals behave when alone. In fact, their thirdhand "body of facts and principles" about crowd behavior was even more impoverished with regard to the form, content, complexity, and variation of what people do together.

A *second problem* with predisposition theories' characterizations of the crowd was the implicit assumption that everyone was exclusively and continuously engaged in the same behavior at the same time.[14] Systematic observations (e.g., McPhail and Pickens 1981) establish that when mutually inclusive behavior occurs, it is ordinarily short-lived. Most crowds are more accurately characterized as consisting of alternating and varied sequences of individual and collective behavior—not continuous and unanimous behavior. I will discuss some of those variations in detail in Chapter 5, but one distinction should be mentioned here.

When two or more persons engage in the same behavior at the same time, I will call this *collective action-in-common* or *collective behavior-in-common*.[15] Mutually inclusive collective action-in-common is more likely in small than in large gatherings. When mutually inclusive collective action occurs in large gatherings it is usually rather simple behavior and is usually short-lived. Noninclusive collective action-in-common may appear in smaller subsets of two or more people scattered throughout a larger gathering.

The predisposition theorists give scant attention to a second form of social behavior that I will call *collective action-in-concert*. I refer to two or more persons engaged simultaneously or intermittently in a sequence of different behaviors that are judged to fit together by participants or observers.[16] (Sociologists often say such sequences involve a division of labor.) Some examples include conversations (speaker; auditor), two-party chanting or singing (part A; part B), or two-party maneuvers (misdirectors; exploiters) such as the jail raid I will describe below. The important points here are that (1) the behaviors of which crowds are composed can alternate between sequences of individual behavior and sequences of social behavior, and (2) sequences of social behavior vary in form, in content, in complexity, in duration, and in the proportion of the gathering that participates.

The *third problem* with predisposition theories of the crowd is that they focused on, and were developed to explain, extraordinary and violent behaviors. Allport characterized crowds as "struggling, fighting, and destroying" (1924:294) and Miller and Dollard characterized crowds as irrational and "patently dangerous" (1941:218) and illustrated their theory with an analysis of a lynch mob. To the contrary, contemporary and systematic studies of political demonstrations (Eisinger 1973; MacCannell 1973; McPhail 1985), sports gatherings (Lewis 1982; Smith 1983), and prosaic gatherings (Edgerton 1979; Whyte 1980) establish that violence is rare. Although there is no comparable systematic evidence on the relative frequency of ordinary and extraordinary nonviolent behaviors, my own observations corroborate those of other field-workers (e.g., Wright 1978): extraordinary behaviors are infrequent. Turner's advice bears repeating: "It would be unwise to adopt the exceptional aberration as the model for collective [or crowd] behavior as a whole" (1964:386). By implication, theories of the crowd and crowd behavior should be judged on the basis of their capacity to account for the full range of behaviors that occur in and by crowds.

The *fourth problem* with predisposition theories in general, and the DFA hypothesis in particular, is that they do not predict, let alone explain, the limited range of phenomena to which they are addressed. For example, one of the first attempts to test the DFA explanation of crowd phenomena systematically was Hovland and Sears's (1940) examination of the relationship between economic deprivation and the incidence of *lynchings*. They reported a strong negative relationship ($r = -.72$) between an index of the cash value of the cotton crop in southern states between 1882 and 1930, and an index of the incidence of lynchings in those states. Mintz (1946) critiqued Hovland and Sears's inappropriate statistical analysis. His own secondary statistical analysis of their data demonstrated a very weak relationship ($r = +.01$) between cotton prices and lynchings from 1882 and 1930, but a slightly stronger one ($r = -.25$) from 1882 to 1913.

Although Mintz's analysis torpedoed the Hovland and Sears claim (Reed 1969), the DFA hypothesis repeatedly has been resurrected in one form or another by psychologists, sociologists, and political scientists. For example, in a recent period of U.S. *riots*, political scientist Gurr wrote:

> The sociological and popular cliche is that "frustration" or "discontent" or "despair" is the root cause of rebellion. Cliche or not, the basic relationship appears to be as fundamental to understanding civil strife as the law of gravity is to atmospheric physics: relative deprivation . . . is a necessary precondition for civil strife of any kind, and the more severe is relative deprivation, the more likely and severe is strife. Underlying this relative deprivation approach to civil strife is a frustration-aggression mechanism, apparently a fundamental part of our psychological make-up. When we feel thwarted in an attempt to get something we want, we are likely to get angry, and when we get angry the most satisfying inherent response is to strike out at the source of frustration. (1968:52–53)

Lieberson and Silverman (1965) were the first sociologists to compare systematically the demographic, socioeconomic, and political conditions of U.S. cities in which 76 *race riots* took place between 1913 and 1963 and those of a control group of nonriot cities. Although Lieberson and Silverman did not set out to test the DFA hypothesis, they did examine the "underlying conditions" of demographic trends, occupations, business ownership, employment, income, and housing of whites and blacks in the riot and control cities. Those variables were selected to provide direct or indirect measures of black-white competition that, by implication, might have led to racial conflict.[17] Lieberson and Silverman established no differences between the riot and nonriot cities, or they established differences opposite from the expected direction. Thus, the hypothesis that competition (and racial discrimination) led to interpersonal conflict and interracial violence was not supported.

The DFA hypothesis was explicitly invoked and extensively tested in many subsequent examinations of the incidence of riots, collective violence, and demonstrations.[18] Socioeconomic and political deprivation yielded very low correlations with the incidence and the intensity of U.S. *property riots* between 1963 and 1972 (Spilerman 1970, 1976; Snyder 1979), and with the incidence of *collective violence* in France between 1830 and 1930 (Snyder and Tilly 1972; cf. Tilly et al. 1975). Socioeconomic deprivation of blacks yielded very low correlations with the incidence of U.S. *civil rights demonstrations* between 1955 and 1965 (McAdam 1982).

Although macroversions of the DFA hypothesis, and related social system strain formulations (e.g., Smelser 1963), were advanced to account for the incidence and intensity of riots and collective violence, the predisposition theories of Allport and of Dollard and Miller were primarily concerned with the individual as the unit of analysis. This DFA explanation was examined for participation in a variety of demonstrations and riots in the 1960s and 1970s. Measures of deprivation and frustration failed to differentiate participants from nonparticipants in the civil rights demonstrations (Orum and Orum 1968; Pinard et al. 1969). A variety of measures of deprivation and frustration failed to differentate participants from nonparticipants in U.S. urban riots (McPhail 1971; Abudu et al. 1972; Miller et al. 1977).[19]

It should also be noted that a variety of measures of other individual attitudes and attributes, from which predispositions or tendencies to behave were inferred, also failed to differentiate participants from nonparticipants in riots (McPhail 1971) and in student demonstrations (Aron 1974).[20] On balance, the predisposition argument in general, and the DFA hypothesis in particular, do not predict or explain the presence of individuals in a variety of crowds, demonstrations, and riots. The DFA hypothesis is not quite the fundamental principle Gurr (1968) would have us believe; it may be no more than a cliché! An alternative explanation is required for individual participation in the formation of crowds.[21]

A *fifth problem* with the predisposition argument is that it does not predict or explain sequences of individual behavior (violent or nonviolent) in social situations. It is important to acknowledge here that the predisposition argument has not been directly examined within crowds, demonstrations, and riots.[22] But those who champion the explanation claim those principles do not change inside or outside the crowd; thus, the argument should stand or fall on the basis of the available evidence, whether gathered inside or outside the crowd.

A large body of experimental data has been generated over the past 20 years on relationships between individual deprivation, frustration, and aggression. That research demonstrates that frustration is neither necessary nor sufficient for individual aggression (Berkowitz 1965a,b, 1969; Geen and Berkowitz 1967). A variety of other factors (e.g., models performing aggressive acts, others making situational demands, or both) must be present if aggression is to follow deprivation or frustration. And those other factors can consistently produce aggression in the absence of deprivation or frustration (cf. Milgram 1963, 1974). Further, Geen and Quanty (1977; Quanty 1976) summarize an extensive body of experimental research that discredits the hypothesized "catharsis" effect of aggression. Persons who engage in aggression are likely to engage in more aggression and more extreme aggression instead of less aggression as claimed by Miller and Dollard (1941). If the DFA hypothesis is empirically suspect at so many different levels of analysis and with so many different units of analysis, what of the stimulus-response learning theory on which it is based?

The strongest version of the predisposition argument in the social and behavioral science literature may well be Thorndike's "law of effect" or B. F. Skinner's restatement of the same idea: "Behavior is a function of its consequences." Miller and Dollard's learning theory falls somewhere between. The fundamental idea is that individuals are predisposed to behave as a function of their reinforcement histories. Between 1950 and 1975 this argument was assigned virtual natural-law status by many social and behavioral scientists. There are more valid criticisms of the argument than I can review here; but one warrants consideration.

Brewer (1974) reexamined more than 150 experiments on classical and operant conditioning of autonomic responses, and motor and verbal behaviors. He concluded that conditioning may occur, but not in the manner or for the reasons that learning theorists have claimed. First, subjects in the experiments learned to make correct responses when they were merely told about, even though they were never exposed to, the conditioned stimuli or reinforcement contingencies (i.e., the rewards or punishments) that the theories say are necessary for those responses to occur. Second, if subjects were told *not* to make a particular response, and were then exposed to the conditioned stimuli or reinforcement contingencies that should have produced the response, the subjects did *not* subsequently make the response the theories predicted should result from such exposure. Third, subjects conditioned when and only when they were aware of the conditioned stimulus response relationships or response reinforcement contingency to which they had been exposed.

In my judgment Brewer's analysis challenges the claim that the law of effect compels human beings to learn or respond in an unwitting manner as a function of conditioning or reinforcement history. Subjects must understand and tell themselves to do what the experimenter asks them to do, or what they understand is appropriate for the conditioning or the reinforcement contingencies with which they are confronted. Perhaps individuals are controlling their behavior by those self-instructions rather than being controlled by the law of effect.[23]

If the law of effect was the strongest theoretical argument underlying the predispositionist explanation of behavior, the most frequently employed indicators of learned individual predispositions have been measures of personality and of attitudes. But knowledge of an individual's personality characteristics (Mischel 1968) or attitudes (Wicker 1969) at time one does not predict that individual's behavior at time two.

Some attitude proponents argue (e.g., Ajzen and Fishbein 1977) that the low correlations between attitude and behavior result from the failure to obtain appropriate measures at time one of specific attitudes (and intentions) toward specific objects in specific situations. When that specificity is introduced at time one, and when very little time lapses before the measurement of behavior at time two, the attitude-behavior correlation greatly increases in magnitude. Conversely, increasing the time lapse allows for the introduction of additional complicating factors. Not the least of these is the presence of other people and their demands on the individual, factors that may provide better predictions of individual behavior in the situation than very specific attitude measures (or personality measures) at an earlier point in time. The Milgram experiments (1963, 1964, 1965a,b, 1974) are a case in point; they also provide evidence for an alternative explanation for violent behavior.

Milgram's subjects were told, and believed, they were participating in a scientific experimental study of the effects of punishment on learning. They were asked to and did administer 15 volt increments of shock each time the pupil made an error (up to a maximum of 450 volts).[24] Virtually all of Milgram's subjects (1965b:61) administered the maximum violence when the pupil did not protest. The percentage of subjects administering maximum violence diminished as pupil protests increased (1965b, 1974).[25] When Milgram's (1965a) subjects were members of a three-person teaching team and were faced with obeying the demands of the experimenter to continue the shocks vs. the demands of the pupil to stop the shocks, subjects continued or stopped the shocks in accordance with the actions of their peers.[26]

Extensive measures of personality characteristics and other individual attributes, from which predispositions are often inferred, did not distinguish between subjects that administered the maximum and subjects that refused to administer any violence (Elms and Milgram 1966; Larsen, Coleman, Forbes, and Johnson 1972). Extensive measures of social attributes, from which predispositions are often inferred, also failed to distinguish between subjects administering maximum and subjects refusing to administer any violence (Milgram 1963, 1964:141, 1965b, 1974).[27] Thus, a wide cross section of human beings, who were neither deprived nor frustrated, engaged on command in progressively more violent behavior against another human being.

The phrase "on command" may imply a misconception about compliance with suggestions, instructions, and commands. Allport attributed compliance with a leader's suggestions, as did Miller and Dollard, to learned predispositions to obey authority figures. An elaboration of this explanation was advanced by Milgram (1974). Milgram argued that his subjects obeyed the experimenter because they believed the consequences of their actions were the authority's responsibility rather than their own. Milgram asked subjects at the end of the experiment to apportion responsibility to the experimenter, the subject (teacher), and the pupil: "How much is each of us responsible for the fact that this person was given electric shocks against his will?" (Milgram 1974:302). Subjects who administered the maximum violence attributed no more responsibility to the experimenter (but more to themselves and less to the learner) than did subjects who refused to administer any violence. The relationship between administering violence and attributing responsibility was not in the predicted direct (Milgram 1974:203, Table 9), was of low magnitude ($r = .14$), and was not statistically significant ($p > .05$).[28]

In sum, the interaction between experimenter, subject, peers, and pupil in the situation explained more of the variance in the subject's aggressive behavior than did the personal or social attributes of the subject. Subjects who received persistent instructions to violate, instructions justified in terms of a higher-level principle (e.g., science), and instructions buttressed by peer support, were very likely to tell themselves to violate another human being (cf. Rigney 1972, 1982). Subjects who received competing instructions were less likely to do so; subjects whose peers advocated nonviolence were least likely to do so.

A *sixth problem* with predisposition theories is their failure to address the range and complexity of social behaviors in which two or more persons engage within gatherings. The predisposition explanation *appears* to fare better with simpler than with more complex forms of collective action-in-common; it does not fare well at all with simple or complex forms of collective action-in-concert.

Collective Action-in-Common

Two studies present evidence (Hastorf and Cantril 1954; Loy and Andrew 1981) that fans from opposing schools selectively perceived the play of a fiercely contested football game between their teams. One team's star player was knocked unconscious in the first quarter; the other team lost a player with a broken leg early in the second half. Fans whose team lost their star saw twice as many rule infractions by the opposing team as by their own, while fans of the opposing team saw about the same number by each team. Fans of the team that lost their star were twice as likely to attribute the start of the rough play to the opposing team as were fans of the opposing team. The latter were more likely to say the rough play began simultaneously.

These two studies complement an analysis by Zillman, Bryant and Zapolsky (1979) of fans' collective action-in-common during a college football game. The home team fans enthusiastically cheered and applauded each successful running and passing play by their own team, but moaned their unsuccessful plays. Their audible evaluation of the runs and passes by the opposing team (or, perhaps, of the home team's defensive play) were in virtually the opposite direction. It may well be that nothing more than fans' preferences for the outcome are required to explain their simultaneous cheering and applause, or moans, groans, and boos during the game. These are relatively simple collective actions-in-common. But it remains to be demonstrated that measures of the presence and extent of individuals' preferences in advance of a game are associated with presence and extent of their collective evaluations (e.g., cheers, applause) of team performance during the game.

Collective Action-in-Concert

It may be unfair to hold predispositionist theories accountable for collective action-in-concert, since this involves two or more individuals fitting together different behaviors into a sequence of social behavior. One of the simplest forms of cooperative concerted behavior (and probably the most frequent in all temporary gatherings) is the two-party conversation. Participants alternate turns as speaker and auditor, intermittently taking, holding, and yielding the floor to one another. Duncan and Fiske (1977:99–122) report that their extensive preinteraction measures of participants' personality characteristics consistently yielded statistically not significant or very low correlations with their equally detailed codes of verbal and nonverbal actions in their sound film records of participants' conversations.[29]

Predisposition theories occasionally refer to interaction but they do not examine it. At best they refer to the interaction of predispositions and responses, and the intensification of the latter occasioned by the sights and sounds of others making similar responses. But there is no attention to or analysis of actors interacting with one another to solve the simplest of problems, for example, carrying on a conversation, let alone the more complex problems of, for example, planning and carrying out a jail raid to capture and escape with a prisoner. Perhaps Miller and Dollard could have explained how a hierarchy of multiple and diverse predispositions could be switched on and off by means of overt verbal and nonverbal cues in relation to the collective actions-in-concert to be explained; but they failed to do so, or even to acknowledge the frequency with which such interaction occurs in crowds. It is difficult, using their scheme, to explain several instances of collective action that occurred before, during, and after the lynching they examined.

The Brewton Jail Raid: Planning. The preparation and implementation of the Brewton jail raid was not spontaneously improvised by a group of strangers. On the Monday following the Thursday murder, a few Jackson County, Florida, residents learned that the accused young black male (hereafter Claude Neal, or Neal) had been transferred to the Brewton, Alabama, jail. No small amount of planning was required to pick competent and trustworthy participants with sufficient time and money, and adequate cars to make the 400 mile round-trip, to arrange for a place and time to plan the raid, and to refine the plan. [McGovern (1982) documents that these "initial aggressors" were hardly the most deprived members in the community; and there is no independent evidence that "their anger drive exceeded their fear drive."] After three days for preparations and planning, the raiding party of one to two dozen men (not the unwieldy 100 reported by Miller and Dollard) left Jackson County on Thursday evening after dark and drove in five or six cars the 200 miles to Brewton.

Ordinarily the preparations and planning for this kind of collective action assume some prior social relationships between the participants, if not membership in some group or organization.[30] At minimum, members of the band of raiders were connected by a social network through which they were contacted, then assembled in planning sessions that yielded a raiding team that subsequently became "the lynch mob":

> Although they probably all knew one another before their expedition to the Brewton jail, they came from several different communities in Jackson County, principally Malone, Greenwood, and Marianna. The nucleus of the group derived from family ties, especially from kinsmen of a local politician, and personal friendships. Key members learned of [Neal's] location very soon after it was divulged. (McGovern 1982:67)

The Brewton Raid: Implementation. McGovern notes "the skill with which [the members of the raiding party] executed the seizure and escape" (1982:65). Some of the raiding party arrived in three cars at the Brewton courthouse shortly after midnight and talked with some police officers outside. The Floridians said some of their party were Florida State Police officers who wanted to talk with the sheriff. They were told the sheriff was at home. They also asked if the jail was in the courthouse and were told it was down the street. Those three cars left and drove to a nearby gas station to fill their tanks. A passerby viewed them with suspicion and called the jail; the jailer called the sheriff, who then drove to the jail. He there encountered three cars from which emerged three men with automatic shotguns, who demanded the release of Claude Neal. The sheriff assured them that Neal was not in the jail and took them on a tour to prove it, confident he had hidden Neal in the jail beyond discovery. Apparently satisfied with the sheriff's account, these men drove their cars away.

The sheriff took the bait and followed them out of town, curious to know the direction they were headed. As he did so, two or three more cars arrived at the jail. Some of their occupants confronted the jailer with shotguns and dynamite, and threatened to blow up the jail unless he surrendered the keys to the cells. He complied. They seized Neal, tied his hands, put him in a car, and left town shortly after 2:00 A.M., returning to Jackson County, Florida, at approximately 6:00 A.M. on Friday. The sheriff was "decoyed out of position," outwitted rather than overpowered (McGovern 1982:64), by a simple misdirection maneuver requiring a division of labor among raiding-party members. These collective actions-in-concert required finesse and coordination, not the crowd intensification by circular reaction set forth by Miller and Dollard (cf. note 8).

Assembling the Larger Gathering.   After the raiding party returned to Jackson County, Florida, they held Neal captive for the next 18 hours. McGovern's (1982) informants report that Neal was not tortured until the last two hours of that period (rather than the ten hours reported by Miller and Dollard.) On Friday morning just before noon, the raiders notified local media where and when the lynching would occur later in the evening. One newspaper printed those directions in a special early afternoon edition, and a radio station broadcast them throughout the afternoon. Whether or not these were cues for aggression, they were essential instructions for assembling the large gathering that began forming late Friday afternoon at the farm of the murdered woman's family. A local reporter wrote of "the invitational lynching":

> For hours as word of the jail storming and seizure spread, the grapevines and telephones of Northwest Florida buzzed and grim faced farmers prepared to make the Cannidy [farm] home their rendezvouz. (McGovern 1982:74)

The Associated Press put the invitational-lynching story on its national wire at 3:00 P.M. The raiders even notified the sheriff in the adjoining county when and where the lynching would occur in Jackson County that evening. There is no evidence the raiders were in contact with the Jackson County sheriff, and he claimed he did not know where they were holding Neal. Thirty special deputies and a dozen police officers were reported unable to locate the raiders and their prisoner.

The Contribution by Authorities. Following the AP wire story, the governor of Florida was bombarded with telephone calls and telegrams throughout the late afternoon, asking him to intervene. When he called the Jackson County sheriff and offered to send the National Guard, the sheriff declined that assistance, claiming he could handle the situation, even while admitting to friends that he could not handle it and that "all hell is going to break loose" (McGovern 1982:75). One of the sheriff's regular deputies told a reporter the mob would not be bothered before or after the lynching. Under this cloak of tacit consent from local authorities, there is little wonder the raiders made no effort to conceal their faces or license plates when they seized Neal from the Brewton jail or when they brought his body to the larger gathering later that evening. Anonymity was not an issue for them.[31]

The Lynching. Lynchings involve two or more persons acting in concert (Raper 1933; Huie 1965; Mars 1977; McGovern 1982; Smead 1986; Whitfield 1988). A variety of actions are required to complete the grisly task of a hanging: getting a rope, finding a secure tree limb, making a noose and tying a hangman's knot, placing the noose around the victim's neck, throwing the other end of the rope over the limb, pulling the victim off the ground and securing the rope until the noose tightens and the victim is suffocated or his neck is broken. Conceding that some individual participants are skilled at one or more of these tasks and others (for example, the Jackson County farmer with expertise in castrating animals), it is virtually impossible that all the tasks could have been performed by one person; it is very likely that several persons contributed different actions. That in turn requires that two or more persons fit those different actions together. Predisposition theories offer explanations for why two or more persons might act together in common; they do not tell us why they should act together in concert; and they do not tell us how either is accomplished.

Dispersal. A wide range of empirical evidence fails to support the claims of the predisposition explanation in general, and the DFA hypothesis in particular, for the incidence of lynchings, riots, and demonstrations, for individual presence at those events, and for individual participation in the behavior sequences that make up those events. The predisposition explanation also fails to account for the termination of events; admittedly, most theories of crowds and crowd behavior do little better on this score. Recall that Miller and Dollard's theory claims aggression reduces drive strength and results in catharsis. But whites' widespread attacks on blacks in the Marianna riot were apparently not sufficient to lower whites' drive strength and terminate the aggression. Thus, Miller and Dollard revive the alternative explanation by resurrecting the fear drive following the arrival of the National Guard. According to McGovern, the arrival of another group of visitors preceded the arrival of the guard by one hour and may provide a complementary if not competing explanation for the termination of this particular riot. It also introduces an element of levity into an otherwise grim event. McGovern quotes a newspaper reporter's account:

> Unexpectedly, at 3:30 P.M., there appeared a motorcade of eighty automobiles returning 350 Chicago delegates from an American Legion convention in Miami. The legionnaires deflated the riot by staging a spectacle of their own. Their presence also deprived the rioters of anonymity, hence dominion over the city. The veterans were convoyed by eight police officers of the Florida Highway Department and three police officers of the Tennessee Highway Patrol, courtesy of the governor of each state. Each driver honked his horn as he came into Marianna while each policeman pulled the siren on his motorcycle. And then in comic-opera fashion, 350 uniformed members of the American Legion stepped out of their cars in the middle of the riot; the mob became so confused it began to retreat. (1982:91)

Extraordinary phenomena are noteworthy. Those who turn and look are distracted, at least temporarily, from the activities in which they were previously engaged. That distraction may provide time for some victims to escape, and thus remove the objects of further aggression. But I concede that this particular distraction of sirens announcing the arrival of 350 similarly costumed individuals might also be perceived as a police force of some magnitude and therefore something to be feared.

Discussion

Predisposition theories of the crowd took us beyond the collective psychologisms of the nineteenth century and demanded that we acknowledge the individuals within the crowd. Regrettably, predisposition theorists gave scant attention to the crowd behavior they claimed to explain. Had they done so they might have advanced different or at least broader explanations of behavior than those reviewed here. The explanations of individual behavior upon which predisposition theories are based are not up to the challenge of predicting or explaining the range of individual and collective behavior of which crowds are composed. A considerable range and volume of empirical data fail to support the claims of the predisposition theorists regarding the incidence of crowds, the individual's participation in those crowds, and specific sequences of individual and collective action—violent and nonviolent—within those crowds. The phenomena to be explained do not succumb to an explanation based on the predispositions individuals carry within them from place to place.

By the middle of the twentieth century most social psychologists had abandoned efforts to identify the "simple and sovereign motives" driving human behavior (Bernard 1924; G. Allport 1954). Human requirements for oxygen, water, food, sex, and shelter were not dismissed; rather, as we have seen, attention was turned to how individuals learn a variety of responses to deal with those requirements. My impressions regarding those efforts are the following. Very few human responses or behaviors are innate; the vast majority are learned in one form or another. Learning is more varied and complex, and probably different, than classic or operant theorists propose. The fact that simple or complex behaviors are learned and become part of an individual's repertoire does not dictate their reappearance in response to some triggering stimulus.

Chomsky (1959) earlier noted another limitation of learning theory explanations of verbal behavior. Young children generate sequences of utterances they have not previously heard or spoken, and therefore sequences for which they could not have been reinforced; moreover, those utterances are understood by competent users of the language. In nonverbal behavior as well, human beings individually and collectively combine and permute learned elements into novel sequences and configurations of behavior to deal with the changing circumstances and problems with which they are confronted.

The predisposition theorists should be credited for raising a related and fundamental issue, despite the shortcomings of their proposed resolution of the issue. They construed groups and crowds as struggle groups. Regrettably they focused on the struggle to satisfy compelling drives, or on the inevitability of released and intensified predispositions, rather than how two or more purposive actors fit their behaviors together to solve the problems with which they are confronted. Allport could not have been more in error when he claimed that "the course of [collective] action is fairly determined from the start . . . [because of the] fundamental reactions upon which the individuals have been launched" (1924:295).

The problems with which human beings are confronted do not always reappear in the same way across space and time; thus, different strategies and tactics are necessary, different combinations and permutations of individual and collective actions are required, to deal with those problems. I noted in Chapter 1 that research on human behavior in problematic situations establishes that critical thinking and purposive control do not disappear. In fact, these may be enhanced rather than diminished as individuals must establish what the problem is, what solutions might work, what is revealed by hypothetical trials of those solutions, what revisions are required in the most probable solutions, and, perhaps, what division of labor is necessary to carry them out: who is to do what, when, where, how, with whom, to carry out the solution.

To understand these issues is to recognize and examine social interaction. It was to this problem that emergent-norm theories of the crowd and collective behavior were addressed, and to those theories that I turn in Chapter 3.

Notes

1.   Allport eventually reversed his position on the fallacy of collective action (1961), and characterized collective structure (1962) as the interdependent behavior of two or more individuals. But his later work neither reports observations of nor develops explanations for the crowd. The irony remains that Allport probably did more work on the problem of collective action than all the early sociologists whose work he called into question.

2.   Ralph Turner (1964a) refers to this perspective as "convergence theory." I use *convergence* to refer to some forms of collective action I want to explain, e.g., the convergent movements of disparate individuals and small groups to form an arc or ring around some object.

3.   Allport's claim may be the source of the hypothesis, restated by Milgram and Toch, that "those who are most intensely motivated to carry out the crowd's purposes will be disproportionately represented at the crowd's structural core" (1969:520). [Cf. Meyer and Seidler 1978; but also see note 22.]

4.   The idea of social facilitation may have originated with Triplett's (1898) observation that sport bicyclists covered a one-mile distance much faster in competition than when riding with a pacer or when riding alone. He then devised the first social psychological experiment in the United States. He asked children to wind up lengths of line on fishing reels. Those who did so (a) alone completed the task at a much slower rate than those who did so (b) in the presence of others or (c) in competition with others.

5.   Zajonc (1965), Simmel and colleagues (1968), and others later extended this analysis to demonstrate similar differences for familiar vs. unfamiliar tasks. This led to a focus upon evaluative apprehension by those performing unfamiliar tasks. Whatever benefits this may have had for other areas of social psychology, it moved social facilitation away from the crowd phenomena with which Allport was earlier concerned. The work of Wheeler (1966) and his colleagues may be closer to Allport's initial concerns.

6.   Dollard et al. (1939) initially defined aggression as any behavior with the goal of injuring another person. Subsequently, Miller and Dollard (1941) recharacterized aggression as simply physical or verbal attack, but acknowledged less conspicuous forms of aggressive action such as hostile thoughts.

7.   The same idea appears in Granovetter's (1978) "threshold theory of collective behavior." He argues that an individual's behavior in a crowd is a function of the individual's predisposition to engage in a behavior, the opportunity to do so, and the threshold of social support that the individual requires to act out that predisposition. Most individuals require no more than the opportunity to engage in mundane behaviors. More extraordinary behaviors require stronger predispositions, more social support, or both; and crowds vary in their distributions of individual predispositions and social support thresholds.

8.   Circular reaction was first introduced by Park (Park and Burgess 1921) and perpetuated by Blumer (1939). It is flawed in the several ways detailed in Chapter 1. Miller and Dollard reproduce all those flaws.

9.   Lynchings have not always involved hangings, their targets have not always been blacks, the alleged precipitating incidence has not always been rape, and the locale has not always been the southern United States. During the American revolution, the revolutionary Continental army was frequently the victim of Tory theft or sabotage. When Tory suspects were caught, the wheels of justice turned slowly if at all on the claims of colonial revolutionaries. Charles Lynch (1736–1796), a Virginia

Colony planter, organized juries of local citizens to try Tory suspects, with Lynch serving as a kind of justice of the peace. Suspects found guilty were usually sentenced to flogging, tarring and feathering, or exile from the community, but never hanging or other forms of capital punishment.

10. Of 4,752 lynchings recorded by The Tuskegee Institute (Williams 1970) between 1882 and 1968 (1,307 white and 3,445 black victims), the alleged crimes of the lynch victim were homicide (41%); rape (19%) or attempted rape (6%); robbery or theft (5%); felonious assault (4%); insult to a white person (2%); and assorted other crimes (23%).

11. In this section I summarize Miller and Dollard's (1941) account of the lynching drawn from an NAACP report by an annonymous white field investigator. McGovern's (1982) *Anatomy of a Lynching: The Killing of Claude Neal* identifies that investigator as Howard A. Kester. His 1934 report reconstructed "The Marianna, Florida Lynching" of Claude Neal on October 26, 1934, in Jackson County, Florida, of which Marianna (population 3,750) was the county seat. McGovern frequently quotes verbatim from Kester the passages that appear in Miller and Dollard (1941). McGovern also interviewed in 1977 a surviving editor of a county newspaper at the time of the lynching, one surviving member of the lynch mob, a surviving member of the murdered woman's family, and several surviving white and black witnesses from Jackson County. Those interviews were supplemented by many local and regional newspaper accounts of the murder, of the jails in which Neal was held and from which he was seized, of the larger gathering to which his corpse was dragged, of the subsequent race riot in Marianna after the lynching, and of the dispersal of that riot. McGovern (1982) makes no mention of Miller and Dollard's (1941) analysis but verifies the accuracy of their general sequence of events, and of the brutality of the castration, self-cannibalism, and mutilation of Neal's body before and after the lynching, and the subsequent race riot. I will note below the few significant discrepancies between the accounts of Miller and Dollard and of McGovern.

12. An economic interpretation of lynching was first suggested by Raper (1933). Hovland and Sears (1940), colleagues of Miller and Dollard, argued that as the price of cotton declined, white competition with and frustration by blacks increased, leading to white aggression against blacks in the form of lynchings. They reported supporting evidence [$r_t = -.70$; but cf. Mintz (1946)].

13. Miller and Dollard primarily refer to Ogburn and Nimkoff (1940), who repeat a litany of second- and thirdhand characterizations of the crowd but report no systematic observations of their own or by anyone else. Kimball Young (1927) at least excerpts some reports (Bentley 1916; Clark 1916; Griffith 1921; Woolbert 1916) of observations of audiences and classrooms by University of Illinois psychologists.

14. Allport (1924:318) does note that crowd members' impressions of universality are probably an illusion, but the crowd behaviors that he "describes" and that he purports to explain are undifferentiated and mutually inclusive behaviors.

15. I will use the terms behavior, action, and conduct interchangeably throughout the book for reasons that I spell out in Chapter 5. I simply note here that the traditional distinction between action and behavior cannot be justified on the grounds that the former is purposive and the latter is not. I assume the overwhelming majority of human conduct is purposive and develop that argument in Chapter 6.

16. Allport uses the terms "concerted action" (1924:295) as well as "common action" (1924:294) but all his examples of crowd behavior refer to what I call behaviors-in-common.

17. The alleged precipitating incidents for Lieberson and Silverman's (1965) 76 race riots were interracial fights (21%); killing, arrest, assault, or search of black males

by white police officers (20%); civil liberties, public facilities, segregation, housing and political events (18%); interracial shooting or murder (14%); robbery, attack, murder, or rape of white female by black male (13%); black-white job-based conflict (7%); black burning of U.S. flag (1%); no information available (6%).

18.   Due to the virtual absence of interracial clashes and the predominance of vandalism, looting, and arson, the riots of the 1960s and 1970s are often termed property riots.

19.   Elsewhere (McPhail 1971) I report secondary statistical analyses of strength of association and statistical significance for 173 tests (from ten studies) of relationship between deprivation, frustration, and/or aggression in the form of participation in five riots: 32 percent were not statistically significant; 61 percent yielded low correlations (between .00 and .29); 6 percent yielded moderate correlations (between .30 and .39); and 1 percent yielded a moderate correlation of higher than .40. I reanalyzed two- and three-variable relationships. Subsequent multivariate regression analyses of attitudes and attributes yielded the same results for individual participation in the Los Angeles Watts riot (Abudu et al. 1972) and in the Detroit and Newark riots (Miller et al. 1977).

20.   I also reexamined (McPhail 1971) more than 100 tests of non-DFA attitudes and attributes in relation to riot participation. The vast majority of those relationships were low or statistically not significant. Aron's (1974) multivariate analyses of the attributes, attitudes, and behaviors of a 10 percent sample of the 1970 University of Chicago student body led him to conclude that students' background attributes explained far more variance in their attitudes than either their attributes or attitudes explained variance in their participation in antiwar demonstrations.

21.   Elsewhere (McPhail and Miller 1973, McPhail and Bailey 1979, McPhail 1983), my colleagues and I have presented an alternative analysis of the assembling process for gatherings. Wilson and Orum (1976) apply this analysis to participation in political demonstrations; Johnson, Choate, and Busin (1984) apply this analysis to participation in religious rallies; Snyder (1979) extends the analysis to the incidence of urban riots.

22.   Meyer and Seidler (1978) claim support for the Milgram and Toch paraphrase of Allport's hypothesis: "those who are most intensely motivated to carry out the crowd's purposes will be disproportionately represented at the crowd's structural core" (1969:520). They examined the core vs. fringe locations of highly committed vs. merely concerned participants, respectively, in one prowar and one antiwar demonstration. My analysis of their data indicates the relationship for the prowar demonstration was low ($r = .25$), and the relationship for the antiwar demonstration was lower ($r = -.18$) and opposite the predicted direction.

23.   It is ironic that predisposition theorists, after rejecting the transformation argument that individuals lose control of their behavior to a crowd mind, turned right around and constrained the individual with drives, response hierarchies, reinforcement histories, or other predispositions that compel and control the individual's behavior.

24.   All Milgram's subjects received a sample shock of 45 volts prior to helping the experimenter attach the electrodes through which the pupil "would receive shock." In fact the pupil, played by a trained actor, received no shocks. The pupil's increasingly agonized verbal protests were audiotape clips prerecorded from a standardized script and activated by the correspondingly higher voltage level levers on the shock generator manipulated by the subject.

25.   In Milgram's "proximity series" (1965b, 1974), the experimenter's instructions and proximity to the subject remained more or less constant while the victim's

protests and proximity were varied. Victim protests are competing instructions. Subjects were most compliant with the experimenter's instructions when there were no victim protests, less compliant when there were verbal victim protests, even less compliant when there were verbal protests from a visible victim, and least compliant when the visible victim verbally protested and physically resisted the shocks. The correlations between victim protest and subject compliance with the victim (vs. the experimenter) range from $r = .46$ (Ofshe, Christman, and Saltz 1981) to $r = .51$ (my secondary analysis) depending on the proximity conditions examined. Ofshe and his colleagues also examined the number of words in the victim's standardized protests after each shock level in relation to the number of subjects dropping out after that level. The correlations ranged from $r = .58$ to $r = .78$, depending on word indexing. McGovern's informants (1982) report the prospective lynching victim neither pleaded for his release nor protested the torture before he was lynched.

26. In two "group pressure" conditions, Milgram (1964, 1965a) placed the naive subject in a three-person team in which the first teacher (a confederate) presented word pairs to the pupil, the second (confederate) teacher judged the pupil's answers right or wrong, and the third (naive subject) teacher administered the punishment. The subject was told he could administer the lowest level of shock recommended by the three. The two confederate teachers raised their recommended levels after each pupil error. Pupil protests increased as shock levels increased.

In one condition, if the subject hesitated or suggested dropping out, his peers urged continuation. In the second, one peer dropped out after the pupil's protests at 150 volts, the second dropped out at 210 volts, both refusing to continue shocking the pupil against his will. The experimenter told the subject to assume the peers' responsibilities and to continue. In the first condition the majority of subjects administered the maximum violence; in the second the majority dropped out *after* their peers did so. Correlations of subject's behavior with peers' behaviors range from $r = .50$ to $r = .63$, depending on cutting points (my secondary analysis). McGovern's (1982) informants reported that the dozen or so men who raided the jail anticipated delivering their prisoner to the larger gathering for punishment. When they decided that was too risky, they were faced with killing the man themselves, a task that all had not anticipated and all did not relish. The informants provided no account of how that was resolved.

27. Milgram reported (1964:141, 1974:205) that subjects who administered the maximum (450 volts) violence were not consistently or significantly different ($p > .05$) from subjects who refused to engage in any violence on the basis of their marital status, occupation, military experience, political preference, religious affiliation, educational history, birth order, or gender. The baseline experiment was replicated frequently and widely in the United States and abroad, with virtually the same results (Miller, A. 1986).

28. Mantell (1971) reports that discrediting the authority status of the experimenter in the presence of the subject reduced but slightly the proportion of subjects who subsequently complied with that experimenter's instructions to increase the shock level after each pupil error. Human beings often comply with instructions from superordinates, but compliance does not presuppose other's superordinate status. Human beings frequently tell themselves to do what their peers ask or tell them to do!

29. Duncan and Fiske (1977) asked subjects to complete the Gough Adjective Check List, the Thorndike Temperament Scale, and two of Schutz's Fundamental Interpersonal Relations Orientation Scales. Their coding of two videotaped interaction sessions between cross-sex and same-sex pairs included measures of the frequen-

cy, duration, and total extent of smiling; frequency and extent of laughing; speaker-auditor turn-taking; auditor back-channel actions; direction of gaze; and gesturing.

30.   The more complex a sequence of collective action, the more likely the necessary prior planning and preparation assume prior social relationships among the participants, and sometimes group membership. When the Jackson County, Florida, men were planning the 1934 Brewton jail raid, there was talk of organizing a local KKK chapter. A front-page newspaper story read as follows:

> Taking a determined stand to protect the honor of womanhood and to champion the oppressed in Jackson County, a group of sober-minded, straight forward men will probably organize a local Ku Klux Klan, it was revealed to the writer the other day by a prominent citizen. The purpose of the Klan is to take over where the law fails, or where the law has no jurisdiction. It will defend and protect the constitution and the flag of the United States and make this section safe for "life, liberty and the pursuit of happiness." (*Mariana Daily Times-Courier*, October 23, 1934, p. 1)

There is no evidence that members of the Brewton raiding party or the subsequent lynching party were KKK members.

In the more recent lynching of three civil-rights organizers outside Philadelphia, Mississippi (Huie 1965), Ku Klux Klan membership and social structure were factors. Testimonies at the subsequent trial (Mars 1977) established that lynching participants were related beyond friendships and family ties. All were members of the local KKK klavern; and the state Klan organization had ordered the execution of the local civil-rights organizers. Thus, plans for abducting and killing the victims, for burying the bodies, and for destroying the evidence were developed in meetings of the local klavern leadership with their rank and file members. KKK klaverns, like other groups, have vertical hierarchies that establish who is expected to assign responsibilities and who is expected to carry them out. Like other political and religious groups, the Klan also has a set of ideological principles to justify whatever actions are taken in the name of the organization.

31.   As I noted in the preceding chapter, a considerable body of research has established that most participants in most temporary gatherings are neither alone nor anonymous; rather, they assemble with family members, friends, or acquaintances, and often encounter more of the same. The anonymous crowd member is a rare phenomenon.

3

Challenging the Myth: Sherif, Turner and Killian

Introduction

The nineteenth-century creators of the madding crowd held that individuals were transformed by and came to act under the influence of a crowd mind. Early twentieth-century critics scoffed at this alleged transformation of the individual. They argued that individuals in crowds are the same as when alone, although in some circumstances more so. Nothing new or different is added in the crowd. Whatever extraordinary behavior occurs there is imported in the drives and predispositions carried into the crowd within individual members. The madness of crowds is not created in the crowd but merely released through the predisposed responses of its members and facilitated by the sights and sounds of others behaving the same.

The first half of the twentieth century also witnessed the development of an empirical social psychology in Europe and the United States. Social psychologists were pursuing answers to Comte's question, How can the individual be both consequence and cause of society? The concerns of this fledgling field of study were to document and understand the influence of society and culture upon the individual, the relationships and interactions between individuals, and the possible influence of individuals upon the culture and society.

This led at least one young social psychologist to recast the polarized argument between transformation and predisposition explanations of the crowd. Muzafer Sherif agreed that individuals were not transformed by the crowd. But he also believed that the presence and actions of other individuals could be of consequence for how any one individual perceives and acts in the situation; and he believed these effects could not be attributed merely to what individuals brought within themselves to that situation as claimed by the predispositionists. Sherif argued that social interaction was of consequence for the development of norms in groups and in ad hoc social situations including the crowd, and that those emergent norms became the standards in terms of which participants perceived those situations, organized, and controlled their behavior. He then developed a series of experimental studies to explore his arguments systematically.

Sherif's autokinetic experiment became a cornerstone in the new discipline of social psychology. Both his criticisms of the transformation and predisposition explanations of the crowd and his theoretical and experimental analysis of emergent norms were embraced by sociologists Ralph Turner and Lewis Killian and later developed as their emergent-norm theory of collective behavior. In this chapter I review and critique the development of Sherif's work and the extension of those ideas and evidence in Turner and Killian's emergent-norm theory.

Muzafer Sherif (1905–1988)

Introduction

In 1935, Muzafer Sherif, a Turkish immigrant, completed a doctoral dissertation at Columbia University, "Some Social Factors in Perception." This was published the following year (1936) as *The Psychology of Social Norms* and became one of the classic experimental studies in the history of the social and behavioral sciences. Sherif's training in experimental psychology was supplemented by extensive reading in sociology and anthropology. This led him to the hypothesis that cultural and social factors, more specifically social norms, had more to do with the individual's perception and behavior than did the physical properties of the world in which that perception and behavior took place.

Sherif's problem was to find "a fluid and ambiguous situation for which individuals did not have previously established standards" (1936:ix), and therefore one in which he could study the development of social norms and their consequences for perception and behavior. He concluded that the autokinetic phenomenon—the apparent movement of a pinpoint of light against a totally darkened field—might provide such a situation. Although this phenomenon, with which he was very familiar, had already been studied in the psychological laboratory and reported in the literature, it was not the source of the idea for his research. Rather, he reports that the idea came from reading sociological accounts of the formation of norms and their effects on individuals, e.g., the small-group field studies of Shaw and Thrasher of the Chicago school, and

> Specifically, Emile Durkheim contributed the fundamental idea that new norms arise when people interact in fluid and extraordinary situations where

behavior alternatives increase beyond those in the compelling grooves of daily routine. (1936:ix)

Sherif's work was also influenced by his reading and rejection of both the transformation and predisposition formulations. Of the former he wrote:

It is emphasized by sociologically inclined authors that the individual in a crowd situation is no longer his individual self; his individual experience is in the powerful grip of the occasion; his actions are no more his; he is simply a tool responding to the whims of the leader or the violence of the group. (1936:70)

Sherif disagreed. He wrote:

The individual in an intense group situation acts as a member of the group; the group situation demands conformity. (1936:70)

Further:

What happens in a group or crowd situation is not restricted to the breaking down of the moral and social norms that regulate one's daily activities, but involves the rise and the incorporation of new norms or slogans in the individual. (1936:75)

Sherif also took sharp exception to Allport's (1924) claim that groups were nothing more than a collection of individuals. Influenced by Gestalt psychology in his study of perception, Sherif cited the classic Hering and Muller-Lyer illusions as examples that no stimulus configuration is perceived independently of its surrounding field. He reasoned:

If the perception of even a line is influenced by other lines around it, it is natural to expect that our perception and subsequent behavior will be modified in a fundamentally similar way when we are in a situation facing other persons in some definite relationship—one of competition, cooperation, or any familiar type of group interaction. (1936:80)

Moreover, Sherif argued that in social situations, unlike arithmetic, the presence and behaviors of other human beings "does something more than add to the perceptual field. The field may be recast" (1936:8) as a new *social psychological gestalt:*

The result is, we repeat, that the properties of any part are determined by its membership in the total functional system. When we extend this general principle to the social field, a new psychological approach to the problems of groups and crowds appears. When we are in a situation with other people, our experience and subsequent behavior are modified by the special social conditions around us. (1936:84)

By social conditions Sherif referred to norms, both those found "wherever we find an organized society, primitive or complicated" (1936:85) as well as those that are established through the interaction of people confronted with the challenge of an unfamiliar, ambiguous, or otherwise problematic situation (1936:86).

The Autokinetic Experiments

Mindful of the greater complexity of the day-to-day world and of the many limitations of the social psychological laboratory, Sherif designed the autokinetic experiments to investigate systematically human behavior in these problematic situations. These are tricky conceptual and methodological issues. I will therefore describe in some detail several of Sherif's experiments to indicate the care with which he proceeded to measure problematic situations, norms, and the subsequent behaviors he believed to be the result of those norms.

Sherif brought individual subjects into a room, seated them at a table containing a signal key, and explained:

> When the room is completely dark, I shall give you the signal READY and then show you a point of light. After a short time the light will start to move. As soon as you see it move, press the key. A few seconds later the light will disappear. Then tell me the distance it moved. Try to make your estimates as accurate as possible. (1936:35)

On the first day, each subject made 100 judgments. Their initial judgments of distance varied considerably. Subsequent judgments varied less and less, the majority converging around a narrower range, unique to each subject. Sherif computed the median of each individual's distance estimates and termed this the individual's norm.

On the second day, three individuals at a time returned to the laboratory, where each made and witnessed one another making another 100 judgments. Each individual's initial judgments clustered around his or her prior individual norm. But subsequent judgments gradually converged in the direction of the judgments given by the other individuals. Sherif reported that no individual returned to his or her initial range or median nor did any individual establish a new or unique range or median. He wrote:

> Where individual sessions came first, divergent norms were established giving rise to "funnel-shaped" figures as a result of the convergence of the subjects' norms in the subsequent group sessions. (1936:102–3)

In a second sequence of experiments Sherif attempted to demonstrate the enduring effects of group norms by reversing the above procedures. He began with three persons making 100 judgments in each other's presence.

After three such group sessions, each individual returned for a solitary judgment session. At issue was whether or not each person would establish a new range of judgments (and median therein), or would give judgments corresponding to those of the group in which he or she had previously participated. Sherif wrote:

> Where the group sessions preceded the individual ones, the convergence of norms was apparent from the first session, and remained throughout including the [final] individual sessions. (1936:102–3)

The median judgments for individuals and groups of three individuals are summarized in Figure 3.1.

Sherif's (1936) autokinetic experiments became true classics in the history of social psychology. But more than a quarter-century passed before very many scholars recognized their relevance to behavior in critical, unstable situations, despite Sherif's discussion of those implications from the outset. He had written:

> [When] a group of individuals faces a new unstable situation and has no previously established interests or opinions regarding the situation, the result is not chaos; a common norm arises and the situation is structured in relation to the common norm. Once the common norm is established, later the separate individuals keep on perceiving it in terms of the frame of reference which was once the norm of the group. (1936:111)

Situations of Varying Instability

In 1952 Sherif and Harvey reported another set of autokinetic experiments that varied situational instability. They argued that the elimination of spatial reference points created uncertainty for the individual and thereby increased "the likelihood of accepting a standard for behavior from a source other than the individual's own" (1952:276).

Sherif and Harvey created three conditions of situational instability and observed the judgments of 20 subjects in each, 10 male and 10 female university students, all previously unacquainted. Each was asked to make judgments of the autokinetic phenomenon while alone and then in the presence of another subject. In condition A, "the experimenter was as friendly and encouraging as possible" (1952:276), telling subjects the task was easy and they would undoubtedly do well. In the alone condition, the experimenter led the subject(s) to a dark room (15 × 28 feet), briefly flashed on the light enabling the subject(s) to see a chair at a table on which the signal key rested, provided brief instructions about the apparatus, then closed the door and allowed five minutes adaptation to the totally dark room.

In condition B the same procedures were followed except judgments were

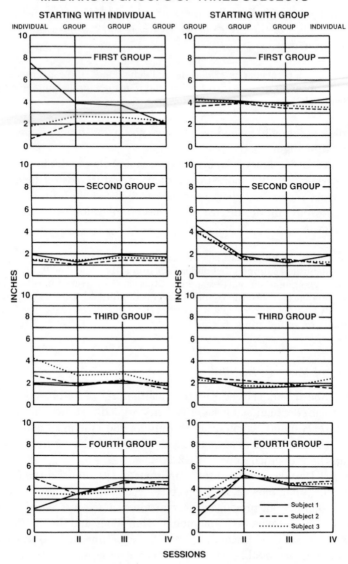

Figure 3.1. Median judgments of the autokinetic phenomenon by individuals and groups (after Sherif 1936).

made in a much larger room (54 × 81 feet) reached by walking down a long, dimly lit corridor. In the alone condition, the experimenter led the subject by the hand down the corridor, into the room, and to the chairs at the table; in the group condition, the experimenter led both subjects, who held one another's hand. Unlike condition A, subjects never saw the interior of the room in which judgments were made.

In condition C, the experimenter engaged subjects in the minimal conversation required to provide instructions but made no further attempt to be friendly. Alone subjects were told to find their way down the corridor, to enter the darkened (54 × 81 feet) room, close the door behind them, and pull curtains over the door to ensure against light seepage. Subjects were then told to stand with backs against the door and walk straight forward (a 12 foot distance) until reaching some steps. After climbing (four) and descending (three) steps, subjects were told to stop, turn left 45 degrees, and then proceed (39 feet) to a table and take a chair. In the group condition, pairs of subjects received the same instructions before proceeding together to the room, entering, and taking their seats. Despite frequent requests for direction and assistance, the experimenter remained completely silent until subjects had reached the table, wandered around for three minutes without reaching the table, or stated they were lost or had given up.

Sherif and Harvey (1952) hypothesized that the more unfamiliar and unstructured the situation (i.e., the fewer opportunities for visual familiarization with spatial references), (1) the more likely individuals would give a broad range of distance judgments, (2) the larger would be the magnitude of median individual judgments (i.e., individual norms), (3) the greater would be the differences between individual judgments, and (4) the greater would be the convergence of judgments among individuals when brought together in a group situation.

The results are summarized in Figure 3.2. The top panel clearly indicates the range of individual judgments was greater than the range of group judgments in all three conditions; and that individual and group ranges were greater in condition C than in B or A.

The bottom panel of Figure 3.2 gives the medians for the ranges of individual and of group judgments. These were highest in condition C and lowest in condition A; and they were higher for individuals than for groups in conditions C and B. In the second column, I constructed an index of convergent (group) judgments by dividing the mean range of group judgments of distance in each condition by the mean range of individual judgments in the same condition; I then standardized these ratios by subtracting from 1.00. Consistent with Sherif and Harvey's hypotheses, these convergence indexes were .17, .25, and .39 for conditions A, B, and C, respectively. Further, on the postexperiment questionnaires, the majority of Sherif and Harvey's subjects (65%) reported more uncertainty in condition C ("com-

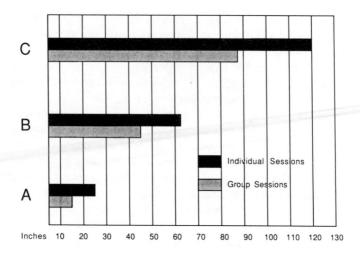

Condition		Judgment median (inches)	Index of individual to group convergence	Report of irritation with other subjects (%)	Those preferring group to individual condition (%)
C	Individual	12.74	.39	45	35
	Group	8.56			
B	Individual	9.04	.25	30	45
	Group	7.24			
A	Individual	4.85	.17	10	65
	Group	5.04			

Figure 3.2. Individual and group judgments in three conditions of uncertainty (after Sherif and Harvey, 1952)

pletely confused"; "lost as heck"), as compared with less than half the subjects (45 percent) in condition B ("bewildered"), and only one-fourth (25%) of the subjects in condition A ("ill at ease but . . . curious").

All the experimental results, however, were not consistent with Sherif and Harvey's theoretical expectations. A higher percentage of subjects in condition A (65%) than in B (45%) or C (35%) preferred the group to the individual situation; and a higher percentage in condition C (45%) than in B (30%) or A (10%) reported irritation or annoyance with the judgments of others in the group condition. Thus, Sherif and Harvey conclude:

The present experimental set-up was not sufficiently conducive to the estab-
lishment of mutual dependence between subject pairs. For this reason our
hypothesis predicting greater convergence in the group situation under conditions of greater insecurity and uncertainty has probably not been adequately
tested in spite of favorable statistical results. (1952:302)

An Assessment

The work of Sherif and his colleagues was impressive when it first appeared and it remains so today, despite Sherif's own reservations and despite
other criticisms, some of which will be reviewed below. Several features of
Sherif's work warrant comment. First, he avoided the perennial problem of
inferring norms from the behavior they are supposed to explain. Sherif and
his colleagues measured individual and group norms prior to and independently of the phenomenon they were supposed to predict and explain. They
construed norm as a measure of central tendency (e.g., median, mode, or
mean) in the individual's (or group's) multiple judgments in a situation.
Thus, norm was treated as a description of what people do, rather than as a
prescription or proscription for behavior. The individual's median judgment
at time one was the best predictor of the individual's initial judgments at
time two. When two or three such individuals were brought together at time
two, however, their subsequent judgments gradually converged and then
stabilized. This provided substantial evidence, then as now, for the hypothesis of social influence on individual judgments in an unfamiliar situation.[1]
Further, the median judgment of these two or three individuals—their
"norm"—was also the best predictor of their behavior when they faced a
similar situation by themselves on a subsequent occasion.

Second, Sherif did not describe nor did he report any measures of the
interaction of those individuals with one another about the light's movement, or about the estimates that should be made. In short, the emergent
norm consisted of no more than the median of converging verbal estimates of
the distance of movement. While this did predict individual judgments in
subsequent situations, it did not predict *collective* judgments, let alone more
complex *collective actions* in the same situation or in subsequent situations.

Third, Sherif and Harvey's work demonstrated that the more unfamiliar
the situation in which people were called upon to make judgments, the more
likely that two or more individuals in such a situation made judgments that
converged in the direction of one another's judgments. This is another very
important demonstration of social influence in problematic situations although, again, there is no demonstration of interaction among the subjects in
the form of questions, answers, challenges, evaluations, qualifications, com-
promises, etc.

Fourth, a conventional interpretation of Sherif's (1936) experiments and
the subsequent experiments of Sherif and Harvey (1952) is that subjects

were exposed to ambiguous stimulus configurations, that they were compelled to reduce uncertainty, and therefore subjects made judgments to impose order on the ambiguous situation. Alexander, Zucker, and Brody (1970) report experimental evidence that dramatically challenges this conventional interpretation. Sherif's instructions to his subjects included the following: "After a short time the light will start to move. As soon as you see it move, press the key. A few seconds later the light will disappear. Then tell me the distance it moved" (Sherif and Harvey 1952:287). Alexander and colleagues believed that those instructions rendered the autokinetic phenomenon more ambiguous than it might otherwise have been judged to be. Thus, in one experiment, they explicitly told subjects the light was actually stationary, that it only appeared to move. In that condition there was virtually no variation in the individual's 100 judgments of the autokinetic phenomenon, and the judgments of two individuals did not converge in the group or "together" judgment situation. In a second experiment, subjects overheard a confederate subject either giving judgments of converging (or diverging) movements of the pinpoint of light. The naive subjects' subsequent judgments of the autokinetic phenomenon corresponded to the type of judgments they overheard the confederate make.

Alexander, Zucker, and Brody's point is a fundamental one. The convergence of individual judgments, or of individuals' judgments, was not occasioned by an intrinsically ambiguous stimulus configuration or unstructured situation; rather, subjects behaved in the situation in accordance with what they were told by the experimenter or by the experimenter's confederate subjects about the nature of the phenomenon under judgment. Alexander, Zucker, and Brody appropriately concluded that "situational cues thus structure the interpretation of events" (1970:120) and not the nature of the events themselves. This illustrates a fundamental contribution of the symbolic interactionist perspective to our understanding of the individual and collective behavior in temporary gatherings: the words used to describe objects influence the way we behave toward those objects. Turner and Killian's emergent-norm theory of collective behavior has attempted to extend that contribution over the last three decades.

Ralph H. Turner (b. 1919) and Lewis Killian (b. 1919)

Introduction

Transformation theorists offered one explanation for behavior away from the crowd and a quite different explanation for behavior within the crowd. Predisposition theorists at least offered a parsimonious explanation for behavior outside and inside the crowd. Differences in their explanations aside, both transformation and predisposition theories assumed and attempted to explain the same phenomenon, viz., that everyone in the crowd was continuously engaged in unanimous or mutually inclusive behavior.

Turner and Killian characterized that assumption as the "illusion of unanimity" (1972:22). In rejecting the assumption they argued that "the crowd is characterized not by unanimity but by differential expression" (1987:26), that is, individual members of the crowd are "feeling differently, participating because of different motives, and even acting differently" (1972:22). Further, "some people express what they are feeling while others do not" (1987:26). But since some members of some crowds occasionally act collectively, Turner and Killian attempt to explain collective behavior as well as "the development and imposition of a pattern of differential expression that is perceived as unanimity" (1972:21; 1987:26).

Their parsimonious explanation for both phenomena is based on the traditional sociological premise that social behavior is the consequence of norms. Conventional and routine social behavior is the consequence of conventional and routine norms; extraordinary social behavior, i.e., collective behavior as they define it, is the consequence of emergent norms that develop from social interaction within extraordinary situations.

Turner and Killian were students of Blumer at the University of Chicago and place themselves in the broader Park-Blumer "collective behavior tradition" (1987:xiii). They write:

> What has endured to characterize the "collective behavior" approach has been the emphasis on the centrality of interaction , . . . (1987:6–7)

But Turner and Killian early abandoned (1957; Turner 1964a) what I have termed Park and Blumer's transformation perspective in favor of their own efforts to extend the normative explanation from routine groups to nonroutine and problematic social situations. In the third edition of their book, they appear more deliberately to draw the theoretical mantle of Blumer's symbolic interaction around their work, while managing to maintain a discrete distance from Blumer's nonsymbolic interaction explanation of collective behavior.

One of the most important sources of ideas and evidence for Turner and Killian's emerging theoretical venture was a social psychologist at the University of Oklahoma where Killian held his first faculty appointment after graduate school. That social psychologist was then midway through three decades of laboratory and field experimental studies of group formation and social influence. And, as Turner and Killian acknowledged across yet another three decades:

> The influence of our colleague Muzafer Sherif, will be evident to any who know his work. (1957:vi; 1972:x)
> From the time when the first edition was being written until now, the

ingenious empirical studies of our colleague Muzafer Sherif have provided
valuable insights into principles of psychological functioning at both individual
and group levels. (1987:xii)

The Emergent Norm Perspective

Collective behavior is defined as:[2]

> those forms of social behavior in which usual conventions cease to guide social
> action and people collectively transcend, bypass, or subvert established in-
> stitutional patterns and structures. . . . Collective behavior refers to the ac-
> tions of collectivities, not to a type of individual behavior. (1987:3)

Although Turner and Killian emphasize that the unusual social behavior with
which they are concerned is "normal, not pathological or irrational" (1987:7)
behavior, they also take great pains to distinguish their social behavior "from
the relatively stable and predictable forms of group behavior guided by
traditional norms" (1987:7).

Turner and Killian contend that routine groups and organizations "are
governed by established [traditional] rules," and have "defined procedures
for selecting and identifying members [and leaders]" (1987:3–4). The collectivities with which Turner and Killian are concerned lack these features.
While those collectivities are "oriented toward an object of attention and
arrive at some shared objective, . . . [neither is] defined in advanced [nor
are there] formal procedures for reaching decisions" (1987:4) about object or
objective as in the case of groups and organizations.

The Focal Theoretical Problems

Turner and Killian claim collective behavior can only be understood if its
distinctive features are explained:

> First, we must *explain how* it is that *people* come to *transcend*, bypass, or
> subvert established *institutional patterns* and structures.
> Second, we must *explain behavior or action contrasted with attitudes*. . . .
> An adequate approach to collective behavior must analyze how perceptions,
> ideas, and feelings get translated into action.
> Third, we must *explain* the fact *that people act collectively* rather than singly.
> (1987:7, emphasis added)

A fourth feature is central to Turner and Killian's concerns:

> In the beginning, *it is [in relation to] events*—an extraordinary condition or a
> precipitating incident—*that a norm* justifying extra-institutional [collective]
> action *emerges*. (1987:10; emphasis added)

Thus elaborated, the emergent norm-theoretical formulation addresses the
following problems:[3]

There must be *group formation related to some event;* [then,] *interaction* and exploration in which a sense of feasibility and timelessness develop; and [finally,] *the formation of an emergent norm defining the situation and justifying* [*collective*] *action.* (1987:50; emphasis added)[4]

In the following pages I will examine in chronological order the components in Turner and Killian's explanation of (1) the formation of collectivities and (2) the interaction processes within those collectivities that give rise to (3) the development of an emergent norm that defines the situation and justifies collective behavior. My analysis of the broad relationships among those components is summarized in Figure 3.3.

The Formation of Collectivities

The first questions that any theory of crowds and collective behavior must answer are: What brings people together? And, how is that accomplished? Transformation theories generally ignored this problem; predisposition theories addressed it but their answer has been refuted repeatedly by the empirical evidence. Emergent-norm theory addresses the problem in a different manner:

> How do people come together to form collectivities? . . . [We] shall stress the combined effect of (1) a condition or event that is sufficiently outside the range of "ordinary" happenings that people turn to their fellow human beings for help and support in interpreting and responding to the situation, and (2) the availability of pre-existing social groupings through which intercommunication can be initiated fairly easily. (Turner and Killian 1987:9)

Turner and Killian locate those extraordinary conditions and events in the physical world or the social order. The *physical world* refers to "the natural environment and material culture" (1987:335) in which sudden changes can create extraordinary circumstances—*events*—with which human beings must cope. Hurricanes, tornadoes, and floods, on the one hand, and explosions, chemical spills, and nuclear accidents, on the other, are examples of the types of disaster that may require emergency evacuation or dispersal of people from the disaster area, as well as the mobilization of existing collectivities or the formation of new ones that converge on the disaster area with a variety of resources and interests.

The *social order* consists of "the normative order," "the social structure," and "communication channels" (1987:36–37).[5] Problems can develop in one or more of these sectors of the social order, just like the physical world, thereby creating *conditions conducive to the formation of collectivities*, interaction within collectivities, and the emergence of collective behavior.

Under the heading of the *normative order*, Turner and Killian include many phenomena: the names, definitions, and classifications of things in the physical and cultural world, which human beings learn in the process of

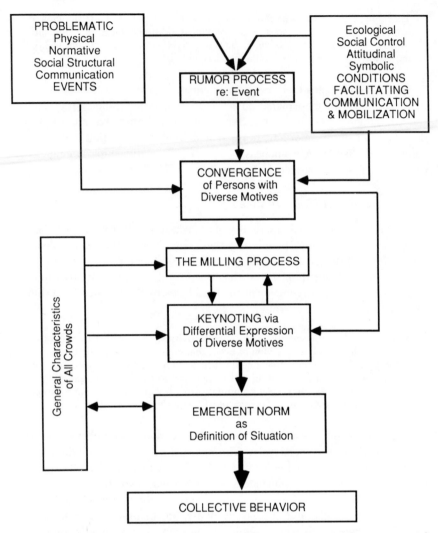

Figure 3.3.   The emergent-norm theory of collective behavior (after Turner and Killian, 1972; 1987).

socialization; the *values* attached to those things which human beings are socialized to seek and avoid; and, last but not least,

> [learned] guidelines for socially approved ways of attaining these values, as well as rules for coordinating their everyday behavior with that of other people. These *norms* include formal laws and regulations, and informal customs, some

with moral implications and others which might be called "rules of convenience." Their existence as shared understandings and expectations constitute an important basis for both individual activity and social order. (1987:37, emphasis in original)

Thus, while the routine normative order (1987:37) offers some standardized solutions to many recurring problems, extraordinary problems can and do occur. However:

[It] is not the existence of what the social scientist may identify as logically contradictory values or ambiguous norms which gives rise to collective behavior. It is the revision of the normative order in the face of events that bring its guidance into question which creates the setting for extra-institutional action. (1987:40)

The normative order is revised through collective redefinition. Accordingly, the long-standing discrepancy between the claims of the U.S. constitution and the treatments of blacks did not bring about the civil-rights movement; rather, it was the collective redefinition of that discrepancy (cf. McAdam 1982).

By *social structure* Turner and Killian refer to "social relationships" in general, and to a "division of labor" in particular; that is, "interdependent *roles*, consisting of stabilized expectations for the behavior of each member in relation to other members" (1987:37). Individual members alternately enact and improvise on those expectations. The emergent-norm formulation argues (1987:44) that social structure, its constituent positions, their connections and occupants, also "depend on socially constructed definitions for their reality" (1987:44). The malfeasance of public officials, police strikes, and presumably assassinations of political leaders as well as coups are all challenges to citizens' confidence in or redefinition of community political structures.

The third component in Turner and Killian's social order is *communication channels* through which individuals are informed by others "what the situation is in which they must act, what norms are appropriate and what roles must be taken into account" (1987:37). If belief in the norms and values and trust in the public officials depend upon open access to and freely flowing communication throughout the community, then impaired or diminished communications have a contrary effect, e.g., strict censorship or the prohibition of free discussion "may give rise to collective behavior" (1987:49). Conversely, where free assembly, free speech, and freedom of the press have long been denied but are suddenly permitted, the conditions and opportunities for collective behavior are dramatically increased.

Turner and Killian argue that "collective behavior emerges out of situations in which changes are perceived as occurring in the normative order, the social structure, or the flow of information" (1987:50). But they emphasize that *problematic events*—conflict, breakdown, declining trust, altered communications—do not of themselves form gatherings or produce collective behavior. Instead:

> It is in the process of communication between individuals who share feelings of uncertainty about reality, whether in their immediate surroundings or in the larger environment of the nation or the world, that the origins of emergent forms of behavior are to be found. (1987:50)

Symbolic interactionists emphasize communication processes. Although Turner and Killian provide no systematic characterization of communication processes in routine situations, they do propose that rumor is "the characteristic mode of communication" (1987:50) in the development of collective behavior.

The Rumor Process.   Rumor has traditionally been viewed (e.g., G. Allport and Postman 1945) as the progressive distortion of initially factually true and uncontaminated information. The emergent-norm theory of collective behavior rejects this view and embraces Shibutani's (1966) characterization of rumor as "a collective problem solving procedure" in uncertain situations where routine channels of communication break down, or do not exist, or cannot be trusted. It is in those circumstances, Turner and Killian argue, that people ask questions, pose answers, make assertions, offer characterizations, and the like. In so doing they construct definitions of the problematic situation that help them to act.

Rumor may develop and spread throughout an entire community by various combinations of mass media, telephone conversations, and face-to-face encounters. Rumor may precede or accompany the convergence of people on a common location, or both. How then does rumor contribute to the formation of a collectivity?

Turner and Killian claim two factors are at work. First, the rumor process develops in relation to extraordinary events, and therefore to events of consequence to many people. Second, "there is differential participation in the rumor process, with different actors advancing different suggestions as to what is going on and what should be done" (1987:59). By "differential participation" Turner and Killian (1987:21) refer to different predispositions or tendencies to behave that bring people to the collectivity and that determine the role they play within it.

Diverse Motivations for Participation.   Turner and Killian (1957; Turner 1964) were among the first sociologists to criticize the explanation that collective behavior resulted from homogeneous predispositions or motivations for participation. They argued instead that "the motivations of individuals for participating in collective behavior are diverse" (Turner and Killian 1972:27, 1987:31) and they set forth (1972:27–29) five different motives for participation:[6]

Turner and Killian refer (1972:27, 1987:88) to "ego-involved" individuals and "concerned" or "committed" individuals. *Ego-involved* individuals are personally involved in, committed to, or perhaps victims of whatever extraordinary event or incident occasions convergence on the common location.[7] *Concerned* or committed persons also have some personal relationship to the event, but they are less involved.[8]

Turner and Killian's third motivation type (1987:33, 1972:28) is *the insecure,* that is, persons who seek out any crowd, regardless of the issue or problem, for the sense of power and security it provides. These persons are said to "derive direct satisfaction from participation in the crowd regardless of the circumstances" (1987:88).

Turner and Killian's fourth category of participant (1987:33, 88, 1972:29) is *the spectator,* that is, the persons "motivated chiefly by curiosity," who gather "just to see what happens."

A fifth category of participant (1987:33; cf. 1972:29) is *the exploiter,* that is, persons who are detached "from the crowd objectives rather than ego-involved in them." Exploiters have no relationship to the problematic event, incident, or issue around which the crowd has formed. They are participating for self-serving purposes; for example, to leaflet or petition or solicit donations for another cause, to sell food, drink, buttons, T-shirts, or perhaps to pick pockets.

Convergence on a Common Location. I have noted that Turner and Killian discuss problematic normative, structural, and communication circumstances (1972, 1987) that can precipitate an event around which a collectivity forms. They further argue that since "collective behavior develops through a communication process and culminates in people acting together in relatively large collectivities, . . . conditions that facilitate communication and mobilization are essential" (1972:61). They identify some variations in ecological arrangements of people, social control policies, and attitudinal/symbolic concentrations that facilitate or discourage communication processes among people and their convergence on a common location.[9]

Interaction in Collectivities

Characteristics Common to All Crowds. Turner and Killian's participants form a collectivity because of their varied interests in some extraordinary event or incident. What they do within the collectivity concerned with that event develops under the influence of elements, conditions, or characteristics that Turner and Killian have long argued (1957:84, 1972:80, 1987:78) are common to all crowds: (1) uncertainty; (2) urgency; (3) selective individual suggestibility; (4) common mood and imagery; (5) constraint; and (6) selective permissiveness. They write:

> The situation is ambiguous and to some degree unstructured; the participants do not initially share clear-cut, pre-existing expectations as to how they should behave; the outcome of the episode appears uncertain. (1972:79, 1987:77)

Turner and Killian have recently added two dimensions that appear to bridge uncertainty and urgency: *feasibility* and *timeliness*.[10] They suggest:

> It is the combination of uncertainty, feasibility, and timeliness which leads to a collective search for a conception of appropriate action. . . . Symbols, emerging out of the milling process, serve to indicate . . . what sort of action is appropriate . . . [and] the kind of coordination of the crowd members' actions that is required. (1987:77–78)

Drawing on Sherif's (1936; Sherif and Harvey 1952) autokinetic experiments, Turner and Killian argue (1987:53) that people confronted with an ambiguous or novel situation are more likely to turn to one another for cues on how to proceed. An examination of the milling process in general, and keynoting in particular, illustrates how the diverse motives of crowd participants interact with the "characteristics common to all crowds" to yield "a conception of appropriate action" in the ambiguous situation. These relationships are sketched in Figure 3.4, an expansion of the relevant sections of the general emergent-norm model.

Milling.   In their early and continuing criticism of the transformation (or contagion) perspective, Turner and Killian rejected the traditional metaphor that compared crowds to milling herds of cattle because "it obscures the fact that with human beings milling is a form of symbolic communication which we have called 'rumor'" (1972:38, 1987:55). They refer to "searching behavior and random restless activity [that] are characteristic of individuals caught in the throes of uncertainty and blocked from satisfying, meaningful action" (1987:55). But milling is "primarily a verbal process." Thus:

> In a crowd engaged in both physical and verbal milling, people ask each other questions about what they have seen and heard and [they] answer [each other] with bits of information, guesses, and theories. In communicating they move about, talking first to one person, then to another. (1987:55)

Turner and Killian suggested (1972:64–65) that *three types of questions* appear to feed the keynoting process, the construction of an emergent definition of the situation, and the launching of collective action. For example,

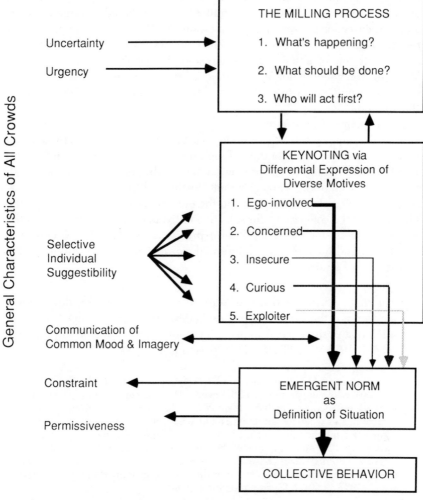

Figure 3.4. Milling and keynoting processes in the development of emergent norms (after Turner and Killian, 1972; 1987).

individuals milling in ambiguous or unstructured situations may be concerned with three kinds of cues.

First, they are said to be concerned (1972:64–65) with what has happened, is happening, or may yet happen. Those concerns seemingly correspond to the general crowd characteristic that Turner and Killian call *uncertainty*. At least it would seem that such concerns might be followed by efforts to define the situation.

Second, people may not be certain about what to do but, according to Turner and Killian (1972:65), they think something should be done immediately. Such concerns seemingly correspond to the general crowd characteristic Turner and Killian call *urgency*, and to concerns with what is an appropriate line of action, e.g.: What should be done? What should we do? What are you going to do? What should I do? The answers provided to these questions would seem to contribute to the development of a "definition of the situation."

Third, people in the milling process are said to be (1972:65) concerned with leadership, that is, Who is going to act first? The answers to these three types of questions posed in the milling process are, according to Turner and Killian, the outcome of an interaction among the different motivations alleged responsible for bringing people to the collectivity. Thus construed, diverse motives play a crucial part in the emergent-norm explanation for the formation of the collectivity, for selective individual suggestibility within the milling process, for the differential expressions that launch and complete keynoting, and for the other differential expressions that contribute to the emergence of a norm.[11]

Keynoting. Turner and Killian state that "emergent norms develop and change through the keynoting process" (1987:10), which involves "the presentation of a positive suggestions in an ambivalent [cf. uncertain] frame of reference" (1972:89, 1987:85). They reason as follows:

> When an unusual, difficult-to-assimilate event occurs . . . individuals entertain a variety of interpretations of the event. They may engage in a brief period of covert restructuring activity, turning over in their minds various possible explanations of what the situation is and what action may be appropriate. A gesture or symbolic utterance made to such an audience may be characterized as a *keynote*. If it embodies one of the competing images held by members of the crowd, it encourages those members to express themselves. The keynote and these supporting expressions shift the balance in support of the keynoted image. (1987:59, 1972:47; emphasis in original)

Thus, the success or failure of any particular keynote presupposes the existence of latent support in the crowd (1972:69). This corresponds to Turner and Killian's general crowd characteristic of *selective individual suggestibility.*[12] Specifically, of the several potential keynotes that may be offered, the one that eventually succeeds presupposes a "convergence of predispositions shared by a significant portion, but not all of the crowd" (1987:90, 1972:95). It is to this problem that the interplay of participants' diverse motivations is connected, as the following discussion will indicate.

On the one hand, there may be some people who believe something must be done but are not certain what to propose and who ask questions like What should we do? On the other hand there are persons "who feel no such uncertainty [and are] capable of proposing definite action tersely and forcibly" (1987:85, 1972:89). The latter are Turner and Killian's *ego-involved* (1972:27) or *committed* (1987:88) participants. These advocates are often called leaders or keynoters: "The leader is important primarily as a keynoter, advancing suggestions that help to resolve the feelings of ambivalence experience by many crowd members" (1987:84–85).

But the keynoters is "not necessarily the person who physically carries out the line of action that develops in the milling process" (1987:85). Those crowd members who believe something should be done—*the concerned*—but are uncertain what to do and therefore unlikely to advocate action (1987:84–5) are likely to carry out another's proposal that corresponds to their motives and to "the common mood and imagery" emerging in the situation (1987:59). This is consistent with Turner and Killian's contention that everyone in the crowd is not equally vulnerable to every suggestion put forth.

Since there may be multiple and competing proposals, the one that prevails will likely be the proposal with (1972:69, 1987:59) the most latent support, that is, the "pre-existing latent tendencies, common to a significant portion of the crowd" (1972:95, 1987:90). The suggestion receiving compliance will "reflect the convergence of predispositions shared by a significant portion, but not all the crowd" (1972:95, 1987:90). Thus, crowd members are said (1972:80, 1987:78) to respond uncritically to suggestions consistent with the emerging common mood and imagery.

Whereas Turner and Killian's theory requires a heterogeneity of motives to form the collectivity and to start the keynoting process, they require a critical mass of homogeneous motives to bring the keynote to fruition. On the one hand they write that: "An emergent norm approach reflects the empirical observation that the crowd is characterized not by unanimity but by *differential expression*" (1972:22, 1987:26).[13] But, on the other hand, they make it quite clear that unlimited differentiation will not suffice:

> It must be remembered, however, that *collective behavior does not develop in a completely heterogeneous aggregate*. Pre-existing, latent tendencies, common to many members of a crowd, facilitate the development of a common mood and imagery. (1972:94, 1987:90; emphasis added)

What is the source of Turner and Killian's general crowd characteristic called *common mood and imagery?* How can the alleged differentiation in motivations be rendered consistent with the requirement that some crowd members share common predispositions or tendencies to behave? My interpretation of Turner and Killian's analysis is that after a sufficient number of *the concerned* carry out a keynote from *the ego-involved*, this is sufficient to attract *the insecure* persons characterized as deriving "satisfaction from participation in a crowd regardless of the circumstances" (1987:88).

At this point Turner and Killian's two remaining types of participants could make their contribution. *The curious spectator* (1972:28, 1987:33) by neither overtly supporting nor opposing the developing modal behavior could contribute tacit approval. This, in turn, could swell the developing common mood and imagery, if not the emerging line of collective action. Last but not least, *the exploiter* could make an unwitting contribution by carefully *not* opposing whatever most people are doing so that their behaviors could be exploited to his or her vested interest, be that selling them food or souvenirs, distributing leaflets or petitions for compatible causes, or even picking their pockets.

The implication of Turner and Killian's argument is that every additional bit of advocacy, participation, and approval of any one course of action by some members of the crowd reduces the uncertainty and hesitation for other members previously reluctant to participate. "As the behavior of an increasing number of crowd members reflects the emergent definition of the situation, it becomes increasingly difficult for the individual to cling to a conflicting conception" (1972:95, 1987:90). Conversely "the silence of dissenters may provide a form of passive support for the emergent norm and contribute to the illusion of unanimity" (1987:28).

The Emergent Norm

Following Turner and Killian's theoretical scenario, we have moved from an extraordinary event, to the formation of a collection of people with diverse interests in that event, to the interaction by some of those people (and the passive observation or active exploitation by others) yielding a keynoting process launched by some types of people for one set of reasons and complemented by other types of people for different reasons. The result is a developing common mood and imagery that imperceptibly becomes a definition of the situation or emergent norm, which in turn encourages or permits some line of collective action. This complex and subtle developmental process warrants careful examination.

Definition of the Situation

The central concept in Turner and Killian's theory of collective behavior is *the emergent norm:*

> We propose that *collective behavior takes place under the governance of emergent norms*. Some shared redefinition of right and wrong in a situation supplies the justification and coordinates the action in collective behavior. (1987:7; emphasis added)

They explain:

> *Since the norm is* to some degree *specific to the situation,* differing in degree or
> in kind from the norms governing noncrowd situations, it is an emergent norm.
> (1987:26; emphasis added)

Some critics (e.g., Tierney 1980) have taken Turner and Killian to task for
their lack of specification of the concept of norm and emergent norm. They
have replied that their conception of norm "does not refer merely to a rule or
a precise behavioral expectation," and, that it "should not be interpreted
simplistically" as a few "do's and don'ts" (1987:26). Emergent norms refer,
instead, to "an emergent *definition of the situation* which encompasses an
extensive complex of factors" (emphasis added). Several are listed:

> First, as a collective definition of the situation *the emergent norm indicates
> what is going on as well as what to do about it,* . . . the sort of action, . . .
> appropriate moods, . . . consistent or inconsistent [behavior.]
> [Second,] it includes *a set of justifications* for both the reconstructed ver-
> sion of reality and the actions defined as appropriate.
> [Third,] the emergent norm includes *an evaluation of various population
> segments* in relation to the situation [e.g., crowd members vs. crowd targets].
> (1987:58; emphasis added)

Simplistic or not, it seems reasonable to assume that overt and audible
answers are offered to the questions noted earlier—What's going on? What
should be done? Who will act first?—and that some subset of those answers
is endorsed by other persons and thus becomes the keynote around which is
constructed the definition of the situation on which the participants act.
Turner and Killian assert:

> *[It] is the reconstructed definition of reality which we designate as "the
> emergent norm."* . . . This definition emerges in the situation and its function
> is to explain and interpret current reality. (1987:58; emphasis added)

The emerging *definition of the situation* is then said to accommodate a
range of acceptable to unacceptable behaviors. Thus (1987:33)

> The emergent norm is not only *constraining;* it is also *permissive.* While some
> specific acts may be required or prohibited, latitude exists for a wide range of
> acts consistent with the definition of the situation. Not uniformity but differen-
> tial expression and participation, with each member "doing his own thing"
> within the bounds of the emergent norm, is the source of the dynamic, creative
> quality of collective behavior. (1987:33; emphasis added)

However, in addition to the permissive and constraining consequences, Turner and Killian also argue (1972:21, 1987:26) that emergent norms result in participants selectively perceiving differential expression as unanimity.

We have now examined the relationships between all of Turner and Killian's general crowd characteristics and the diverse motives of their participants in the development of the emergent norm. We turn now to the critical question. To what end?

Collective Behavior

To repeat, Turner and Killian define this central concept as:

> those *forms of social behavior* in which usual conventions cease to guide social action and people collectively transcend, bypass, or subvert established institutional patterns and structures. (1987:3; emphasis added)

Further recall Turner and Killian's (1987:7) contention that to understand collective behavior is to "single out its [three] distinctive features for explanation," two of which are that "people act collectively," and that collective "behavior or action [not] attitude" is the phenomenon to be explained. My repeated examination of three statements of the emergent-norm formulation (1957, 1972, 1987) located few examples and no criteria by which to know Turner and Killian's *collective behavior* when I see it or hear it, no criteria by which to make the judgment that people have acted collectively. Thus, if we require further specification of Turner and Killian's forms of social behavior, we must look elsewhere. I turn to their treatment of crowd types and tendencies.

Crowd Types and Tendencies[14]

Turner and Killian (1957) early adopted Swanson's (1953) modification of Blumer's (1939) distinction between acting and expressive crowds, to which they added their own distinction between individualistic and solidaristic crowds. The combination yields the fourfold taxonomy of crowd types I have represented in Table 3.1. Turner and Killian now subsume these distinctions under two sets of crowd processes of tendencies they believe are found in some form or combination in all crowds: "One [is] related to the [solidaristic or individualistic] *coordination* of the behavior of crowd members, the other to the [acting or expressive] *symbolization* of the objective of the crowd behavior" (1987:77, emphasis in original).[15] I discuss their four tendencies in turn.

Acting Symbolizing Tendencies. Blumer (1939) distinguished between *acting crowds* that establish some object for mutual attention to which their

Table 3.1.   Crowd Types by Coordinating and Symbolizing Tendencies

Symbolizing Tendencies	Coordinating Tendencies	
	Solidaristic	Individualistic
Acting	Lynching crowd	Looting crowd
Expressive	Holiness Crowd	Celebrating crowd

(After Turner and Killian 1987).

actions are then directed, and *expressive crowds* whose objective was said to be a release of tension rather than the realization of a goal. Guy Swanson, a student of Blumer, distinguished (1953:523) between crowd members acting to manipulate objects external to themselves and crowd members acting to manipulate their self concepts as objects, calling the former acting and the latter expressive crowds. Turner and Killian embrace Swanson's modification:

> Thus, both forms of crowd may be said to have an *objective*, in the sense of a goal, contrary to Blumer's implication. Only acting crowd behavior, however, has an *object* in the sense of a part of the environment which the crowd attempts to manipulate or change. (1987:92, emphasis in original)

Turner and Killian illustrate *individualistic acting crowds* by collective but parallel looting, involving the manipulation of external material objects, or simultaneous and parallel entry and exit stampedes. They illustrate *solidaristic acting crowds* by the division of labor involved in a lynching.

Expressive Symbolizing Tendencies.   One referent Turner and Killian offer for this concept is the collective "feeling of ecstasy" (1987:97) portrayed in Liston Pope's (1942) cursory account of "waves of ecstatic rhythm sweeping over [a Holiness religious] congregation." They illustrate the *solidaristic expressive crowd* with the minimal division of labor among minister and congregation producing collective praising, weeping (and in pentecostal services, collective glossolalia). Turner and Killian do not limit expressive tendencies to religious phenomena. They illustrate the *individualistic expressive crowd* with cheering and dancing street gatherings celebrating sports victories or the end of a war. Other conceivable examples might be fans who surge forward to glimpse, touch, or grab a piece of clothing from a movie idol, pop music star, or political or religious leader, as well as the dancing, swaying, singing, cheering fans at pop music concerts; for example, the fans of Sinatra (in the 1940s), Presley (in the 1950s), the Beatles (in the

1960s), and the Grateful Dead (in the 1970s and 1980s and probably the 1990s).

Individualistic Coordinating Tendencies.   Turner and Killian's referent for this concept is similar individual behaviors occurring at the same time, "parallel, but competitive behaviors that give an appearance of unity" (1987:77). They argue that "the members of the collectivity are each trying to gain an objective whose attainment is problematic for each of them" (1987:81). The very presence of multiple individuals seeking the same objective "lends urgency to such a situation," lends uncertainty to the outcome, "causes the situation to be perceived as a contest, and thereby changes the behavior of individuals" (1987:81).

Looting and panic are offered as illustrations of individualistic and competitive but parallel behaviors regarding an external object. Looting is said to involve the individualistic and competitive seizure of external property objects. Thus, according to Turner and Killian "individualistic tendencies lead to parallel and competitive behavior [by the looting crowd]" (1987:93–97).

Panic is said to involve individualistic and competitive but simultaneous and parallel movement toward or through some portal, door, or passageway. Acknowledging that panic is a rare event, Turner and Killian nonetheless illustrate individualistic tendencies in acting crowds with the entry surge that killed seven and injured more participants prior to a rock concert by The Who at Cincinnati's Riverside Coliseum. They state:

> There is clearly an emergent norm which legitimizes this type of behavior for the actors—a definition of the situation as one in which it is "every man for himself and the devil take the hindermost!" (1987:82)

Further:

> A new norm arises, collective support for untrammeled pursuit of individual survival or gain, and the behavior of the crowd becomes individualistic and competitive. (1987:82)

And:

> Normative pressure builds up for people to act in parallel ways and to experience the same sort of emotions—impatience, anger, fear—as other people are feeling. (1987:82)

Solidaristic Coordinating Tendencies.   Turner and Killian define solidaristic collective behavior as "cooperative behaviors involving a division of labor" (1987:77). They note two further characteristics:

[First, the emergent definition] suggests an objective that an individual could not accomplish alone. Such an objective demands that the individual members of the crowd cooperate with each other even though their behavior may be differentiated. This type of coordination may be characterized as *solidaristic*. [Second,] a division of labor develops. Instead of being parallel and identical, the actions of the crowd members are differentiated and supplement each other. (1987:83, emphasis in original)

Further:

Some members act as leaders, exerting marked influence in the defining of the situation. Others are very active and vigorous in carrying out the suggestions of the leaders. Yet others may appear to be mere spectators, limiting their activity to shouting, cheering, or clapping. There is differential participation and an emergent division of labor . . . [that] contribute to the unified action of the crowd. (1987:84)

Turner and Killian's illustration of *solidaristic acting crowds* briefly alludes (1987:93) to a minimal division of labor and differential participation in a looting crowd. They refer to a crowd of rioters, some of whom "being practiced criminals" pulled down metal grates protecting store windows and doors, and others being "bystanders who took advantage of an unusual situation" to engage in trashing and looting.

Turner and Killian's discussion of *solidaristic expressive crowd* tendencies again draws on Pope's (1942) cursory account of a "holiness" religious service. They suggest there may be "a careful staging of the crowd setting, and . . . a definite division of labor between the worshippers, the minister, and the musicians" (1987:98). Indeed there often is. The music director invites the congregation to stand and sing songs of praise; the minister may invite the congregation to stand and pray aloud, "each in your own individual way"; or congregation members may be invited to stand and give individual praise and testimony. In pentecostal gatherings, the minister often invites the congregation to stand and lift their hands overhead in praise and preparation to receive the visitation of "the holy spirit," which in turn is sometimes followed by collective speaking in tongues (glossolalia).

Casual and Conventional Crowds. The emergent-norm theory of collective behavior, by definition, is addressed to crowds confronting extraordinary situations and the development of collective behavior in relation to such situations. Turner and Killian acknowledge, nonetheless, that some crowds face slightly less extraordinary situations, and many crowds face very ordinary ones. They call the former *casual* and the latter *conventional* crowds.

According to Turner and Killian, *casual-elemental crowds* have the general characteristics of all crowds although they do "not develop sufficiently to engage in a distinct, differentiated type of crowd behavior" (1987:78). An example of this is the:

> automobile accident . . . a [fire] or police arrest in a public place [that] draws spectators, and the extraordinary nature of the event moves people to attend to the reactions of others at the scene and initiate a limited exchange of comments. But many of the people at a typical scene of this kind have assembled as pairs and in small groups of friends or family members. (1987:9)

Elsewhere:

> In the elemental crowd a norm does not emerge in the sense that agreement is reached on what is happening and how to cope with it. Lacking the agreement, the crowd may continue to mill until it gradually disperses or until some new event creates a renewed sense of urgency. (1987:78)

And, again:

> Many assemblages . . . do not develop into crowds, or they only go through the early stages of crowd development before dispersing. They may be audiences or expressive crowds. Such assemblages include participants in political rallies and religious gatherings; spectators at athletic events or parades; merrymakers at picnics or festivals; and sightseers who gather at the scene of an accident, a fire, or a crime. (1987:127)

According to Turner and Killian (1987:105), *conventional crowds* do not manifest the characteristics alleged common to all crowds. However, "the distinguishing feature of the conventionalized crowd is that it arises when the participants gather with the hope that their assemblage will be transformed into a crowd" (1987:105). Therefore:

> It is likely that at least a portion of them have experienced similar situations before [e.g., sports fans, churchgoers, partygoers]. . . . Furthermore, the people who gather in a setting conducive to conventionalized crowd behavior are likely to share a common cultural background. Because of these prior experiences, the collective behavior which does take place may be regularized by becoming repetitive from one occasion to another, even though it represents a deviation from the usual norms. (1987:106)

Thus, Turner and Killian argue on the one hand that "collective behavior, in spite of its spontaneity, may be expressed in established and regularized ways" (1987:105). And yet, on the other hand, they suggest that much behavior that occurs in conventional audiences is not truly collective behavior. For example: "Much audience behavior is *not collective behavior at all* . . . [since people are engaging in mere "ritualistic" or polite applause as opposed to a]. . . genuine outpouring of unusual approval" (1987:106–7; emphasis added).

The Emergent Norm Hypothesis: An Assessment

Sherif's experimental work and Turner and Killian's theoretical work made significant advances beyond the explanations offered by the transformation and the predisposition perspectives. Turner's (1964) penetrating critique of those perspectives, and his (1964a:390; Turner and Killian 1972) identification of the illusion of unanimity that those perspectives attempted to explain, laid the groundwork for a fundamental breakthrough in describing and explaining crowds and collective behavior. If these emergent-norm scholars did not achieve the breakthrough, they at least offered some provocative conceptual openings.

Turner and Killian's emergent norm perspective addresses a very wide range of collective phenomena and offers a sociological explanation of routine and nonroutine collective behavior with the same principle: socially generated norms. As comprehensive and parsimonious as the emergent-norm perspective may be, it shares some problems with both transformation and predisposition perspectives, and has several problems of its own. Before assessing the coherence and scope of emergent-norm theory and comparing its claims against the evidence, Turner and Killian's formulation should first be evaluated in terms of their own objectives.

Turner and Killian's Objectives

Turner and Killian claim that collective behavior cannot be understood unless several distinctive features can be explained: "*First, we must explain how . . . people* come to *transcend,* bypass, or subvert established *institutional patterns. . . . Second, we must explain behavior or action contrasted with attitudes.* [And, an] adequate approach to collective behavior must analyze how perceptions, ideas, and feelings get translated into action. . . . *Third, we must explain the fact that people act collectively* rather than singly" (1987:7; emphasis added).

The first feature is not a distinguishing characteristic of collective behavior at all; rather, it is an implicit explanation. In fact, Turner and Killian beg the question of what governs ordinary social behavior. Is it ordinary, traditional norms? Does it therefore follow that extraordinary social behavior is governed by extraordinary, by emergent norms? To what the extent does knowledge of any norm at time one enable *pre*diction of individual or social behaviors at time two (as opposed to ex post facto inference of the norms from the behavior to be explained). Sherif finessed the problem with independent measures; Turner and Killian's resolution of the problem is less consistent. I mention these points because norms are one of the oldest stumbling blocks in sociological theory, a problem that has been repeatedly and severely criticized (Blake and Davis 1964; Gibbs 1965; Tierney 1980).

Turner and Killian's second feature is commendable on both counts. However, a review of their statements suggests that they give far more attention to attitudes or other cognitive variables than they do to individual or collective behaviors, a point to which I will return. Further, it is incumbent upon them to demonstrate if and how attitudes, perceptions, norms, definitions of the situation, or any other cognitive processes are causally connected to the behavior they are said to produce. In my judgment, they do not present a persuasive theoretical argument or empirical evidence connecting *their* cognitive variables to individual or collective behavior. After two decades of criticism (Wicker 1969), controversy and revision (Ajzen and Fishbein 1977), and reexamination, attitudes remain very poor predictors. McGuire concludes: "[Only] within quite limited circumstances do attitudes account for more than 10 percent of behavioral variance except when they are correlated not with behavior per se but with self-reports of intention to behave" (1985:252).

Third, Turner and Killian must be held accountable to the primary objective of addressing collective phenomena. But in one sense, stating the problem in this manner poses a false dichotomy between individual and collective behavior. My observations of temporary religious, political, sports, and casual gatherings persuade me that the most characteristic feature of such gatherings is alternating and varied sequences of individual and collective behavior. An adequate theory should account for both, as well as for alternation between the two. Whether Turner and Killian accept my observations or not, it is incumbent on whoever offers a theory of collective behavior at least to specify how they (and others) can know a *collective* phenomenon when they (and others) see one. Turner and Killian give little attention to the specification and description of the phenomena they claim to explain.

Finally, Turner and Killian submit (1987:7) that their distinguishing features of collective behavior are questions rather than answers. In my judgment the relevant questions might be posed as follows: What forms and variations of human actions are to be explained? If collective action is among them, what are its defining characteristics, and how do we know the various forms of collective action when we see them? What is responsible for, what are the sources of, those forms and variations of collective action?

Turner and Killian's emergent-norm explanation cannot be stretched to fit every form of collective action in which human beings engage. But it does address some forms of collective phenomena and should be evaluated in terms of how well it fit those forms, as well as the extent to which it is supported or can be assessed by empirical evidence. I will do that in three areas of the theory's concerns: the formation of collectivities; interaction within collectivities; and the collective behavior that derives from that formation and interaction.

The Formation of Collectivities:
Participants' Diverse
Motivations

A fundamental flaw in Turner and Killian's formulation is their failure to describe or explain the convergence of people on a common location. First, although they properly reject the argument that people converge because of similar motivations, they then draw an erroneous conclusion; namely, if people who converge on a common location do not have similar motives, they must converge because of diverse motives. This assumes that motives, predispositions, or tendencies to behave, whether similar or dissimilar, are responsible for producing convergence, or any other behavior.

Second, Turner and Killian offer no independent evidence for the particular motives they claim bring people together. They infer those motives from the behaviors taken by people who have converged. Their *ego-involved* person is one who makes suggestions; their *concerned* person is one who carries out those suggestions; their *exploiter* is one who sells food and drink or who picks pockets; their *insecure* person is anyone else who joins in the behavior launched by the committed and supported by the concerned. Their *spectators* are those who stand and watch. In short, Turner and Killian's evidence for these diverse motivations appears to be based on circular reasoning.

Third, when independent measures of motives personality, attitudes, or any other predispositions or attributes have been examined in relation to participation in riots (McPhail 1971; Miller et al. 1977), in protest demonstrations (Aron 1974), or in gatherings celebrating upset victories (McPhail and Miller 1973), the evidence has consistently varied from weak to negative!

Fourth, while similar motives, similar personality types, or other such similar predispositions appear to have little to do with people coming together, this does not mean we should abandon our search for other circumstances, sequences of events, or behaviors distinguishing those who do converge from those who do not converge on a common location, for example, the ecological and social-control conditions to which Turner and Killian early referred, the interpersonal networks or group memberships of participants and nonparticipants, and the communications through those networks or groups of participants and nonparticipants.

Finally, Turner and Killian's emphasis on *individual* motives in the formation of collectivities obscures the basic empirical fact that most people do not converge individually; rather they converge in small groups of family, friends, or acquaintances (Aveni 1977; Miller 1973; Woelfel, Woelfel, Gillham, and McPhail 1974; Wimberly, Hood, Lipsey, Clelland, and Hay 1975; McPhail 1985) and remain with them throughout the duration of the gathering (Miller 1973). The interaction and communication within these groups may have more to do with the initiation and completion of convergence than the motives of the individuals who do or do not participate (cf. Quarantelli and Hundley 1969; Singer 1970; McPhail and Miller 1973).[16]

Rumor as a Unique
Communication Process

Turner and Killian argue that rumor emerges as a unique communication process in the development of collective behavior because ordinary sources and channels of communication have been rendered problematic. Thus, rumor is said to feed the formation of collectivities. However, the few studies we have of communication processes in problematic situations do not support Turner and Killian's interpretation. For example, Singer's (1970) study of communication processes among 500 persons arrested in the 1967 Detroit riot indicates that some people learned of the riot and its location from direct observation (27%), some learned from radio (16%), and, a few learned from television (9%); more learned, however, by word of mouth: either face to face (39%) or by telephone (9%). There is little indication that extraordinary sources or channels of communication were involved in learning about the riot. Singer's study also suggests that these ordinary sources of information were related to whether or not these people informed someone else about the riot. Thirty-nine percent did so. Only a small percentage of those who learned at the scene (28%) or face-to-face from other persons (37%) informed someone else. A much higher proportion of persons informed another person after learning of the riot by telephone (51%), television (51%) or radio (54%).

Turner and Killian properly reject traditional and commonsense views of rumor and endorse Shibutani's (1966) view that rumor is better conceived as "the development of a collective definition [of a problematic event, issue, or situation] through symbolic interaction" (Turner and Killian 1972:41). This recharacterization is useful; but all definitions of all situations involving two or more persons are constructed, recalled, reviewed, revised, and repeated through symbolic interaction. The construction of a definition of the situation with symbols is hardly unique to collective behavior. If rumor does not refer to anything unique, it may not be of any unique value. If it does refer to something unique, that remains to be specified.[17]

Conditions Facilitating Communication and Mobilization. Turner and Killian were somewhat closer to the mark when they argued that since "collective behavior develops through a communication process, . . . [then] conditions that facilitate communication and mobilization are essential" (1972:61), e.g., ecological concentrations and arrangements of people, social-control conditions that allow or preclude the formation of collectivities, and significant symbols (cf. note 9, above). Inexplicably this argument is conspicuously absent in their most recent discussion.

The ecological argument was clearly borne out by the Kerner Commission Report that most U.S. urban riots in the 1960s and 1970s broke out in close proximity to high-density housing and/or high-density vehicular and pedestrian traffic flow. Another example is the concentration of large numbers of people on college campuses. Social-control limitations on assembling are relatively foreign to Americans except for infrequent curfews and very rare declarations of martial law. A form of social constraint, if not social control, can be indexed by variations in the availability of people to form collectivities or participate in temporary gatherings. For example, U.S. urban-riot activities *commenced* after the end (5:00 P.M.) of the workday, or on weekends, developed to a peak shortly after midnight, and then declined sharply. This pattern was repeated throughout the workweek.

Students have large blocks of unscheduled time, in which they can be mobilized for rallies and demonstrations. Even so, there is variability here as well. Student demonstrations in the 1960s, as today, almost never begin before noon; they fluctuate in size almost hourly throughout the afternoon; they peak between 4:00 and 6:00 P.M. and then drop sharply until 7:00 or 8:00 P.M., after which they grow in size until about midnight. In short, there is evidence here of variation in the competing demands of work and classes, of family and dormitory mealtimes, all of which are forms of social constraint if not social control.

What is also missing from Turner and Killian's symbolic interactionist formulation, in all the editions, is any specification of the form or content of communications between individuals or existing groups (1987:9) that might nurture the formation of collectivities under various ecological arrangements or conditions of social constraint.

Selected Communication Processes and Conditions

David Miller and I (McPhail and Miller 1973) examined several of the variables implied by Turner and Killian's earlier (1972) discussions of the conditions that facilitate communication and mobilization. We also examined respondents' reports of the communications by which they learned what was to happen at an alternative location in space and time and by which they were then invited or directed to assemble there.

We first attempted to establish where people were located and the number of people who were present—*social density*—when the announcement came of an upset road victory over a rival basketball team and the impending arrival of the victorious team at the local airport. We then attempted to learn if anyone proposed to our respondents that they move to that location at the estimated time of the team's arrival, and how frequently such proposals—*assembling instructions*—were made to respondents between the time they first learned about and the time of the proposed gathering. We further inquired about respondents *availability*, i.e., their relative freedom from competing demands at the time of the proposed gathering, and whether they had the means of transportation—*access*—to carry out the instructions and travel to the site of the gathering. Finally, we inquired about our respondents' histories of attending games and listening to game broadcasts as well as their gender, year in school, age, and the like.

A multiple-regression analysis determined that our index of social density was the best predictor (Beta = .33), followed by attendance at prior home games (Beta = .27), of the respondents who received the most assembling instructions ($R = .57$; $R^2 = .325$).[18] Our index of assembling instructions in turn was the best predictor (Beta = .38), followed by transportation access (Beta = .18), prior home game attendance (Beta = .17), and availability (Beta = .14) of respondents who did or did not assemble ($R = .67$; $R^2 = .449$). The significance of interpersonal communications, specifically, assembling instructions, in predicting participation in this temporary gathering, is consistent with Singer's (1970) research on how people learned about and came to participate in the Detroit riot, as well as with research on participation in impromptu campus demonstrations (Quarantelli and Hundley 1969). Equally important, the contributions of assembling instructions, availability, and access in these informal interpersonal networks are consistent with what we know of how political and religious organizers mobilize participation in rallies and demonstrations through formal organization and informal interpersonal networks (cf. Bruno and Greenfield 1971; Wimberly et al. 1975; Wilson and Orum 1976; Johnson et al. 1984). This body of research is consistent with the conditions for and processes of communication to which Turner and Killian earlier (1972) called attention but did not develop.

Interaction within Collectivities: General Crowd Characteristics

Turner and Killian's characteristics common to all crowds do not characterize several hundred crowds I have observed. For example, *uncertainty* conveys the notion that people do not know what they are supposed to do. Unanticipated events, disrupted social structures, intense value conflicts, or sudden changes in communication channels or systems all create situations with which many people have no experience. But experience *is* a variable; some people have more than others. Some such continuum of experience more closely corresponds to my *impressions* of participants in the variety of temporary political gatherings I have observed. Many participants have no experience; some have a little experience; and a few have extensive experience in large collective actions, in confrontations with belligerent opponents or with hard-nosed police. Thus uncertainty is a characteristic of the experience of people, not of crowds or situations. More important, to repeat, it is a variable, not a constant. Most important, as Alexander, Zucker, and Brody's (1970) experiments demonstrate, uncertainty can be reconstructed by statements participants make in the situation. Veterans can and do redefine situations for novices, e.g., "Walk, don't run." "Stay calm." "Don't rub your eyes."

Turner and Killian's crowd characteristics of *urgency* is similarly problematic. I have observed some manifest expressions of urgency from some people when running from the police, from some people when diving behind and beneath cars at the sound of gunshots, and from some people when evacuating buildings during bomb threats or fire alarms. But those manifestations of urgency do not characterize the majority of the gatherings, let alone all the people in the gatherings, I have observed. Such manifestations have been the exceptions rather than the rule. More frequently, even in temporary gatherings confronting immediate or impending problems, people seem to be waiting around to see if anything will happen. An evaluation of Turner and Killian's remaining general crowd characteristics requires a general assessment of milling and keynoting.

Milling

Turner and Killian's initial effort to recast "the milling process" as collective problem solving was an important contribution. Over the years that emphasis appears to have shifted. They now describe milling as verbal "searching behavior and random restless activity . . . characteristic of individuals caught in the throes of uncertainty" (1987:55). They explain milling as a product of the interaction between "characteristics common to all crowds" and the diverse motives of participants. I have already indicated the reservations I have about the alleged presence and effects of uncertainty and urgency. I have also indicated the host of logical and empirical problems with the diverse motives that drive Turner and Killian's explanation for the formation of collectivities. All of those problems are present in their explanation of milling, keynoting, selective individual suggestibility, and the development of a common mood and imagery that becomes the definition of the situation that becomes the emergent norm. There are additional problems as well.

First, recall that Turner and Killian's formulation requires a diversity of motivations to drive and secure the keynoting process.[19] According to their argument, the ego-involved person is more likely to propose, the concerned person is more likely to comply. Further, given the lack of opposition and hence tacit consent from the curious spectator, a modal behavior can develop sufficient to attract the insecure person; and, all of this provides a cover for the exploiter to pursue surreptitious interests.

Second, since there is no independent and prior evidence of the diverse motives in question, all of the motives must be inferred after the fact from the behavior to be explained.[20] Turner and Killian's general crowd characteristic of *selective individual suggestibility* appears to reduce to nothing more or less than circular reasoning and thus a very flexible source of evidence in support of their theoretical claims.[21]

Third, after renouncing the homogeneous predisposition argument, and claiming that heterogeneous motives form a collectivity and launch the keynoting process, Turner and Killian reverse their position and argue that too much heterogeneity will not permit the resolution of the keynoting process and the development of collective behavior. Instead, they require a critical mass of motives that are similar, or at least not antagonistic, to the keynote. I am at a loss to understand how a coherent, cogent, and consistent theory can have it both ways. The predisposition argument that Turner and Killian earlier rejected now reappears at the core of their own emergent-norm formulation. Reicher (1984) argues that Turner and Killian's explanation of keynoting is nothing more than "an elitist version of Allportian individualism." The keynote is offered and supported, and the emergent norm is thereby constructed, by the personalities of a dominant few.

Regrettably, in my judgment, Turner and Killian abandoned their initial line of explanation, which focused upon questions members of a collectivity posed and answers they offered about the problem with which they were confronted. In their second edition Turner and Killian discussed (1972:64–65) three types of cues sought by people confronted with unstructured situations. First, there is an attempt to define the situation: What's going on? Second, there is a concern with rules or directions: What are people supposed to do in such situations? Third, there is a concern with leadership: Who will act first? These are deleted from Turner and Killian's third edition, although I cannot see that their relevance to the emergent-norm formulation has diminished in any way. And, regardless of their relevance to emergent-norm theory, people in problematic situations do raise, and other people do propose answers to, precisely those kinds of questions (cf. Wright 1978). My impression is that discourse within such gatherings proceeds on the basis of what is required to identify and solve the problem at hand; i.e., the criterion for selecting among alternative or competing proposals is a pragmatic one. Will it solve the problem?[22]

One of the mysteries in Turner and Killian's symbolic interactionist formulation is that they champion symbolization and yet they do not provide a *pragmatic* analysis of how things get done with words (cf. Bruner 1983). For example, they call attention to the external objects and the internal objectives of acting and expressive crowds and yet they do not indicate how those objects are established, nor how individuals organize their behavior toward those objects, let alone how two or more individuals coorganize their respective behaviors toward objects established in common.

Turner and Killian could well draw upon George H. Mead's (1936) principle of organization to describe if not explain how, by means of significant symbols and taking the attitude of the other, two or more people can establish an object in common (e.g., the problem) and can direct their mutual behaviors for movement toward, away from, or with respect to that mutual object. These are some of the tools of collective problem solving!

These ideas offer a strategy for observing and analyzing the actions by which two or more people in problematic situations (1) establish what the problem is, (2) propose solutions, (3) entertain the hypothetical implementation of those solutions, (4) evaluate and debate the advantages and limitations of the projected outcomes, (5) combine, revise, compromise, then select a solution, (6) propose who will do what, individually or collectively, when, where, and how, to implement the solution.

Turner and Killian's communication of a common mood and imagery is also a difficult concept with which to deal. Since it is not clear how one sees or hears an imagery when it occurs, it is even more difficult to decide when one has been communicated. It is possible that Turner and Killian mean nothing more here than the modal lines of verbal behavior and nonverbal gestural display that follows from the endorsement of a keynote. If so, then displays of emotion—e.g., joy, sadness, or anger—can be observed, identified, and recorded. These emotion displays are sometimes called "moods" (cf. Lofland 1981, 1982b). But when these emotions are displayed within or across a gathering, they are seldom mutually inclusive, and almost never continuous; instead, the displayed emotion is more often intermittent and may alternate with neutral or sometimes even opposing displays of emotion. For example, the vocal utterances, facial displays, and gestures of a joyous section of football spectator-fans (Zillman et al. 1979) can quickly change to displays of disappointment with the failures of their own team, to a neutral silence when the opposing team succeeds, or to anger and hostility (Greer 1983) when the officials penalize the team the spectators support. Common moods are more often variables than constants. The widespread and continuous grief displayed after the death of national heroes (cf. Manchester 1964) may be an exception rather than a rule.

The Emergent Norm as Definition of the Situation

Norms are prevalent sociological explanations; they are even more problematic. There has been little consensus on what constitutes a norm (Gibbs 1965). Sometimes norm refers to modal patterns of behavior and sometimes to prescriptions (or proscriptions) for behavior. Too frequently norms refer to both at the same time. Blake and Davis argued:

> The difficulty of proving the existence of the norm is great. As a consequence, there is a tendency to take regularities in behavior as the evidence of the norm. When this is done, to explain the behavior in terms of the norm is a redundancy. (1964:464)

It is also circular reasoning.

Repeated examination of Turner and Killian's earlier (1957, 1972) work establishes that norms sometimes referred to prescriptions or proscriptions for behavior (a la Durkheim), and sometimes to modal patterns of behavior (a la Sherif). Either use is appropriate. And, if properly and independently specified, one could examine the relationship between a normative prescription for behavior (e.g., a verbal or written suggestion, command, or instruction), and the subsequent absence, presence, or extent of a corresponding modal behavior pattern among the people to whom the prescription was addressed; or, like Sherif, one could examine the relationships between a modal pattern of behavior at time one and the subsequent presence or extent of a corresponding behavior pattern at time two among people exposed to the mode at time one. But Turner and Killian have not done this. In their earlier work they inferred the presence and operation of the norm from the modal behavior it was supposed to explain. As others have noted (Tierney 1980), this was tautological.

In their most recent statement Turner and Killian (1987) addressed these criticisms in two ways. On the one hand, they explicitly distanced the concept of emergent norm from "precise behavioral expectations" or "simplistic do's and don'ts" (1987:59). They argued that emergent norms are complex ranges of acceptable and unacceptable behavior. It is difficult to imagine that anything so complex does not have some verbal or nonverbal behavioral referents, particularly when two or more persons are involved and neither can penetrate the consciousness of the other. It is puzzling that Turner and Killian eschew the specification of behavioral referents for their central concept. The actors in the problematic situations I have observed verbally and gesturally advocate or disapprove certain courses of action, not infrequently accompanied by subtle if simplistic "Yes, yes, that's it," or, "No, no, not like that."

Turner and Killian's second response to the criticism was to reconstrue the emergent norm as a definition of the situation. They do not use that concept in the traditional sense.[23] Instead, their concept refers to (1) a characterization of the situation (e.g., "That arrest procedure involved illegal and immoral police brutality"); (2) an evaluation of the category of objects to which the crowd target belongs as opposed to the category of objects to which crowd members belong (e.g., "That cop's just like all the other lousy [majority group members]; we decent [minority group members] aren't gonna take it any more."); (3) a recommended course of action (e.g., "We should [object to, resist, intervene in] this illegal and immoral action"); (4) a justification for the characterization and recommendation (e.g., "The police can't legally do that; it is outrageous that they continue to treat us this way").[24]

I think these are important developments for emergent-norm theory. Turner and Killian here direct attention to some observable classes of action by which definitions of the situation are constructed rather than dwelling on the hypothesized cognitive consequences of definitions of the situation. That those classes of action are multiple, and may appear in various combinations, makes the concept more complex but no less concrete. The emergent-norm concept is now potentially available to systematic empirical scrutiny. It may now be possible to determine if emergent norms, as definitions of the situation, have the consequence of constraining some behaviors and permitting other behaviors as Turner and Killian claim. This reconstructed version of emergent norm might be examined in relation to the collective behavior for which it is said to be responsible, were it not for one *major* remaining problem.

Collective Behavior

Emergent-norm theory offers little help to the student of collective behavior who wants to go into the field to see or hear the collective behavior that Turner and Killian claim to explain. They provide no systematic descriptions and no working definition of the collective behavior to which their theory is addressed. They tell us what is (e.g. Turner, 1964b:132; Turner and Killian 1987:7) and what is not (1972:10, 1987:112) responsible for collective behavior. They tell us the goals (1987:236) and the consequences (1987:6) of collective behavior.[25] We are told that collective behavior is the "coordinated" (Turner 1964b:132; Turner and Killian 1987:77) or "cooperative" (1987:10, 77) action of collectivities (1972:4–5, 1987:3); but we are not provided with even the most elementary criteria for (1) recognizing a collectivity when we see one, or for (2) judging when collective, coordinated, or cooperative behavior has occurred within or by a collectivity, or for (3) identifying recurring elementary forms of collective behavior.

While Turner and Killian have developed a complex and comprehensive explanatory formulation, they have given virtually no attention to the fundamental task of specifying and describing what that formulation claims to explain. They emphasize that collective behavior is different from routine social behavior but they distinguish between the two in terms of the types of norms alleged to produce them (1987:112), not in terms of attributes or forms of the behaviors that are collective in one instance and social in the other. In short, there are no recipes or guidelines here for the field-worker who wants to attempt to identify, observe, and describe collective action, let alone for the researcher who wants to test Turner and Killian's hypotheses about the sources of collective action.

Crowd Types

Turner and Killian's taxonomy of crowd types cannot resolve these problems, even when the types are relabeled as tendencies. They recently acknowledge the basic problem, even if they do not offer a solution: "Changes in a crowd are the rule, not the exception" (1987:102).

The most characteristic feature of the crowds I have observed is alternating sequences of individual and collective behavior. The sequences of behaviors to be explained in most gatherings are variable indeed; they are neither continuously nor exclusively collective. A satisfactory explanation must acknowledge that variation; it must account for sequences of individual behavior, for sequences of collective behavior, for variation within and alternation between the two. Emergent norms are no more up to that challenge than are the individual predispositions from which Turner and Killian construct those norms. A brief examination of the flaws in Turner and Killian's crowd types and tendencies illustrates the complexity of the task facing the student of collective behavior.

Acting versus Expressive
Crowd Tendencies

Turner and Killian distinguish between acting and expressive crowds and crowd tendencies in terms of the external or internal objectives of the collective actors. Thus, once again, the phenomenon to be explained is defined or distinguished in terms of the factors alleged responsible for the phenomenon, a very problematic if not unacceptable basis for identifying and differentiating the object of study.

All of the examples Turner and Killian offer of *expressive* crowds, or *expressive* tendencies, appear to involve people *acting!* Indeed, because they are often acting with respect to some visible object or target, Turner and Killian eventually qualify their position and argue that some crowds engage in actions toward external objects in order to realize internal, expressive objectives. For example, they cite Muslims' actions toward the Kaaba, the shrine located in the center of Mecca's Grand Mosque. By focusing on the objectives of the actors, however, Turner and Killian do not attend to or describe the actions in question, nor do they indicate the criteria by which we might judge the actions to be collective, coordinated, or cooperative. This is regrettable, since Islamic prayers may be the most frequent, sometimes the largest, and among the most spectacular sequences of collective action on the face of the earth.

Five times daily, all devout Muslims (approximately one-sixth of the world's population) turn in the direction of the Kaaba and utter very similar prayer sequences while engaging in very similar sequences of nonverbal behaviors (*rakas*), in a convergent direction, at the same time (at least by those located in the same time zone). On Fridays Muslims assemble in their local mosques and pray collectively in the direction of the Kaaba, but do so in a elementary division of labor with an imam (prayer leader). Further, during the pilgrimage (*hajj*) to Mecca that every devout Muslim is expected to make once in a lifetime (and has occurred every lunar year for 13 centuries), there are three occasions on which pilgrims circle the Kaaba seven times, reciting prayers and gesturing in the direction of the cornerstone (said to be a remnant of the first place of worship built by Abraham). These prayers are said in unison, but differ in content for each circuit around the Kaaba. As many as 10,000 pilgrims at a time complete the seven circuits, repeating the prayers that are first uttered by their *mutawwif* (*hajj* guide). On the ninth day, the most holy day, of the *hajj*, more than two million gather on the Plain of Arafat where they pray continuously toward Mecca from noon to sunset. By performing these rather complex collective actions, in striking unanimity of movement, gesture, and utterance in the direction of this symbolic object, Muslims do seek the salvation of their souls and the reaffirmation of their self-conceptions as children of Allah. Thus, while Turner and Killian's interpretive distinction between external and internal objectives may well be illustrated by Islamic prayers, their scheme ignores—indeed it cannot describe—the magnificent form and content of this collective action.

Individualistic versus Solidaristic Tendencies

Turner and Killian distinguish between individualistic and solidaristic tendencies in crowds:

> At one extreme the goal sanctioned by emergent norms is strictly individual survival, as in [*looting or*] collective panic. At the other extreme a lynching mob may only be able to storm a prison and hang their chosen victims by working together. (1987:391)

I am puzzled that Turner and Killian emphasize the individualistic and competitive features of looting, even while reprinting (1987:94–97) Quarantelli and Dynes's careful (1970; cf. Dynes and Quarantelli 1968) analysis of the collective character of civil-disorder looting: "Looters often work together in pairs, as family units, or in small groups." Even then, both individual and collective acts of looting occur in the same gathering, often occurring alternately by the same participants. The problem is, once again, that, "changes in a crowd are the rule, not the exception." The crowd is simply too crude and cumbersome a unit of analysis to describe those changes; an emergent norm is not sufficient to the challenge of explaining the ongoing alternation between and variation within sequences of individual and collective action.

Turner and Killian also treat entry and exit surges as examples of individualistic and competitive crowd tendencies, and do so in the face of three decades of evidence to the contrary. Equally disturbing is their contribution to the perpetuation of the myth of panic. For example, they draw on journalistic accounts of the now famous tragedy at Cincinnati's Riverfront Coliseum and offer this as an illustration of their claim that individualistic and competitive behavior is driven by panic:

> A group or *a mere aggregate of people* routinely going about their work, shopping or *standing in line waiting* for a store to open *can quickly explode into crowd action* given certain conditions. (1987:78–79; emphasis added)

Perhaps Turner and Killian did not have prepublication access to Johnson's (1987a,b) careful secondary analyses of interviews with survivors of The Who concert entry surge. By that point in time, however, there was abundant evidence from the earlier work of Quarantelli (1954, 1957, 1960, 1981) and others (Guten and Allen 1972; Smith 1976; Sime 1980; Bryan 1981, 1982; Keating 1982) that individuals do not lose self-control in the face of life-threatening problems. They may be momentarily stunned; they may be afraid; they are not incapacitated by shock or fear. They may not be able to see clearly because of smoke or dust; they may not be able to hear clearly because of noise; and they may not be able to move freely because of debris or the density of the gathering around them. But participants report, and observers confirm, considerable evidence of self-control and rational problem solving in these difficult circumstances.

Further, and contrary to popular myths of unregulated individualistic competition, panic, and stampede, there is considerable research evidence for cooperative and altruistic behavior in entry and exit surges, in the advent, in the course, and in the aftermath of various natural and human-made disasters. Johnson (1987a,b) presents a convincing argument and illustrative data for regulated as opposed to unregulated competition, for very civil behavior, for helping behavior, and for cooperative behavior during The Who concert incident.

Casual and
Conventional Crowds

Turner and Killian's discussion of this most frequent form of temporary gatherings makes it ever more difficult to determine when, by their criteria, an assemblage, a gathering, a collectivity constitutes a crowd. Is it only when collective behavior occurs? And does collective behavior occur only when the norm that governs it is an emergent norm? It appears that the overriding and continuing distinction between Turner and Killian's collective behavior and routine social behavior, between true crowds and mere elemental crowds, is the emergent norm. Thus, the basic criterion in terms of which they define crowds and collective behavior is also their basic explanatory device for crowds and collective behavior.

Conclusion

The most serious limitation of emergent-norm theory is one shared with all its predecessors and most of its successors. All the theorists have set out to develop an explanation before familiarizing themselves with the phenomena to be explained. Thus, they have sometimes developed explanations for phenomena that do not occur; more frequently they have developed explanations for phenomena that occur rarely; to date, they have failed to develop explanations for the most frequent actions, and therefore the full range of actions, in which people do collectively engage in temporary gatherings.

Emergent-norm theory addresses a very real collective phenomenon but hardly the only one. Some of the collective action in which some people engage in some temporary gatherings does result from their confronting a mutual problem, from their interaction with one another and their construction of an ad hoc solution to the problem. And this may well develop in some approximation of the manner Turner and Killian set forth. But a lot of collective action in which people engage in temporary gatherings is much simpler, is preceded by minimal if any interaction among those people before they engage in the collective action, e.g., the cheering, the applause, the laughter of sports spectators, political supporters, religious zealots. Still other collective action is far more complex and sustained and requires extensive planning and preparation and mobilization of people and resources for its implementation within the temporary gathering in question.

While Sherif and Turner and Killian challenged the myth of the madding crowd in a very clear and consequential manner, their alternative characterizations and explanations have addressed only part of the problem; and, as I have argued here, their proposed explanation has at least as many limitations as advantages. Other scholars have identified some additional problems and offered some different solutions. I turn to their work in Chapter 4.

Notes

1. There is evidence that the presence and judgments of others would have had even greater impact on the individual subject's judgments had those others been

family, friends, or acquaintances—the usual companions in temporary gatherings—rather than the unacquainted strangers that Sherif's experiments involved (cf. Sampson 1968a,b).

2. Turner and Killian initially defined collective behavior as the "study of the behavior of collectivities" (1957:4), which they in turn defined as "that kind of group characterized by the spontaneous development of norms and organization which contradict or reinterpret the norms and organization of the society." Turner subsequently wrote that "the study of collective behavior is the study of the processes through which coordinated behavior arises and changes under the control of emergent normative definitions when the conventional normative structure is internally conflicting or inapplicable to the situation at hand" (1964:132). Turner and Killian similarly referred to collective behavior as an area of study in which groups are classified "according to the nature of the social norms that govern them" (1972:5), and as "the action of collectivities" (1972:4–5) that "operate without clear cut [normative] direction from their culture" (1972:10). Thus, their characterization of collective behavior remains essentially unchanged across a 30-year period.

3. I elected not to reproduce Turner and Killian's (1987) diagram of the emergent-norm model because I find it more confusing than helpful in understanding their explanation of collective behavior. Further, that diagram implies more fundamental changes in the components of Turner and Killian's earlier theoretical formulation than I can find in their 1987 edition. My examination of that statement locates some new labels for old components, and some deletions of earlier components, but no fundamental changes.

4. Turner and Killian also argue (1972:21, 1987:26) that emergent norms are responsible for collective behavior and are the source, as well, of participants' selective perception of differential expression as unanimity.

5. In the previous edition, Turner and Killian wrote of "specific kinds of situations that, given a relatively high state of conduciveness, set off the rumor process and thereby give rise to various forms of collective behavior" (1972:64). These included: *challenges to the normative order,* such as a sports team's unanticipated upset victory over a powerful traditional rival; the *disruption of the social structure,* e.g., a police strike (and one would presume here such things as the assassination of a president); a *value conflict between opposing groups,* (e.g., stances of pro- and anti-racial integration groups or pro- and antiabortion groups); and *sudden change in communication processes,* for example, opening up channels of communication may put people in touch and dispel pluralistic ignorance or closing channels may accentuate differences in existing viewpoints of two groups (cf. Jackman 1957; Denzin 1968). The first, second, and fourth of these sources of problems are mentioned in Turner and Killian's latest (1987) edition.

6. Turner and Killian have been criticized (e.g. McPhail and Miller 1973; Reicher 1984) for their extensive reliance on diverse individual predispositions, a reliance that is prevalent in their earlier work (1972) and is pervasive and persistent throughout the most recent (1987) edition. Turner and Killian write: "Just as the motivations of individuals for participating in collective behavior are diverse, attempts to classify participants are many and varied. All of these attempts [such as Fritz and Mathewson (1957)] result in typologies which are tentative, incomplete, and almost certain to be challenged and revised. Hence we will not claim to be advancing a definitive classification of participants" (1987:31).

Although Turner and Killian (1987:33, 88) recast their discussion of participants' motives, their typology of diverse motivations, and the importance of those diverse motives to emergent-norm theory, remains fundamentally unchanged. They make

(1987) some minor modifications in their earlier (1972) position by rearranging and relabeling some of the motives on which their current formulation depends, and by attributing some types of motives to other scholars, e.g., "To emphasize the argument that participants are heterogeneous, some of the types identified by different theorists will be mention" (1987:31). But the diverse types of motives that are so central to Turner and Killian's emergent-norm formulation were and are their own creations.

7. Turner and Killian (1987:32) cite McCarthy and Zald's (1973) discussion of "potential beneficiaries" of movement success as one category of social movement participants, and imply this corresponds to their ego-involved participants.

8. Turner and Killian (1987:32) refer to McCarthy and Zald's (1973) "conscience constituents" as altruists who do not personally benefit from movement success but are nonetheless committed to the cause, and imply this corresponds to their concerned or committed participants who are present in crowds and movements out of loyalty to their group, whether or not they agree with the particulars of the action in question.

9. Turner and Killian (1972:61) earlier noted three important conditions. First, some *ecological concentrations and arrangements* of people permit their ready access to and communication with one another, the possibility of mobilization, and the opportunity for others to witness them converging on some common location. University campuses, urban ghettos, and many prisons and mental hospitals meet those criteria.

Second, certain *social control arrangements* allow freedom of assembly and free speech, impose no curfews, and allow the publication and distribution of printed materials. Campuses and ghettos more often meet these criteria than prisons or mental hospitals (cf. Jackman 1957; Denzin 1968).

Third, certain *attitudes and symbols held in common* by people provide a common basis in terms of which they can act together; e.g., the photograph of a murdered ideological leader for a revolutionary group, an aborted fetus for an antiabortion group, or the photograph of a rat-bitten child for a community tenant group. All of these conditions are said by Turner and Killian to facilitate the development of the rumor process that is set in motion by challenges to the normative order, disruption of the social structure, a conflict in values, or sudden changes in communications. I am puzzled that these three conditions were eliminated from Turner and Killian's recent (1987) analysis, a point to which I will return.

10. *Feasibility* refers to the "shared perception that something can be done, even at some risk" (1987:77), that the resources are available, including social support, to do something despite opposition. *Timeliness* "also includes such elements as urgency, the feeling that something must be done now if at all, and a sense of cultural appropriateness" (1987:77–8; cf. 1987:241).

11. Turner and Killian wrote: "[The] unity [a crowd] achieves must result from the interaction of these different [motivations and predispositions]. The key to the emergence of the situationally specific norms is differential expression" (1972:29). Although this statement does not appear verbatim in Turner and Killian's third edition (1987), their analytical argument remains unchanged.

12. Turner and Killian write: "The heightened suggestibility which characterizes individuals amounts to a tendency to respond uncritically to suggestions consistent with the mood, imagery, and conception of appropriate action that have developed and assumed a normative character" (1987:78).

13. Turner and Killian's initial characterization of differential expression (1972:22) was that different individuals in the crowd (1) feel different, (2) participate because of

different motives, and (3) even act different. More recently the emphasis in differential expression shifts to "some people expressing what they are feeling while others do not" (1987:26). The variation in motives now appears to be centered in Turner and Killian's concept of differential participation, although their examples for that concept vacillate between a diversity of inferred motives or predispositions and, occasionally, diverse behaviors.

14.   I have elected not to consider here at any length Turner and Killian's distinction between and discussion of diffuse vs. compact crowds. This corresponds roughly to Park's earlier distinction between mass and crowd, where the former involves a number of physically separated people who are giving attention to the same object or engaging in the same behavior regarding that object. The latter more closely corresponds to my concerns in this book; that is, two or more persons occupying the same location in space and time.

Turner and Killian argue (1987:155) that diffuse crowds (i.e., a mass or a public) can give rise to compact crowds, and suggest several ways in which that might come about. They do not discuss the consequence of compact gatherings for a diffuse mass or for public opinion, a relationship for which the evidence is equally compelling. For example, we know that individual attitudes and opinions do not predict participation in demonstrations. Mobilization through interpersonal networks or organizations, however, does produce participation; and Skolnick (1969:24) documents the relationship between increased frequency and size of antiwar demonstrations (compact gatherings) and increased polled public opinion (a diffuse mass phenomenon) against the Vietnam war.

15.   Regarding the first, they write (1987:77): "The *coordinating* tendencies, processes which give the crowd an appearance of unity, range from highly *individualistic,* parallel, but competitive behavior, to *solidaristic* behavior which involves cooperation and a division of labor" (1987:77; emphasis added).

After the second, Turner and Killian write: "It is important to remember that all crowds, as well as other types of collectivities, act on the basis of *symbolization* of both the external environment and their own behavior" (1987:92; emphasis added). In particular they use symbolization to refer to objects external to the acting crowd and to objects that are internal to the expressive crowd.

16.   Turner and Killian do note that within the milling process, after a gathering has formed, "pre-existing groupings" are probably "the critical channel through which communication is sustained and the translation into action is monitored" (1987:10). The available research (Woelfel et al. 1974; Singer 1970; McPhail and Miller 1973) suggests this critical channel is in operation both prior to and throughout the participation in temporary gatherings.

17.   Rosnow and Fine (1976) define rumor as "unsubstantiated information on any issue or subject." I question whether this distinguishes rumor. Much of the information upon which we organize our daily actions is not verified; some is not even verifiable. Journalists may verify against a second or third source; more frequently than not other folks act on the basis of unverified information. Conceivably this varies as a function of the credibility of the source of information. Singer (1970) does not report the relationship between his respondents' source of information about and their participation in the riot. But his respondents were more likely to inform others about a riot in progress if they had received their information from radio or television (or telephone) rather than from face-to-face conversations or direct observation of the riot. Of course there is less apparent requirement for direct observers to tell other direct observers what they too can see and hear.

18.   Multiple regression analysis examines several independent variables in relation to a dependent variable to ascertain the contribution that each of the former

makes to the latter. A *Beta coefficient* is a standardized regression correlation coefficient. The value of the Beta coefficient for any one independent variable indicates how much of the variation in the dependent variable can be attributed to that one independent variable net the contributions of all the other independent variables in the analysis.

19. Recall too that all these diverse motives are inferred, after the fact, from the behavior they are alleged to explain. Turner and Killian offer no independent or prior evidence for the motives.

20. Meyer and Seidler (1978) examined the relationship between participants' independently measured predispositions (verbal attitudes) and their spatial location at the core or toward the periphery of a political demonstration gathering. My secondary statistical analysis of their reported data yielded nonsignificant or very weak associations.

21. Johnson and Feinberg (1977) have simulated collections of people composed of homogeneous and heterogeneous predispositions, exposed them to suggestions for actions of varying extremes, under conditions of varying ambiguity. They report that collections composed of persons with similar and extreme predispositions shifted more readily in the direction of extreme suggestions even under conditions of low ambiguity. Collections with normally distributed predispositions (i.e., some radical, some conservative, most moderate) were reported to shift slowly but in the direction of extreme suggestions under conditions of high ambiguity. These simulations support Turner and Killian's claims, but they are simulations (and may or may not correspond to the distribution or interaction of predispositions in actual gatherings). Further, the shifts Johnson and Feinberg produce are shifts in opinions, not shifts in behavior. Computer simulations are invaluable (Feinberg and Johnson 1988; Johnson and Feinberg 1989), all the more so when they simulate behavior patterns that have also been identified and systematically described by field-workers.

22. Turner and Killian do, in fact, allude to something like this line of analysis. They write that "during the preliminary stages of collective behavior tentative actions, 'trials,' are undertaken, obstacles are encountered, and both resources and resistance are weighed. Hence an impression of the feasibility of action itself and of different types of action is formed. If action appears justified and feasible in the definition of the situation developed by the collectivity, collective behavior follows" (1987:10). Regrettably, Turner and Killian fail to develop this promising line of analysis.

23. Turner and Killian cite W. I. Thomas's concept "definition of the situation": "Whatever people believe to be real is real in its consequences" (1987:26). This is a hypothesis about the consequences of a definition of the situation rather than a specification of the actions involved in defining a situation (cf. McHugh 1968), that is, in the construction of a definition. To their credit, Turner and Killian's recent treatment of definition of the situation gives somewhat more attention to the actions involved in its construction and thus to the actions an observer could see and hear and examine in relation to the hypothesized consequences.

24. Perhaps it is actions and utterances such as these that not only define the situation but also contribute to the selective perception of differential expression as unanimity.

25. The central premise of emergent-norm theory is that collective behavior results from an emergent norm-as-definition of the situation. But Turner and Killian also claim that "collective behavior of all kinds is in large part a collective effort to formulate and implant a consensus about the nature and meaning of situations" (1987:236). Construed in this fashion, collective behavior is both the consequence and the cause of definitions of the situation.

4

Moving Beyond the Myth:
Couch; Berk; Tilly; and Lofland

Introduction

Turner and Killian challenged the traditional models of collective behavior long before the civil-rights and antiwar movements or the urban riots provided frequent opportunities for more students to observe the bases for the earlier challenges, to add to and move beyond them. Turner and Killian called attention to the importance of interaction within the crowd even if they did not examine it in any detail. They also called attention to the implications of macro social, political, and demographic considerations for the micro incidents of, and for the substance of, interaction within crowds. In this chapter I briefly review and assess the contributions of four more students of crowds and collective action—Carl Couch, Richard Berk, Charles Tilly, and John Lofland—who have critiqued, built upon, or superseded the Turner and Killian formulation.

Five themes run through these four characterizations and explanations. First, Couch, Berk, and Tilly explicitly recharacterize individual crowd members as purposive and rational actors rather than as individuals transformed by the crowd or driven by some predisposition to behave.

Second, Couch, Tilly, and Lofland extend one aspect or another of Turner and Killian's recognition that rationality and emotionality are not mutually exclusive. Couch and Tilly argue that crowds are not distinguished by their emotionality, and that emotion may be coincidental with or the consequence of collective action rather than its driving force. Lofland's claim that crowds *can* be characterized by a pervasive emotion challenges students of collective behavior to reconsider this controversial issue.

Third, Berk offers an explanation of why and Couch an explanation of how individual members interact within the crowd to yield collective action; Couch acknowledges and Tilly concentrates on the interaction between crowds and other individual or collective actors, for example, status quo authorities or their agents of social control.

Fourth, Couch, Tilly, and Lofland are concerned with identifying or explaining different forms (or repertoires of forms) of collective action in contrast to traditional concerns with the substantive content of crowds and collective action.

Finally, Couch by implication, Tilly by practice, and Lofland by taxonomic specification advocate further attention to the important connections between micro and macro levels and units of analysis in the study of crowds and collective action.

Carl J. Couch (b. 1925)

Couch's (1968) powerful critique of then current stereotypes of crowds and collective behavior was quickly and widely acclaimed by most scholars and requires but few qualifications today. He demonstrated those stereotypes were empirically false or that they did not distinguish crowds from other collectivities. More significant, in my judgment, was Couch's recharacterization of crowds first and foremost as social phenomena. He reasoned (1968:321) that: (1) social behavior is any individual action that incorporates the acts of another into the individual's own action; (2) some crowd members clearly incorporate the acts of others into their actions; therefore, (3) acting crowds are instances of social behavior.

Couch made a big leap here, and perhaps a questionable one, from a sequence of social behavior involving two or more persons within a crowd to the crowd as a whole. The leap was compounded when he further characterized political-protest crowds as "social systems human beings adopt to take action with reference to other systems" (1968:322). In his zeal to avoid the fallacies of individual crowd psychology, Couch bordered here on the sociological illusions of crowd unanimity and continuity. He subsequently tempered the social system hyperbole (Couch 1970; Miller, Hintz, and Couch 1975) by returning to the analysis of sequences of social behavior within gatherings. Before examining those analyses, it is well worthwhile to review briefly his critiques of several traditional stereotypes of the crowd and collective behavior. Those commonsense misconceptions haunt us still!

Stereotypes of Collective Behavior

Couch argued that crowds are not distinguished by extraordinary *emotional displays;* wherever human beings are located they display emotion, and these displays are occasionally extraordinary. Perhaps this is because whenever human beings engage in individual or collective purposive actions, they also evaluate the success and the failure of, the threats to or blockages of, their actions. I will argue below that those evaluations are displayed as emotions by individuals and by collections of individuals.

Couch argued that crowds are not distinguished by *violence* and destruction. I noted earlier that most political-demonstration crowds are seldom disorderly, let alone violent. When violence occurs, civilians engage in most of the violence against property; social-control agents (police and military) engage in most of the violence against persons. While most violence against persons probably evolves from interaction between protest crowds and social control agents [see Tilly (1978) and below], Couch noted that those agents are authorized, organized, trained, and equipped to engage in violence. Civilians are seldom a match.

For Couch, the phrase *antisocial crowd* is a contradiction in terms, a true oxymoron. Political-protest crowds do criticize and oppose society (as does "the loyal opposition party") and may thus be construed as anti–status quo; but crowds are hardly antisocial. To the contrary, Couch argued that crowds are fundamentally social. They are made up, in large measure, of many instances of social behavior, and only intermittently constitute a mutually inclusive social action of the majority, let alone of the whole; when that occurs for political crowds they can be construed, as Couch suggests, as social systems that human beings adopt to take action regarding other social systems.

Given these social features of crowds, Couch's *criticisms of transformation explanations* of crowds were both unique and significant. For example, he argued that political-protest crowds do not form from *spontaneous* combustion. Instead, some of the prospective members engage in some prior interaction, considering when and where protest might take place, often planning and preparing to assemble the remaining participants.[1] Further, members of political-protest crowds do not experience a *loss of self-control;* instead, they frequently refuse to control themselves with directions from authorities, controlling their behavior instead with directions from within their own ranks.[2] Similarly (1968:315), the individual pursuit of most political goals would be far more *irrational* than pursuing them via collective action. Thus, "if we tentatively accept the definition of rational action as that action which represents the most effective means for achieving some goal, then [political-protest crowds] are frequently highly rational endeavors" (1968:315).[3] Moreover, political-protest crowds can hardly be dismissed as highly *suggestible* since they frequently refuse authorities' suggestions to cease and desist and disperse.[4] Finally, recall that transformation psychologists concluded that the cumulative effects of spontaneity, loss of self-control, irrationality, and suggestibility rendered crowds "a kind of device for indulging ourselves in a kind of *temporary insanity* by all going crazy together" (Martin 1920:6; emphasis added). But Couch eliminated the transformation premises, and thus rejected the transformation conclusion as well. Crowds are "no more and no less pathological or bizarre than other systems [human beings] have developed" (1968:322).

Couch's most explicit *critique of predisposition explanations* centered on what he then believed to be the most strongly entrenched of all crowd stereotypes, viz., their *lower-class composition*. Authorities often discredit demonstrations or riots as the work of riffraff, ne'er-do-wells, or malcontents.[5] That explanation is demonstrably false. Couch cited Rude's (1964) historical evidence to the contrary regarding the socioeconomic class composition of French revolutionary and English industrial revolutionary crowds (cf. Tilly et al. 1975). This was further substantiated by the research on U.S. urban riots in the 1960s and 1970s. As I noted earlier, measures of socioeconomic status did not distinguish between riot participants and nonparticipants (McPhail 1971; Miller et al. 1977).[6]

Couch (1968) was the first to challenge a fundamental premise of *emergent-norm theory* (Turner 1964a; Turner and Killian, 1957, 1972, 1987; cf. Weller and Quarantelli 1973), viz., that the defining characteristics of collective behavior and crowds are their *emergent properties*. Given his long-standing concerns with explaining how two or more persons fit their actions together, that is, how they act collectively, Couch recognized early on that routine social behavior does not simply and automatically derive from routine social structures, from routine norms, or from routine roles. The participants in routine social behavior must actively construct what they do together; therefore, routine social behavior will always have some emergent features. Thus, the collective behavior cannot be distinguished from routine social behavior in terms of emergent properties. "The crowd is no more emergent than other forms of interaction" (1968:320). But Couch did not claim there were no unique characteristics of crowds and collective behavior. To the contrary!

Dimensions of Association

Couch suggested that "a crowd does involve people relating themselves to each other in a fashion *different* from that of routine relationships" (1968:320; emphasis added). And he subsequently wrote that "if the crowd is unique or distinctive it is not because of an absence of aligned conduct but rather in *how the alignment occurs*" (1970:458; emphasis added). In *reciprocal alignment* (1970:462) two or more persons fit together different behaviors (e.g., a speaker and an auditor in conversation). In *parallel alignment* two or more persons fit together the same or similar behaviors (e.g., singing in unison, synchroclapping, marching together). Couch argues that participants in these two forms of collective behavior engage one another in different ways.

In *reciprocal alignment* a relatively small number of participants are positioned more or less face-to-face, as in Figure 4.1. Because each individual can directly monitor every other individual, Couch calls this "particularistic monitoring"; when acknowledged by the other, this becomes "reciprocal acknowledgment." In face-to-face conversations "each participant has his own distinctive perspective [e.g., speaker vs. auditor; and each] retains a clear separation of identity between the self and the other[s] (1970:464). Couch argues that particularistic monitoring and differentiated identification increase the accountability of persons in reciprocal alignments. Some social psychologists (e.g., Festinger et al. 1952; Zimbardo 1969; Diener 1977, 1980) refer to this as *individuation*.

Conversely, *parallel alignments* involve a larger number of participants who are ordinarily positioned, more or less, side by side and face to back as in Figure 4.2. Each individual can monitor those persons located to either side, and the backs of those located to the front. Couch calls this "global monitoring." At minimum the individual can see that these others are orienting in the same direction as the individual; the individual may also be able to hear them singing, chanting, praying, shouting, cheering, applauding, or booing the same as the individual, or see them gesturing or marching in common with the individual. Couch claims that these parallel alignments, at minimum, encourage the individual's adoption of the other's line of orientation, the other's perspective, the other's focus. He further claims these alignments lend themselves to the identification of self and other in similar terms, e.g., we are engaging in this (these) behavior(s) together. Some social psychologists call this *deindividuation* (cf. Festinger et al. 1952; Zimbardo 1969; Diener 1977, 1980). Finally, Couch claims that "to be held accountable, persons must be differentiated and identified"; those who cannot be differentiated cannot be held accountable; and "those who cannot be held accountable are more likely to commit irresponsible acts" (1970:466).

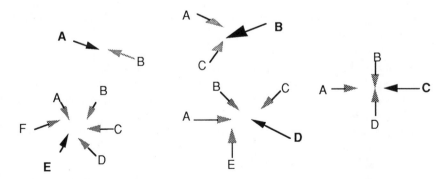

Figure 4.1. Reciprocal alignment in clusters (after Couch 1970).

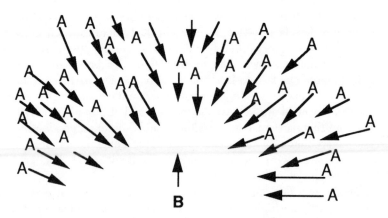

Figure 4.2.   Parallel alignment in crowds (after Couch 1970).

Whether this variation in monitoring, acknowledgment, self/other identification, or accountability is cause, consequence, or merely coincidental with
parallel and reciprocal alignment, it is far more important at this point to
acknowledge that both forms of collective behavior occur. Popular impressions to the contrary, most crowds consist of more than parallel behavioral
alignment: "Within nearly all, if not all, . . . [crowds] there is some differentiated and reciprocal [collective] behavior" (Couch 1970:463).

Not only can both forms occur but, when they do occur, they do so more
or less intermittently. For example, even in semiconstrained parallel behaviors, e.g., in gatherings seated on fixed and tiered benches, standing on
terraces, or marching in a street action, all the individuals who are orienting
straight ahead (parallel alignment) still can and do peripherally monitor their
neighbors. Further, during games, worship, concerts, lectures and marches,
they also intermittently orient in the direction of their neighbor(s) for verbal
or nonverbal conversation (reciprocal alignment). In standing gatherings
without built constraints, probably more time is spent in face-to-face or face-
to-side reciprocal alignment than in side-by-side and face-to-back parallel
alignment with neighbors.[7]

Finally, in view of the fact that some of the individual's neighbors in
crowds are friends, family, or acquaintances, conversations (reciprocal alignment) may be far more frequent than any parallel alignment across the
gathering; and most important, those companions (with whom the individual
assembles and remains throughout the gathering and then disperses) are
readily identifiable by, differentiated from, and accountable to one another.

Couch (1970) was well aware that these variations in monitoring, acknowledgment, self/other identification, and accountability were (and are) not
sufficient to explain either form of collective behavioral alignment. Thus, he

added some additional variables—e.g., identifying, directing, and evaluating actions—but failed to specify the necessary and sufficient relationships among them to produce collective behavior. Rather than belaboring the limitations of Couch's preliminary theoretical efforts, it is more useful to review his subsequent empirical examination of the initiation of collective behavioral alignment.

Constructing Openings

The concept of "opening" (Schegloff 1968) derives from a simplifying strategy of decomposing complex social actions into opening, middle, and closing phases. Miller, Hintz, and Couch write:

> Opening refers to the activity of two or more persons moving from a condition of behavioral independence to one of inter-dependence. It is thus the first necessary activity two persons must perform successfully if they are to do anything else together. (1975:479)

Drawing on Couch's (1970) theoretical paper on dimensions of association, Miller, Hintz, and Couch (1975) argued that five elements are necessary and sufficient for two or more persons to move from independent behavior to interdependent behavior.[8] *Mutual availability* refers to two or more individuals in the same setting with sensory access to one another. Sometimes those individuals scan the setting and in the course of doing so may note each other's movement or focus of attention. *Mutual attention* is established when each acknowledges attention from the other (cf. reciprocal acknowledgment, above). This may occur by simultaneous eye contact, by sequential touch, or by one person summoning and the other looking in the direction of or speaking to the summoner. Mutual attention can also, but need not at this point, incorporate a third object of mutual focus. *Mutual responsiveness* is an elaboration on mutual attention, that is, reciprocal touching, eye contact, facial expression, talk, or gesturing between the two parties who have already acknowledged one another. It may include one party's proposal for action that is either not acknowledged or is rejected by the other. *Mutual futures* refers to one or both parties proposing or projecting some immediate future action regarding a third object and the acknowledgment of that proposal by the other party. This may involve a verbal or nonverbal directive for behavior, for an outcome, or for both. Miller, Hintz, and Couch term that third object the *mutual focus,* which, if it has not been established by now, must be made specific since proposals for action—the mutual futures—are always in regard to some object.[9]

The construction of openings is at the core of interaction that can develop into collective action within a gathering of people. Sherif established the importance of social interaction for understanding behavior in problematic

situations. Turner and Killian sustained attention to the importance of interaction in a variety of such situations. Miller, Hintz, and Couch (1975)
examined how that interaction opens and develops into collective action in a
problematic situation.

A Quasi-Experimental
Examination

These theoretical ideas were elaborated and examined in a replication of
Latane and Rodin's (1969) woman-in-distress study. A female experimenter
told pairs of subjects seated in parallel arm-desks to write descriptions of a
Rorschach inkblot while she shelved books in an adjoining room. Two minutes later the noises of a crashing ladder and bouncing wastebasket ema-
nated from that adjoining room. After 16 seconds of silence, a groan was
heard and then a request for help (the two totaling 9 seconds); then after 8
seconds of silence, another request: "Please help me. I'm really hurt. Someone out in the hall?"

The Dependent Variable.   Miller, Hintz, and Couch were concerned with
a continuum bounded on one end by both pair members doing nothing
about the extraordinary incident, and on the other end by both pair members standing up and moving together in the direction of the door to the
adjoining room. The latter was Miller, Hintz, and Couch's criterion for
collective action.

The Method.   Miller, Hintz, and Couch videotaped these subjects from
the time they entered the room until the time both moved toward the
adjoining room or until it became apparent both were not going to do so.
They searched the videotapes with refinements of the analytic concepts
Couch had proposed (1970), and coded for the presence or absence of verbal
and nonverbal referents for dimensions of association and for collective
action.

The Control Variable.   Miller, Hintz, and Couch were curious about the
effects of relationships between subjects for their actions (or inactions) in the
research situation. They studied 23 pairs of subjects who were complete
strangers and 23 pairs of subjects whose friendship ranged from a few weeks
to many years.

The Hypothesis.   If two or more persons are to engage in a line of cooperative action, they must establish mutual attention, be mutually responsive,
and (sooner or later) establish a shared focus with regard to which they
project mutual future activities.

Results. Collective action occurred in 22 (11 stranger and 11 friend) pairs out of 46. The details are summarized in Figure 4.3 and are discussed below.

1. Mutual Availability; No Collective Action. In ten pairs (eight stranger, two friend), the members did not attend to one another, mutually acknowledge the extraordinary incident, or call (give directions) for the attention of the other. In one pair (stranger), neither member was distracted from the writing task. In six pairs (four stranger, two friend), one member oriented in the direction of the incident, but the second member oriented neither toward the incident nor the other member. In three pairs (stranger), one

mutual availability but no interaction   (n=10; 2F; 8S)

A   B

mutual attention re: mutual focus   (n=9; 6F; 3S)

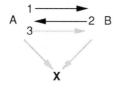

mutual responsiveness re: mutual focus   (n=5; 4F; 1S)

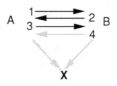

mutual futures re: mutual focus   (n=22; 11F; 11S)

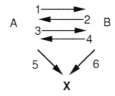

Figure 4.3.   Dimensions of association in opening collective action (after Miller, Hintz, and Couch 1975).

member oriented toward the extraordinary incident and then took action without orienting or calling to the second member who did nothing before or after. There was no collective action.

2. *Mutual Availability, Attention, and Focus; No Collective Action.*   In nine pairs (three stranger, six friend), both members first made eye contact and then laughed. Miller, Hintz, and Couch judge that "the participants established reciprocally acknowledged attention and recognized they had a shared focus" (1975:486). They also claim the laughter was not mere ridicule since the laughing member deflected the other member, thereby creating an opportunity to develop an opening. (Further, laughter and collective action toward the adjoining room were positively if weakly correlated: $r = .10$.) The missing element was a proposal to do something more about the mutual focus than just laugh about it.

3. *Mutual Attention, Focus, and Responsiveness; No Collective Action.*   In five pairs (one stranger, four friend), there was both "a reallocation of attention and the tentative negotiation of mutual responsiveness" (1975:486). One member was deflected and called for the attention or response of the other, who acknowledged the call but declined to project a mutual future regarding the incidence. Pair members moved neither individually or collectively in the direction of the adjoining room. For example:

A: "Shouldn't we go?"
B: "No! (Breaking off eye contact and returning to writing task.)
A: "But if someone calls for help, wouldn't you help them?"
B: (Silently continues writing task.)
A: (Returns to writing task after a few seconds.)

4. *Mutual Attention, Focus, Responsiveness, and Futures; and Collective Action.*   Twenty-two pairs (11 stranger, 11 friend) stood up and moved in the direction of the door to the adjoining room from which the sounds of the extraordinary incident had come.

In 19 pairs (11 stranger, 8 friend), one or both members gave a startle response to the incident, then oriented toward the other member, or the adjoining room, or both in rapid succession, thereby enabling reciprocally acknowledged attention by both members. (In a few instances, for which details are not provided, one member verbally summoned the other, who then oriented toward the first.) Miller, Hintz, and Couch claim there were various combinations of visual, vocal-auditory, and tactile cues by which mutual attention was established, further responsiveness developed, and futures subsequently projected. Regrettably they provide no examples, let alone detailed evidence.

Finally, in three pairs (all friend), Miller, Hintz, and Couch could not distinguish the sequencing of mutual attention, responsiveness, and futures regarding a focus. They nonetheless claim that all those elements were present but that they were merged into a near-simultaneous sequence:

> Both persons simultaneously evidenced a startle or freezing response, [then] turned to each other and established eye contact, rose from their chairs simultaneously, and moved toward the door together. (1975:489)

All three pairs had known each other for years, two pairs since high school, and one pair were twins; all three pairs were current roommates.

Miller, Hintz, and Couch had expected to find striking differences in the manner in which friends and strangers constructed collective action. They found but one: pairs of friends acted together more than twice as quickly (mean = 6.7 seconds) as pairs of strangers (mean = 15.2 seconds). Friends' prior interaction with and knowledge of one another may have increased their shared repertoire of succinct and subtle verbal and nonverbal directions for behavior, thereby increasing the speed with which they could communicate and construct collective action.

Discussion. In Table 4.1, I have arrayed Miller, Hintz, and Couch's 46 cases in a bivariate relationship between the presence (or absence) of the necessary and sufficient elements, and the presence (or absence) of collective action. If we classify the three instantaneous cases as undifferentiated and therefore insufficient, the strength of association with collective action is still impressive: $r = .88$. If we concede Miller, Hintz, and Couch's interpretation that those three cases contained the necessary and sufficient elements, the association is even stronger.

An Assessment

Although Couch devoted far more attention to the development of an explanation for collective behavior than to the specification and description of the varied forms of collective behavior to be explained, he did not ignore

Table 4.1. Necessary and Sufficient Elements for Collective Action (After Miller, Hintz, and Couch 1975)

Subjects constructed	Sufficient necessary elements present	Insufficient necessary elements present	Total
Collective action	19	3*	22
No collective action	(?)	24	24
Total	19	27	46

*$X^2 = 35.94$, $p < .001$, $r = .88$

the latter problem. Even more important than Couch's critique of stereotypes was his recharacterization of the crowd as a social phenomenon and his subsequent distinction between parallel collective behavior and differentiated collective behavior. In each case, Couch properly emphasized that *collective* behavior involves two or more persons fitting their behaviors together. The explanatory problem then became one of explaining how alignment takes place.

Couch claims (1984:7; Miller, Hintz, and Couch, 1975) to have identified the necessary and sufficient, the generic elements for constructing collective action. There are two flaws in that claim. First, those generic elements (the various "mutuals") are descriptions of phases in the development of collective action rather than specifications of classes of action that will produce collective action. Miller, Hintz, and Couch's claims would be more persuasive if they could *also* have manipulated some (or all) of those inductively identified elements and thereby produced a sequence of collective action.[10]

Second, Miller, Hintz, and Couch readily concede that what may hold true for the construction of collective action by two participants is more problematic if not different for larger numbers. They wrote:

> In situations involving large numbers, successful openings to coordinated action are much more problematic. When those involved do not have a history of prior social action together, the coordination of attention, . . . responsiveness, . . . [futures] and focus are still required, but often are nearly unmanageable. This condition explains the high proportion of unsuccessful openings for collective behavior episodes (cf. McPhail 1969). It is this condition that also explains the presence of persons who dedicate themselves to "managerial" tasks within large scale organizations. (1975:497)

The implicit assumption here is that instead of the face-to-face alignments and interaction possible within small groups of two to five or six members, *larger numbers* require the interaction between many persons and one person who nurtures mutual responsiveness, who establishes a mutual focus, who proposes mutual futures regarding that focus, and who oversees and nudges the development alignment of the behaviors to which those mutual futures referred. I will argue in Chapter 6 that the larger the number of people involved, and the more complex and sustained the collective action that is proposed and implemented, the more necessary will be prior planning, preparation, and off-site rehearsal of those plans, and deliberate on-site, *third-party* management and implementation of those plans (cf. McPhail 1985).

Nonetheless, Miller, Hintz, and Couch examined a fundamental form of micro–collective action within temporary gatherings and they called attention to some important aspects of the construction of that form of collective action. It is a recurring form of collective action within temporary gatherings as small groups of companions, initially interacting among themselves, direct one another's attention to actors and actions outside their group, and sometimes propose and occasionally carry out collective movement in the direction of (or away from) those other actors and actions. The work of Couch and his colleagues is an important theoretical and methodological contribution to our understanding of the structure and dynamics of this elementary form of collective action.

Richard A. Berk (b. 1942)

Berk's field observations and analyses of both interracial confrontations (1972a,b) and antiwar demonstrations (1974a) convinced him of the limitations of transformation and predisposition explanations for the crowd (1974b). Although he acknowledges the advances offered by the emergent-norm perspective, he also identifies several problems.

Berk's Critique

First, Berk argues (1974b:67) that Turner and Killian fail to examine the interaction process within the crowd, and its development into collective behavior. Second, he therefore claims (1974b:66) that Turner and Killian fail to specify the sources of and processes by which norms emerge. Berk suggests both of these shortcomings reflect the minimal attention Turner and Killian give to the environment or setting within which the crowd interacts and develops, e.g., the effects of terrain, elevation, light, sound, and density on what members of the crowd can see and hear one another do (1974b:67). Finally, Berk takes sharp exception to Turner and Killian's assumption of the individual's "heightened suggestibility" under the influence of the emergent norm, and the "tendency to respond uncritically to suggestions that are consistent with the mood, imagery, and conception of appropriate action that have developed and [that] assume a normative character" (Turner and Killian 1972:80, cited in Berk 1974b:355). Turner and Killian, therefore, attribute collective behavior to the "crippled cognition" of individual crowd members (Berk 1974b:67).

Berk's Alternative: Rational
Calculus Theory

Berk's alternative explanation is based on Raiffa's (1970) decision making theory. Berk writes:

Gaming approaches to crowds try to delineate the theoretical mechanisms through which crowds respond to their environments and to each other. Rest-ing heavily on Decision Theory, the gathering of a crowd is viewed as an opportunity in which individuals can experience certain rewards and certain costs. Each individual tries to maximize rewards and minimize costs. (1974b:67)

This reduces to a sovereign principle of "the minimax strategy." Individuals attempt to get information about any situation in which they have to act. They attempt to estimate different developments that might occur in that situation and to arrange them in some likely sequence of developments. They then attempt to estimate where they figure in those developments, what their options are in those sequences of development, and how well they like the probable outcomes of those options. They then estimate the likelihood that any of these developments and outcomes will occur and choose a course of action that maximizes their rewards and minimizes their costs.

Berk contends this individual decision-making process operates in all situations. The crowd is no exception. However, a critical variable in crowd situations is what other people do. Their actions can create rewarding or costly outcomes for the individual:

Crowd members are engaged in a "game" in which each "player's" payoff matrix depends on the actions of others on the scene. Opportunities to be highly satisfied depend on people acting in unison. (1974a:363)

The central proposition in Berk's argument is the relationship between the behavior the individual believes would yield the greatest rewards and least costs, and the extent of support for that behavior the individual believes is present or forthcoming from others in the situation. He summarizes that proposition: "The probability that a person will initiate action is a function of the product of net anticipated payoffs (the rewards for acting minus the rewards for not acting) and the certainty of support" (1974b:70).

Several contingencies may be involved (1974b:70–71). The greater the anticipated rewards for an action, the more likely that action will be taken. The greater the anticipated support from others for an action, the more likely that action will be taken. If anticipated rewards are low for an action, it will not be taken even if anticipated support is high. If anticipated support is low for an action, it will not be taken even if anticipated rewards are high. The critical issue is the mix of rewards and support.

Thus, like Granovetter (1978), Berk argued that the individual's estimation of others' support is very important. Several characteristics of the crowd situation may affect that estimation: the number of persons already engaging in a particular behavior; the visibility of that particular behavior (affected by crowd shape, density, location of the behavior within the crowd, amount of light, terrain on which the behavior occurs); the coherence of the particular behavior; and the proximity of persons engaging in the behavior. The relationship between the number of people engaging in the behavior and perceived support is graphically represented in Figure 4.4. Berk writes:

> The effect of [the number of others already acting] may be "S" shaped (a logistic function) such that it alters the probability of support mostly through changes in its middle ranges (a tipping effect). If only a few people are acting, the effect on perceived support may be minimal. When most are acting, the probability of support is already high. (1974b:71)

The collective behavior in which people engage may range from cooperative [e.g., building a barricade during a street action (Berk 1974b)] to competitive [e.g., looting (Berk and Aldrich 1972)], but the focus is upon what two or more people are doing with or in relation to one another. Berk summarizes his position as follows:

> We have come a long way from herd-like descriptions of crowd activity, and if there is one overall conclusion, it is that collective behavior is not some unique type of human interaction. Collective behavior occurs every day in a variety of situations. We are constantly being bombarded by informal group pressures and many of our contacts with others approximate cooperative and/or competitive games. Hence, human rationality is no less operative in crowds than in any other

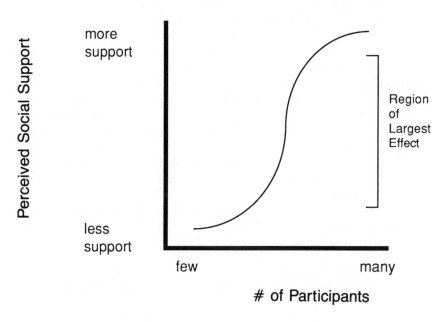

Figure 4.4. Number participants in a sequence of collective action by extent of perceived social support (after Berk 1974b).

circumstances. We all operate with blinders and though they may differ from situation to situation, they obscure the world nonetheless. (1974b:75)[11]

An Assessment

Berk's formulation is a welcome alternative to the tradition of the madding crowd established by the transformation theorists, indirectly maintained by the predisposition theorists, and only recently challenged by the emergent-norm theorists. If the coherent individual statements and the coherent conversations overheard in hundreds of crowds are acceptable evidence of coherent thought, there is little indication that crowds cripple the cognitions of their members.

Perhaps Berk's judgments remain valid that Turner and Killian (1957, 1972) neither examined the interaction process nor provided a satisfactory description or explanation of emergent norms (cf. Turner and Killian 1987). I have already indicated my own reservations. Berk's third criticism of emergent-norm theory is debatable. He lumps Turner and Killian with the rest of the madding-crowd theorists who argue that an individual's critical ability is diminished and suggestibility is increased under the influence of the emergent norm. In my judgment, Turner and Killian do not say that people fail to evaluate critically *all* suggestions; rather, they claim people are "uncritical of suggestions consistent with the mood, imagery, and conception of appropriate action that have developed and assumed a normative character" (1987:78). It may be that suggestions consistent with what people are already doing create no problems and therefore do not occasion critical scrutiny. I will return to this point in Chapter 6.

Although Berk's rational-calculus formulation shares some features with the cost-reward formulation of Miller and Dollard, there is one striking difference. Whereas Miller and Dollard placed the individual under the control of a reward history and the resulting response hierarchy, Berk's formulation places the individual squarely in control of his or her own behavior. The individual is not driven by a predisposition, but rather organizes and controls his or her own behavior with regard to a minimax principle and to estimates of social support.

The problem, of course, is the absence of independent measures of anticipated payoff and probability of support by others. Berk acknowledges the problems with both causal variables in his basic proposition:

Because both independent variables are unobservable mental states, the formulation is fraught with epistemological problems. Analyses of their impact risk circularity. (1974a:365)

This is not the sole limitation of Berk's two variables.

To say that human beings sometimes select a course of behavior on the basis of what has previously been rewarded or the basis of anticipated future rewards is not to say they always do so. Nor is it to say that any who do so accomplish whatever they do solely on the basis of anticipated (or past) rewards and costs. Exchange theorists and rational-calculus theorists imply this is the most important if not the sole set of instructions human beings give to themselves. I submit the minimax principle is but *one* set of instructions people in our culture may learn and may give themselves in some situations. But it is a very limited set of instructions, insufficient for virtually all the complex individual and social behaviors in which human beings engage.

Minimax instructions only tell us why we should engage in one behavior rather than another; this is an important question. In choosing between alternative solutions to problems, human beings will more frequently than not choose the solution that appears to have the best chance of working. However, this presupposes that we have first established what the problem is, that we have then entertained one or more possible solutions to the problem, that we have further considered what behaviors would be required, by one or more persons, to put that solution into operation. The minimax instruction does not establish problems, formulate solutions, or tell us what the behaviors should be, or when they should occur, where, how, by or with whom. Thus, minimax instructions are but a subset of the instructions with which an individual organizes and controls his or her own behaviors, not to mention the instructions required for two or more individuals to fit their respective behaviors together into social behavior. It is conceivable that two or more individuals might participate in some very simple sequences of social behavior solely on the basis of anticipated (or prior) rewards. But as the complexity of the social behavior increases, the respective behaviors of the two or more individuals cannot be focused, merged, and adjusted without instructions to self and other that go beyond the minimax principle. Situations must be assessed; objectives must be established; behaviors regarding those objectives must be proposed and enacted; the results must be assessed; adjustments must be made; and frequently one or more of these steps must be repeated several times before people accomplish what they set out to do. The minimax strategy is not sufficient to these tasks; it is frequently tangential; it is sometimes unnecessary.

The probability of support by others is the second variable in Berk's main proposition. He defines this as "actions by crowd members which decrease the anticipated costs for a given individual" (1974a:366). Anticipated costs are, in Berk's words, an "unobservable mental state." But the presence and actions of other crowd members are observable. Thus, the simple syllogism: (I) The greater the number of others already engaging in action X, the less an individual's anticipated costs for engaging in action X. (II) The less the anticipated costs for engaging in action X, the more likely the individual will engage in action X. Therefore, (III) The greater the number of others already engaging in action X, the more likely the individual will engage in action X.

Both terms in proposition III are observable in principle. Most social psychologists would agree with the plausibility of the relationship asserted by proposition III, a slightly different statement of Berk's own description of the S-shaped curve in Figure 4.4.

The problem is not with proposition III, of course, but with the connecting link between the number of others already engaging in the behavior and the likelihood of the individual engaging in the same behavior. Past or anticipated costs and rewards are problematic connecting links, for the reasons already stated. It is not that the behaviors of others are irrelevant; it is simply that we need a better explanation for how others' behaviors, and which ones, are of consequence for the individual's behavior in crowds and in other situations of copresence.

Finally, Berk's detailed descriptions of an aborted interracial confrontation (1972b) and of a student antiwar demonstration, in particular, movement through the streets and the construction of a barricade (1974a), are among the best in the literature. But those substantively rich accounts imply an alternation between and a variation within sequences of individual and collective behavior in the gatherings that simply overwhelms the explanatory formulation Berk sets forth. Other sociologists have also put forth rational and proactive explanations for collective action in lieu of irrational and reactive emphases of transformation and predisposition theories. One of those scholars is Charles Tilly.

Charles Tilly (b. 1929)

Tilly's work on collective action is highly regarded by sociologists and historians alike, by quantitative and qualitative scholars, by those who work at both macro and micro levels of analysis. Tilly explicitly embraces a rational model of collective action, but is concerned with the macro sources of the particular interests that actors pursue at the micro level of analysis as well as the macro conditions in which micro collective actions are more likely to succeed or to fail. The distinctions he draws among categories of actors, the forms of interaction between those categories (including the development of collective violence from nonviolent interaction), and the repertoires of collective action upon which those actors draw all contribute to our understanding of temporary gatherings.

An Explanation for Collective Action

Tilly defines *collective action* as "people acting together in pursuit of common interests" (1978:7). The primary components in his explanation of collective action are the interests of a group of actors, the extent of their organization, the extent to which they can mobilize their personnel and other resources in the pursuit of their interests, and the opportunities they have to do so. Tilly's explanation is outlined in Figure 4.5. In general, group mobilization is a function of interests and organization, as well as the opportunities for mobilizing and the extent to which the group is repressed, tolerated, or facilitated because of its interests. Collective action results from a group's power, its capacity for mobilization, the opportunities for (and the threats to) the pursuit of its interests. These theoretical elements are briefly summarized below.

Interests. Tilly is "trying to explain why people behave as they do" and he argues that "the goals they have fashioned for themselves appear to influence their behavior even when those goals are trivial, vague, unrealistic, or self defeating" (1978:61). Thus, Tilly assumes a purposive actor even though he does not tell us how those goals result in behavior; fortunately, others have addressed that piece of the problem in theories of cognition and behavior to which I will return in Chapter 6. What Tilly does

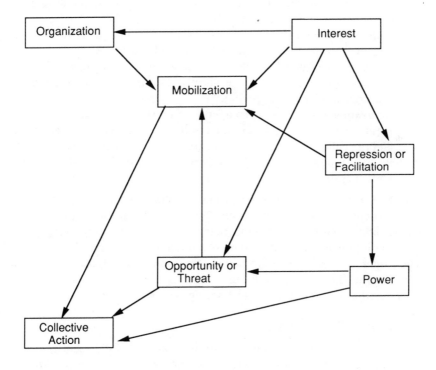

Figure 4.5. Tilly's model of collective action (after Tilly 1978).

address are matters that cognitive theories often ignore, viz., the forms of social organization as well the larger social and political circumstances that increase or diminish the prospects for acting on those goals.

Organization.   Drawing on some of Harrison White's ideas, Tilly (1978: 62–68) characterizes organization as the product of *category attributes* shared by and the *networks* (of contacts, interactions, and relationships) among two or more individuals. The most important category attribute is often the name with which member actors collectively and publicly identify themselves; but a variety of "standard symbols, slogans, songs, styles of dress or other marks" may be used as well.

The cumulative extent of relationships among such actors can be indexed by the extent to which one or more members: has the authority to speak for the entire group; controls spaces or structures open to group members; controls money, labor, weapons, information, or other resources held in common for group use; controls the time and energy members spend in the name of the group; and (occasionally) controls the primary relationships among group members (cf. Young 1966).

> *Mobilization* is defined as the extent to which a group can control and deliver resources in behalf of its interests. Tilly explains mobilization as a function of organization.
>
> *Opportunity* refers to the chances a group has to pursue its interests or, negatively, to encroachments upon those chances.
>
> *Power* is construed by Tilly as a relationship between two or more competing interest groups, specifically, the extent to which one group can prevail over its competitor.
>
> *Repression* can come from competing interest groups, from the government, or from both. Government is likely to repress mobilization by and the collective actions of those groups whose interests conflict with its own, unless those groups are very powerful or their actions are not very threatening.

In Figure 4.5, repression was represented as influencing group power; but Tilly recognizes (1978:115) the relationship is reciprocal. Governments often ignore those groups with nonconflicting interests. When interests do conflict but groups pursue them with actions of limited scale, they are also tolerated. The larger the scale of group action, the more likely repression by the government; the more powerful the group, the less likely such repression. Tilly's representation of these relationships appears in Figure 4.6.

Forms of Collective Action

These "forms," Tilly reminds us, are the analytic tools of scholars, not to be confused with the descriptions or distinctions made by participants in those actions. He writes:

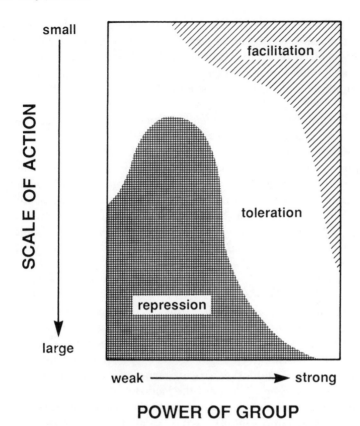

Figure 4.6. Government response by group power and scope of collection action (after Tilly 1978).

Real people do not get together and act collectively. They meet to petition parliament, organize telephone campaigns, demonstrate outside of city hall, attack powerlooms, go on strike. (1978:143)

Tilly has examined volumes of archival descriptions of such actions, gatherings, and events in the construction of his particular analytic tools. His characterization of collective action has three distinctive features. First, he limits collective action to collective claims, thereby deliberately excluding collective action involving "pure recreation, contemplation, [or] escape" (1978:144).

Second, Tilly argues that group claims are rarely unilateral actions; that is, they involve interaction between one acting unit (e.g., a challenge group) and at least a second active unit (e.g., a decision maker). In contemporary episodes of collective action, several categories or groups of actors are frequently involved in addition to the challenge group: police, media, spectators, and often counterchallenge groups. (Tilly subsequently refers to these multiple and diverse collections of actors within gatherings as formations.)

Third, Tilly sorts *collective claim making* into one of three categories: competitive, reactive, proactive. *Competitive collective actions* "lay claim to resources also claimed by other groups which the actor defines as rivals, competitors, or at least as participants in the same contest" (1978:144). These range from the *shivaree* (*charivari*) in which male suitors competed for scarce brides, to contests between guilds for order of precedence in public processions, to competitions between rival villages for natural resources, to combat between religious or ethnic groups for territorial dominance, to brawls between civilians and soldiers or between student groups for other resources.

Reactive collective actions "consist of group efforts to reassert established claims when someone else challenges or violates them" (1978:145). A frequent example from eighteenth-century Europe and nineteenth-century America involved one group tearing down new fences built by another group around spaces previously used by everyone for pasture, gleaning, or firewood. Another example from the English Industrial Revolution involved handworkers (the Luddites) destroying new power looms that threatened to displace those workers. Tilly cites the food riots as a third example. [12]

Proactive collective actions "assert group claims which have not previously been exercised" (1978:146). The oldest example is the work stoppage for better working conditions or higher wages, an action as old as the employment of one party by another. [13] A much newer example is the demonstration rally or march. Both are by-products of the development of nineteenth-century mass electoral politics. The general strike, the dumping of surplus crops, and the sit-down or sit-in are twentieth-century products.

Claims are collectively stated within or by gatherings. Thus, Tilly refers to *contentious gatherings* that is, "occasions in which ten or more persons outside the government gather in the same place and make a visible claim which, if realized, would affect the interests of some specific person(s) or group(s) outside their own numbers" (1978:176). Two additional and related distinctions are important: the form of the gathering and the form of the claim.

Gatherings in which contentions are made range from assemblies and carnivals to celebrations and parades, to rallies and demonstrations, to strikes, union meetings, and related activities. The actual claims or contentions range from statements of aspirations, complaints, demands, dissatisfactions, grievances, and interests, to petitioning a government, to opposing a government policy or its agent, to supporting a government enemy. [14]

Repertoires of Collective Action

Repertoires are lists or supplies of available pieces, parts, skills, devices, or ingredients with which an individual or group is familiar and may be prepared to perform. Tilly argues there are repertoires of collective political actions:

> Within any particular time and place, the array of collective actions that people employ is (1) well defined and (2) quite limited in comparison to the range of actions that are theoretically available to them. (1979:131)

For example:

> Hijacking, mutiny, machine breaking, charivaris [shivarees], village fights, tax rebellions, food riots, collective self immolation, lynching, and vendetta have all belonged to the standard collective-action repertoires of some group at some [earlier] time. (1978:153)

Group members were familiar with these forms; they knew how to use them; they considered them legitimate ways of stating their claims and seeking redress of their grievances.

In the late twentieth century, many citizens around the world are familiar with some form of the demonstration. They may not have studied demonstrations or even directly participated in one, but they have observed them as onlookers, read about them in the newspapers, or viewed them on television. Writing of Americans, Tilly notes that:

> They know that a group with a claim to make assembles in a public place, identifies itself and its demands or complaints in a visible way, orients its common action to the persons, properties or symbols of some other group it is seeking to influence. With those general rules, most Americans know how to carry on several different forms of demonstration: the massed march, the assembly with speechmaking, the temporary occupation of premises. Moreover, there are some specifiable circumstances in which most Americans would actually apply their knowledge by joining a real demonstration. (1978:151–2)

Tilly suggests that, faced with the necessity of stating a claim or seeking a redress of grievance, most contemporary Americans (and other nationalities as well) would be more likely to rally, march, picket, or sit in, than to engage in a *charivari*, a food riot, machine breaking, or a vendetta. Tilly argues that at any given point in time, the existing standardized repertoire "significantly constrains the strategy and tactics of collective actors" (1979:131).

Repertoires vary in the extent to which they are known to all members of the group; they enable the group effectively to convey their claims to those who can do something about them; and they are more or less successful in realizing some of those claims. Tilly suggests a wave may develop involving a particular tactic because:

[One] group gets somewhere with the tactic [and this] spreads the expectation that [other] employers or governments will be vulnerable to the same tactic in the hands of other similar groups. (1978:155)

One example, to which I will give more attention below, is the wave of sit-in demonstrations that spread across the southeastern United States in February and March of 1960 as part of the civil-rights movements' efforts to secure equal access to public accommodations (McAdam 1982; Morris 1984).

Public officials who are the repeated targets of this or any other tactic sometimes devise responses that make the tactic less effective, if not useless. A group's continued use of the same tactics exemplifies what Tilly calls a *rigid repertoire* of collective actions. Conversely, a group's development and employment of alternative tactics to press its claims in new and different ways exemplifies what Tilly calls a *flexible repertoire*. Flexibility is preferred (cf. Alinsky 1972); and flexibility is associated with success (McAdam 1983).

Changes in Repertoires

Repertoires ordinarily are slow to change. Tilly notes several factors that can contribute to change in repertoires. The successful repression of one form may require the development of alternatives if the movement is not to die.[15]

A government that guarantees the rights of free assembly and free speech will probably tolerate a greater variety of protest forms than a government without such guarantees. Daily routines of life may provide opportunities to state claims in certain ways but not in others—indeed may allow only for the statement of claims in limited ways. For example, Tilly notes that for centuries prior to 1800, the only legitimate opportunities for civilian assembling were market days, festivals, and holidays. On these occasions the authorities created the opportunity for and gave approval to people coming together. Then:

During the festivities [the people] often expressed their collective opinions of the day's heroes, villains, and fools. They paraded effigies, floats, charades, and placards. Hangings, funerals, exits from prison, royal birthdays, [and] announcements of military victories often drew crowds and, sometimes, [also drew] concerted expressions of demands, sympathies or complaints. (1978:168)

Tilly documents this pattern in England as well as in the American colonies. Whatever statements of claims were made were limited to street theater and other forms of symbolic protest.

With the development of electoral politics, however, the forms of collection action began to shift dramatically. Tilly hypothesizes that "the growth of elections promotes the crystallization and spread of the demonstration as a form of collective action" (1978:167). The legalization of elections protected the process by which elections took place, including the formation of associations or special-interest groups to promote particular candidates, and the use of special gatherings for the purpose of speech making in behalf of and by those candidates, the development of petitions in behalf of candidates, and the mass petition march to deliver those petitions to Parliament. Tilly argues that the legal umbrella hoisted over the electoral process extended protection to other associations and gatherings "not quite electoral, not *only* electoral or not *now* electoral" (1978:167). All these process were significant steps "toward the creation of the demonstration as a distinctive form of collective action." In England and subsequently in the American colonies, there was, on the one hand, a decline in street theater and symbolic protest and, on the other hand, a growth of special-interest associations and specific assemblies for the purpose of stating claims.

Collective Violence

Sociologist Charles Tilly, historian Louise Tilly, and economist Richard Tilly examined newspaper accounts and other archival records of tens of thousands of contentious gatherings and thousands of incidents of collective violence from the eighteenth through the twentieth century. Their research challenges many long-standing stereotypes about collective political violence. I noted Couch's early criticism of the stereotypical belief that political demonstrations are typically violent. Couch's claims are born out by the Tillys' data. Over the past two centuries (Tilly et al. 1975) as in the past two decades (Eisinger 1973; MacCannel 1973; McPhail 1985), violent demonstrations have been the exception rather than the rule!

A second stereotype holds that when political violence occurs it is the product of unilateral planning and implementation (if not the unilateral predispositions) of the demonstrators. To the contrary "violence is rarely a solo performance. It usually grows out of an interaction of opponents" (Tilly 1978:175). More specifically, demonstrators undertake a large action that nonviolently, although sometimes illegally, states a claim. The target of the claim is more likely to resist if its own interests are threatened by the claim. Its resistance constitutes, at minimum, a counterclaim. The two sides may struggle. The target may "call the cops"—the police, the troops, a posse, a vigilante—to act in its behalf. Whether the target is the state, or simply status quo constituents, the state has the authority to order its agents of social control to use whatever means are necessary to resist and disperse the contentious demonstrators. Those agents are equipped to use violence; they are trained to use violence; when they are given authority to use collective violence, we should not be surprised if they do so (cf. Stark 1972)! And, Tilly contends, "the standard structure of collective violence . . . [is the] by-product of the play of claim and counterclaim" (1978:174). For evidence supporting, Tilly's analysis, see Kritzer (1977).][16]

A third stereotype holds that violence is driven by passionate emotions. But there is now good reason to suspect that emotion is more often coincidental with or the consequence of violence rather than its cause. Tilly does not suggest that collective violence takes place in an atmosphere of "calculating calm. Far from it" (1978:182). There may be considerable anger, resentment, retaliation, exhilaration, and the like. Tilly simply claims that emotions are not the cause of the collective action:

> Collective violence is not, by and large, the result of a single group's possession by an emotion, sentiment, attitude, or idea. It grows for the most part, out of strategic interaction among groups. (1978:183)

What these facts and this line of analysis lead Tilly to conclude is that the student of collective violence must deal with a paradox: "to understand and explain violent actions, you must understand nonviolent actions" (1978:184). Whenever violence occurs it develops within a sequence of actions or gatherings that are very much like the majority of nonviolent demonstrations. Tilly's analysis suggests that it is the combined power of the group making the claims, the scope of the collective actions with which the claims are made, and the extent to which the claims threaten status quo interests that affects the development of the interaction, and the play of claim and counterclaim from which violence emerges.

An Assessment

Tilly argues that organized collections of rational actors mobilize and then engage in forms of collective action selected from the repertoire of forms with which they are familiar. Tilly's work reminds us that gatherings take place within a larger spatial-temporal framework that can affect the formation of the gathering, what takes place there, and how the gathering is ended. Tilly does not examine how the mobilization of gatherings or the organization of collective action within gatherings is accomplished. His concerns are with the political conditions that facilitate or impede the occurrence of contentious gatherings, and whether the interaction by which those claims are delivered and received develops violently or nonviolently. These are important questions, but they are neither more nor less important than the question of how (and why) sequences of collective action are organized within gatherings, and how gatherings are mobilized in the first place. And, if it is important to study nonviolent gatherings in order to understand the development of collective violence, then by the same logic it is also important to study gatherings and collective action in which claims are not made in order fully to understand those in which and by which claims are made. The conclusion to which I am drawn is that students of gatherings and collective action must recognize the validity and the interdependence of a variety of levels and units of analysis. One of the first scholars to give systematic attention to this issue was John Lofland.

John Lofland (b. 1936)

Lofland writes in the introduction to his essays on collective behavior and social movements that "scholars of collective behavior are on the verge of a significant breakthrough [in] what they are studying and, therefore, in the acuity of their analyses" (1985:31). Lofland's own contributions to this potential breakthrough are considerable. I examine four here: Lofland's (1981) call for attention to "forms of elementary collective behavior" and his own analyses (1982b) of forms of collective emotion and (1982a; Lofland and Fink 1982) of forms of political protest; his (1985) endorsement of gatherings rather than crowds as a basic unit of analysis; his (1985) proposed cumulative continuum of micro to macro units of analysis in the study of collective phenomena; and his (1985) recognition of the necessity of more complex if not alternative explanations for these varied units of collective phenomena.

Forms of Collective Behavior

Lofland correctly notes that in their preoccupation with the causes and consequences of collective phenomena (and with the particulars of substantive content), sociologists have given little attention to *forms of collective phenomena* per se. "This pronounced neglect of forms is having a critically retarding effect on the development of the field of collective behavior" (1981:411). One effect is the failure to develop a systematic taxonomic scheme to direct and organize the results of pertinent empirical studies. That void, in turn, tolerates debates over the conceptual merits of different theoretical explanations (e.g., contagion, convergence, emergent norm, rational calculus) without any agreement on the forms each presumes to explain, or the relevant evidence regarding the explanations of specified forms.

Consequently, Lofland undertook the development of a taxonomy of some elementary forms of collective phenomena. He did not specify what he meant by "forms." Thus, I will here construe *form* rather broadly as the distinctive configuration or structure of the component elements of a phenomenon. Form is not independent of substantive content; instead, form transcends diverse and particular substantive contents.

Lofland (1981:415) further argued that contemporary emphases on cognition and on behavior have resulted in ignoring emotion. He wrote:

My concern is that stress on the cognitive [and the behavioral] commits the opposite error [viz.,] that of reducing the field to exercises in cognitive theory [e.g., emergent norm, rational calculus, symbolic interactionist] or even more extreme, to a species of behaviorism in which the study of collective behavior is merely the study of human coordination (e.g., Couch 1970; McPhail and Wohlstein 1983). (1981:415)

Elsewhere Lofland suggested that:

Both [cognitive and behavioral] approaches seem suffused with the fear that discussion of emotion . . . inevitably drags us back to the likes of Gustave LeBon, Sigmund Freud or even Herbert Blumer and imputations of assorted irrationalities and group mind perspectives. (1982a:377)

Lofland properly argued that students of human behavior must give attention to cognition *and* behavior *and* emotion, the traditional "holy trinity" of social psychology. Given the lack of attention to emotion, and given his concern with collective forms, Lofland developed a taxonomy of elementary forms of collective emotion. Whatever the merits or flaws in Lofland's treatment of forms of collective emotion, he must be credited for calling attention to *forms* of collective behavior and for resurrecting *collective emotions* as legitimate objects for study by students of collective phenomena. With those two strokes he significantly recast the agenda for students of the crowd and collective behavior.

Forms of Collective Emotion.   Lofland focuses on three of the primary emotions: joy, anger, and fear (cf. Ekman 1982). Then, following Tarde, Park, and subsequent generations of sociologists and social psychologists, Lofland differentiates collective phenomena among assembled individuals (the crowd) from collective phenomena across dispersed individuals (the mass). Combining those two dimensions, Lofland generates six "master forms" of collective emotion phenomena: joyous crowds, joyous masses, hostile crowds, hostile masses, fearful crowds, fearful masses. Into this taxonomic scheme, Lofland masterfully sorts a comprehensive review of the "dominant [forms of] emotional arousal" reported in the literature on crowds and masses. He does all this even while acknowledging the danger of "the illusion of unanimity" (1985:32).

One example of Lofland's treatment of forms of collective emotion is his essay, "Crowd Joys" (1982b). Students of collective behavior have long been preoccupied with protest (by implication, the emotion of anger), and only slightly less concerned with panic (by implication, the emotion of fear).[17] Lofland's examination of sacred crowd joys (e.g., joyful revival crowds, ecstatic pentecostal congregations, or reverent gatherings awaiting the appearance of a virgin saint) and of profane crowd joys (e.g., partisan sports spectators, reveling carnival participants, or celebrants of a war's end) provides a salutary balance. Explicitly noting the illusion of unanimous emotion within crowds, Lofland specifies some of the dimensions along which displays of elementary collective emotion could (and do) vary within any crowd: the number, the complexity, and the intensity of overt motor activities; the proportion of the crowd displaying those actions; and the continuity and linkages across separate sequences of emotional display. Despite Lofland's repeated acknowledgment of the illusion of unanimity, it is very difficult for him to avoid sliding into that illusion. It is even more difficult to avoid an illusion of continuity, a point to which I shall return.

Forms of Collective Protest. Lofland divides political activity into three categories: polite (i.e., conventional) politics; violent (e.g., terrorist) politics; and the middle ground of protest politics. Following Sharp (1973), Lofland distinguishes between *symbolic protest* (e.g., rallying, marching, picketing, or vigiling demonstrations), *noncooperation protest* (e.g., slowdowns, strikes, or boycotts), *intervention protest* (e.g., harassing, overloading, blockading, or occupying), and *alternative institution protest* (e.g., communes).

Lofland has studied two forms of symbolic protest at some length. He calls the first *crowd lobbying,* that is, "the lobbying organization tactic of circumspectly assembling large numbers of its grass roots constituency at governmental centers for the purpose of promoting policy preferences in direct contacts with officials, a combination of polite politics and protest intervention" (1982a:i). Crowd lobbies combine politics with protest politics. They are "polite" by virtue of their indoor locations, their use of dignified settings, and their constrained forms of expression. But they draw upon what Lofland insightfully notes as "the special meanings of crowds, per se; [that is,] any reasonably large number of gathered humans sends messages that are not entirely transmittable by any other device of social struggle" (1982a:6). The very presence of the collection of people makes their message both personal and powerful; their shared status characteristics make their message a concrete embodiment of the abstract category they represent, for example, "the steelworkers *are here,*" and the "common fear" that the "crowd might 'turn [people] on' who are not its members" (1982a:6) makes the collective message vaguely threatening. [18] Lofland observed three major subtypes at the California state capitol: *crowd cryptolobbies* (for example, meetings of statewide chamber of commerce members in the capital city were used as occasions for exchanges with legislators on "matters of mutual interest"); *emergency crowd mobilizations* (for example, packing a legislative hearing room in which a related issue is under discussion); and, the highly planned, prepared, and programmed *annual assemblies* (for example, a periodic gathering of a state realtors' association received association position briefings and lobby packets, addresses from legislative leaders, luncheon visits and photographs with legislative members, and individual visits with their own district legislative representatives.

The second form of protest investigated by Lofland (Lofland and Fink 1982:vii) is *the symbolic sit-in*, that is, "protest occupations or 'seizures' of places or spaces that draw on the ideology, rhetoric and posture of historic sit-ins but which lack the classic, additional earmarks of those actions; namely, true disruption of the settings in which they occur, an atmosphere of crisis, the threat of (and actual) violence, and extensive involvement by bystanders and other third parties" (Lofland and Fink 1982:vii). Lofland and Fink provide detailed descriptions of five variations of symbolic sit-ins: the lone-in, the long-term vigil, the one-night stand, spirited sieges, and pack-ins.[19]

It is clear that Lofland initially used forms of collective behavior primarily to refer to the crowd as a unit of analysis. This has the advantage of encompassing a larger unit of space over a longer unit of time and thereby enabling the characterization or description of some forms of collective phenomena that might not otherwise be possible. But it has the disadvantage of succumbing to the illusions of unanimity and continuity of crowd behavior. Lofland was not oblivious to these problems, as indicated by his examination of specific but varied forms of political protest within protest crowds. Further, he subsequently adopted the concept of gatherings rather than crowds as a unit of analysis. Finally, and perhaps most important, he proposed a continuum of units of analysis of protest actions and gatherings that has great potential for transcending the illusions of unanimity and continuity.

Gatherings versus Crowds. Lofland (1985) abandoned the concept of crowd in favor of the concept of gathering, a shift initially suggested by Goffman (1963) and later advocated by McPhail (1972, 1978; McPhail and Wohlstein 1983). As noted above, gatherings simply refer to a number of people in the same place at the same time. Lofland notes three consequences of using this "at once obvious and obscure notion of 'the gathering' as [a] key starting point" (1985:31). He writes: "Again following McPhail, the concept of "the crowd" drops out for several reasons:

> (1) It is too general, abstract, and vague to serve as a unit of human association.
> (2) It carries too much excess conceptual baggage, such as "the illusion of unanimity."
> (3) Most important, it is the central concept of the classic "collective behaviorist" tradition descended from LeBon's [1895] *The Crowd* with all the emotional baggage of irrationality, irritability, excess, fickleness, and violence. (1985:31)

The third point has received more than sufficient attention by now. The first two points are far more important, in particular, the question of what may be a useful unit of human association. Recognizing the varied complexities of human association that challenge the interests of sociologists at different of levels of analysis, Lofland set forth a cumulative continuum of analytical units.

Units and Levels of Analysis

In the introduction to his (1985) collected essays on crowds and movements, Lofland identified and briefly discussed "six units of reference" for the student of protest action. *These units consist "of progressively more complex, populated, and temporally prolonged series of actions"* (1985:3; emphasis added):

- *acts:* which Lofland explicitly limits to "specific, circumscribed acts of *individuals"* (1985:3; emphasis added)
- *gatherings:* "a large number of people in the same place at the same time . . . as in marches, rallies, pickets, sit-ins, riots, stormings, and so forth" (1985:13).
- *events:* "gatherings combined with organized action carried out over weeks, months, or slightly longer, make up protest events, as in a boycott, strike, or vigil" (1985:3)
- *campaigns:* "an interrelated series of . . . protest events taking place over some months . . . as in the one guided by Martin Luther King Jr. and centered on Selma, Alabama in the spring of 1965" (1985:3).
- *waves:* "a series of campaigns focused on a common objective and taking place over many months in diverse locales, reaches the level of a protest wave, as in the sit-down strike wave of industrial workers in 1936–1937 and the sit-ins of civil rights activists of 1960–1961" (1985:3).[20]
- *cycles:* following Tarrow (1983), Lofland here refers to "some few waves combined with other waves in periods of a 'general heightening of social conflict' and the invention of 'new weapons . . . of protest' that diffuse through several sectors of the public arena" (1985:3).[21]

It is instructive for the student of nonprotest collective phenomena to identify analogs for each of these units of analysis in other arenas. One example is provided by the *wave* of "streaking" (that is, running naked through public places) that spread over many U.S. college communities over a period of several weeks in the spring of 1974 (Evans and Miller 1975; Aguirre, Quarantelli, and Mendoza 1988).[22] That wave consisted of college community level *campaigns* (Anderson 1977) in which, over a period of two or three days, various student residential groups (both independents and fraternities/sororities) literally competed with one another for the largest, longest, and most novel form and location of streaking in that community campaign. Those campaigns were sometimes composed of multiple gatherings connected in spatial-temporal sequence and thus constituted streaking *events* (e.g., nude parades passing through and proceeding to other stationary gatherings of clothed and nude persons themselves witness to and participants in a variety of repetitious and novel forms of streaking.) On still other occasions, streaking occurred within or by single *gatherings*.

But at the level of the *gathering*, however, Lofland's continuum requires expansion. On my campus at least, the gatherings consisted of spectators who were intermittently silent, then laughing at, then applauding and cheering various participants who intermittently engaged in the *sequences of individual action* (e.g., solitary nude runners, solitary nude horseback riders, solitary nude motorcycle riders, solitary nude wheelchair operators, solitary nude flagpole climbers/handstanders), interspersed with numerous *sequences of collective action* (e.g., nude cancan lines atop buildings, nude conga and bunny-hop lines snaking across the center campus quadrangle, smaller clusters of four or five nude friends and acquaintances running together, and occasional nude pairs pushing/riding in grocery carts. (Field notes, C. McPhail, Urbana, IL., March 7 and 8, 1974.) Lofland notes the former (i.e., sequences of individual action) but not the latter (i.e., sequences of collective action); moreover, his definition of collective behavior is inadequate to the task of characterizing or describing those sequences.

A Definition of Collective Behavior

In Chapter 5 I discuss the advantages and limitations of the various definitions of collective behavior advanced by scholars over the past 65 years. Several of those problems are manifest in Lofland's definition of collective behavior, "the idealized profile of [which is 1] the unanimous and maximum suspension of the attitude of everyday life in a collectivity, combined with [2] uniform and maximal emotional arousal, and [3] universally adopted [4] extraordinary activities" (1981:413–414, 1985:29–34).

To his credit, Lofland recognizes that each of his criteria can range from partial to widespread manifestation in a collectivity. The problem is what Lofland includes and excludes. First, and most problematic, he includes elements of his explanation of collective behavior (e.g., "the attitude of everyday life," or definition of the situation) in the criteria by which he defines collective behavior. Such amalgams fail to describe and they lend themselves to tautological explanations. Second, Lofland's definition excludes ordinary social behaviors, implying that routine social life need not be treated as a problem to be explained, and further implying a discontinuity of routine and nonroutine social phenomena as well as the requirement for different explanations. Third, whether emotions or behaviors are involved, whether they are extraordinary or ordinary, Lofland's definition does not include criteria for judging when two or more persons can be said to engage in those phenomena together, that is, collectively. None of these problems are addressed by the distinction Lofland draws between collective behavior (as defined above) and "collected behavior," that is "the occasion of a number of people being in the same place at the same time acting together under some encompassing definition of the situation" (1985:3). By what criteria can we say that they act together and what are the forms that such action take?

Changing in Explanations

I am in complete agreement with Lofland that it is futile to debate competing explanations in the absence of a useful specification of the phenomena to be explained. I am less confident than Lofland that existing explanations, e.g., contagion, convergence, emergent-norm, and rational-calculus views, are up to the task of explaining the varied and alternating individual and collective actions within gatherings, not to mention the gatherings themselves, the events they make up, the campaigns of events and gatherings that may develop, and the waves that sometimes result therefrom.

Although Lofland may have fewer reservations than I do about existing theories, he is well aware of their limitations and that students of collective behavior are revising not only their units and levels of analysis but their explanations as well. Lofland writes:

> The aborning shift I have described is one of the more recent and technical-scholarly manifestations of the larger and longer-term trend in collective behavior which stresses its similarity to ordinary life along such dimensions as viewing its participants as rational rather than irrational, acting in solidarity rather than in atomized disorganization (a [stress upon] "build-up" versus . . . "break down"), obeying (emergent) norms rather than breaking out of the bonds of control, creating new organization rather than reacting to its lack, pursuing goals and policies rather than goal-less tension-release and expressive emotionality. (1985:32)

An Assessment

Lofland's call for renewed attention to *emotions* is an extremely important contribution. He also calls for the integration of cognitive, behavioral, and emotional dimensions of collective phenomena. Not only can they be integrated, they must be integrated. Cognition, behavior, and emotion are potentially connected in every purposive action in which human beings engage. Individuals invariably evaluate their purposive actions as achieving or falling short of the goal to which they were directed; they evaluate the circumstances in which those actions occur, including the actions of others, as either facilitating or thwarting the achievement of their goal. These evaluations are frequently displayed as the emotions of happiness or disappointment or anger about the outcomes, or of uncertainty or fear about prospective outcomes. When two or more individuals share the same purposes, and when their own behaviors or their representatives' behaviors realize those goals, we often see collective displays of joy. When their behaviors or their representatives' behaviors fall short of the goals, we often see collective displays of disappointment. When goals are deliberately thwarted by others, we may see collective displays of anger. When the prospects of injury or death loom in the offing, when the goals of health and life are imminently threatened, we may see collective displays of fear.

I examine this cycle of cognition, behavior, and emotion again in Chapter 6, but one point should be noted here. Since thoughtful goals, the behaviors required to achieve them, and the evaluations of the relationships between goals and behaviors change across time, so too will change the emotional displays of those evaluations. Thus, variation and discontinuity of emotions are more likely than unanimity and continuity. With rare exceptions, to speak of the joyful crowd, the hostile crowd, or the fearful crowd is likely to exaggerate the unanimity and continuity of emotions displayed. The constituent individual and collective sequences of cognition, behavior, and evaluation may be the more appropriate units and levels of analysis at which to assess emotions within and by the gathering.

Lofland's specification of a continuum of formal units of analysis can become an extraordinarily valuable tool for students of gatherings and collective action. These analytic *forms* can be applied to a wide range of substantively different phenomena, for example, new chants and gestures and tactics in political gatherings, events, campaigns, and waves; new vocalizations and gestures such as glossolalia in religious gatherings, events, campaigns, and waves; and new chants and gestures such as "the wave" in sports gatherings.

The primary shortcoming in Lofland's taxonomic continuum is at the lower end. Gatherings are composed of varied and intermittent sequences of individual and collective actions, not merely the "specific, circumscribed acts of individuals" (1985:3). Only by acknowledging this variation in individual and collective action across the space and time frame of the gathering can one avoid the illusions of unanimity and continuity. To his credit, Lofland abandoned the concept of the crowd for the gathering and he recognizes that gatherings are composed of actions. But they are composed of individual actions and collective actions; unfortunately, Lofland's criteria for *collective* do not help us address that fact.

Lofland restricts *collective behavior* to what he alleges to be extraordinary, although he offers no criteria for distinguishing between the ordinary and the extraordinary, let alone between sequences of individual and collective behavior. It is an empirical question whether there is more individual than collective action, and whether there is more ordinary than extraordinary action. Those questions can and must be answered, but not until conceptual and operational criteria are offered by which to make the necessary empirical judgments. To repeat my earlier question: By what criteria can we say that people act together and what are the forms that such action takes?

There is yet another reason for rejecting "the extraordinary" as the defining characteristic of collective behavior. For many years collective behavior languished in the "back wards" of sociology, a circumstance that has stunted its theoretical development and its systematic empirical study. Over the past two decades many sociologists have called for, and some argue there is a perceptible trend in the direction of, examining the similarities of and continuities between collective behavior and ordinary social behavior in everyday life. The accumulating evidence favors this stance, as do most contemporary students of collective behavior.[23]

Moving Ahead

This chapter concludes a review of the principal twentieth-century theories of crowds and collective behavior. All have posed some important problems, even if their proposed solutions were often conceptually or empirically flawed. Virtually all their proposed solutions were methodologically flawed; that is, most proceeded to develop explanations of the crowd or collective action without first specifying the range of behaviors to be explained and indicating to which subset of those phenomena their explanations applied. Future theoretical and empirical work should not repeat that mistake.

The early social psychologists and sociologists were concerned only with explaining the individual's behavior in the crowd; subsequent scholars have offered explanations for how two or more persons fit together sequences of collective behavior within gatherings; and a few have even recognized that sequences of individual and collective action occur intermittently within the gathering. Still others have been concerned with the gathering itself as a unit of analysis. Last but not least, we must not ignore Lofland's "progressively more populated, complex and prolonged forms" of collective action—events, campaigns, waves, and cycles—which are composed of the gatherings that consist of sequences of individual and collective action. No one of these units or levels of analysis of collective action can be defended as more important than another. The description and explanation of each derives from or contributes to the others.

One of the most important but often unstated assumptions in the social and behavioral sciences is that every theory of the social presumes some theory of the individual, and vice versa. Thus, explanations of individual and collective action assume some model of a larger social system, just as theories of society and theories of social behavior assume some model of individual actors.

There is no consensus on any one theoretical model of the individual actor that emerges from the contemporary theories of collective behavior and collective action reviewed here, but two things seem clear. The archaic notion of crowds composed of individuals possessed of or driven by simple and sovereign motives is not sufficient to explain the complexities of intermittent individual and collective action. Second, and almost without exception, contemporary students of collective phenomena assume some model of a rational individual actor, albeit one whose cognitions involve more than mere minimax calculations. But, having said this, it must be emphasized that rational actors are not emotionless actors. Contemporary scholars have simply abandoned the naive traditional assumption of individual or collective actors driven by some single emotion. What remains to be specified are the sequential connections between rational cognition, action, and the displays of emotion that often follow.

Rational actors are not controlled by predispositions or tendencies to behave; they organize their actions to achieve their goals; they sometimes act in common or in concert with one another. They are more likely to do both intermittently, than either one continuously or exclusively. Because of this fact, we are confronted with two fundamental problems, which must be addressed if we are to move beyond the myth of the madding crowd. Students of collective phenomena must specify the range of collective actions to be explained; and they must develop an explanation that can account for individual and collective action with the same set of principles. I turn to the first problem in Chapter 5 and to the second in Chapter 6.

Notes

1.   Students of collective action (e.g., Tilly 1978:158–9) who champion rational, purposive action are at the same time wary of spontaneity's antithetical stereotype: conspiracy. The truth probably lies somewhere between. For any sizable gathering to form there must be some interaction among some of the members who therein call the attention of one another to, and perhaps propose or invite convergence on, the site of an impromptu celebration (McPhail and Miller 1973), an arrest, fight, fire, or accident (McPhail and Bailey 1979), or even a riot in progress (Singer 1970). But in each of these cases there were multiple sites vs. one single central site of interaction and proposals, and this could be true for other impromptu political gatherings and protest actions (Quarantelli and Hundley 1969). For any sizable, sustained, and complex collective political action, however, some central planning, preparation, and organization is more likely (McPhail 1985).

2.   Couch cites Turner's assertion that "normal social control is effective largely because the individual is known and identified and held responsible for his actions" (1964a:386). To and by whom is the individual known, identified, and held account-

able? In political demonstrations (McPhail 1985) as in most other temporary gatherings (Aveni 1977; Miller 1973), individuals do not assemble alone but with family, friends, or acquaintances; sometimes, individuals assemble with their companions within even larger units of social organization, e.g., neighborhood, community, or regional chapters, committees, and associations. It is to those primary and secondary groups within demonstration gatherings that the individual is known, identified, and held responsible for his or her actions, and not to outsiders in general or authorities in particular.

3. Alinsky (1972) argued that what is rational is relative. Rationality must always be situated in space and time and viewed from the vantage point of the actors in the arena rather than from the perspective of status quo authorities, let alone the perspective of persons even further removed.

4. Compliance with another's suggestions is ubiquitous among acquaintances. Workers comply with their employers' suggestions, students with their teachers', and children with their parents'. Sociologists attribute their compliance not to suggestibility but to asymmetrical power-dependency relationships.

People in problematic situations may be more open to suggestions from strangers. Swanson (1953) demonstrates that individuals who have not previously worked together and who have no prior experience with a problem are much more receptive to strangers' suggestions than are those individuals who have previously worked together on a problem (cf. Sherif 1936; Sherif and Harvey 1952).

5. Even Couch remarks on the inexperience if not inability of the lower-class individuals to organize collective action. Given his own working-class origins, Couch would be the first to agree that most lower-class individuals have considerable experience with organizations; however, they are more likely to have experience as the objects or targets of organizing, whereas middle-class individuals have experience as the subjects or agents of organizing.

6. Couch is probably wrong when he claims that "the formation of crowds and other protesting collectivities depends upon a plurality having common dissatisfying experiences" (1968:319). Even if a plurality of participants is dissatisfied, it is unlikely that dissatisfaction distinguishes them from nonparticipants (cf. McPhail 1971; and Chapter 2).

7. One exception may be the rock concert audience members standing in a high-density gathering, perhaps singing, swaying, or gesturing collectively with the music, throughout the concert. The individual's immediate neighbor(s) are likely family, friends, or acquaintances but the high density prevents them from turning face-to-face and the noise precludes much conversation. The extent to which these physical circumstances are approximated in other settings is an empirical question. I suspect they are exceptional; I am confident they are not the rule.

8. I have tried to simplify, clarify, and render consistent the conceptual apparatus with which Couch and colleagues refer to their dimensions of association. The concepts I have used here are followed in parentheses by those used in Miller, Hintz, and Couch (1975; cf. Couch 1984): mutual availability (mutual availability or copresence); mutual attention (reciprocally acknowledged attention); mutual responsiveness (mutual responsiveness); mutual futures (congruent functional identities); mutual focus (shared focus).

9. Miller, Hintz, and Couch (1975; Couch, 1984) distinguish between the proposal of collective action (mutual futures) regarding some third object (mutual focus) and the nature of the collective action (mutual or shared objective) that is proposed, i.e., who will do what, when, where, and how. I have lumped mutual futures and objectives together as mutual futures.

10.   The fact that others (cf. McPhail and Wohlstein 1986) have experimentally manipulated similar conceptual elements with similar results adds credibility to both efforts.

11.   What is implicit here is the implication that collective behavior refers to the ubiquitous phenomenon of social influence in every aspect of everyday social life and not just to the crowd. If my interpretation is correct, then Berk joins a long list of sociologists who construe collective behavior as an explanatory variable rather than as something that people do together and therefore as a social phenomenon to be explained.

12.   Food riots are frequently misunderstood. They were a frequent form of collective action between 1750 and 1850 but they more frequently involved grain than edible food, they seldom escalated to violence, and they ordinarily took one of three forms, none of which correspond to popular stereotypes: Sometimes citizens attacked individuals or merchants thought to be hoarding or profiteering from grain. They often seized the grain, sold it publicly for what was considered a fair price, and then returned the funds to the individual or merchant. Even more frequently, local citizens blocked the shipment of grains from their own locality to other regions or cities (Tilly 1975, 1978:185).

13.   A useful history of strikes, strikebreaking, and violence in the United States is provided by Taft and Ross (1968:270–376).

14.   Tilly's diverse but specific examples of these taxonomic distinctions derive from a three-decade search of thousands of national daily newspapers in France, Italy, Germany, England, and the United States from 1750 to the present for examples of contentious gatherings and collective actions. Newspaper reporters were and are more likely to identify the groups or formations present in a gathering, their claims, and the collective form of claim making than they were and are to specify other sequences of individual and collective action that compose the larger portion of the temporary gathering in question.

Nonetheless, Tilly's coding procedures are impressive with regard to the specific identification of various *formations* (groups or sets of individuals who act together or interact with another formation) and the various action-phases in which they engaged. Tilly codes the latter in terms of action verbs that appear in newspaper accounts.

15.   McAdam (1983) documents the new and shifting tactics of the civil-rights movement from 1960 to 1965 in response to the successful thwarting of their earlier tactics by targeted governments and their agents of social control.

16.   The historical record should come as no surprise: state agents of social control do most of the killing and most of the violence against persons; whatever violence demonstrators engage in is more frequently directed to property.

17.   One critical caveat here. Lofland frequently uses the word *panic* and cites several anecdotal accounts and theoretical explanations of it. Regrettably he references neither the early (e.g., Quarantelli 1954, 1957, 1960) nor the more recent (Sime 1980) critiques of *panic*. This misbegotten concept implies incapacitating fear, crippled cognition, and uncontrolled flight in the face of life-threatening danger, implications that are *not* supported by evidence from numerous systematic studies of evacuation behavior in disasters (Wenger, Dykes, Sebok, and Neff 1975), fires (Canter 1980; Bryan 1981, 1982), and other problematic situations (Johnson 1987a,b). Although the emotion of fear is quite real, it *is* a variable. Fear rarely incapacitates to the extent of crippling cognition or causing loss of control. Flight behavior is more often orderly than disorderly; choices are rationally calculated within problematic situations, although perceptions of escape routes and exits can be distorted by poor

visibility and audibility; and deaths result more frequently from asphyxiation than from mindless actions or fear-filled immobility. In short, *panic* is neither a useful description or explanation; the concept should be expunged from the language of social and behavioral science.

18.   Lofland here implies the LeBon-Park-Blumer view that the combined presence, behavior, intensity, and emotion of the crowd are sufficiently powerful and overwhelming that in one fell contagious swoop those forces might spread to, capture, and "turn-on" onlookers and passersby. I suspect that Lofland does not share this transformation interpretation but is merely attributing it to commonsense thinking about and fear of the crowd.

19.   I have arrayed Lofland's five variations from large to small gatherings. Lofland and Fink (1982) also consider variations in *duration* (from hours to days) and in what they term *flex level*, a promising concept that warrants further development. Lofland's flex level refers to a variation in the overall intensity of behavior in the gathering: in low flex, participants are simply sitting, reading, chatting, sleeping, and waiting; moderate flex might involve interviews between protestors and media crews, or a meeting between a subset of protestors and authorities, or perhaps a discussion meeting among the protestors; and high flex might involve a noisy debate between the gathering of protestors and authorities, or singing and/or chanting and/or marching "crowds" of protestors).

20.   Lofland provides a very useful account of four waves of sit-in interventions. Morris (1981) and McAdam (1982) provide the definitive empirical studies of the wave of community sit-in campaigns that spread across the southeastern United States in February and March of 1960.

21.   McAdam's (1983) analysis of tactical innovations in the civil-rights movement provides an excellent illustration of cycles of protest. The basic idea is that once a new tactic (whether it be sequences of individual and collective action, gatherings, events, or event campaigns) has been introduced and is successful, the tactic becomes an exemplar that others elsewhere adopt to use in their own local struggles (cf. Tilly 1978:155). Similar adoptions are repeated; their spread across space and time creates a wave. When status quo authorities devise a way of absorbing or repressing the tactic (or participants can otherwise no longer sustain it), the wave subsides. Thus, the beginning, middle, and ending of one cycle of protest (campaigns, events, gatherings, sequences of collective and individual action, etc.) transpire. After a period of time a new tactic is developed, and a new cycle begins. McAdam (1983) demonstrates this for sit-ins, ride-ins, jail-ins, and community campaigns.

22.   A second example is the Ghost Dance Movement that spread across Native American Plains tribes in 1890 (Mooney 1965). The Ghost Dance was a form of collective action that involved a number of people dancing together in a continuous moving circle. This sequence of collective action was interspersed with other individual and collective actions that made up the religious ceremonial gatherings, the events, and the campaigns of which the wave was composed. Wevoka, the Paiute messiah whose mountaintop vision had revealed the divine imperative for the ritual, sent the following message to other tribes: "When you get home you must make a dance to continue five days. Dance four successive nights, and the last night keep up the dance until the morning of the fifth day, when all must bathe in the river and then disperse to their homes. You must all do in the same way. . . . I want you to dance every six weeks. Make a feast at the dance, and have food that everybody may eat. Then bathe in the water. That is all. You will receive good words again from me some time" (translated by Mooney 1965:23). See Landsman (1978) for a social organization explanation of the spread of the Ghost Dance across Plains tribes.

23.   Lofland (personal communication, March 1990) takes exception to my rejection of the extraordinary as a defining characteristic of collective behavior. I do not retreat from my conviction that we should be concerned with continuities and similarities in forms of social behavior across all manner of temporary gatherings rather than continuing to celebrate the unspecified bizarre nature of collective behavior.

Lofland argues that his concern with the extraordinary is a concern with departures from the ordinary, not a concern with the bizarre. I agree that concerns with the extraordinary are perfectly legitimate concerns; however, one must first offer criteria for establishing ordinary social or collective action of behavior before one can mark extraordinary departures and examine their consequences (cf. note 7, Chapter 6).

5

What Phenomena Are to be Explained?

Introduction

> Although the demarcation of [the objects of study] is not an end in itself, and is not so intriguing as the inquiry into causes and consequences of collective behavior, it is of prime importance. Before we can pose questions of explanation, we must be aware of the character of the phenomena we wish to explain. (Smelser 1963:5)

The wisdom of this earlier counsel notwithstanding, students of collective behavior have persisted in their preoccupation with developing explanations to the exclusion of establishing the phenomena to be explained. This misplaced priority is not without its costs nor, as Robert K. Merton (1987) recently reminds us, is it unique to the study of collective behavior.[1]

These misplaced priorities in the study of collective behavior have resulted in developing explanations for phenomena that rarely occur, ignoring the description and explanation of the forms of collective behavior that occur most frequently in temporary gatherings. Some sociologists even regard collective behavior as a type of explanation rather than as phenomena to be explained.

But even if everyone agreed on these priorities for where investigations should begin, it is unlikely they would agree on what to describe and explain. Some scholars study what people do within gatherings; others study variations across gatherings; others study strings or campaigns of gatherings; others study the spread or waves of collective behavior, of gatherings, or of campaigns across regions or nations; and others study the cyclical rise and fall of some or all these collective phenomena across longer periods of time. In short, there are a number of legitimate but nonetheless quite different interests in different units of analysis at different levels of analysis. But we cannot develop explanations for any of those phenomena until we have first specified, observed, and described what is to be explained.

In this chapter I examine a wide range of sociological concerns with what people do collectively, and with some of the relationships between those different units and levels of analysis. I begin with a discussion of the sociological birthright of collective behavior and call attention to the continuum of social forms that were Park's initial referents for the phenomena to be explained. Second, I examine traditional and contemporary sociological definitions of collective behavior and their limitations. Third, I discuss the life cycle of temporary gatherings: assembling processes, the assembled gathering (within which a variety of forms of collective behavior may occur), and dispersal processes. Fourth, I offer an alternative definition of collective behavior and identify 40 elementary forms that have been the focus of my own and other colleagues' field research in a wide range of gatherings over the past 20 years. Fifth, I examine some relationships between the different units and levels of analysis with which students of collective behavior have been concerned: the sequences of individual and collective behavior within gatherings, the sequences of gatherings that constitute events, the gatherings and events that constitute campaigns within communities and waves across regions, and, the cycles of gatherings, events, campaigns, and waves that rise and fall across time.

The Sociological Birthright of Collective Behavior

For many sociologists collective behavior has become a pejorative term that evokes one of two images. One image is that collective behavior is a class of explanations (cf. Gamson 1975:130–136) more than a class of social behaviors to be explained. The collective behavior explanation is that people are transformed by the madding crowd, therefore lose control over their own behavior, and engage in behaviors quite different from those in which they ordinarily engage. Another explanation is that people flock together because of similar psychological or ideological predispositions, which also compel them to engage in behaviors within the crowd that correspond to their madness-in-common. In both explanations, collective behavior is construed as primarily a psychological phenomenon and an unacceptable one at that.

A second image of collective behavior alludes to a residual category of social epiphenomena—fads, crowds, crazes—that do not easily fit into the various sociological schema, and are therefore considered trivial and inconsequential problems on the sociological agenda.

It is not difficult to understand why these two images have led many sociologists to view collective behavior in a negative manner. It is ironic that the sociologist who formulated the concept of collective behavior to refer to a continuum of fundamental sociological phenomena to be explained was also a major contributor to the development of a psychological explanation for those phenomena. When the majority of sociologists eventually rejected that psychological explanation, they also abandoned, unfortunately in my view, the sociological phenomena to be explained.

Robert Ezra Park was a student of Simmel. Park was therefore concerned with establishing the fundamental *forms* of social life. His doctoral dissertation (1904) examined the crowd as one "basic form of sociological entity." Park placed the crowd within an array of social forms along a continuum of collective behavior. "The most elementary form of collective behavior seems to be what is ordinarily referred to as social unrest" (Park and Burgess 1921:874). Further along that continuum he placed the implicitly more complex social forms of the crowd, mass movements, and, finally, social institutions.

I do not claim here the discovery of some long overlooked but implicit definition and taxonomy in Park's writings. Indeed, such specification is conspicuously absent from his work. Rather, my point is that at the outset, Park characterized the crowd and collective behavior as sociological and not psychological phenomena. The crowd was construed as one elementary form on a continuum ranging from very simple to increasingly complex forms of collective behavior. Unfortunately, Park provided neither a working definition of collective behavior nor a delineation of its forms and variations. He did offer a definition, but his emphasis was upon explanatory factors and not upon the phenomena to be explained. Park and Burgess defined collective behavior as "the behavior of individuals under the influence of an impulse that is common and collective" (1921:865). Park then turned right around and drew on those same common impulses to explain the collective behavior the impulses had defined. Park's failure to separate the phenomena from the explanation yielded a bad definition and a bad explanation. Such conceptual mergers always generate circular explanations and they provide neither specification nor description of the phenomena to be explained. Park's particular conceptual merger may have led many scholars to dismiss collective behavior as a legitimate *sociological* phenomena to be explained at the same time they rejected Park's *psychological* explanation for collective behavior as both ideologically repugnant and empirically false.

While Park's characterizations of the crowd and collective behavior were never as negative or pathological as LeBon's, Park's explanation for these phenomena was virtually the same. Individuals were treated as the victims of psychological transformation. Individuals were construed as irrational and uncritical pawns of a common impulse that derived from the condition of social unrest that dominated and directed their behavior within the crowd. This psychological transformation explanation of LeBon's and Park's was subsequently adopted, expanded, and perpetuated by Herbert Blumer (1939).

The LeBon-Park-Blumer transformation hypothesis was sociology's prevailing explanation for the crowd and collective behavior until the 1960s, when it was finally subjected to extensive critical scrutiny and empirical examination.[2] Too many students (Turner 1964a; Couch 1968; McPhail 1969; Milgram and Toch 1969; Berk 1974b) found too many flaws in the psychological transformation hypothesis. The result was near categorical rejection (but see Lang and Lang 1961; Klapp 1972; Zimbardo 1969; Diener 1980). Moreover, the critics rejected the reactionary political implications of an explanation that impugned the rational capacities of individuals engaged in protest against and demands for changes in the status quo (cf. Bramson 1961; Currie and Skolnick 1970; Gamson 1975). Regrettably, the rejection of the LeBon-Park-Blumer psychological explanation for collective behavior was tantamount to the repudiation of collective behavior as a legitimate sociological phenomenon to be explained.[3]

The concept of collective behavior has a legitimate sociological birthright. The phenomena to which it refers warrant serious examination as elementary but fundamental forms of social life. To reclaim these phenomena as worthy objects for sociological study is not to embrace the traditional psychological explanations nor the ideological biases of early scholars. Rather, it is a call for the study of a continuum of sociological phenomena ranging from the formation of temporary gatherings, to sequences of collective behavior within gatherings, to variations in the sociological complexity of gatherings, to the sequences of gatherings that constitute events, to the gatherings and events that constitute the local campaigns, the regional and national waves, of which cycles are composed. It is therefore a call to pursue with greater specificity the task that Park abandoned.

The focus of this chapter is primarily on sequences of collective behavior that occur within gatherings. But I will also attempt to show the how that focus provides a means for characterizing variations across gatherings and will thereby attempt to forge a relationship between my concerns and those of colleagues who are primarily concerned with gatherings, events, campaigns, waves, and cycles of collective phenomena (cf. Lofland 1985). To place my concerns with collective behavior sequences within in a somewhat broader context, I will discuss first the life cycle of gatherings.

The Life Cycle of Temporary Gatherings

Many sociologists speak of the crowd and collective behavior interchangeably. Indeed, many think of the two as synonymous. This is unfortunate. Just as the concept of collective behavior has specified too little, the concept of the crowd has implied too much. The concept of the crowd conveys an image of homogeneity and continuity of behavior. But many crowds never engage in homogeneous or mutually inclusive behavior and, no crowd does so continuously. Thus, the crowd should not be equated with homogeneous behavior; it merely provides an opportunity for such behavior to occur. I prefer the alternative concept of gathering, i.e., a collection of two or more persons in a common place in space and time. Gatherings are opportunities for collective behavior; they do not guarantee it.[4] I will defer until the following section an examination of what sociologists have meant by collective behavior. The important point here is that gatherings lend themselves to, but must not be equated with, people behaving collectively. And even when collective behavior occurs, it is seldom mutually inclusive, it is rarely complex, and it is never continuous.

Neither are gatherings. They are temporary. People come together; their gatherings have lifespans of shorter or longer duration; then people disperse. Unlike human settlements and total institutions, the gatherings addressed in this chapter are temporary.

There are three phases in the life cycle of temporary gatherings: the assembling process, the assembled gathering, and, the dispersal process. Assembling processes vary in the extent of space and amount of time over which they develop. They vary in the number of people who participate. Some are periodic; some ad hoc. But all share the essential feature that two or more people move from different locations in space at time one to a common location in space at time two (McPhail and Miller 1973).

Dispersal processes also vary. The vast majority are *routine dispersals* and unproblematic. That may be the main reason they have been studied so seldom and that we know so little [but cf. Pauls (1977, 1980)]. Some problematic dispersal processes have been studied extensively. I refer to *emergency dispersals* from buildings, stadiums, and communities in the wake of bomb threats, explosions, fires, chemical spills, nuclear meltdowns, tornadoes, hurricanes, floods, etc. (Quarantelli 1981; Quarantelli and Dynes, 1977; Drabeck 1968; Bryan 1981, 1982). A third class of dispersals falls somewhere between the routine and the emergency in the amount of work that has been done and the resulting amount of information. I refer here to *coerced dispersals* by police, the military, or other agents of social control. With few exceptions (e.g., Lohman 1947; Bayley 1976; Erickson and Flynn 1980), most of what we know derives from the work of social-control agents (Applegate 1969; Thornton 1971; Vandall 1973) rather than social scientists. Routine, emergency, and coerced dispersal processes all entail the movement of two or more persons from a common place at time one to one or more different places at time two. In general, the dispersal process that brings the gathering to an end is the reverse of the assembling process responsible for its beginning.

Between assembling and dispersal is the gathering of two or more persons in a common location in space and time. Members of gatherings are engaged in ongoing sequences of individual behavior and may engage in one or more sequences of collective behavior. These sequences vary in content, form, complexity, duration, and the proportion of the gathering participating. The next two sections of this chapter will consider what sociologists have had to say about what constitutes collective behavior and about some variations in the content, form, complexity, duration, and participation in sequences of collective behavior.

Extant Definitions of Collective Behavior

My contention that collective behavior was initially construed as a sociological phenomenon is not to suggest a doctrine of inherent or intrinsic subject matter. Nothing is inherently sociological or intrinsically collective behavior. Assertions that some phenomena are truly collective behavior or that other phenomena are not really collective behavior at all are simply not defensible. The meanings of any phenomenon are all the responses ever made to it. But some responses are made more consistently than others. Consistent responses are established and stabilized by cultural and subcultural instructions for identifying and responding to phenomena. In the behavioral sciences, definitions are supposed to provide those instructions for response. They should provide criteria for identifying and differentiating the phenomena under investigation; unfortunately, they do not always do so (Miller, 1985).

Definitions are arbitrary. Whether they are good or bad depends on the extent to which they solve the problem at hand. Definitions that suffice for academic conceptual exercises may not hold up to empirical scrutiny in the field. Definitions judged useful by scholars working at a micro level of analysis are not always satisfactory to scholars working at a macro level of analysis, and vice versa.

My initial survey of the sociological literature on this matter was prompted by my attempt to observe and record behavior in demonstrations in the late 1960s and early 1970s. Our research group sought criteria that would help us systematically judge that two or more participants were behaving collectively. Examination of the sociological literature, then and now, yielded six different categories of definitions of collective behavior.

What Collective Behavior Is Not!   At least three distinguished scholars emphasized what collective behavior is not. Lang and Lang (1961:4) asserted it is neither structured nor organized behavior. Smelser contended (1963:11) it is not defined by physical, temporal, or psychological characteristics, nor by any unique type of interaction or communication among participants. Elsewhere (1964:117) he reiterated his contention that collective behavior is not institutionalized behavior. While such criteria may eliminate certain phenomena from consideration, they do not provide much help in recognizing or judging phenomena to be included. Negative criteria will not suffice. We require criteria to answer the question, How will we know collective behavior when we see it?

What Collective Behavior Is Not Caused By. A second group of definitions in the literature distinguished collective behavior with factors alleged *not* responsible for its occurrence. Blumer (1939, 1957) argued that collective behavior does not result from preestablished understandings or traditions, or from prior prescriptions or social definitions. Turner and Killian (1957:12) suggested that collective behavior occurs without guidance from the culture or from broader norms in the larger society. They further contended that it occurs without procedures for establishing membership, leadership, objectives, or decisions. Lang and Lang (1968:556) subsequently defined collective behavior as that which occurs in situations without adequate guides to conduct. All these criteria are problematic in at least two ways. Again, negative criteria do not tell us what to include. But, in addition, it is even more problematic to define a phenomenon in terms of what is alleged to be, or not to be, its cause. These problems are particularly evident in the next category of definitions.

What Collective Behavior Is Allegedly Caused By. One of the oldest and most common ways of defining collective behavior is with criteria or factors also used to explain the phenomena they define. Thus, as I have noted, Park and Burgess (1921) defined collective behavior in terms of common impulses that were also alleged responsible for such behavior. Blumer (1939:169) and the Langs (1961:4) defined collective behavior as "spontaneous behavior." Spontaneity, of course, is a kind of "immaculate causation" hypothesis, an assertion about the cause of the behavior. Turner and Killian (1957:12) defined collective behavior (and then subsequently explained it) in terms of "spontaneous" or "emergent norms." Turner subsequently characterized collective behavior as that which "arises and changes under the control of emergent normative definitions" (1964b:132). Turner and Killian also referred to collective behavior as an area of study in which groups are classified "according to the nature of the social norms that govern them" (1972:5). Turner and Killian now define collective behavior as "those forms of social behavior in which usual conventions cease to guide social action and people collectively transcend, bypass, or subvert established institutional patterns and structures. . . . Collective behavior refers to the actions of collectivities, not to a type of individual behavior" (1987:3).

I noted earlier that Smelser (1963) recognized the importance of establishing the phenomenon to be explained before proceeding to explain it. Nevertheless, he defined collective behavior as "mobilization on the basis of a belief which redefines social action" (1963:8), and he further identified and classified collective behavior as "purposive behavior in which people are trying to reconstitute their social environment on the basis of a generalized belief" (1964:117). Unfortunately, Smelser also used the generalized belief as a central component in his explanation of collective behavior.

There are fatal flaws with all attempts to define any phenomenon in terms of the same factors alleged to explain or produce it. First, they provide no useful information about the alleged causal or explanatory relationship. If collective behavior is defined in terms of X, one then judges that collective behavior has occurred when and only when X is present. But if X is also the alleged cause of collective behavior, one can only examine collective behavior when X is present, and vice versa. There is no possibility of observing collective behavior in the absence of X nor of observing X in the absence of collective behavior. There is always a perfect relationship between X and collective behavior. There can be no negative cases. It is a perfectly circular argument that can neither be confirmed nor refuted. It is therefore of limited utility.

Second, this strategy provides no information at all about the phenomenon to be explained. It abandons the standard procedure of scientific inquiry in which one first attempts to become familiar with the primary characteristics, with the range and variation, of the phenomenon to be explained. One then proceeds to locate or to devise or adopt an explanation that bears some logical correspondence to what one understands to be the characteristics of the phenomenon to be explained. But these advantages are lost if a scholar defines the phenomenon in terms of its alleged explanatory or causal factors. Others cannot know because the scholar cannot say, or at least does not say, what is to be explained. An explanation cannot be useful when it is not clear what is being explained!

Collective Behavior as Copresence.   Several students of collective behavior have suggested physical copresence or awareness of copresence as defining characteristics. Park (1904; Park and Burgess 1921) introduced analyses of collective behavior with the condition of "people coming together in the most casual or informal way," thereupon becoming aware of one another's presence. Turner and Killian (1957) made similar reference to people who are interacting and who sense that they "constitute a unit." Couch suggested that collective behavior occurs "when participants attend to the actions of each other and fit their actions together" (1970:459).

Although most of my field research has concerned forms of collective behavior by people who are in one another's presence, the copresence criterion excludes the assembling process that brings people together in the first place (McPhail and Miller 1973).[5] It also excludes many instances of mass behavior in which people collectively engage in the same behaviors at the same time although physically separated (e.g., Muslims' daily prayers). Finally, it excludes a growing number of instances where mass and gathering are electronically merged. I will return to this point below.

Collective Behavior as Social Behavior.   Blumer (1957), Turner and Killian (1957, 1972, 1987), and Weller and Quarantelli (1973) all referred to collective behavior as *group* behavior or the behavior of collectivities. Turner (1964), Couch (1970), Turner and Killian (1972, 1987), and Weller and Quarantelli (1973) also referred to *social* behavior and to *concerted* or *coordinated* or *cooperative* behavior. Lang and Lang (1961), Smelser (1964), Weller and Quarantelli (1973), and Perry and Pugh (1978) refer to social interaction or to social action.

There can be little objection to any of these adjectives provided those who use them attach criteria by which others can judge that group, social, concerted, or coordinated behavior or action has occurred. Each requires the specification of categories of behaviors in which people engage, and the criteria for judging when and how those behaviors can be said to be group, social, concerted, or coordinated.

Nothing of distinguishing value is gained here by substituting the concept of action for the concept of behavior. Collective action is often favored by those who criticize the collective behavior (explanatory) perspective (e.g., Gamson 1975). The use of the word *action*, as opposed to *behavior*, is usually accompanied by the assertion that action is purposive human conduct whereas behavior is merely mindless movement. This is another example of defining the phenomenon to be explained in terms of some element of its explanation.[6]

Collective Behavior as Extraordinary Social Behavior.   This final category of definitions includes a variety of efforts. One is the traditional and dubious practice of treating collective behavior as the residual category for all the unwieldy leftovers that fall between the cracks of conventional sociological concerns. Evans (1969:2) reports "the key historical element in collective behavior [has simply been] that any behavior that is *unusual* is by itself of interest, and its heuristic appeal is multiply enhanced if many people exhibit it—and in fact, these two criteria define the substance of the field" (1969:2; emphasis added).

More recently there have been some very deliberate efforts to forge definitions and/or taxonomies of extraordinary collective phenomena. Gary Marx (1980:270–271) defines collective behavior as group behavior that (1) is "new to the culture" (i.e., novel behavior); (2) is "prohibited or not supported by" the culture (i.e., taboo behavior); (3) "seeks goals which are not institutionalized" (i.e., anti–status quo behavior); or (4) "has a high degree of culturally sanctioned openness" (i.e., anything goes).

John Lofland pursues a similar line of reasoning. Acknowledging that collective behavior varies, Lofland suggests the "idealized [collective behavior] profile is unanimous and maximum suspension of the attitude of everyday life in a collectivity, combined with uniform and maximum emotional arousal, and universally adopted extraordinary activities" (1981:413–414).

The common denominator across these traditional and contemporary efforts is an emphasis upon the extraordinary substance if not the form of the behavior(s) in question. This, of course, raises a critical empirical question. Of all the behaviors within a gathering, what proportion are extraordinary and what proportion ordinary? To answer that question presumes answers to a series of prior questions. By what criteria are we to recognize or judge the presence of ordinary vs. extraordinary behaviors? By what criteria are we to judge either type of behavior collective rather than individual? Then and only then can we make a determination of the proportion of behaviors that yield the various combinations of ordinary, extraordinary, individual, and collective behaviors. The proponents of extraordinariness have not provided us with the conceptual tools with which to make the judgments required by their arguments.[7]

A Working Definition of Collective Behavior

Given the limitations of existing definitions of collective behavior, our research group required alternative criteria for judging and recording what we saw and heard people doing collectively in our direct observations of political, sports, and religious demonstrations and the prosaic gatherings we studied between 1967 and 1987.

After people assembled, some of them occasionally engaged in what we intuitively thought was social behavior. By social, we agreed with Wallace's judgment that the common denominator in virtually all theoretical definitions of social phenomena is "the regular accompaniment of the behavior of one organism by the behavior of one or more additional organisms" (1969:5; cf. 1983:14–15). The organisms of interest to us were human beings. They engaged in behaviors with or in relation to one another. But we still had to specify those behaviors in which we were interested and the criteria by which to judge variations in the accompaniment of those behaviors.

We attempted to answer two questions: What behaviors did we see and hear people engaging in "collectively" in the gatherings we were investigating? And, what were the bases for saying their behaviors were collective, that those behaviors accompanied one another? We combed our field notes, film, and audio records. We made lists of behaviors and dimensions on which to judge those behaviors collective. We reexamined our notes and records. We advanced a tentative specification of behaviors and dimensions. We observed more gatherings and repeated the same procedures. After several revisions we arrived at a reliable working definition to confront the problems with which we were concerned (cf. McPhail 1972, 1978; McPhail and Pickens 1975, 1981; Pickens 1975; Smith, McPhail, and Pickens 1975; Wohlstein 1977a,b; Wohlstein and McPhail 1979; McPhail and Wohlstein 1982, 1983, 1986). With but slight modification, that definition is repeated here. By *collective behavior* I refer to:

- two or more persons,
- engaged in one or more behaviors (e.g., locomotion, orientation, vocalization, verbalization, gesticulation, and/or manipulation),
- judged common or concerted,
- on one or more dimensions (e.g., direction, velocity, tempo, or substantive content).

Definitions always raise ontological and epistemological issues. This one is no exception. Without discussing any of these issues here, I will simply state my assumptions. [For more discussion, see McPhail and Rexroat (1979, 1980).] First, I cannot know if an observer's knowledge of collective behavior corresponds to the true nature of collective behavior independent of that knowledge. Second, there is no way anyone can know if an observer's judgment of the presence or extent of collective behavior corresponds to the participants' experience of those behaviors. Their experience is impenetrable, although observers and participants can, of course, compare reports. Third, I do not expect participants to judge their behaviors collective in the same way that an observer does unless both use the same criteria.[8]

Criteria for Judging Behaviors Collective: Two or More Persons. A minimum of two persons is required for a sequence of collective behavior. The number can range from two to *n* persons within the gathering. The larger the gathering, the less likely all members will be involved in any one, let alone all, sequence(s) of collective behavior.

It is not uncommon for several separate sequences of collective behavior to occur simultaneously within a large gathering. These may be similar (e.g., multiple conversation clusters), or different (e.g., conversation clusters in one section, spectators applauding a speaker in another section, newly arriving participants marching into another section, queues for food, drink, or toilets in other sections, and, one or more rings developing around arguments, fights, or arrest in yet other sections of the gathering). The appropriate metaphor for the gathering is less frequently a blanket of uniform behavior than it is a patchwork quilt of multiple and diverse sequences of individual and collective behaviors.

Engaged in One or More Behaviors.   By *behavior*, I mean the movement of the entire body (e.g., jumping, walking, running) or movements of a portion of the body (e.g., orienting or facing, laughing, shushing, whistling, talking, chanting, pointing, grasping, carrying, or throwing). Many of the behavior sequences in which I am interested often involve several behaviors occurring simultaneously. Nonetheless, it is prudent to classify the behaviors in mutually exclusive categories, enabling their examination separately or in various combinations.

Orientation refers to facing behavior, specifically, to the direction or inclination of the nose on the individual's face. This is a crude behavioral indicator of the range of objects, persons, or events to which the individual might be giving attention.

Vocalization refers to oohing, ahhing, ohhing, yeaaing, booing, hissing, laughing, crying, shushing, whistling, and humming.

Verbalization includes speaking, chanting, singing, praying, pledging, and reciting.

Locomotion refers to the movement of the entire body in space. *Vertical* locomotion includes bowing, kneeling, kowtowing, sitting, standing, falling, lying, and jumping. *Horizontal* locomotion includes crawling, walking, marching, jogging, dancing, and running.

Gesticulation refers to the movement and configuration of the fingers, hands, arms, shoulders, head, and face (including the brows, eyes, nose, and mouth) in a manner recognized by the user and one or more observers as a significant symbol.[9]

Manipulation includes using the hands in applauding, in striking other objects (e.g., drums, pots and pans, other persons), in grasping, lifting, and carrying objects (e.g., flags, banners, handkerchiefs, placards), in throwing objects (e.g., hats, cushions, bottles, rocks), and in pulling, lifting, and overturning objects (e.g., autos, trucks, buses, barricades).

Judged Common or Concerted.   Nothing is inherently collective. Some observer judges that two or more persons are engaged in similar behaviors, or different behaviors that mesh together. Sociologists distinguish parallel (Couch 1970; Turner and Killian 1987) from reciprocal (Couch 1970) or solidaristic collective behavior (Turner and Killian 1987). I refer to the first as collective behavior-in-common, the second as collective behavior-in-concert.

By *collective behavior-in-common* I mean:

- two or more persons,
- all of whom are engaged in one or more behaviors,

- that are judged common,
- on one or more dimensions.

I describe below 40 elementary forms of collective behavior-in-common. By *collective behavior-in-concert* I mean:

- two or more persons, of whom one or more engage in one behavior (A),
- while one or more additional persons engage in one or more different behaviors (B, . . . , n),
- and the two or more different behaviors are judged concerted,
- on one or more dimensions.

With the sole exception of the conversation cluster, collective behavior-in-concert occurs less frequently in temporary gatherings than does collective behavior-in-common. Some familiar forms of collective behavior-in-concert, e.g., conversations, two-party chants, songs, and card stunts, are discussed below.[10]

One or More Dimensions.   The dimensions listed here are merely illustrative. Additional criteria will be required to deal with some phenomena of interest to other investigators.

Direction refers to the line or course upon which an object (e.g., a body or body part) moves or in which it points. This criterion has been used to judge orientation (e.g., Milgram, Bickman, and Berkowitz 1969; McPhail and Pickens 1981), gesticulation (e.g., D. Morris 1985), and collective locomotion (e.g., McPhail and Wohlstein 1982, 1986).

Velocity refers to the rate of change of position of a body or body part in a specified direction per unit of time. This criterion has been used to judge collective locomotion (McPhail and Wohlstein 1982, 1986).

Tempo refers to the relative rate of movement or sound per unit of time. This criterion has been used to judge the tempo or rhythm with which two or more persons are chanting or gesturing (e.g., D. Morris 1981, 1985), or synchroclapping (e.g., Marsh 1981), and whether their chants, gestures, and clapping are in tempo with their locomotion behaviors (e.g., McPhail and Wohlstein 1986).

Substantive content.   In accordance with the investigator's criteria, two or more persons can be judged to chant or sing the same words, make the same gestures, or wear the same apparel or symbols.[11]

There is a considerable range in spatial and temporal frames of analysis of the various units of collective behavior examined by different scholars (cf. Lofland 1985). The majority of research I refer to here assumes a *spatial frame* with two or more individuals in sufficient proximity that one or more observers can see or hear them behave in more or less the same time frame. That time frame varies for different forms or sequences of behavior. Most of my research has examined sequences of behavior developing across a number of seconds or minutes. I will discuss variations in macro spatial and temporal frames below.

The Crowd and Collective Behavior: A Recharacterization

The definition of collective behavior advanced here has implications for several long-standing misconceptions about the crowd and collective behavior. One misconception has been that when collective behavior occurs, every member of the gathering is involved. Collective behavior and the crowd have too long been treated as synonymous. It is rare for everyone in the crowd to engage in any one mutually inclusive sequence of collective behavior. The exception may be the assembling process that produces the gathering; even then, it is rare for everyone to assemble at the same time.

Once assembled, sequences of mutually inclusive behavior are comparatively infrequent despite the impressionistic reports of participants and casual observers. Turner and Killian (1972) properly refer to such reports as "the illusion of unanimity." Assembled gatherings merely provide the opportunity for sequences of collective behavior to occur. The number of participants in any sequence can vary from two to n members. Most sequences involve fewer than the majority of the gathering. Any sequence that involves the majority is comparatively simple and short-lived.

A second and related misconception has been that if any collective behavior occurs within a gathering, only one sequence occurs. More frequently, people in various sections of the gathering are engaged in multiple sequences of collective behavior. Some are similar in form and content; some are different. The result is a patchwork quilt of various sequences of individual and collective behavior rather than a blanket of behavioral uniformity.

A third misconception has been that when collective behavior occurs it continues indefinitely. In fact, extended sequences of collective behavior are rare, even when only a few participants are involved. And when members of a gathering are not involved in some sequence of collective behavior, they are engaged in some sequence of individual behavior. This alternation between individual and collective behavior is a characteristic feature of most temporary gatherings. It is a formidable challenge to describe and explain.

A fourth misconception has been that all collective behavior is simple if not simplistic. It may be true, in general, that the greater the number of people participating in a sequence of collective behavior, the more likely that sequence will be simple. But it is also true that most sequences of collective behavior do not involve the majority of the gathering and that some are more complex than others. Sequences of collective behavior vary in complexity as a function of the number of behaviors in which two or more persons are engaged and the number of dimensions required to judged those behaviors common or concerted.

A fifth misconception of the crowd and collective behavior is that it frequently involves competition if not conflict. Indeed, it was a concern with conflict, in particular, violence against person and property, that launched our research program in the 1960s. But we soon learned from observing dozens of political demonstrations that violence against property or person is rare, a fact borne out by other research (Eisinger 1973; MacCannell 1973). Violence is similarly rare in sports gatherings (Smith 1983; Lewis 1982). Collective violence is rarer yet. Collective competition and conflict may be more frequent within sports gatherings than within political gatherings. Cooperation occurs more frequently than any other form of collective action in all temporary gatherings. An understanding of competition or conflict between sports, political, or religious groups first requires an understanding of how they cooperate among themselves to compete or engage in combat against one another. Therefore, the majority of my concerns here will be with describing and explaining how two or more persons act together in cooperation rather than against one another or others in competition or conflict. But this descriptive approach can be extended to competition or conflict, as can the explanatory model set forth in the following chapter.

Thus, collective behavior within human gatherings is not a constant. It should not be equated with the crowd. Gatherings merely provide opportunities for various sequences of collective behavior to occur. Those sequences vary in the number of participants, in content, in form, in duration, in complexity, and in the proportion that are cooperative, competitive, and conflictive, in that order.

Collective Behavior within Gatherings: Some Elementary Forms

Table 5.1 lists 40 forms of collective behavior-in-common that are frequently observed in a variety of temporary gatherings. These are very simple forms of collective behavior. Most consist of one behavior engaged in by two or more persons. Whatever criticisms may be leveled at anyone's explanation for these elementary forms, it is difficult to deny that people collectively engage in these behaviors in a great variety of gatherings around the world.

Collective Orientation. We cannot ascertain what individuals are thinking by observing the direction they are facing. But the direction they face provides a crude indicator of a range of objects to which they might give attention. These orientation behaviors take several forms.

Table 5.1   Some Elementary Forms of Collective Behavior-in-Common

Collective orientation	Collective vocalization	Collective verbalization
1. Clustering	1. Ooh-, ahh-, ohhing	1. Chanting
2. Arc-ing, ringing	2. Yeaing	2. Singing
3. Gazing, facing	3. Booing	3. Praying
4. Vigiling	4. Whistling	4. Reciting
	5. Hissing	5. Pledging
	6. Laughing	
	7. Wailing	

Collective gesticulation
(nonverbal symbols)
1. Roman salute (arm extended forward, palm down, fingers together)
2. Solidarity salute (closed fist raised above the shoulder level)
3. *Digitus obscenus* (fist raised, middle finger extended)
4. #1 (fist raised shoulder level or above, index finger extended)
5. Peace (fist raised, index finger and middle fingers separated and extended)
6. Praise or victory (both arms fully extended overhead)

Collective vertical locomotion	Collective horizontal locomotion	Collective manipulation
1. sitting	1. Pedestrian clustering	1. Applauding
2. standing	2. Queueing	2. Synchroclapping
3. jumping	3. Surging	3. Finger-snapping
4. Bowing	4. Marching	4. Grasping, lifting, waving object
5. Kneeling	5. Jogging	5. Grasping, lifting, throwing object
6. Kowtowing	6. Running	6. Grasping, lifting, pushing object

Clustering.   A great deal of research has been done on the frequency of companion clusters of varying size in standing (e.g., James 1951, 1953; Bakeman and Beck 1973; Whyte 1980) and in some seated gatherings (e.g., Edney and Jordan-Edney 1974; Edgerton 1979; Smith 1981) around the world. Clustering can be identified in one or more of three ways: by the common or convergent direction of orientation of two to five adjacent persons—here termed orientation clusters; by the direction and velocity of locomotion of two to five adjacent persons—here termed pedestrian clusters (cf. McPhail and Wohlstein 1982); or, by the alternating direction of speech and orientation plus nonverbal gestures among two to five persons—here termed conversation clusters. For all three types, researchers consistently report an inverse, linear relationship between cluster size and the frequency with which they are observed: dyads are the most frequent and clusters of six or more are very rare. [These distributions are discussed at length in McPhail (1987).] In fact, the majority of members of most gatherings assemble with one or more companions (Aveni 1977; Miller 1973; Woelfel et al. 1974; Wimberly et al. 1975), remain with them throughout the gathering, and then disperse together (Miller 1973). On some occasions, cluster members walk and orient in a common direction and converse with one another at the same time (McPhail and Wohlstein 1982). They often engage in two of those behaviors in common. More frequently they are engaged only in orientation or facing behaviors in common.

Arcs and rings (arc-ing and ringing). When a half-dozen or more persons are judged to orient in a convergent direction, they tend to be arrayed in an arc or series of arcs around the focal point on which their orientations converge, e.g., street performers, political and religious speakers, accidents, arguments, arrests. Descriptions and analyses of arcs and rings have been reported by several investigators (e.g., Milgram and Toch 1969; Milgram et al. 1969; Knowles and Bassett 1976; Wright 1978; Whyte 1980; Harrison 1984).

Facing. The direction and the proportion of the gathering engaged in collective orientation or facing behaviors varies greatly among spectators to sports, political, and religious demonstrations, among audiences in lecture halls, and probably in all gatherings. For basketball game spectators, mutually inclusive orientation is rare, is short-lived when it occurs, and small patches of collective orientation scattered throughout a gathering are much more frequent than larger ones (McPhail and Pickens 1981). This varies for other spectator sports, e.g., professional tennis matches as compared with baseball or soccer games.

Vigiling. To vigil is to watch or guard. Unlike the queue in which members stand more or less face-to-back, vigilers stand side by side and orient in a common direction. The vigil line is a frequent form of political demonstration. It is also a form in which police sometimes align at demonstrations; it is a common form at religious ceremonies.

For example, each lunar year since 1970, on the ninth day of the month of *Hijjah*, at high noon, more than one million pilgrims stand on the Plain of Arafat in Saudi Arabia and face in the direction of the Mount of Mercy from which the Prophet Mohammad delivered his final sermon in 631 A.D. This is followed by a vigil in which the pilgrims face in the direction of the *Kaaba* in Mecca, pray, and meditate until sunset. This is probably the longest continuous sequence of collective behaviors (orientation, verbalization, gesticulation and vertical locomotion) by the largest proportion of persons in the largest gathering on the face of the earth.[12]

Collective Vocalization. Two or more persons are often judged to engage in common *vocal* sounds (albeit not articulate speech) at more or less the same time. Sometimes the additional judgment can be made that their vocalizations rise and fall together in pitch.

Researchers have examined the vocalization behaviors of sports spectators, e.g., collective *ooh-ing, ahh-ing, ohhing and yeaing* (Zillman et al. 1979) and *booing* (Greer 1983). These behaviors are often mixed with *whistling* and *hissing*, respectively, and mixed applause (Gambrell 1979; Aveni 1985).

Another frequent form of collective vocalization is *laughing* (Levy and Fenley 1979). *Crying* at funerals is universal. Collective weeping and wailing, comparatively infrequent in the Western world, is frequently observed at funerals and burials in the Middle East.

These various forms of collective vocalization are examples of the forms of collective emotion to which I referred above, e.g., surprise (oohs), joy (yeas, whistles, laughter), disappointment (ohhs), and anger (boos, hisses).

Collective glossolalia (speaking in tongues) involves two or more persons simultaneously uttering strings of nonsense syllables. The effect of *glossing* is one of muted collective babel. On rare occasions the tempo and pitch of glossing-in-common takes the form of choral modulation (cf. Laurentin 1977:63–64; Samarin 1972:179, and 1987, personal communication).[13]

Collective Verbalization. Two or more persons are frequently judged to engage in the same substantive speech or song at the same time. Routinized collective verbalization occurs in the form of collective *reciting and praying* (e.g., in religious gatherings), collective *singing and chanting* (e.g., during sports and political gatherings), and collective *pledging and oath taking* (in many religious, sports, and political gatherings). The flexibility of human imagination yields many variations and innovations in the collective singing and chanting heard at sports and political gatherings. Fewer collective variations and innovations are heard in religious gatherings. Extensive research on sports demonstration chanting is reported by D. Morris (1981).

Collective Gesticulation. Collective gestures are frequent companions of collective vocalization and verbalization. Fingers, hands, arms, or other body parts are positioned or moved to form significant symbols. These are performed individually and collectively. Some of the more frequent and familiar collective gestures are noted here.

One ancient and familiar collective gesture extends the right arm, 45 degrees from the shoulder, fingers extended and touching in the fascist or *Roman salute.*

Another familiar collective gesture is the *raised clenched fist* (sometimes shaken overhead). The signification varies from time to time, but is more frequently used to indicate a common bond among those who display the gesture (e.g., solidarity, "power to the people") than to indicate a threat toward or negative evaluation of others.

Conversely, collectively raised *fists with middle fingers extended* upward (or fists with thumbs extended downward) typically signify a negative evaluation of the person(s), behavior(s), or object(s) to which the gesture is addressed.

An increasingly frequent collective gesture in sports gatherings over the past decade is *fist(s) with extended index finger(s) raised overhead* signifying "We're number one!" Among evangelical Christians the same gestures signifies "Christ is the one" or "one way."

Another ancient collective gesture is one of celebration, exhilaration, or praise and involves *both arms and hands raised overhead,* sometimes repeatedly thrust overhead, sometimes waved from side to side. This is frequently observed among sports spectators celebrating successful plays, scores, or victories, among political demonstrators signifying victory, and among religious practitioners praising their god (cf. Psalms 134:2), or testifying to or inviting a religious experience.

A subtle variant of the preceding gesture is the *raised fist with extended and separated index and middle fingers.* When the heel of the hand is turned away from the body, in Great Britain as in the United States, the gesture signifies victory (cf. Winston Churchill during World War II) or peace (cf. the antiwar movement of the 1960s). When the heel of the hand is turned toward the body, in Great Britain at least, the gesture is a negative evaluation of the person, behavior, or object in whose direction it is pointed, the equivalent of the extended middle finger (*digitus obscenus*) in the Roman Empire (ca. 100 B.C.) and today in the United States and elsewhere (Morris 1985). An extensive record of collective gestures in British football gatherings is reported by D. Morris (1981).

Collective Vertical Locomotion. The most frequent forms are *sitting* and *standing.* The completion of most assembling processes temporarily results in a standing gathering. Thereafter, sitting and standing vary considerably across different gatherings.

Standing and sitting. Some gatherings (e.g., at fires, accidents, arrests, and street performances) stand from the completion of assembling to the start of dispersal. In other gatherings (e.g., religious, concert, theatrical, and academic) the majority of the gathering sits soon after arrival. But since arrival is sequential, simultaneous sitting is rare. Most academic gatherings remain seated until shortly before dispersal. Many religious gatherings sit and stand intermittently and do so more or less simultaneously. Sports spectator gatherings also sit and stand intermittently, but do so sequentially.

[Golf galleries may be an exception (cf. Bogardus 1924).] Even this varies by sport (cf. tennis vs. basketball, football, and baseball).

Jumping.   Sports spectators frequently jump for joy when their team has scored points. According to D. Morris (1981) British soccer fans have routinized a vertical "pogo jump" that gives the appearance of "heaving and swelling rough seas." (A recent form of collective vertical locomotion at U.S. sports gatherings—the wave—also involves collective orientation and collective gesticulation, and is discussed below with more complex forms of collective behavior-in-common.

Sitting.   Political demonstrators have engaged in sit-in or sit-down tactics for nearly a half century (cf. Fine 1969). This involves occupying and sometimes blockading a space or thoroughfare by sitting in close proximity (and sometimes linking arms/or legs to thwart easy dispersal by police).

Bowing and kneeling.   The most complex and routinized forms of collective vertical locomotion may occur in religious demonstrations; for example, genuflecting, sitting, standing, kneeling, and sitting sequences in a Catholic mass, or the standing, bowing, kowtowing, kneeling, and standing sequences in the Muslims' Friday noon prayers (Al-Khateeb n.d.).

Collective Horizontal Locomotion.   From hunting and gathering societies through the diaspora, to the crusades, to wedding, funeral, and other religious processions, collective locomotion is an established pattern of social behavior. It is not surprising that this ordinary form of social behavior was coopted for political purposes in the form of labor, suffrage, civil rights, antiwar, women's rights, pro- and antiabortion, and antiapartheid marches (cf. Tilly 1978, 1979). But marches and processions are not the most frequent form of collective locomotion observed in or by temporary gatherings.

The most frequent form of collective locomotion within gatherings is the *pedestrian cluster.* People frequently assemble with one or more friends or acquaintances. They intermittently stand in orientation and conversation clusters and may occasionally move or mill about the area. Two or more pedestrians are judged to move together—to be "with" one another (Goffman 1971)—on the basis of mutual conversation or touch (James 1951, 1953; Berkowitz 1971), or the spacing, direction, and velocity of their locomotion behaviors (McPhail and Wohlstein, 1982).

Mann (1973) contends the *queue* "is the most ordered and cooperative, the most highly structured" elementary form of collective behavior. Queueing involves two or more persons standing face-to-back, with orientation in the direction of some potential point of service, commodity, or entry. Queues take different forms (Leibowitz 1968). Some are single lines with single servers (e.g., at ticket booths); others are a series of lines and servers (e.g., grocery stores); one line with multiple servers (e.g., bank tellers); and, occasionally, interconnected queues (e.g., university registrations). Queues are found throughout the Western world (cf. Hraba 1985) and have been studied in a variety of settings for more than a decade (Mann 1969, 1977; Hraba 1985; Milgram Liberty, Toledo, and Wackenhut 1986).

The direction of orientation of queue members varies. While standing, members often face and talk with companions and even to adjacent strangers. They occasionally face in the direction of passing pedestrians, vehicles, or other surrounding activity. What *is* more or less constant is the order of their position in the queue, and the direction of the queue's intermittent locomotion in the direction of the point of service.

Surging involves the sudden movement of a portion of a gathering in a common direction at a more or less common velocity. The surge is typically in the direction of what has previously become a focal point for orientation, e.g., an accident, argument or fight, an arrest, an arriving speaker, ambulance, police car, or newly arrived contingent of demonstrators, or an opening or closing entry or exit.

It is not unusual for surges to end in the formation of arcs or rings around the focal point of orientation and locomotion. Surges that do not end in arcs and rings include entry and exit surges (cf. Johnson 1987a,b), as well as the assault and siege of buildings, assaults against groups of counterdemonstrators, assaults on weak points in police lines.

The most familiar forms of horizontal collective locomotion are *marches and processions*. These range from street actions (variants of surges and assaults), to protest marches, parades by veterans, ethnic groups, patriots, and politicians (cf. Davis 1986), to religious (Crawley 1918) and state (Burrage and Corry 1981) processionals. All share the common feature of two or more adjacent persons moving in a common direction at a common velocity (cf. Wohlstein and McPhail 1979; McPhail and Wohlstein 1982). The social organization of these various forms of collective locomotion is discussed by McPhail and Wohlstein (1986). Various combinations of collective locomotion with singing or chanting and gesturing are discussed below with more complex forms of collective behavior.[14]

Collective Manipulation.   The most frequent form is *applause*. Most collective applause involves two or more persons clapping their hands at approximately the same time but not in tempo (cf. Atkinson 1984a). Desmond Morris (1981) refers to applause in tempo as *synchroclapping*. This form of collective behavior is observed at sports (D. Morris, 1981) and political gatherings (Atkinson 1984b; Heritage and Greatbatch 1986) throughout the world and at theatrical and musical performances in Great Britain and the Soviet Union. The slow synchroclap is a sign of derision in the former country, a sign of high praise in the latter. A variant of synchroclapping is collective *finger-snapping*.

Perhaps the next most frequent form of collective manipulation involves *grasping, raising waving, shaking, or rotating* flags, placards, pom-poms, banners, scarves, car keys, rosaries, candles, etc., at a variety of political, sports, and religious gatherings. One variation is the complex sequence of several hundred persons simultaneously grasping, lifting, rotating, and lowering separate colored cardboard squares to form large and often spectacular pictograms across a section of or sometimes an entire stadium. "Card stunts" originated among football fans at the University of Illinois in 1921. They have since spread to large U.S. colleges and universities, and have been adopted and performed in large gatherings by many political and religious organizations throughout the world.[15] One spectacular stunt—a pictograph of the flags of all participating nations—involving more than 100,000 spectators was performed at the opening ceremonies of the 1984 summer Olympic Games in Los Angeles. Techniques for producing these complex sequences of collective manipulation are examined elsewhere (McPhail 1986).

Collective manipulation often takes the form of people *grasping, raising, and throwing objects* in a common direction. Political and sports demonstrators celebrate victories by throwing paper streamers, confetti, and more frequently, whatever is at hand, e.g., hats, banners, cushions, programs, or drink containers. In the 1970s and 1980s, U.S. and British football fans threw rolls of toilet paper high into the air, resulting in long white streamers floating down over the stands and playing fields. Sports and political demonstrators sometimes throw any available object at speakers, performers, political representatives, referees and umpires, members and supporters of opposing teams, opposing groups, and, the police. One meaning of this elementary form of collective behavior, a response made by participants, targets, and observers alike, is the indication of disapproval of the targeted persons or their activities. (Conversely, flowers thrown in the direction of actors, ballet dancers, and opera singers indicate approval and affection.)

Another category of collective manipulation involves striking any available surface with open palms or with fists (e.g., protestors or celebrators pounding on a car roof or hood), grasping an object with one hand and striking it with the other hand (e.g., passing motorists honking their horns in support of demonstrators or in celebration of their team's sport victory), or holding an object in one hand and striking it with another object held in the other hand (e.g., house occupants banging spoons on cooking pots in protest or celebration).

A more complex but infrequent form of collective manipulation involves two or more persons *grasping, lifting, and pushing and overturning* autos, trucks, buses, kiosks, barricades, etc. These behaviors are observed in demonstrations of protest and of celebration.

More Complex Forms

Most of the elementary forms of collective behavior in Table 5.1 are, taken separately, rather simple. But people frequently engage in two or more of these behaviors at the same or at sequential point(s) in time. This increases the complexity of the collective behavior sequence.

Complex Collective Behavior-in-Common. Often two or more persons engage in more than one behavior-in-common at the same time, and those two or more behaviors are performed in the same direction or at the same tempo or velocity, or are otherwise judged common to the two or more persons on one or more of these or other dimensions. Several examples follow.

1. Two or more persons, seated or standing, face in a common direction and chant a common content at the same tempo, "Pot's an herb; Reagan's a dope."

2. Two or more persons, standing or seated, face in a common direction, raise their index fingers overhead, and chant in tempo, "We're number one!"

3. Two or more persons, standing, face in a common direction, raise and/or snap their index fingers overhead, and dance in tempo with, and occasionally sing the words or hum the melody line of, a rock song performed by a singer or group in concert.

4. Two or more adjacent persons march in a common direction and at a common velocity, and thrust clenched fists overhead in tempo with their chant, e.g., "The people united will never be defeated."

5. Two or more persons stand in a vigil line, grasp the hand of the person on either side (or a ribbon running the length of the line) to form a "human chain" in protest or celebration of some person, principle, or circumstance, e.g., the antinuclear demonstrator chains in England and Europe in 1984 and 1985, or "Hands Across America" for the homeless in 1986.

6. An individual seated in a stadium or arena filled with people faces forward and upward as she stands and raises both arms overhead. She then faces forward and lowers her arms as she sits. She performs this sequence of behaviors immediately after the same behaviors are performed by the persons seated in the rows immediately to her front and to her right (or left). When this is repeated by the person seated behind her and to her left (or right), and by "every" individual in every column and row of seats (to her rear and left), it results in what has come to be called "the wave" around a stadium or arena or a section thereof.

7. At noon each Friday, in mosques around the world, two or more Muslims face in the direction of Mecca and collectively engage in a minimum of four *rakaa*s of postures-and-prayers. Each *rakaa* consists of the following sequence: (a) standing with bowed head with hands raised to shoulder height with thumbs behind the earlobes; (b) placing the hands, right over left, just below the naval; (c) bowing from the waist with hands touching the knees; (d) returning to standing posture but with arms at side; and then (e) kowtowing (i.e., kneeling and touching the forehead to the ground); (f) raising the torso to a sitting posture with head bowed; (g) repeating the kowtow; and (h) returning to the sitting posture. Each of these positions is held for a specified number of seconds and is accompanied by specified prayers. During the pilgrimage to Mecca, as many as 500,000 assemble in the Grand Mosque and another 500,000 or more assemble in the surrounding streets for these collective prayers. (Amin 1978).

8. Two or more adjacent persons, uniformly dressed, march in a common direction, in step, at a common velocity, separated by equal spacing, flags or weapons grasped in a common manner and pointed in a common direction, and face to the right upon approaching and then straight ahead after passing the review stand during ceremonies celebrating a state anniversary (McDowell 1974; Lane 1976).

Complex Collective Behavior-in-Concert.   These forms of collective behavior involve the merger of different behaviors by different individuals at the same or at different times. With one exception, collective behavior-in-concert is relatively infrequent in most temporary gatherings. Some examples follow.

1. The exceptional form of collective behavior-in-concert is also one of the most prevalent forms observed in all human gatherings. I refer to *the conversation cluster.* This form consists at minimum of one sequence involving one speaker and one or more auditors. Ordinarily there is intermittent orientation of speaker and auditors in one another's direction, occasional gesturing on the part of the speaker, affirming, negating, or questioning vocal and verbal utterances by the auditor(s), and ordinarily one or more alternations of "speaking turn" among the various members of the cluster. No conversation occurs without this elementary division of labor between speaker(s) and auditor(s) (cf. Duncan and Fiske 1977; Kendon 1982). Conversation clusters are the most frequent form of collective behavior-in-concert. They are found wherever temporary gatherings occur.

2. Another simple form of collective behavior-in-concert is the *two-party chant.* Person or persons A chant one word or phrase at time one; person or persons B chant a second word or phrase at time two; and, the sequence is

often repeated, sometimes with variation. An example from a political gathering:

Person(s) A: "What do we want?"
Person(s) B: "Peace!"
Person(s) A: "When do we want it?"
Person(s) B: "Now!"
Person(s) A: "What?"
Person(s) B: "Peace!"
Person(s) A: "When?"
Person(s) B: "Now!"

These can take on more complex forms of content and rhythm:

Person(s) A: "We're fired up!"
Person(s) B: "Won't take it no more!"

Religious gatherings provide similar sequences of interspersed two-party responsive readings and liturgical chants by a clergy and the congregation. Sports gatherings provide similar sequences of interspersed two-party chants by cheerleaders and fans, or by separate groups of fans:

Person(s) A: "I-L-L"
Person(s) B: "I-N-I"

3.   A more complex form of collective behavior-in-concert is the *card stunt* that involves each of several hundred or thousand individual participants simultaneously and sequentially manipulating small colored cards to form a large pictograph. A simple hypothetical example follows. Three 18-inch-square cards (red, white, and blue) are distributed among 300 persons with written and verbal instructions to perform one or more of three different manipulations, at three successive points in time.

A circular core of 50 persons, in the center of a section of 300 persons seated on risers, grasp the blue cards in both hands, raise them to eye level at time one, flutter the cards rapidly backward and forward at time two, and lower the cards at time three. Persons 51–125, seated in a circular band around the first 50, grasp the white cards in both hands and raise them to eye level at time one, slowly but alternately rotate them to the left and then to the right at time two, and lower the cards at time three. Persons 126–300, seated around the circumference of the section, grasp the red cards in both hands and raise them to eye level at time one, hold them steady at time two, and lower the cards at time three. The result is a three-dimensional, red, white, and blue pictograph of a bullseye. Sports, political and religious rally organizers design, rehearse, arrange, and implement vastly more complex, multidimensional, and serial renditions of these sequences of collective actions involving thousands of card manipulators.

4.   Another complex sequence of collective behavior-in-concert involves demonstrators marching alone or with their own band. If demonstrators merely chant (e.g., "The peo-ple u-ni-ted will ne-ver be de-feat-ed") and gesture (e.g., raised clenched right fists on every other footfall), in tempo with their footballs as they march down the street, the result is a relatively complex form of collective behavior-in-common. But if demonstrators merge those same behaviors with music played by their own marching band, this constitutes an elementary form of collective behavior-in-concert. The majority of the demonstrators are engaging in one set of behaviors-in-common in tempo with another set of collective behaviors by the remaining demonstrators: the band. The latter may play their music in common (e.g., all instruments playing in unison) or in concert (e.g., different instruments playing different notes in harmony); the complexity of their play varies accordingly.[16] In all these examples, collective behavior-in-common and collective behavior-in-concert are said to increase in complexity as a function of an increase in the number of similar or different behavior(s) that two or more persons perform, and the number of dimensions required to judge those behaviors common or concerted.[17]

In summary, the alternative definition and characterization of collective behavior I offered addresses three problems. First, it provides guidelines for observing and systematically describing a number of elementary forms or sequences of collective behavior that occur within temporary gatherings. Second, it organizes a wide range of research on those forms by scholars in several disciplines. Third, by providing a preliminary summary of the variety of behaviors in which human beings collectively engage, it sets a target to which explanations and tests of explanations of collective behavior can be directed.

I hope this alternative definition and characterization of collective behavior also addresses a fourth problem. It may enable the "specification of our ignorance" (cf. Merton 1987) about the characterization, composition, and comparison of temporary gatherings. This might provide a first step toward program of research to alter our current state of knowledge. A context for this problem is provided in the following discussion of the relationships between collective behavior, temporary gatherings, and the macro levels and units of analysis of collective action that have been the focus of considerable sociological research over the last two decades.

Other Levels and Units of Analysis

The behavioral variation within gatherings that challenges one group of scholars is set aside by other scholars who are more intrigued with case studies of single gatherings or with the various relationships between types of gatherings and other social, economic, and political considerations. This is as it should be. Different scholars work at different levels of analysis. Some work at one end of a continuum, focusing on the alternating sequences of individual and collective behavior of which gatherings are composed. Others work at the level of the gathering, or they examine campaigns or waves of gatherings. Still others are concerned with longer trends of campaigns, waves, and gatherings.

The common denominator across these diverse interests is some unit of *social* phenomenon. The alternative definition and characterization of collective behavior I have presented was developed to deal with the problem of observing and recording sequences of collective behavior within gatherings. I do not presume this definition and characterization solves all the descriptive problems of all my colleagues working at all levels of analysis. But someone must start somewhere to bridge the gap between the levels of analysis separating studies of micro from studies of macro phenomena. More will be gained by examining the continuity and relationships across these levels and units of analysis than by continuing to emphasize the differences between them.

Figure 5.1 presents a simple matrix of the spatial and temporal levels of analysis at which students of crowds and social movements have examined a range of related collective phenomena (cf. Lofland 1985). Across the horizontal axis I have arrayed units of space from geographical–political locales (e.g., nations, states, counties, communities) at the macro end of the continuum, to coordinate points at the micro end (cf. Collins 1981). Down the vertical axis, I have arrayed units of time from years, months, and weeks at the macro end, to minutes, seconds, and split seconds at the micro end of the continuum. At the intersects of these spatial and temporal frames are the units of analysis investigated by different scholars.[18]

A few scholars do examine sequences of individual behavior or of collective behavior, or the variations within and alternations between *sequences of individual and collective behavior* within gatherings (cf. Milgram and Toch 1969; Mann 1977; Wright 1978; McPhail and Wohlstein 1983, 1986; Heritage and Greatbatch 1986). Some sociologists are concerned with *gatherings* as the unit of analysis (e.g., MacCannell 1973; Lofland 1981, 1985; Snow et al. 1981; Aguirre 1984) or with sequences of related gatherings constituting *events* that develop over a continuous period of hours. Still others are concerned with more extended sequences of behavior sequences, gatherings, and events aggregated at the level of *campaigns* (e.g., A. Morris 1981), *waves* (e.g., Aguirre et al. 1988; McAdam 1983), and *trends* (e.g., Tilly et al. 1975; McAdam 1982). In this section I briefly examine some of the relationship between these units of analysis by aggregating micro units to form macro units (or by disaggregating the latter to identify the former).

By *individual behavior* I mean the movement of the entire body (e.g.,

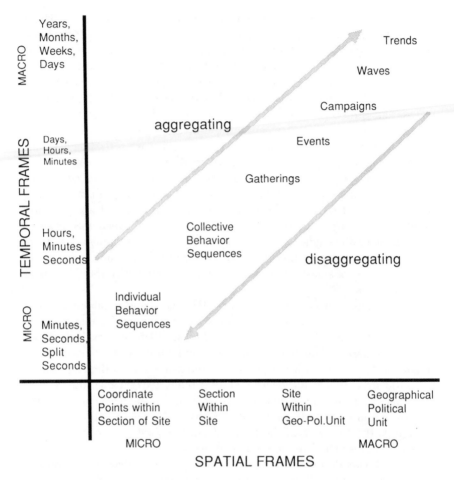

Figure 5.1.   Units of analysis by spatial and temporal levels of analysis.

horizontal or vertical locomotion) or portions of the body (e.g., orientation, vocalization or verbalization, gesticulation, or manipulation) across adjacent coordinate points in space and time. Examples include all of the behaviors previously mentioned in which two or more individuals may also occasionally engage collectively, plus scratching, stretching, eating, drinking, smoking, reading, writing, photographing, and such behaviors that are not often performed collectively.

By *collective behavior* I refer to any behavior(s) by two or more individuals that can be judged common or concerted by the criteria given earlier. I will not repeat here the numerous examples of elementary and more complex forms of collective behavior-in-common and collective behavior-in-concert discussed above.

By *gatherings* I mean a temporary collection of two or more persons occupying a common space and time frame. Here I follow Goffman (1963, 1971, 1983), who struggled for two decades with the problem of how to draw boundaries for the study of temporary gatherings in public places. In both his first and his final work on the problem, he resorted to virtually the same criteria I have used to define gatherings.

But how are gatherings, thus defined, to be further specified or characterized so as to permit their systematic examination, description, and comparison? Various social scientists have classified gatherings with regard to their size (Newton and Mann 1980), the presence or absence of violence and arrests (Tilly et al. 1975), participants' motives inferred from their modal behaviors (Turner and Killian 1972), predominant emotional displays (Lofland 1981), and the selected characteristics of various categories of participants (MacCannell 1973). I have suggested throughout this chapter that gatherings are composed of a variety of sequences of individual and collective behaviors; I have identified some recurring elementary forms of sequences of collective behavior; and I have argued, therefore, that gatherings may be characterized and compared in terms of the sequences of collective behavior of which they are composed.

Thus construed, some gatherings are very simple; others are very complex; but most probably fall in between. On such a crude hypothetical continuum I would provisionally mark the simple end with what I call prosaic gatherings, the complex end with ceremonial gatherings, and I would place most demonstration gatherings (political, religious, and sports protests and celebrations) in between.

By *prosaic gatherings* I mean two or more persons in a common space-time frame in a public or semipublic gathering. Substantively the modal individual and collective behaviors in such gatherings are socializing, people watching, or simply "hanging out." Prosaic gatherings range from casual and transitory gatherings in parks, plazas, and squares, on beaches and campus quadrangles, to occasional gatherings at the scene of fires, accidents, and arrests, to recurring gatherings outside skating rinks, swimming pools, movie theaters, dance floors, drive-ins, malt shops, and the like. If collective behaviors occur in a prosaic gathering they will likely be one of the simple forms, e.g., clusters (either orientation, pedestrian, or conversation), queues, arcs, or rings (and therefrom, occasional collective vocalization—oohs, ohhs, ahhs, boos, laughter—or applause), and, on rare occasion, surges of collective locomotion (cf. McPhail 1987).

By *demonstration gathering* I refer to two or more persons in a common space-time frame whose modal individual and collective behaviors involve the protest or celebration of some principle, person, collectivity, or condition (cf. McPhail 1985). In addition to the more familiar political demonstration, I include religious and sports demonstrations as well. There are youth rallies for sacred figures (and protest rallies against satanic figures, activities, and objects), just as there are pep rallies and victory celebrations for athletic teams (and protests against alleged injustices to players, coaches, teams, etc.).

All the aforementioned simple forms of collective behavior also occur in demonstration gatherings, e.g., all the various forms of clustering, queues for food, water, toilets, literature, and other concessions before and after rallies, and arcs or rings with attendant vocalization and applause during the rallies. But in addition, demonstration gatherings routinely include forms of collective behavior almost never found in prosaic gatherings, viz., chants, songs, pledges and prayers, synchroclapping, collective gesticulations, and the collective manipulation of banners, flags, placards, scarves, pom-poms, noisemakers, candles, prayer books, logos, emblems, icons, and other symbols. Moreover, beyond the prosaic gatherings' simple pedestrian clusters, queues, and occasional surges, demonstration gatherings have street actions, protest marches, victory parades, and processions in which participants also engage in collective chanting or singing, gesturing or synchroclapping, or hoisting the various objects noted in the preceding sentence. Not infrequently, demonstration gatherings include musicians engaging in complex sequences of collective vocalization and/or manipulation of instruments, sometimes while engaged in collective locomotion. Frequently the musicians, and occasionally other segments or delegations within the gathering, are uniformly costumed.

By *ceremonial gathering* I refer to two or more persons in a common space-time frame whose modal individual and collective behaviors celebrate or mourn the status passage of some individual, or group, or some event (Van Gennep 1909).[19] Thus defined, ceremonies range from very small gatherings in private or semiprivate places (e.g., christenings, family weddings, anniversaries, birthdays, and funerals) to very large gatherings in public or semipublic places. I am primarily concerned here with ceremonial gatherings of varying size in public or semipublic places.[20] Such gatherings ordinarily involve such matters as celebrating the anniversaries of the birth of states, of religions, or of their leaders; inaugurating, coronating, or investing political and religious leaders; funerals and burials of political and religious leaders; celebrating the marriages of political and religious leaders; and, last but not least, the opening ceremonies for the Olympic Games that honor the participants in the competitions to determine the swiftest, strongest, most skilled athletes in the world.[21]

In the gatherings immediately preceding and following ceremonial sequences, one observes virtually all the simpler forms of collective behavior observed in prosaic gatherings, particularly clusters, queues, arcs and rings, occasional collective vocalization, and applause. As ceremonies proceed, the more complex forms of collective behavior noted in demonstration gatherings are observed as well (McDowell 1974; Lane 1976; Aguirre 1985): collective chanting, singing, gesturing, applauding, and various forms of collective locomotion ranging from single- and double-file processions by some members of the gathering, to other delegations arranged and proceeding in multiple, very symmetrical ranks and files. But, in addition, ceremonial gatherings appear to have far more delegations in uniform dress than do demonstration or prosaic gatherings. And ceremonial delegations are more likely to carry and collectively manipulate arms, flags, banners, and symbols, or to engage in collective gestures. They are more likely to chant or sing, or recite oaths or pledges of allegiance, etc., in unison or in concert. Marching political or sports delegations in ceremonial gatherings are likely to orient collectively in the direction of and to salute rulers, elites, and other dignitaries in reviewing stands, just as religious processions are likely to bow or genuflect sequentially or collectively in the direction of sacred leaders, icons, or altars. In short, there are more separate delegations in ceremonial gatherings than in prosaic or demonstration gatherings; they are more likely differentiated from one another, and perhaps from onlookers, by their uniform costumes; they are more likely to engage in more sequences, and in more complex and sustained sequences of collective behavior than will be found in prosaic or demonstration gatherings; and onlookers may engage in more, albeit simple, sequences of collective behavior (e.g., vocalization, verbalization, applause, gesticulation) than onlookers to demonstration gatherings.[22]

By the preceding discussion I intend to suggest that prosaic, demonstration, and ceremonial gatherings crudely mark three points along a hypothetical continuum of the collective behavioral complexity of temporary gatherings. Furthermore, I suggest that the elementary forms of collective behavior discussed in connection with each of those gatherings take the form of an ordinal scale, a hypothetical representation of which is presented in Figure 5.2.[23]

All gatherings, the simplest prototype being the prosaic gathering, contain the same elementary forms of collective behavior if they contain any form of collective behavior at all.

Some gatherings, the familiar prototype of which are political, religious, and sports demonstrations, contain all of those elementary forms plus more complex forms of collective behavior in common and in concert.

A few gatherings, the proposed prototype being the public ceremonial gathering, contain the previously noted elementary and complex forms, and more. By the latter I mean more sequences of collective behavior (including uniform costumes) by more members of the gathering, and more complex sequences of collective behavior by some members of the gathering.[24]

PROSAIC GATHERINGS				DEMONSTRATION GATHERINGS								CEREMONIAL GATHERINGS		
SIMPLE ->	->	->				->	->	->	->	->	->	->	-> ->	COMPLEX
clst	clst	clst	clst	clst	clst	clst	clst	clst	clst	clst	clst	clst	clst	clst
	que	que	que	que	que	que	que	que	que	que	que	que	que	que
		arc	arc	arc	arc	arc	arc	arc	arc	arc	arc	arc	arc	arc
			voc	voc	voc	voc	voc	voc	voc	voc	voc	voc	voc	voc
			apls	apls	apls	apls	apls	apls	apls	apls	apls	apls	apls	apls
				chn	chn	chn	chn	chn	chn	chn	chn	chn	chn	chn
					sng	sng	sng	sng	sng	sng	sng	sng	sng	sng
						gst	gst	gst	gst	gst	gst	gst	gst	gst
							plc	plc	plc	plc	plc	plc	plc	plc
								mar	mar	mar	mar	mar	mar	mar
										uni	uni	uni	uni	uni
											bnd	bnd	bnd	bnd
												cbn	cbn	cbn
													???	???
														???

LEGEND

clst	-	clusters
que	-	queues
arc	-	arcs and rings
voc	-	vocalization (oohs; ohhs; ahhs; laughs)
apl	-	applause
cht	-	chanting
sng	-	singing
gst	-	gesturing
plc	-	hoisting placards, banners, flags
mar	-	marching (collective locomotion)
uni	-	uniformed delegations
bnd	-	musical band
cbn	-	various combinations of the above
???	-	other complex forms social behavior

Figure 5.2.   Collective behavioral composition of temporary gatherings.

Most readers will think of exceptions, e.g., some prosaic gatherings that are more complex than some demonstrations, and some demonstrations more complex than some ceremonial gatherings. The problem is that we simply do not know the collective behavioral composition of these gatherings in any systematic fashion. Until now we have not had even the most rudimentary criteria for observing, comparing, and scaling temporary gatherings in terms of their component sequences of collective behavior. Building upon my efforts at the outset of this chapter to establish the phenomenon of collective behavior, I have attempted to specify our ignorance of the collective behavioral composition of gatherings, and I have suggested a way in which that ignorance might be reduced in a systematic fashion (cf. Merton 1987).

This could enable the comparison of a variety of prosaic gatherings, of political, sports, and religious demonstrations, of the Olympic Games opening and closing ceremonies, the Nuremberg rallies, July 4 parades in the United States, November 7 parades in the USSR, and the inaugurations and funerals of heads of state, to mention but a few. With a comparative measure of gathering complexity in hand, we could proceed to examine relationships with gathering size, with periodicity, with the organizing and mobilizing efforts of interest groups and state agencies, and with variations in macro social, economic, and political circumstances.

By an *event* I mean a related sequence of two or more gatherings spread across different spatial frames within a single continuous time frame of up to 24 hours. One example is the college football game that is preceded by tailgate parties outside the football stadium while the marching band moves from its point of origin across campus to a location inside the stadium, where two competing teams take their pregame warm-ups, spectators locate their seats, journalists assemble in the press box, the officiating team checks its assignments and the ground rules, all prior to the start of the contest between two teams, the efforts of cheerleading teams, cheering spectators, band music, etc. [Cf. MacAloon's (1987) simultaneous gatherings making up the Olympic Games.]

Another example involves the 10,000 pilgrims who simultaneously pray and gesture while circling seven times around the sacred Kaaba inside the Grand Mosque of Mecca, while thousands more wait to take their place; in an adjoining structure, having completed their seven circumambulations, another 10,000 engage in a ritual of seven runs between the symbolic mountains of Safa and Marwa (cf. Amin 1978; Kamal 1961).[25]

A third example is the political demonstration consisting of a sequence of two or more different forms of protest or celebration gatherings. The modal behaviors in political demonstrations ordinarily take one or more of five forms. The *rally* is a seated or standing gathering in which the majority of participants are located in arcs or rings around one or more speakers and performers. Speeches and songs by the latter are followed and often accompanied by applause, cheers, chants, and songs by the former. The *vigil* line involves two or more persons standing side by side and facing in a common direction, often carrying placards stating the focus of their protest or promotion. The *picket* involves one or more persons carrying placards stating a protest or principle. Picketers stand, or walk single file (but sometimes two or three abreast) in an elliptical path. The *march* was described above in some detail (also cf. McPhail and Wohlstein 1986). *Civil disobedience* can take a variety of forms (Sharp 1973). The familiar sit-down blocks pedestrian or vehicular traffic or otherwise obstructs routine movements in a thoroughfare, entryway, or place of business.

Sometimes these forms of political demonstration occur separately as single gatherings, sometimes as a sequence of two or more forms but in various combinations. In 1983 I observed an available sample of 46 political demonstrations in Washington, D.C. For this set of demonstrations, the most frequent form of protest or promotion was the rally (45 percent), followed by the march (25 percent), the vigil (13 percent), and the picket (8 percent). Civil disobedience occurred in six gatherings (8 percent): five in the context of a rally or picket; one—a sit-down— in the middle of a long march. The various combinations I observed are reported in Table 5.2. The most frequent sequence was some combination of rally and march. These demonstrations are examined in greater detail elsewhere (McPhail 1985).

The 46 demonstrations consisted of a total of 75 gatherings spread over different but contiguous locations in space and time. These various combinations of protest forms illustrate my definition of an *event:* related sequences of gatherings that spread across separate but contiguous space and time frames within a single geographical-political community.[26]

By *campaign* I refer to a recurring sequence of events, gatherings, and/or sequences of collective behavior that are repeated in the same and in different space and time frames, ordinarily within a single community, across a period of several days, weeks, or months. Religious campaigns, also known as revivals or crusades, have been studied extensively by historians (McLaughlin 1959) and sociologists (Lang and Lang 1960; Whitam 1968; Johnson 1971; Wimberly et al. 1975; Clelland, Hood, Lipsey, and Wimberly 1974; Althiede and Johnson 1977; Johnson et al. 1984). The organization of gatherings and events in the election campaigns of political candidates has been described by campaign managers (Bruno and Greenfield 1971) but has not yet been examined by social scientists for the wealth of information it can yield. Sports teams' season campaigns of home and away games, the attendant gatherings, and component sequences of collective behaviors by spectators in general, by bands, cheerleaders, pep clubs, etc., have yet to receive the attention they warrant by social scientists.

The community campaigns of social movements have been described by participants and journalists (King 1958; Raines 1977;Branch 1988) and investigated extensively by sociologists (A. Morris 1981, 1984; McAdam 1982, 1983) and by political scientists (Garrow 1978).[27] Those accounts correspond to my own observations of a hospital workers' strike in Charleston, South Carolina, which served as the crucible for a civil-rights movement campaign between March and July of 1969. The campaign consisted of almost daily rallies in a local church, followed by marches to each of three hospitals where additional brief rallies were held with striking picketers before the marchers returned to their point of origin for a final rally. On some occasions the initial rally was followed, or the final rally preceded, by a march through the

Table 5.2.   Political Events: Sequences of Demonstration Gatherings, Washington, D.C., 1983 (McPhail 1985)

Sequence of Gathering Type					Totals	
1	*2*	*3*	*4*	*5*	*Gathering*	*Event*
R					14	14
V					9	9
P					5	5
M	R				8	4
R	M				4	2
M	V				2	1
M	P-CD				2	1
R	M	R			12	4
R	M	R-P-CD			6	2
M	CD	M			3	1
R	B*	R-P-CD			2	1
P	M	R			3	1
R	M	R	M	R-CD	5	1
				Total:	75	46

*B: bused

Frequency of Political Demonstration Gatherings by Type

Abbreviation	Type	Frequency
R	rally	34
M	march	19
V	vigil	10
P	picket	6
R-P-CD	rally-picket-civil disobedience	3
R-CD	rally-civil disobedience	1
P-CD	picket-civil disobedience	1
CD	civil disobedience	1
	Total:	75

downtown business community to supplement continuous picket lines, encouraging all citizens to join the demonstrators in boycotting local merchants until the strike was settled (C. McPhail, field notes, 1969). The combination of boycott, picket lines, rallies, and marches (with attendant arrests) continued, sometimes on a daily basis, for five months (Bass 1969). Thus, this campaign consisted of several simultaneous forms of protest, e.g., boycott, multiple picket lines, and demonstration events. The latter, in turn, consisted of a sequence of gatherings (e.g., initial rally, march, rally with picketers, march, rally with picketers, march, and rally). Each form of demonstration gathering, in turn, consisted of various sequences of collective behavior (e.g., chanting, singing, placard bearing).

By *wave* I refer to a spread—a repetition—of similar campaigns, events, gatherings, and/or sequences of collective behavior across different communities, states, regions, or countries, within a time frame of weeks or months. This phenomenon is well known to sociologists under another rubric—the diffusion and adoption of innovations—and waves of tactical innovations in the civil-rights movement have been analyzed as such by McAdam (1983). Other specific and familiar examples include the wave of civil-rights sit-in demonstrations in the southeastern United States in February and March of 1960 (McAdam 1982; A. Morris 1981); the wave of antigovernment demonstrations on U.S. college campuses in May 1970 after four students were killed during a gathering at Kent State University on May 4 (Peterson and Bilorusky 1971); the wave of individual and collective streaking sequences within and by gatherings on U.S. college campuses in March 1974 (Aguirre et al. 1988); the wave of antiapartheid demonstrations across U.S. college campuses during the 1985–86 academic year; and, the wave of "the wave" among spectators to collegiate and professional football, baseball, and basketball games during 1985 and 1986.

By *trends* I refer to the rise and fall in the frequency of waves, campaigns, events, gatherings, or sequences of collective behavior that occur across states, regions, or nations across a time frame of several years.[28] Tilly et al. (1975) examined the rise and decline of gatherings and events in which there was collective violence (including, no doubt, some waves and campaigns of events and gatherings in which violence occurred) in France, Germany, and Italy between 1830 and 1960.

McAdam (1982) plotted trends of demonstration gatherings, events, and campaigns in the U.S. civil-rights movement between 1960 and 1965. He suggests that "peaks in movement activity correspond to the introduction of new protest techniques" (1982:165) and, as I noted earlier, represent waves of tactical innovation that spread across states, regions, or nations in a short period of time. Tactical innovations in various forms of collective protest expanded to campaigns and waves: the sit-in campaign of 1960; the jail-in campaign in the winter and the freedom ride campaign in the summer of 1961; the boycotts, rallies, marches, and pickets in the communities of Albany, Georgia, in 1962, Birmingham, Alabama, in 1963, Selma, Alabama, in 1965, and, the voter registration campaign in Mississippi in 1964. These are trends of campaigns, events, gatherings, and of sequences of collective behavior.

Summary and Discussion

The concepts of crowd and collective behavior have been used interchangeably in the sociological literature for more than a half-century. Neither has proven fruitful. The traditional concept of crowd has been useless because it connoted too much. Traditional conceptions of collective behavior have been equally useless because they denoted too little, more frequently implying an explanatory perspective than specifying, describing, and classifying the social phenomena to be explained.

The common denominator in most dictionary definitions of *crowd* is a compact gathering or collection of people. Unfortunately, the additional suggestion or connotation ordinarily conveyed is one of the homogeneity of that collection of people or the unanimity of their behavior, or both. Neither popular nor scholarly usage has allowed for, let alone recognized, variation in behavior across the collection of people at any one point in time, let alone variation across successive points in time. In short, the concept of crowd has prevented recognition of alternation between and variation among collections of people behaving individually and collectively. In failing to recognize this variation and alternation, students of the crowd (and of collective behavior) proceeded to develop explanations for unanimous and homogeneous behaviors, i.e., for phenomena that rarely occur and are short-lived if and when they do.

People do behave collectively; but what they do together varies greatly in complexity, in duration, and in the proportion of the gathering that actually participates. In one sense, recognition of this variation would appear to make more difficult the task of the student of crowds and collective behavior. But, in fact, the task is made more manageable and therefore simpler. Attempts to describe and explain the crowd have been an impossibly large task to date. By breaking that task into smaller components, the problem is reduced to several tasks, each of more realistic proportions.

First, I proposed the alternative concept of gathering, i.e., a collection of two or more persons in a common space and time frame who may behave collectively, although not necessarily so. I further noted that just as behaviors within gatherings vary across space and time, so does the gathering itself. I therefore proposed recasting gatherings into a simple three-phase life cycle: the assembling or formation process, itself a form of people behaving collectively; the assembled gathering of people, within which a variety of sequences of individual and collective behavior may occur; and the dispersing process.

Second, I set forth a working definition of collective behavior, of collective behavior-in-common, and of collective behavior-in-concert. I specified and briefly described 40 elementary forms of the former and 6 forms of the latter, illustrated by the work of sociologists and social psychologists who have systematically examined what people do collectively within temporary gatherings. I also discussed variation in the duration and complexity of these forms of elementary collective behavior, and in the proportion of the gathering participating.

If comparatively few sociologists have given attention to what people do collectively within gatherings, an increasing number have given attention to larger units of analysis, at more macro levels of analysis, e.g., gatherings, events, campaigns, waves, and trends. The relationships between what people do collectively at micro and macro levels of analysis are too important to ignore. These must be considered in relation to rather than at odds with one another.

Third, to demonstrate some of those relationships, I first suggested a way of characterizing gatherings by scaling variation in their collective behavioral complexity. Thus, establishing the phenomena to be explained—in effect, disaggregating the crowd into the varied and alternating elementary forms of collective behavior that occur within gatherings—provides a way of specifying our ignorance about the composition of and variation across gatherings. It also enables the systematic recharacterization and comparison of gatherings in terms of the forms of collective behavior of which they are composed.

Finally, I reported some research examining various sequences of protest demonstration forms into political events, and noted the relationships between these units of analysis and the campaigns, waves, and trends investigated by other sociological colleagues. This chapter is a micro step toward examining the relationships between the various units and levels of analysis of what human beings do collectively, ranging from sequences of behavior, to gatherings, to events, to campaigns, and to waves of and trends in those phenomena. I invite my macro colleagues to join me in that examination. In the next chapter I turn to the task of proposing the elements of an explanation for the range of individual and collective phenomena described here.

Notes

1. Merton writes: "In the abstract, it need hardly be said that before one proceeds to explain or to interpret a phenomenon, it is advisable to establish that the phenomenon actually exists, that it is enough of a regularity to require and to allow explanation. Yet, sometimes in science as often in everyday life, explanations are provided of matters that are not and never were" (1987:2).

2. One of the earliest critiques of the collective behavior approach of LeBon, Park, and Blumer was by Bramson (1961). This was followed by critiques by Turner (1964a), Couch (1968), Currie and Skolnick (1972), Gamson (1975), and others. Turner and Killian (1957, 1972, 1987) reject the transformation (contagion) explanation of Lebon, Park, and Blumer, but continue to align themselves with what they call *the collective behavior approach* of Park and Blumer. They write: "What has endured to characterize the 'collective behavior' approach has been the emphasis on the centrality of interaction, the emergent nature of social order, and the normality of collective behavior as the vehicle through which social change comes about" (1987:6). In my judgment they construe collective behavior more as a type of explanation than as a sociological phenomenon to be explained. Perhaps they do both.

3. Quarantelli and his colleagues have persistently called for the convergence of social organization and collective behavior perspectives (Dynes and Quarantelli 1968), and for the recognition of collective behavior as a legitimate sociological phenomenon for investigation (Weller and Quarantelli 1973; Aguirre and Quarantelli 1983).

4. It should be noted that all temporary gatherings are formed by some type of assembling process and that assembling processes, in turn, are a form of collective or convergent behavior involving two or more persons moving in a common or convergent direction. But once the gathering has formed there is no guarantee that any additional collective behavior will occur although it does provide the opportunity for that to occur.

5. If one had the necessary vantage points—an aerial perspective or participants' retrospective reports—one could observe or reconstruct the converging paths of the assembling process from disparate points of origin to a common destination. The assembling process is the form of collective behavior that spans the gap between the diffuse mass and the compact gathering.

6. I assume the majority of human behavior is purposive (McPhail 1986; McPhail and Wohlstein 1986). Therefore, I do not wish to use an element of my explanation to define the phenomenon to be explained.

7. Lofland takes exception to the bizarre characterization I attach to his use of *extraordinary* and argues (see note 23, Chapter 5) that his concern is rather with departures from ordinary forms of social behavior and the consequences of those departures. My impression is that if one established baseline frequency distributions of routine or ordinary forms of social behavior across space and time (cf. Table 5.1), Lofland would accept significant departures from those baseline distributions (e.g., spikes and troughs) as examples of the extraordinary. But my fundamental point remains: one must first have criteria for establishing the presence of ordinary social behavior before one can construct the baseline frequency distributions required to measure sharp departures from the ordinary, and before one can examine the consequences of those extraordinary departures.

Elsewhere (McPhail 1987; and Chapter 6) I outline a theoretical framework for the hypothesis that extraordinary phenomena are noteworthy and can result in orientation in the direction of such phenomena. I offer some illustrative evidence.

8. I am not indifferent to participants' meanings for (i.e., their responses to) their own sequences of individual or collective behavior. At this point, however, I must first establish what I mean by, i.e., how I will judge the presence of, collective behavior. At a later point I or others may want to compare observers' and participants' judgments. I recognize at least two additional and important questions about participants' meanings: Do participants intend to behave with others? Do participants have a sense of *solidarity* in behaving with others? The first is a question about the source or cause of collective behavior. This is obviously a crucial question but separate from the question of what we must see or hear before we can judge that collective behavior has occurred. The second is a question about the consequences of behaving collectively. This question often arises for observers and participants *during* a sequence of collective behavior. It is one referent for Floyd Allport's (1924) notion of social facilitation, viz., the claim that the sights and sounds of others behaving as the individual is behaving or contemplating behaving encourages the individual's behavior. Those sights and sounds are said to produce "a rush" of recognition, togetherness, solidarity. But the collective behavior comes first. Knowing this, organizers work hard to get people to behave collectively, recognizing that collective excitement derives from collective participation, not the other way around (Durkheim 1912)!

9.   Following G. H. Mead (1922), a significant symbol is any verbal or nonverbal gesture that calls out in its user responses that are similar to those called out in the person to whom the gesture is addressed.

10.   The relative absence of sequences of collective behavior-in-concert *within* most gatherings is not to say that a division of labor is never involved. On a micro scale, e.g., in conversation clusters, there is almost always a division between speaker and auditor(s). On a larger scale, particularly in demonstrations and ceremonial gatherings, a complex division of labor is often involved in planning and assembling the gathering and in implementing sequences of collective behavior within the gathering.

11.   Critics of this formal definition of collective behavior should note that substantive content is a dimension on which the behaviors of two or more persons can be judged collective.

12.   The largest gathering may be the six million people who assemble for the Hindu festival of *Kumbh Mela* at Alahabad on the Ganges river in India. They engage in ritual bathing in the river, but only a few thousand can do so at once; the remainder must queue to participate in the ritual or await their turn to queue for participation (cf. Rai 1986; Oki 1989).

13.   Glossalalia, speaking in tongues, occurs in some pentecostal religious gatherings. These sounds fall between vocalization and verbalization. They are not significant symbols, even among speakers and auditors. They consist primarily of sequences of consonants from the language of the speakers, uttered at what sociolinguists characterize as the level of regressive or infantile babbling (cf. Samarin 1972). Glossolalia ordinarily parallels or alternates with other sequences of individual and collective behavior, e.g., praying, singing, and testifying. While two or more persons may engage collectively in glossalalia, it is rare for more than a small proportion of the gathering to do so. The exception may occur at national conventions of the charismatic movement where the more inclusive collective babel has been observed (cf. Laurentin 1977). It further should be noted, however, that as meaningless as sociolinguists may consider these utterances to be, they are construed by charismatics or pentecostals as signs of the in-dwelling of the Holy Spirit.

14.   Another form of collective locomotion is the road race run by hundreds and often thousands of men, women, and children. For many of the celebrated races (e.g., the 10 K in Atlanta on July 4, the annual marathons in Boston, New York, and Chicago) there are thousands of participants, hundreds of thousands of spectators lining the routes, and millions watching on television.

15.   Eastern European countries have perfected and regularly performed spectacular card stunts at annual party rallies, youth rallies, and sporting events (e.g., the 1986 Goodwill Games in Moscow) over the past three decades. Similar card stunts are observed at political and religious rallies in Asia. The Nichiren Shoshu Gakkai religious movement in Japan has become particularly adept in using this technique.

16.   Any band with a drum plus other musical instruments constitutes an instance of simple collective behavior-in-concert if the drum provides a rhythm and one or more other instruments provide a melody. The more different instruments that play different harmonic notes, the more complex the collective behavior-in-concert becomes.

17.   An index of complexity can be constructed for the combination of behaviors and dimensions in which people are judged to engage in common or concert. First, make a matrix consisting of columns of 1 to n behaviors by rows of 1 to n dimensions. All of the dimensions will not apply to all of the behaviors. Second, determine which dimensions are applicable to which behaviors, whether or not those dimensions

happen to be present in the case in point. Third, calculate the dimensions that are present as a proportion of all applicable dimensions. Fourth, multiply that proportion times the behavior. Fifth, repeat the third and fourth steps for each behavior. Sixth, sum the products across all behaviors. The result is an index of complexity for that sequence of collective behavior.

18. I am indebted to John Lofland (1985) for the concepts that I use to refer to some of these units of analysis; we do not always put those concepts to the same uses.

19. I am attempting to avoid the problem of defining ceremony or ritual in terms of the same criteria required to explain what is being defined, e.g., "ritual: rule-governed activity of a symbolic character which draws the attention of its participants to objects of thought and feeling which they hold to be of special significance" (Lukes 1975:291). In my judgment, rules—rather, some detailed textual and verbal directions—are essential in the production of routinized individual and collective sequences of behavior. Therefore, one cannot use rules to define the same phenomena those rules are used to explain!

20. As gatherings increase in size, it is more likely that some sequence of collective behavior will occur. As more sequences occur, it is more likely that some will be more complex than others. Controlling for the size of the gathering, I suggest that the complexity of the collective behavioral composition will increase across prosaic, demonstration, and ceremonial gatherings, in that order.

21. For a discussion of the opening and closing ceremonies of the modern Olympic Games, and variations in the form and complexity of sequences of ceremonial collective behavior, see MacAloon (1984).

22. There are, of course, additional features of both stationary and mobile ceremonial gatherings that distinguish them from demonstration gatherings and that cannot be reduced to sequences of individual and collective behavior *in process*. The settings in which ceremonial gatherings occur are often draped with buntings in state colors and festooned with flags and banners, and frequently display massive photographs of current or past state leaders and heroes, all residues or products of behavior sequences. State processions often include a variety of floats and large military vehicles and weapons, and flyovers by military aircraft frequently occur.

23. The necessary database could be constructed from observer records of sequences of these forms of collective behavior occurring in a sample of gatherings (plus the additional forms I have overlooked). In addition, observers could record the proportion of the gathering engaging in the sequence, the identity of the category of participants engaging in the sequence and the duration of the sequence of collective behavior. These procedures should yield scales comparable to those for riot behaviors in the 1960s (cf. Wanderer 1968, 1969) and selected aspects of political demonstrations in the 1970s (cf. MacCannell 1973; Kritzer 1977).

24. Separate scales will be required to deal with the detailed and distinguishing features of different categories of gatherings, e.g., mundane gatherings, religious, sports and political demonstrations, and state ceremonies. Elsewhere (McPhail 1985) I have described an ordinal scale of the collective behavior composition of political demonstration marches. There will undoubtedly be differences in the order of various forms of collective behavior between religious, sports, and political demonstrations. My guess is that the general ordinal pattern I have described can still be established; that is, the simpler forms of collective behavior (clusters, vocalization, arcs and rings, etc.) will be the most frequent in all the ordinal scale patterns, and these will be followed by the more complex and less frequent forms of collective behavior. Of course, these are empirical questions. I have suggested some tools with which to proceed.

25.   These gatherings are preceded by the initial procession from Mecca to Arafat, and followed by the subsequent "standing on the plain of Arafat", and by the symbolic "stoning the devils" at Mina, as part of the total set of ceremonial gatherings making up the event known as the pilgrimage to Mecca or, more simply as, "the hajj".

26.   An event of a much different magnitude has been created by technological innovations of the last decade. Radio made it possible for a mass audience to hear, and television to see and hear, behavior sequences, gatherings, and events in progress: sports contests, demonstrations, papal masses, state inaugurations, weddings, funerals, anniversaries, and a variety of other gatherings. But participants in those gatherings, while often aware that "the whole world is watching," were unable to monitor their audience. More recent technological developments have made dramatic changes in that state of affairs. Satellite transmission and massive video screens have made it possible for large gatherings in different locations to see and hear one another engaging in a variety of sequences of individual and collective behavior regarding a common object; indeed, they are able simultaneously to engage in collective behavior regarding a common object. Seventy thousand persons gathered in London's Wembley Stadium and a corresponding number gathered in Philadelphia's JFK Stadium to watch a cast of star performers in the Live Aid concert for starving children in Biafra. Members of both gatherings swayed, gestured, clapped their hands, and sang along to the music of the performers, and they watched one another engage in those behaviors simultaneously on the massive video screens by way of satellite transmission. This electronic merger of mass and gathering is the epitome of McLuhan's "shrinking global village."

27.   Lofland's (1982b; Lofland and Fink 1982) examination of lobbying campaigns of interest groups in the California state capitol warrants replication in every state capitol.

28.   I deliberately use *trend* here instead of Lofland's *cycle* because I use the latter to designate *the life cycle* of temporary gatherings.

6

Elements of an Explanation

Introduction

Auguste Comte posed the quintessential social psychological question: How can the individual be both consequence and cause of society? The offspring of human beings are the most dependent creatures in the animal kingdom. They cannot survive without continuous nurturing by parents or other caretakers. In the course of that nurturing they acquire language, which in turn enables them to learn the culture of the society more rapidly, to direct (and be directed by) the behavior of others, to organize and direct their own behavior, and to fit their behavior together with the behavior of others. This analysis of becoming a human being was set forth by George Herbert Mead (1924, 1936) and others as well.

Too often sociologists and social psychologists think only of Mead's analysis of the genesis of self, and fail to appreciate his analyses of the individual act and the social act, and the extension of those analyses to the problem of collective action. His analysis of the act was a precursor to many of the basic features of the cybernetic models of human behavior that are at the cutting edge of cognitive science today. One of those models, developed by William T. Powers, will be presented below. When combined with Mead's equally powerful analysis of the role of language in fitting together the behaviors of two or more persons, the elements are present for a cybernetic model of social behavior.[1] This allows the possibility of developing an explanation, with the same basic principles, for the varied and alternating sequences of individual and collective behavior that take place in temporary gatherings. It also enables us to move beyond the analysis of cooperative behavior to consider elementary forms of competition, conflict, and violence.

I first summarize Mead's theories of self and of the individual act. Then I summarize Powers's cybernetic theory of purposive individual behavior. I return to Mead for a discussion of his "principle of organization"—the role of significant symbols and taking the attitude of the other in coordinating the behaviors of two or more individuals. I then recast Mead's argument in terms of Powers's cybernetic model and develop three ways by which two or more purposive actors can generate a sequence of collective action. I briefly discuss the relationship between cooperation, competition, and conflict, and I conclude with a brief discussion of how this cybernetic model of social behavior can be extended to micro levels and units of analysis in the gathering, the event, and, the campaign.

George Herbert Mead (1863–1931)

Mead's Theory of Individual Behavior

The "Social Self." The most fundamental idea in George Herbert Mead's theory of human behavior is that people talk to themselves and to one another. The former enables the individual to organize and control his or her own behaviors. The latter enables each of two or more individuals to organize their respective behaviors in relation to a common object and to one another. Humans learn to do the latter before they can do the former (Bruner 1983). Through interaction with others, the infant learns the animate and inanimate objects in its culture, subsequently learns the names given to those objects and that those names are effective ways of referring others to those objects and vice versa, and thereby learns a powerful means of establishing objects in common with others.

Young children learn about their own bodies and behavior experiences in the same way, namely, through the nonverbal and verbal behaviors others take toward those objects. Infants and children have no other knowledge of who or what they are apart from the actions others take toward them. When the infant and child behaves toward his or her own body, behavior, and experiences as others behave, the result is a social self, or what Mead called a "me."

Mead (1924) referred to this as a social self because of the correspondence between others' behaviors and the individual's own behaviors. Others label or identify or designate what the individual has done, is doing, or proposes to do, and the individual subsequently designates his or her own behaviors (or body, or experiences). Others evaluate the individual's past, present, or proposed behavior, and the individual subsequently evaluates what he or she has done, is doing, or proposes to do. Others prescribe or proscribe certain behaviors by the individual toward him or herself, other people, and other objects, and, the individual subsequently prescribes or proscribes behaviors for him or herself.

The correspondence between others' behaviors and the individual's behaviors is seldom complete.[2] Sometimes the individual does not quite understand what others have said, or at least does not "get it right"; often there are multiple others who direct slightly different or even competing behaviors toward the individual creating uncertainty or confusion; and, in other instances, the individual simply resists what others have said. But at the outset and in general, the individual's behaviors, the individual's body, and the individual's experiences are constructed just like all other objects. They have no intrinsic or inherent meaning. Like other objects, whatever meanings they have are acquired through the responses people make to them. And the more consistent others' responses toward the individual's behavior, body, and experience, the more likely the individual behaves toward those objects as others behave.

This argument is not unique to Mead. In many ways it is simply another version of a basic sociological principle; namely, the more frequently we interact with others across time, the more likely we will behave as they do toward objects of mutual consideration. We come to adopt the same beliefs, biases, and behaviors toward those objects. Mead emphasized that there are as many different social selves as there are contexts of behavior and experience in which the individual is engaged (some with others, and some alone). These social selves are of consequence in one very fundamental way. When the individual encounters situations like those encountered in the past, the individual has some bases for knowing who he or she is, what such a person should or should not do, and how well he or she can (or cannot) do it.

The "Individual Self."   If the preceding were all there was to Mead's theory of self, it would be like many other theories of social learning, and it would be subject to the same criticisms. One of the most telling criticisms is that from time to time most individuals encounter new situations with which they have little directly applicable prior experience, and no prior responses from others telling them who they are, what to do, or how well they do it in those situations. What does the individual do then?

Mead's answer to this question was his theory of the individual act, more specifically, a theory of problem solving. This theory also illustrates the frequently overlooked, but even more frequently misunderstood, aspect of Mead's theory of self: "The I." By this Mead refers to the efforts of the individual to solve the range of problems not addressed by "the me." This does not mean the individual abandons those repertoires of behavior and experience that make up the multiple social selves. Rather, the individual must draw upon bits and pieces of information from this and from that repertoire, and bits and pieces from the ongoing situation (including the behavior of others), to formulate a solution to the problem at hand. Thus,

Mead's concept of "the I" refers to the synthesizing and improvising—the problem-solving—facet of the individual's self or selves.

Mead defines a problem as "the checking or inhibition of some more or less habitual form of conduct, way of thinking or feeling" (1938:22). No phase of behavior or experience is immune. According to Tucker and Stewart (1983:6–9), Mead's formulation addresses *five classes of problems* which I summarize here.

1. Ongoing behavior may be deflected or stopped by an intrusion (e.g., sudden crosswinds when driving down the interstate), by an obstacle (e.g., the back doors of the trailer truck one is following on the interstate swing open, dumping dozens of cartons onto the roadway), or by a malfunction (e.g., one has a blow-out).
2. A routine and familiar problem solution may no longer produce routine and familiar results (e.g., the antiseptic used in a hospital may no longer eliminate deadly bacteria).
3. A routine problem solution may continue to work but may now create previously unobserved, unanticipated, and presently undesirable consequences (e.g., womens' prolonged use of birth control pills increases the likelihood of certain forms of cancer).
4. Phenomena may be observed that are exceptions to, or cannot be explained by, existing theories (e.g., Unidentified Flying Objects).
5. Existing theories or belief systems may predict the occurrence of phenomena which have yet to be observed by anyone.

The discussion that follows focuses upon the first of these; namely., the disruptions of and disturbances in every individual's everyday behavior and experience. These problems were the principal focus of Mead's theory of "the act."

The "Individual Act."   Shibutani (1968:331,332) argues the act is the basic unit of analysis in Mead's theory of human behavior.

> All the things [human beings] do can be broken down, for purposes of analysis, into a succession of acts. There are many kinds of acts; they vary in length; they may overlap one another; and may be delayed or even truncated. . . .
> . . . Each act is constructed as [the individual] makes a succession of adjustments to conditions (external and internal) that are undergoing constant change. Overt behavior is generally only the final phase of an act; in most cases it is preceded by a number of preparatory adjustments. (1968:331,332)

Mead's analysis divides the act into four phases: impulse, perception, manipulation, and consummation. One or more of these may be repeated in the course of adjusting to the conditions that have created the problem in question.

a. The impulse phase. An impulse can be characterized as a "distur-bance" (Shibtuani (1968:332). Mead noted two classes of disturbances. The individual does not have what she or he wants at the moment; or the indi-vidual is doing what she or he wants but that ongoing behavior is deflected or blocked. Both require the individual's attention to and assessment of the problem.

Mead advanced no set of sovereign motives. He acknowledged biological requirements for oxygen, liquid, and food, as well as innate sexual, ag-gressive, and parenting impulses. But he also recognized that whatever innate needs the individual might have are readily modified by one another as well as by experience; and Mead emphasized experience! Human beings acquire a great number and variety of impulses, interests, and behaviors by participating in the group into which they are born and the other groups and social relationships through which they pass throughout life.

Mead wrote that "the situation out of which the difficulty, the problem springs is a lack of adjustment between the individual and his world" (1938:6). But what occasions that lack of adjustment? Mead suggests at least two ways in which a lack of adjustment might be produced by the disruption of ongoing behavior; he has less to say about the lack of adjustment deriving from the individual not having what she or he wants at the moment. In the case of the former, some disruption might come from a change in the indi-vidual's physical environment, or from the presence or the behavior of an-other person. In the case of the latter, the individual might complete the organization of one sequence of behavior—one act—and ask, "Now what remains to be done?" Unless the individual says, "Nothing!" there is a lack of adjustment between the individual's many interests and the status quo. What the individual wants has not yet been satisfied, or what was satisfactory is no longer so. What has worked until now no longer suffices. The indi-vidual's attention is directed to the disparity. It is in relation to such prob-lems that consciousness arises and problem-solving behaviors are under-taken.

b. The perceptual phase. Here the individual entertains one or more hypothetical solutions to the problem, hypothetically projects their imple-mentation, and assesses the hypothetical outcomes of those solutions. Should none of those appear to work, the individual may return to the first phase of the act for a reassessment of the problem before attempting to formulate further hypothetical solutions.

Mead construed human perception as the purposive efforts of a sensing organism grappling with the solution of a problem. He distinguished (1938) between two classes of perception: "immediate experience" and "reflective analysis." In discussing the former Mead emphasized the variety of behav-iors in which the sensing organism might be engaged. For example, visual perception requires moving the head and eyes, focusing the lens, and adjusting for binocular focus. Tactile perception involves contouring the hands and fingers to engage objects, moving the hands and fingers over the surface(s) of the object(s), and often varying tactile pressure against object surface. Aural perception involves inclining and orienting the ear, and making minute muscular adjustments in the tension of the eardrum. Olfactory perception requires maneuvering the nose and regulating the inhalation of air over the nasal sensory receptors. Oral perception requires the deliberate maneuvering of the fluids in the mouth over the taste buds.

Thus, for Mead, perception is purposive! The individual actively engages its environment rather than merely passively receiving it. Moreover, perception is selective! The individual is seeking stimuli that will solve the problem or contribute to the development of a possible solution. The problem and its solution may not necessarily be in the individual's immediate space and time frame experience. Hence, Mead's second category of perception: reflective analysis. Human beings frequently deal with problems that are removed in space and time. Mead argued that language makes this possible. Humans can talk with others, and with themselves, about objects that are removed in space and time. They can consider, examine, and rearrange objects that are not present, that have no existence except in the conversation underway. But, as Mead noted, "the process of identifying the object and correcting our attitudes [i.e., gestures] in the presence of unsuccessful conduct through the use of significant symbols (social in origin) in inner conversation, is as immediate as any other" (1938:17).

By means of covert conversation, therefore, the individual can establish, consider, and fit a variety of hypothetical pegs in a variety of hypothetical holes. In the course of doing so, the individual may visibly alter its own posture, the position and contour of its hands, etc., even though no physical referents are present for the object(s) under consideration (cf. Jacobsen, 1931, 1973).

Whether the individual is attempting to solve an immediate and visible problem in ongoing behavior or an abstract problem with no immediate physical referents, the perceptual phase of the act consists of one or more hypothetical trials of possible solutions to the problem. Language enables the individual to transcend time and space, to draw upon repertoires of experience and behavior for elements of possible solutions, and hypothetically to project those solutions into the future, thereby to imagine and assess their possible outcome.

   c. The manipulatory phase.   Once the individual has identified a plausible hypothetical solution to the problem, the next step is to test the hypothesis. Here the individual attempts to carry out the probable solution considered in the perceptual phase. For problems of immediate experience, the reality of the perceptual object is found in the contact experience. Mead wrote:

> The physical thing arises in manipulation. There is in manipulation the greater fineness of discrimination of the tactual surfaces of the hand, the three dimensional experience which comes from grasping, and of more critical importance, there is the instrumental nature of the manipulation experience. (1938:24)

In this third phase of the act, the individual presses the hypothesized solution against the problem. The manipulatory phase of the act provides an empirical and pragmatic test.

If a solution works, the problem is resolved; the hypothesis has been consummated. Consummation is not always accomplished immediately. The individual frequently has to revise or adjust and then try the modified solution. This may involve a repetition of cycles through the manipulatory phase of the act. Failing there, the individual may have to return to the perceptual phase, reassess the problem, and consider one or more different hypothetical solutions before returning to test one of them in the manipulatory phase. The individual may even quit the problem for the time being and return to it later, e.g., with abstract problems of reflective analysis. Or the individual may abandon the problem altogether.

d. The consummatory phase. To consummate is to sum up, to complete the act. Once a solution is in place, whatever was problematic is no longer so; the individual's interest is satisfied; the disrupted behavior goes forward. For the moment!

Mead also wrote of a subsequent phase in the act, one he termed "the aesthetic phase" in which the individual assesses the solution to the problem, and perhaps the problem-solver as well. I will return to this phase later for it provides a basis for understanding the expression of evaluation, that is, emotion (cf. McPhail 1989a).[3] Mead argued that virtually all human behavior is purposive. There is no one simple and sovereign purpose such as power, profit, altruism, or self-esteem maintenance. Rather, the individual's varying purposes are the solutions of the varying problems with which it is confronted. The perceptual and manipulatory phases of the act are the consideration, revision, implementation, and further revision of solutions to those problems.

Thus, as Shibutani suggests:

> Purposive behavior requires negative feedback. The principle is relatively simple: the results of one's own action are included in the new information by which subsequent behavior is modified. Thus, by responding to what he observes [to be the results] of his own activity, a person makes necessary corrections. Although this principle appears over and over in the work of Dewey and Mead, it has been largely overlooked, perhaps because they failed to coin a striking term to designate it. (1968:333)

Norbert Wiener (1948, 1954) coined a very striking term—cybernetics—to refer to self-governing systems, and he came to be known as the father of cybernetics. Shibutani (1968:330) contends the first cybernetic model in social psychology was proposed much earlier in the century in John Dewey's (1896) critique of the stimulus-response "reflex arc" and in George H. Mead's subsequent and related development of pragmatic theory of the individual problem-solving act. The correspondence between their ideas and those of contemporary cybernetic models will become evident as we examine the work of William T. Powers.

William T. Powers (b. 1925)

Control Systems Theory

Introduction. Powers (1973a, 1978, 1988) argues that human beings are very complex, self-governing, *control systems;* more accurately, human beings consist of thousands of hierarchically arranged control systems in the brain, down the spinal column, and out to the 600–800 voluntary muscles whose contractions move the parts of the body that produce every behavior in which human beings engage. Human beings are not controlled; human beings control. Human beings are not mechanical automations; they design, build, and use electromechanical control systems to further their own purposes.

For example, a control system with which readers are familiar is the wall-mounted thermostat used to control the temperature in their living rooms. It is a control system designed by one human being to do what another human would have to do if he or she could stand watch 24 hours a day with one hand in the living room to register room temperature and another hand on the furnace or air conditioner to adjust the source of hot or cool air into the living room to regulate that temperature.

Control Systems. All control systems—human and electromechanical—share several features in common, four of which are illustrated in Figure 6.1. The first is *an input function* that registers features of that control system's environment. In the wall thermostat the input feature is a thermometer that registers room temperature. In human control systems Powers calls the product of this input component *perceptual signals (p).*

The second feature of a control system is *a comparator function.* This compares those perceptual signals against some purposive human being's objective or goals. Powers terms those objectives *reference signals (r).* Thus, comparators in human control systems compare where the individual senses that she or he is p with where she wants to be, r. The wall thermostat

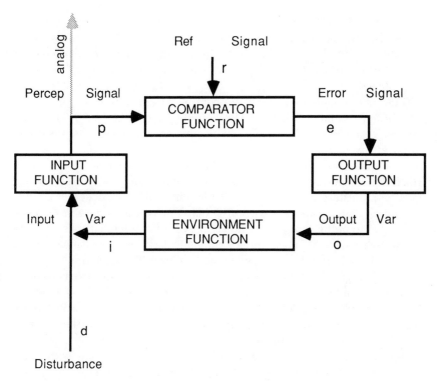

Figure 6.1.   Generic control system (after Powers 1973).

contains an electromechanical comparator. Some purposive human being sets the thermostat on the wall to regulate the room temperature at a desired 65 degrees in the winter months. The thermostat then compares the current room temperature sensed by the thermometer p against the preset desired temperature level r.

A third feature of control systems is *an output function*. A discrepancy between perceptual and reference signals is called an *error signal* (e). When there is a discrepancy in the thermostat, e.g., when room temperature falls below 65 degrees, the thermostat puts out an electric signal and turns the furnace on; the furnace heats air, which rises or is blown through the duct system into the living room. Similarly, error signals in human control systems occasion instructions for adjustments in behavioral output.

Just as the output of the thermostat control system affects the living room environment of that system, so the behavior of the individual control system takes place in some environment and behavioral output affects that environment. In both cases, the control system senses those environment effects through its input component, compares the resulting perceptual signals with its reference signals, and, if a discrepancy remains, makes further adjustments until perceptual signals match reference signals. Thus, in the words of the title to Powers's (1973a) book, human beings behave to control their perceptions. They adjust their behavior to make their perceptions match their objectives.

There is one additional feature of control systems designated in Figure 6.1: the environment function. The output of a control system enters an environment that will also be affected by other agents, forces, and processes. Furnaces may continue to work at peak capacity over long periods of time and use enormous amounts of energy if they are heating air in a room in which the thermostat is set for 65 degrees, but someone has left the window open on a blustery day when the outside temperature is 32 degrees.

Similarly, an individual's purposive behavior output occurs in environments that sometimes physically impair or resist the intended consequences of that behavior (e.g., noise, bright sunlight, darkness, fog, icy pavement, crosswinds, population density, equipment failure). Those environments frequently include other human beings contributing their respective behavioral outputs. The effects of those disturbances are registered in the individual's perceptual input, require further comparisons of perceptual against reference signals, and often result in error signals that require further instructions for behavioral adjustments.

One of the most important ideas in Power's formulation is one with which we are all familiar from repeated personal experience but one that has escaped virtually all the theories of human behavior that have come to my attention. The adjustments in behavior an individual must make at one point in time to achieve a particular result are not the same adjustments she or he must make must make at subsequent points in time to maintain the same result, let alone the adjustments required to reproduce the same result at a later point in time. Similarly, the behavioral adjustments individual A must make to achieve a particular result at one point in time are not the same adjustments individual B must make to achieve the same result at the same point in time. One reason is that factors other than the individual's purposive control over its behavior may prevent the intended consequences from taking place, and those disturbances change across time and space, *requiring variable behavioral output to achieve the same end result.* Similarly, two or more persons in the same situation occupy slightly different points in space and may have to negotiate and overcome slightly different disturbances to achieve the same result.

A Hierarchy of Control Systems.   Figure 6.1 vastly oversimplifies the individual as a single control system. Powers (1973a, 1979, 1988) convincingly argues the individual is more accurately viewed as thousands of control systems arranged hierarchically. He (1988) hypothesizes 11 levels of control systems, in ascending order: intensities, sensations, configurations, transitions, events, relationships, categories, sequences, programs, principles, and systems. My primary concerns, like those of most social and behavioral scientists, are with higher-order systems; however, lower-order control systems are required to produce the actions called for by higher systems. My cursory description of Powers' control systems hierarchy follows.[4]

Whatever phenomenon or process any particular system controls, it does so by creating a perception of that process or phenomenon that matches the reference signal operating the control system (Powers, 1979:45). Higher-order control systems do this by changing the reference signals for lower-order systems. A discrepancy between reference and perceptual signals creates an error signal. Error signals call for adjustments in the reference signals of lower-order control systems. This is illustrated in the left-hand hierarchy (behaving) in Figure 6.2. If the perceptual signals of the next lowest control system do not correspond to the newly adjusted reference signal, the resulting error signal in that system will call for changes in the reference signal for the next lowest control system, and so on in descending order, until perceptions are created that match the reference signals.

First-order control systems are the only systems that can produce behaviors that result in changes in the external environment. They control the 600–800 voluntary muscles in the human body. The contraction of those muscles make the movements that have effects in the body's environment. Those effects are registered as intensity signals by first-order kinesthetic receptors and compared against first-order intensity reference signals.

Frequently the individual must make continuing adjustments in the loop of behavioral output, environmental effect, perceptual input, and comparison, until first-order perceptual signals match first-order reference signals. Analogs of first-order perceptual signals are then transmitted up the hierarchy, providing each higher-level control system with the ingredients for creating appropriate perceptual signals to compare against that control system's reference signals. In Powers's theory, the ascending hierarchy of perceptual signals is therefore cumulative: the perceptual signals at each order are composed of some aspect of lower-order perceptual signals.

It should be emphasized that, in this hierarchical model, first-order control systems can register nothing about environmental stimuli except variations in the magnitude of their *intensity*. First-order sensory receptor signals must be transformed before they are of consequence elsewhere. Thus analogs of first-order signals are transmitted to second-order control systems where they are grouped into *sensations*, e.g., of sound, or light, or of kinesthetic effort. Similar transformations occur up the ascending hierarchy of control systems. Second-order sound sensation signals are grouped into third-order perceptual *configurations* of phonemes; light sensations are grouped into shapes. Multiple-configuration signals are transformed into fourth-order perceptions of

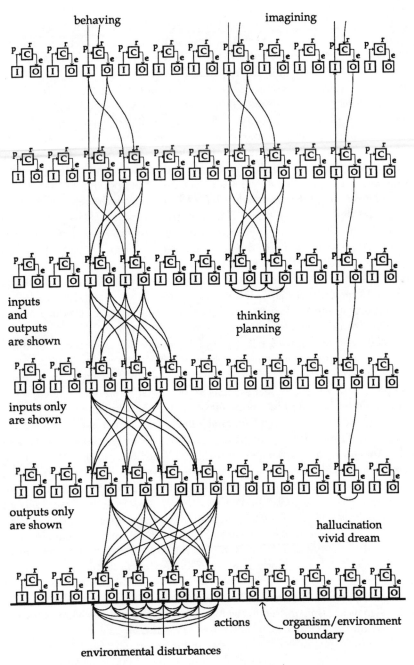

Figure 6.2. Hierarchies of control systems (after Powers 1988).

transitions, e.g., softer to louder sound configurations, smaller to larger shape configurations. Transition signals are transformed into fifth-order perceptions of *events*, that is, transitions with beginnings and endings. Multiple-event signals make possible sixth-order perceptions of the *relationships* of one event, transition, or configuration to another, e.g., one event is on, above, below, beside, or in front of the other.

Seventh-order control systems may be unique to human beings because they arbitrarily group lower-order perceptual signals—relationships, events, transitions, configurations, sensations, intensities—into *categories* of experiences that are tagged with and distinguished by *symbols*. Symbols are verbal or nonverbal gestures that arbitrarily stand for a category of experiences (or a category member), e.g., raised fist with extended index finger, Arabic [1] or Roman [I] numerals, or alphabetic letters [E-N-O].

Eighth-order control systems arrange symbols into ordered *sequences* that are both conventional and familiar. Words are ordered sequences of alphabetic symbols, e.g., the word O-N-E (cf. E-N-O), or, the word W-R-I-T-E. Sentences are ordered sequences of words.

Symbols—letters, words, and sequences of words—enable us to imagine, to think about, and to adjust the reference signals for all the lower-level control systems required to connect higher-level control systems to actions in the world. Symbols enable human beings to establish objects or targets removed in space and time, and to give directions to others and to themselves for movements regarding those objects or targets. Consequently, symbols are *the* crucial means by which two or more persons can communicate, by which they can set and adjust similar reference signals, and can thereby adjust their respective individual actions to yield collective action. Sometimes this is accomplished by symbol sequences alone; sometimes it requires higher-order reference signals, themselves constructed of symbols or symbol sequences.

Ninth-order control systems organize symbol sequences into *programs*. Programs are contingent directions for behavior, exemplified by Miller, Gallanter, and Pribram's (1960) TOTE units: test-operate-test-exit. For example: does the letter [W] appear on the screen? No? If not, depress the key marked [W] on the keyboard. Is the letter [W] on the screen now? Yes! Go to the next letter. Is the letter [r] on the screen? No? If no, depress the key marked [r]. Is the letter [r] now on the page? Yes! Next, perform the same TOTE for the individual letters [i], [t], [e]. Similar TOTEs can be executed for sequences of numbers, of words ("I am pleased to write this letter of recommendation"), and of sentences (e.g., this paragraph).

Tenth-order control systems are called *principles*. These are abstract, symbolic standards in terms of which choices are made between programs as well as standards for formulating, revising, evaluating, and rejecting programs. For example, there are a number of programs for communication:

talking face-to-face, telephoning, writing. There are a number of writing programs, among them handwriting, typewriting, and word processing. Selection among these programs might be made in terms of one or more principles such as familiarity, competence, efficiency, or clarity. Other programs are formulated, revised, evaluated, selected or rejected in terms of such principles as problem solution, honesty, consistency, loyalty, verifiability, parsimony, majority rule, first come first served, or minimax.

Powers names the highest-order control systems in his hierarchical model *systems level* control systems. Systems are *interrelated constellations* of principles, programs, sequences, categories, relationships, events, transitions, configurations, sensations, and intensities. If self is treated as reflexive actions the individual takes toward its own body, behaviors, and experiences (past, present, and future), then *self-systems* (cf. Mead 1924) may be viewed as a constellation of principles, programs, sequences, and categories pertaining to the individual's reflexive actions. There are, of course, other systems upon which individuals draw to organize and control their behaviors and experiences, e.g., various theoretical systems (Newtonian mechanics, the genetic code, operant conditioning, structural linguistics), philosophical, theological, and ideological systems (e.g., pragmatism, Calvinism, democracy), language systems (English, Urdu, Japanese, ASL), not to mention social systems (family, peer group, bureaucracy, society).

Some students of purposive human action will be less familiar with Powers' first six levels of control systems; most will be more familiar with the last five. Most social and behavioral science theories incorporate some aspect of these higher-order reference and perceptual signals in their explanations of individual and collective action; e.g., systems (social or self), principles (values, laws, norms), programs (calendars, schedules, scripts, roles, directions), sequences, and categories (symbols). But as I noted earlier, the problem with such abstract elements is that they cannot produce overt behavior by themselves. They contribute by adjusting reference signals for lower-order control systems. Conversely, the lower-order control systems cannot select what behaviors to produce or when. They depend on higher order control systems for the necessary reference signals. A hierarchical model of human action is essential!

Adjustments in higher-level reference signals (**for example, the program level reference signal for typing the parenthetical phrase you are now reading**) set in motion adjustments in the lower-order reference signals necessary to produce perceptions matching those higher-level reference signals. This enables this typist to produce the words in the parenthetical phrase you just read, and to do so in seconds; indeed, to do so far more rapidly than this typist can utter the commands for the actions required to type the *16 words, the punctuation mark, and the 15 intervening spaces inside those parentheses,* let alone the total *103 marks and spaces* of which the phrase is composed. These particular words appeared on this typist's computer monitor at approximately 100 words per minute, averaging three to seven letters each. This typist cannot utter 300–700 letters per minute, let alone the instructions to position, raise, and lower the appropriate fingers over the appropriate keys to produce those letters, spaces, and words, or the phrase they compose. But this typist can speak, read, or think 100 words per minute and, at a program level, call for their appearance on the paper or the monitor; and that program resets the reference signals for the lower-order sequences, categories, relationships, events, transitions, configurations, sensations, and intensities that strike the keys and produce the words, phrases, and sentences on the paper or the monitor. Similar hierarchies are involved in the familiar and "simple" actions of walking, hand-clapping, singing a melody, writing one's signature, driving a nail, hitting a ball, and the like.

I note one further and invaluable feature of hierarchical control systems. As the middle hierarchy (imagining) in Figure 6.2 suggests, higher-level reference signals may call for imagining the hypothetical execution and consequences of one program of action or another. That is, the reference signal for which the individual is controlling involves imagining, planning, thinking through, and revising before choosing between two programs for the best solution to the particular problem with which the individual is confronted. By merely imagining "how it might work," the lowest-level adjustments feed back to the level of transitions or configurations but not at the level of intensities that result in overt actions.[5]

The experimental evidence for Powers's control systems model of individual behavior is impressive (Powers 1978; Marken 1980, 1986, 1988). An individual subject manipulates a joystick or mouse (the behavioral output) to move a cursor (one perceptual signal) in relation to some point or configuration (another perceptual signal) on a computer monitor, in accordance with a reference signal established by the experimenter's instructions to the subject. The environment in which the tracking efforts take place is an electronic one, which the experimenter has programmed with a variety of random disturbances. Notwithstanding those disturbances or changes in those disturbances, the individual subject maintains the perceptual signal against the reference signal with impressive persistence and accuracy. The correlations between the predictions of the theoretical model and the individual's behavior, recorded every 1/30th of a second across 1,200 successive data points, are consistently in excess of $r = .955$. That evidence persuades me of the merits of this model of purposive individual behavior as a basis upon which to proceed to develop a model of purposive social behavior.

Symbolic Control. To control for a symbol is to create a specified perception of that something; it is to see, hear, touch, taste, or smell the members in the category to which the symbol refers, or to the category itself. As the typing example suggests, symbols are powerful means of adjusting the reference signals for lower-order control systems that occasion complex observable movements in the environment. For several additional reasons as well, I believe it is difficult to exaggerate the importance of symbols, symbol sequences, programs, and principles in the production of purposive individual and collective action.

First, symbols are the means through which individuals can talk with themselves (and others) about their experiences. Presymbolic organisms can discriminate and experience a wide range of intensities, sensations, configurations, transitions, events, and relationships (Plooij 1984), but symbols enable humans to transcend space and time, to recall, stabilize, and analyze complex past experiences, and to connect them by hypothesis to prospective future experiences.

Second, the relationships between symbols and referents are not only arbitrary, they are also conventional; that is, they were constructed by human beings, and they can be deconstructed and reconstructed. But at any one point in time we can estimate the meanings of a particular symbol by observing the responses made to it. There may be a range of responses to that symbol; but more frequently than not, there will be modal responses, that is, those responses most frequently made to that symbol by most members of the language community. I construe those conventional uses of that symbol as its shared meaning in the community.

Third, it is by virtue of the shared meanings of symbols within a language community that two or more members of that community can communicate with one another, about which more later.

Fourth, a language system exemplifies what Durkheim (1895) called a "social fact." Language systems are both exterior to and and independent of any one individual member of the community, but they are also constraining on all members of that community. Newcomers must acquire the language and its conventional usages if they are to survive within the community; they invariably do so through interaction with accomplished users (Bruner 1983). As they progressively do so, they can more readily establish mutual objects with other individuals, they can more readily direct and be directed by others regarding such objects, and they can more readily direct their own actions.

A Sociocybernetic Theory of Social Behavior

Powers's control systems theory argues that purposive action involves the comparison of perceptual signals to a reference signal, and the adjustment of behaviors to make perceptual signals correspond to that reference signal. It follows that purposive collective action requires that two or more persons set similar reference signals with respect to which they adjust their individual actions to make their respective perceptions correspond to those similar reference signals.[6] The observed result is collective action in common and/or in concert. Thus, I will refer to what follows as *a sociocybernetic theory of collective action* (cf. Prologue, note 2).

We cannot see the perceptual signals those individuals are adjusting nor the covert reference signals against which those adjustments are made. But I think there are at least three ways, each in part observable, by which two or more persons in the same environment can set similar reference signals and give themselves related instructions for adjustment. The results are actions that an observer can judge to be collective. These are summarized below:

1. Two or more persons can *independently* generate similar reference signals and make adjustments (to control their perceptual signals) yielding very elementary forms of collective action.

2. Two or more persons confronted with a mutual problem can *interdependently* generate similar reference signals and make similar or differentiated adjustments yielding somewhat more complex forms of collective action for a relatively small number of people.

3. Two or more persons can adopt the reference signals developed by a *third party*, along with directions for similar or differentiated adjustments that, in combination with third-party preparations and arrangements, can yield very complex forms of collective action for larger numbers of people

Although these sources of similar reference signals and related directions for adjustment are listed separately, I recognize they sometimes develop in sequence or in combination to yield sustained or complex collective actions. I now turn to some examples and empirical illustrations of the three sources of collective action.

Independently Generated
Similar Reference Signals

Some of the simplest sequences of collective action in temporary gatherings occur when two or more persons engaging in separate courses of action shift to a common course of action such as orienting in a common direction, vocalizing in common (e.g., laughing, cheering—yeaing, oohing, ahhing, ohhing, booing), or applauding in common.

What is striking about these very elementary forms of collective action is the apparent lack of contact or consultation between the two or more participants immediately prior to the development of the sequence. I infer that those participants, e.g., person A and person B in Figure 6.3, independently establish similar reference signals and control for those reference signals by

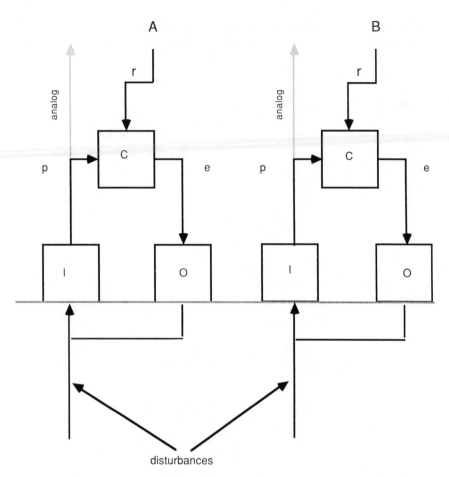

Figure 6.3. Two or more individuals (A,B) independently set similar reference signals (r).

adjusting their respective actions (which we can observe) to make their
respective perceptual signals (which we cannot observe) match those reference signals. I base this inference on evidence from the following two types
of situations.

First, when two or more individuals in the same environment independently perceive departures from what is ordinary in that environment, they
often take one or more steps regarding the correction of that error. Powers
writes of a related phenomenon:

> To say that behavior exists in order to control perceptions is not to say that all
> perceptions are under control. Much that we can see happening around us
> happens without benefit of our advice or effort. But we do come to "expect" the

world to be a certain way; that is, even without specifically intending to do so, we set up reference signals against which we compare perceptions even when we have no direct way of affecting them: an inner model of how the world should be. As long as the world matches those expectations, we experience no error and go about our affairs normally. But just let the sun rise in the west one morning, and see how much error you would experience, and how frantically you would start to act to try to do something about this gross mistake. (1988:24)

I have in mind less cosmic errors and less frantic adjustments.

For example, when the reference signals of two or more individuals for ordinary sounds, light, behavior, or behavior configurations in a public setting are not matched by their perceptual signals for sound (e.g., explosions, or even "falls off ladders"), for light (e.g., dark clouds), for behavior (e.g., fistfights), or even for an extraordinary number of people engaging in collective action (e.g., configurations of more than six people), those individuals are momentarily startled by the error. *The extraordinary* sound, light, behavior, or configuration *is noteworthy.* Those two or more persons turn in the direction of the extraordinary to ascertain what is going on (McPhail 1987). Although this involves controlling for an error, it does not correct that error; but it is a first step. Further, noting the extraordinary frequently occurs independently, i.e., without initially consulting with companions or proximate strangers (Darley, Teger, and Lewis 1973; Miller et al. 1975).[7] When the two or more persons engage in those changes in orientation in the same direction at more or less the same time, an observer notes collective or convergent orientation.

Second, simple collective actions in temporary gatherings can also be produced when two or more persons in the same environment independently control for the same desired outcome, albeit one they cannot directly affect. Some familiar examples are provided by spectators at sporting events. All the spectators do not see the game (Hastorf and Cantril 1954; Loy and Andrews 1981). Fans who assemble to observe a game between their team and a rival team are likely to control for the perception of selected categories of actions by selected categories of actors. They want to see their team score and win. Thus, partisan spectators sometimes chant for their team's successful offensive play that will move the ball across the goal line for a score; they sometimes chant for their team's successful defensive play to thwart the opponent. They also evaluate the outcomes!

A study by Zillman and colleagues (1979) demonstrated that fans systematically cheered and applauded their team's successful running and passing plays (and perhaps jumped up and down as well); the same fans moaned their team's failures and shortcomings. They moaned the opposing team's success and cheered their failure. Partisan fans also see more rule infractions and dirty play by the opposing team than by their own (Hastorf and Cantril 1954).

Greer's (1983) research documented that fans booed when an opposing player fouled, when an official failed to impose a penalty, or when an official was perceived to impose a penalty unjustly on the fan's team. Home team fans sometimes chant "bullshit" when officials make unfavorable or incompetent calls. Home team fans also raise the general ambient noise level by cheering, applauding, and whistling when the opposing team has the ball at the home team's one-yard line or when the opponents shoot a free throw, or by chanting "defense" when the opposing team has the ball or chanting "air ball" when opponents miss the rim and the backboard. In short, the proverbial home court advantage may turn out to be a visiting team disadvantage by virtue of the disturbances home team fans introduce (cf. Silva and Andrew 1987).

Collective whistling, cheering and applause, collective boos, ohhs, and and ahhs, are extremely simple forms of collective action. Most readers will probably accept my characterization of those actions as evaluations of some sequence of individual or collective action by an individual player or the team. I believe it is consistent with control theory to argue that these vocalizations (yeas, boos, oohs, ohhs, ahhs) and manipulations (applause) result from two or more individuals independently controlling for similar reference signals (objectives, goals), and then independently evaluating the extent of correspondence between those reference signals and their perceptual signals for what subsequently transpires.[8]

For example, partisan fans of a college sports team may operate with self-systems that include self-identification in terms of a particular team (e.g., "I'm Sooner born and Sooner bred, and when I die I'm Sooner dead"), principles of loyalty to the team (e.g., "Hail to the Orange, hail to the Blue, ha-il to Ill-i-nois, ever so true"); programs for demonstrating that loyalty by assembling when their team competes against opposing teams (e.g., when there is a Saturday home football game, any and all other commitments and obligations are superseded); and additional programs for cheering the successes and moaning the shortcomings of their team's performance on the playing field during the game. Regarding the latter, fans cannot hit home-runs, make baskets, or score touchdowns or goals. But the fans are represented by their team. In addition to singing the fight song, chanting "defense, defense," and synchroclapping while chanting "Go! Go! Go! Go!" to urge their team onward, fans also independently evaluate the success or failure of their team's collective actions to realize the reference signals for which the fans (and the team) are both controlling; namely, scoring points, stopping the opposition from scoring points, and winning the game.

When the team scores a touchdown or drops a pass in the end zone, the fans do not first consult with one another or look around to see what others are doing, nor are they asked at that point by third parties to cheer the good fortunes or moan the bad fortunes of their team. Instead, their perceptual signals regarding the team's actions either correspond to or fall short of their independent but similar reference signals. When they correspond, the individual fan displays positive evaluations by cheering and/or applauding; when the perceptual signals fail to correspond, the disappointed fan displays a negative evaluation by sighing or moaning. When the perceived lack of correspondence is attributed to foul play by the opposition or to incompetent or biased rulings by the officials, the angry fan displays a negative evaluation by booing, cursing, or throwing objects in the direction of the disturbing opponent or official. Having displayed those evaluations, the sights and sounds of others doing the same may affect the individual's adjustments in the intensity, volume, or duration of his or her applause, cheers, boos, throwing, and the like.[9]

Interdependently Generated Similar Reference Signals

Although two or more individuals can independently generate similar reference signals and make behavioral adjustments to match perceptual signals to those reference signals, such procedures seldom yield more than simple and brief collective action. For more complex and sustained collective action to occur, the two or more persons must either interact with one another or with some third party to establish or adopt the necessary reference signals in common, the directions for behavior output, or both. This is crudely described in Figure 6.4.

One circumstance in which such interaction occurs is when two or more persons are confronted with a *mutual problem*. Problems range from encounters with an extraordinary or unfamiliar phenomenon (cf. Sherif 1936), to encounters with an accident or an emergency involving another person (Latane and Darley 1970), to the disruption or blockage of some ongoing activity in which the two or more persons have been engaged (e.g., Alinsky 1972; Gamson Fireman and Rytina 1982).

This can begin with one companion noting the extraordinary, nudging the other, and—with a nod of the head—directing orientation toward the extraordinary phenomenon. Those two or more persons might then identify the phenomenon and isolate what is problematic from what is not; they might further estimate some possible solutions to the problem, anticipate the possible outcomes of those solutions, then pursue what appears to be the most feasible solution. At several points they might have to decide who among them can and should do what, when, where, and how, to implement that solution (Latane and Darley 1970).

Individual onlookers intervene more frequently than onlooking collections of strangers (a phenomenon Latane and Darley named "diffusion of responsibility"), but not significantly more frequently than onlooking pairs of friends (Latane and Rodin 1969; Miller et al. 1975). It is important to note here that

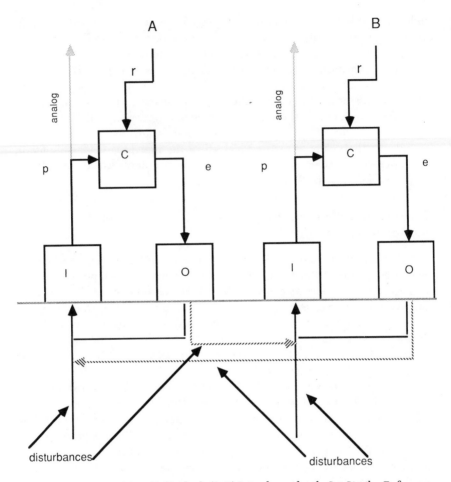

Figure 6.4.   Two or More Individuals (A,B) Interdependently Set Similar Reference
    Signals (*r*).

the majority of people in public places (McPhail 1987), sports (Aveni 1977),
religious (Wimberly et al. 1975), and political gatherings (McPhail 1985) are
not alone. Rather, they assemble, remain together, and disperse in the
company of one or more friends, family members, or acquaintances. Therefore, most temporary gatherings are composed primarily of small groups of
companions. This does not mean that all the purposive action is collective
action; it is not. It does mean that individuals are seldom alone, not to
mention anonymous, in most temporary gatherings.

   When confronted with an extraordinary or problematic development,
friends are far more likely than strangers to turn to one another for confirma-

tion, to talk with one another to determine what the problem is and to decide whether, how, and when to intervene (Miller et al. 1975). The early portions of these exchanges may turn on registering one another's facial displays, e.g., surprise or the startle response noted earlier (Darley et al. 1973). Rudimentary proposals for action can be made with nothing more than a nod of the head. More frequently questions are posed (Is something happening?), assertions or proposals are made ("Sounds like trouble to me," "It's nothing," or "Maybe we should check that out"). Finally, when friends intervene, they do so almost twice as quickly as pairs of strangers (Miller et al. 1975). I have suggested that friends are able to do so in part because of shared past experiences and their familiarity with one another's skills, but more so because of the rich vocabulary of verbal and nonverbal symbols friends share. That vocabulary enables the two or more persons to establish more quickly a mutual object (and the characteristics of that object), and to propose and implement some course of action regarding that object.

Mead (1936) used the concept *significant symbol* to refer to verbal or nonverbal gesture that call out similar responses in members of a language community. Those symbols enable one individual to establish, by naming or labeling or identifying an object for consideration by another. The individual initially may have to scrutinize the other and take the context into consideration before selecting the symbols to direct to the other. While a variety of symbols might be used, the individual is likely to select those symbols that evoke modal responses in the language community the individual believes to be shared with the other. Having made that selection, and having directed those verbal or nonverbal symbols to the other, the individual can hear or see the symbols at the same time they are heard or seen by the other.

Mead hypothesized that the significant symbols the individual directs to the other call out similar responses in the individual, ordinarily the modal response of the language community (cf. note 5). That modal response may serve as the individual's reference signal against which to judge the other's response to the symbols. If the other responds as the individual responds or fails to respond to the contrary, the individual has evidence of shared meaning and a basis for assuming that some object in common has been established with the other.

George Herbert Mead (1924, 1936, 1938) avoided the fallacy of suggesting or requiring that one individual get inside the mind or experience of another. Instead, he advanced the argument that by using the significant symbols of a language community one individual can give directions to another and that such symbols call out in the individual responses similar to the responses those symbols call out in the community at large; if the other does not respond to those symbols as the community does, the individual can repeat, rephrase, or recast the directions until the other does so respond (or until the individual abandons the effort).[10]

Mead recognized the highly complex but innate and therefore fixed forms of collective action engaged in by ants, bees, and termites. In contrast, he called attention to the enormous flexibility with which two or more human beings can establish varied objects and directions for related behaviors in common or concert corresponding to the varied problems with which they are confronted. Mead (1936) termed this "the principle of organization" and referred to it as the "principal method of organization." However, as flexible as this interdependent resolution of problems may be, it does not work as well for more than about six persons (Hare 1981). With an increase in the number of people, it is increasingly difficult for every person to monitor every other person, thereby to negotiate and confirm understanding or agreement. Thus, as the number of persons increases, mutually inclusive interdependent interaction among all persons decreases. One frequent consequence is that some small subset of a larger collection of persons engages in the majority of the interacting, proposing, debating, revising, and compromising among themselves while, for all practical purposes, ignoring surrounding others.

If the excluded others are uncertain of what to do, or if they are dependent on or loyal to the principals, they may continue to monitor (in arcs or rings around the principals) what is taking place and they may await further instructions for behavior. When this occurs, in effect the onlookers adopt the reference signals and instructions for behavior adjustment provided by the third-party principals. More frequently, however, the excluded others turn away and interact among themselves, forming small groups of their own (Bales, Strodtbeck, Mills, and Rosenborough 1951; Bray, Kerr, and Akin 1978; McPhail 1987). In sum, complex and sustained sequences of collective actions by large numbers of people are not generated frequently by mutually inclusive interaction with one another.

Adopting Similar Reference
Signals from a Third Party

Complex and/or extended sequences of collective action, particularly those involving large numbers of people, are more likely produced when participants adopt the reference signals and related directions from some third party. This is crudely described in Figure 6.5. What distinguishes third parties from the sources of reference signals already discussed? When are third-party reference signals and directions required? Why should anyone adopt the reference signals and directions offered by a third party? How do variations in third-party reference signals and directions relate to variations in collective action?

What Distinguishes Third Parties?   When two or more individuals independently generate similar reference signals, they do so as onlookers to

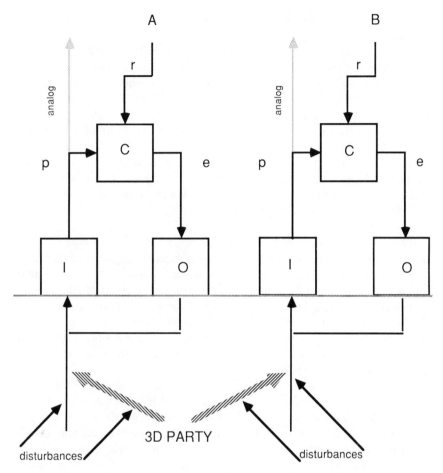

Figure 6.5   Two or more individuals (A,B) adopt from a third party (*r*).

phenomena in their environment that are often indifferent to them. When two or more individuals interdependently generate similar reference signals and related directions regarding some mutual problem, they are active participants in establishing the characteristics of and a solution to that problem; but, again, the problematic phenomenon is often indifferent to them.

Third parties are not indifferent to onlookers. They deliberately attempt to manipulate verbal and nonverbal symbol sequences to produce collective action by two or more members of the gathering. They do so by carefully selecting significant symbols, by stating those symbol sequences simply and repeatedly, and often by making them redundant across sensory modalities (e.g., audible, visible, and sometimes tactile). Third parties also frequently supplement the program level reference signals they direct to gatherings by offering higher-level ideological principles as justification for adopting the program.

The use of significant symbols, higher-level principles, and related rhetorical devices to manipulate audiences has been documented in analyses of sales convention rituals (Peven 1968) political speeches (Atkinson 1984b; Heritage and Greatbatch 1986), fundamentalist preachers' sermons (Rosenberg 1970), and stage comedians routines (Tomlinson 1981). Other examples of third-party manipulation of reference signals for more complex collective actions by smaller collections of actors is found in the work of football coaches and quarterbacks, band directors and drum majors, orchestral conductors and choral directors, political demonstration organizers and marshals, and, experimental psychologists and social psychologists who study collective action (cf. note 6).

When? I have asserted repeatedly that for sustained and complex collective actions to occur, two or more persons must either interact with one another interdependently developing the necessary similar reference signals and related directions for behavior adjustment, or they must adopt those reference signals and directions from a third party. As the number of people increases, it is increasingly difficult for all of them to interact and increasingly unlikely they can reach consensus on the reference signals and directions. If they are to act together, they must adopt the reference signals and directions from a third party.

For example, the organizers and directors of large religious, sports, and political gatherings, events, and campaigns, must plan for the assembling of participants,[11] for the sequences of collective action in which they will engage, for the arrangement of settings that will facilitate the initiation, development, and completion of those sequences, for the provision of equipment or props, costumes, scripts, and communication devices that are necessary to those sequences. Preparations for the Nuremberg Party Day Rallies during the Third Reich are one prototype (Burden 1967); those of the pilgrimage to Mecca are another (Long 1979; Azim 1985). But it could be argued that I am stating the problem from the perspective of the organizer who is attempting to produce and direct sustained and complex collective action. Why should the participants adopt the reference signals and directions offered by a third party?

Why? The more experience an individual has in a situation, the more likely that individual knows what to do regarding the range of problems or opportunities encountered in that situation. An individual with less experience is more likely confronted with the question, "What am I supposed to do here?" Performances by or instructions from another who demonstrates or claims knowledge of what to do in the situation are likely to be considered by the individual who does not know what to do. Further, an individual confronted by the question of what to do, or whether to pursue one course of action or another, is more likely to pursue that course advocated or performed by family, friends, or acquaintances. And, in many religious, sports, or political gatherings, the individual not only assembles, remains, and disperses with one or more family members, friends, or acquaintances, that small group of companions may be part of a larger group or organization responsible for producing or participating in the gathering. By virtue of those group memberships, the individual is more likely to adopt the directions offered by a third party who speaks for the group, particularly when those objectives and directions for behavioral adjustment (program level) are justified in terms of religious or political ideological principles (principle level).

Last but not least, individuals, small-group members, and organizations sometimes adopt the objectives and directions of third parties on whom they are dependent for resources ranging from liberty, to jobs and salaries, to food, water, oxygen, to life itself. That is, individuals sometimes choose between alternatives, they often do as they are told, even when they do not embrace the actions they are asked to carry out because they are dependent on the individual or group that is the source of those directions. Power is the ability to carry out actions or to compel others to carry out actions, over and against resistance. Power is a function of dependency. Those who are dependent are more likely to tell themselves to do what they are asked or told to do by those on whom they depend.

If one or more of these circumstances lead two or more individuals to adopt the reference signals offered by a third party, how are those objectives and related instructions of consequence for the behaviors in which those individuals engage together? McPhail and Wohlstein (1986) report research addressing that question.

How?   McPhail (1972) trained a team of observers to make records of a variety of forms of social behavior in political demonstrations. Several dozen demonstrations were observed. More than 100 sequences of collective locomotion were recorded, in field notes and on film, involving two or more adjacent persons walking, running, or marching together in the same direction and at more or less the same speed: pedestrian clusters, collective surges by individuals and clusters within gatherings, impromptu street actions by large portions of gatherings, and announced marches by entire gatherings. Both small and large numbers of participants were observed moving over short and long distances, in both simple and complex forms of collective locomotion in a wide variety of settings. Sometimes the collective movement commenced simultaneously; more frequently initiation was staggered. Sometimes participants sustained their movements together; more frequently there were gaps and surges.

A system was developed for making and systematically coding film records of locomotion behaviors (Wohlstein and McPhail 1979; McPhail and Wohlstein 1982). A unit of collective locomotion was defined as two or more adjacent persons (within 7 feet of one another), locomoting in the same direction (plus or minus 3 degrees), at the same velocity (plus or minus .5 feet per second). Criteria were developed for reliably measuring three dimensions of collective locomotion: the simultaneous initiation of movement by two or more adjacent persons; the extent to which the direction and velocity of their movements were connected; and the extent to which they moved in step. Each measure ranges from .00 to 1.00. The mean of the three measures constitutes an *index of coordination*.

The theoretical framework for describing and explaining collective locomotion was more Meadian than cybernetic, but there were continuities and overlaps as my earlier comments suggest. McPhail and Wohlstein (1986) assumed that for collective action to occur, two or more individuals must have similar objectives and give themselves similar or related directions for behavior. The greater the similarity and specificity of those self-directions for who is to do what, with whom, when, where, and how, the more coordinated their actions should be. A quasi-experiment was devised to examine this argument.

Five groups of 12 subjects each were given different sets of written instructions to read and to carry out. All received instructions in common for assembling (CA) at point X. Each received different instructions for what to do at point X.

The first group (CADL) received diverse instructions for locomotion: two to wait at X for further instructions; two to walk to Y, and two to run but only after everyone had assembled at X; two to move to Y but not in a straight line; two to move to Y but only after half those at X had begun to move; and two to move to Y only after a whistle had blown. Each of these written instructions (in CADL) concluded with the request, "Please *don't discuss these instructions* or show them to anyone else."

The second group (CAL) received minimal instructions in common for assembling and for locomotion. They were informed that when everyone had assembled at point X, they were to move to point Y. This group and all remaining groups were further informed that everyone in their group had the same instructions and that *they could discuss those instructions* while assembling at point X.

The third group (CALI) received instructions in common for assembling, for locomotion, and for initiating locomotion. They were informed that when everyone had assembled at point X and a whistle was blown, they were to move to point Y.

The fourth group (CALIA) received instructions in common for assembling, for locomotion, for initiating locomotion, and for aligning their locomotion. They were informed that when everyone had assembled at point X a whistle would be blown, whereupon everyone should begin chanting aloud and in unison, "left, right, left, right"; further, when a second whistle was blown, they were to move to point Y starting with their left foot on the chant of left, their right foot on the chant of right; and, finally, to stop at point Y.

The fifth group (CALIAS) received instructions in common for assembling, for locomotion, for initiating and aligning locomotion, and for spacing their locomotion. They received the same instructions as the fourth group plus the additional instruction to stay in step with and maintain equal spacing from adjacent persons while moving to point Y.

Continuous film records were made of each group assembling at point X, of behaviors within that gathering, and of any locomotion to point Y. The film records were then coded for the three dimensions of collective locomotion summarized above. Results are detailed elsewhere (McPhail and Wohlstein 1986) and are summarized in Table 6.1. The index of coordination varied from .01 in the first group (CADL) to .88 in the fifth group (CALIAS). Although differences between all treatments were not statistically significant, the results support the hypothesis that extent of coordination should increase with the specificity of similar self-instructions for behavior.

Discussion.   Individuals must set similar reference signals if they are to act together; they must set increasingly specific reference signals if they are to initiate movement together and to maintain similar direction, uniform velocity, and spacing as they continue their movement together. As the number of people in a band or military unit increases, their interaction with one another decreases and with it the likelihood of their interdependently setting similar reference signals, not to mention the likelihood of their doing so independently. If similar reference signals are required, they will have to be set by a third party, adopted by those who are to move together, and perhaps reiterated by counting cadence, by drumbeat, or by both.

Table 6.1.   Collective Locomotion by Self-Instructions Adopted from a Third Party (After McPhail and Wohlstein 1986)

Dimensions, collective locomotion	*Self-instructions adopted from third party**				
	CADL	CAL	CALI	CALIA	CALIAS
Initiation	.00	.36	.73	.93	.91
Connection	.02	.49	.58	.86	.81
In-step	.00	.30	.27	.75	.91
Index of coordination	.01 [a]	.38 [b]	.53 [bc]	.84 [cd]	.88 [de]

* Treatment group instructions are summarized in text.

[a-e] Index of coordination scores with no superscript in common are significantly different ($p < 0.5$).

Elementary collective locomotion may seem trivial until we realize that most preschoolers cannot yet move together from place to place. How do they come to do so? When such movements are necessary, double files of preschool children are sometimes tied together with ropes and led to their destination by an adult. Kindergarten children and first-graders hold hands (or hold onto a rope) and can thereby move together, under adult supervision, to a specified destination. Older children are capable of regulating the direction, velocity, and spacing of their movements in accordance with their teacher's specification of the reference signal: "Stay together." Precision marching and maneuvering in a school band or a military unit represent a further point along this continuum of similar and specific self-instructions.

Third-party directions are seldom so comprehensive or clear that those to whom they are directed can do what is requested or required without further interaction among themselves, with the third party, or both. In the collective-locomotion study, participants were sometimes required to give attention to one another because the experimenter's instructions asked them to do so (CALIA, CALIAS), and sometimes because the experimenter's instructions were simply inadequate, e.g., specifying what to do but not when or how (CAL), or what to do and when, but not how (CALI).

Summary and Discussion

This analysis has touched on but a few of the many and complex problems of explaining individual and collective action in temporary gatherings. In the preceding chapter I argued that temporary gatherings consist of alternating and varied sequences of individual and collective action, a feature that traditional theories of the crowd and collective action have ignored or cannot explain. In this chapter I have presented Mead's and Powers's explanations of purposive individual action, an explanation that can be extended to purposive collective action. That extension is made possible by means of symbols, more specifically, systems of significant symbols enabling two or more persons to establish objectives (reference signals) in common and to direct or adjust their behaviors to bring their perceptions (perceptual signals) in line with those reference signals. It is primarily for this reason that I refer to this formulation as *a sociocybernetic explanation of collective action*. Although I did not demonstrate the extension of this model to the alternation between and variation within individual and collective sequences of action, I did offer some empirical evidence for the claim that control systems theory addresses a range of collective actions, from simple to complex, involving small numbers and large.

While most psychologists are concerned with purposive individual action, or occasionally with elementary purposive collective action, most sociologists are concerned with far larger and more complex collective phenomena, none of which I address here and only some of which I have addressed elsewhere (McPhail 1988).[12] I suggest that just as simple sequences of collective actions consist of merged or joined individual actions, more complex collective phenomena (e.g., political, sports, and religious gatherings) can be construed as the repetition and/or combination of individual and collective sequences of action. Larger events, such as an initial rally followed by a march to another location, where a second rally is then followed by a sit-in involving civil disobedience, can be construed as a combination of sequences of gatherings, extended in space and time. Campaigns involve the repetition of multiple events and gatherings across longer periods of time and multiple locations in space.

I view these gatherings, events and campaigns, as purposive actions, even though they are seldom controlled by the same purposes, let alone the same purposive actor. The sequences of individual and collective behavior of which they are composed are ordinarily alternating and varied: heterogeneity is the rule rather than the exception. When entire gatherings, events, or campaigns *are* designed, prepared, rehearsed, and implemented by one person or a small group of persons from a common script with a common or related set of reference signals, the resulting sequences of coordinated, symmetrical, and integrated collective actions can be spectacular; e.g., the Nuremberg party rallies, the opening and closing ceremonies of the Olympic Games, state funerals, state weddings, state coronations and inaugurations, or the religious rituals making up the *hajj* in and around Mecca.

Members of groups, organizations, and societies may share more reference signals in common with fellow members than they do with nonmembers, because they are likely to be working on the solution of more mutual problems with one another than with nonmembers. Purposive action is problem driven (Tucker and Stewart 1989). But no two members of even the smallest group always agree that a problem exists, or which problem to solve, let alone how it should be solved. Nor do they always have equal access to or control over the resources that may be required for problem solutions. Different problems, different solutions, and different resource control lend themselves to competition and to conflict, issues I have not addressed until now, and will do so here but briefly.

The mere presence and actions of others can present obstacles to the pursuit of individual and collective objectives, obstacles that frequently can be circumvented or overcome without conflict. Competition, on the other hand, can be defined as the presence of two or more parties pursuing mutually exclusive objectives: one party's success is the other's failure. Some competition is regulated by rules or laws (i.e., principles or systems of principles) to which the competitors agree and which more or less regulate or prevent the kinds of clashes between competitors that would lead to dangerous levels of violence. This is true of most contact sports competitions, e.g., in boxing, hockey, basketball, and football. It is sometimes true of political demonstrations (and counterdemonstrations) regulated by permits granted by police agencies in many larger U.S. cities.

When competition for mutually exclusive objectives is not regulated in some fashion, hostility and conflict between competitors is probable if not inevitable. This holds true for small groups and for nation-states (Sherif and Sherif 1953). That conflict can be reduced or eliminated by identifying or establishing what Sherif termed "superordinate goals," i.e., objectives that are necessary to each competitor but cannot be obtained by either short of their collective efforts (Sherif 1966). Through those collective actions in common and/or concert, hostility and conflict can be reduced. Control systems theory appears to offer a means of increasing our understanding how cooperation, competition, and conflict can be produced as well as reduced. A great deal of work remains to be done; the prospects are promising. I address these issues at greater length in another book.

Notes

1.   My efforts to forge this connection and extension have been informed repeatedly and immeasurably by the ideas of my colleagues Robert Stewart (1981a,b; Stewart and Tucker 1983) and Charles W. Tucker (Tucker and Stewart 1989; McPhail and Tucker 1990).

2.   There is probably very high correspondence between parents' behaviors and the child's self-behaviors. There is some evidence that the correspondence declines as the child grows older, and comes in contact with a greater number and variety of others in different settings. There is further evidence that correspondence is both mixed and fragile between parents' behaviors and adolescents' self-behaviors, but appears to be stronger and more stable between spouse's behaviors and the individual's self-behaviors.

3.   It also provides a basis for understanding the individual's contribution to self-conceptions. New selfing activities—the improvising and synthesizing activities Mead called the I—are undertaken in relation to new problems. If the individual solves those problems, he or she has the basis for a new conception of self, or reevaluation of self, in relation to the solution of the problem. In this way the individual's notion of self is not restricted to the mere reflection of the appraisals of others. Having engaged in some behavior for the first time that the individual knows others call x-ing, the individual can deductively label him- or herself an X. Of course, it may be difficult for the individual to sustain this new notion of self in the face of others' disagreement, their disapproval or rejection of what the individual now presents or claims his or her self to be.

4.   For a more detailed discussion of this hierarchy of control systems, see Powers (1973a, 1979, 1988) and Plooij (1984).

5.   Jacobsen (1931, 1973) demonstrated that when subjects deliberately imagine making the movements of walking, running, or skiing, the relevant large muscles contract even if, as in the case of amputees, subjects cannot possibly carry out the

movements. Smith (1971) and O'Toole and Dubin (1968) demonstrate that when we give directions to others to perform certain actions, we exhibit truncated versions of those actions. G. H. Mead argued (1936) that when we give directions in significant symbols to others, we simultaneously hear and see those same significant symbols and respond to them ourselves, albeit in truncated fashion. He called this "taking the attitude of the other." Mead's student Cottrell (1971) demonstrated that when subjects scrutinized the actions of someone clenching his or her jaw, the subject's own masseter muscle contracted; when they scrutinized the actions of someone squeezing a rubber ball, their own flexor carpi radialis muscle contracted (for summaries, see McPhail and Rexroat 1979:460–62). Berger and Hadley (1975) report that subjects showed greater arm electromyographic (EMG) activity while scrutinizing others arm wrestling than while watching another stutter, and greater lip EMG activity while scrutinizing another stutter than while watching arm wrestling.

6.   For another control systems analysis of how two persons purposefully fit their behaviors together in relation to a similar reference signal, and resist disturbances in doing so, see Bourbon (1989). His subjects adopted the reference signal provided by the experimenter (a third party), namely, the horizontal alignment on a CRT of their respective cursors with a target cursor. But they had to negotiate interdependently the adjustment of their respective cursors to bring their perceptual signals in line with the reference signal. The important contribution of Bourbon's research is that it makes visible both the reference signal and the actions of the two persons, as well as providing systematic observations and measurements of the relationships of these phenomena vis-à-vis the disturbance.

7.   Correction of the problem, or the investigation and analysis that precedes it, often involves interaction among companions within the temporary gathering. I discuss this in the following section under the interdependent generation of similar reference signals and instructions for adjustment of behaviors to make perceptual signals correspond to those reference signals.

8.   Elsewhere (McPhail 1989a) I have discussed at somewhat greater length, these relationships between *cognition* (i.e., the individual's goal, objective, purpose, or reference signal), *behavior* (i.e., the adjustments the individual makes to realize that reference signal), and *emotion* (i.e., the individual's evaluation of the extent of correspondence between perceptions of behavioral consequence and the reference signal). Thus, my hypothesis is that displayed emotions are evaluations of the outcome of purposive actions. This offers one possible general solution to the age-old problem in social psychology of the relationships between cognition, behavior, and emotion. Instead of placing reason and emotion at odds with one another, this formulation makes them part of the same purposive loop of adjusting behavior to make perceptions match reference signals and evaluating the extent of their correspondence. Frequently that evaluation is displayed as emotion.

9.   Similarly, knowledgeable opera, theater, and concert fans applaud and cheer at the end of arias, acts, and symphonies. Like sports fans, they ordinarily do so independently at the outset, although they subsequently may adjust their actions to the sights and sounds of others' similar actions.

Less knowledgeable fans may not know when to applaud, and may await the actions of others to provide those directions. This fact perhaps led to the practice of performers (or their agents) hiring persons (claquers) to stand or sit in opera houses and theaters to commence vigorous applause at the end of an aria or speech by their performer-employer, thus signaling the less knowledgeable or uncertain members of the audience to applaud and, in turn, conveying a message to the critics, directors, and producers (cf. Wechsberg 1945). Claques are often used today in political and religious gatherings to prompt approving responses from "naive" members of the gathering.

10.   Repetition is probably the most frequent strategy, but repetition and recasting may not suffice. The other still may not understand; may understand but disagree; or may simply refuse to comply. The individual may abandon the effort; or, if the individual has (or is thought to have) resources that the other wants or requires, the individual may attempt to bargain, e.g., "If you will do X for me, I will do Y for you." The other may still refuse. This can discourage further efforts to extract agreement or compliance; it can also occasion attempts to coerce, i.e., "If you do not agree or comply, I will force you to do what I request." Individuals may attempt this through the direct application of physical force.

Individuals engaged in collective action may attempt to withdraw resources from or disrupt the activities of the other and then offer to exchange that withdrawal or disruption for compliance. For example, striking workers withdraw labor from their employers; boycotting consumers withdraw revenue from a merchant; or demonstrators occupy an intersection or an administrative office to prevent routine activities from taking place in those locations. In each case, the withdrawal or disruption makes the other dependent on the collective actors. Power is a function of dependency. Those who engage in collective action to make another dependent upon them are in a position to compel the other's agreement or compliance with their demands in exchange for terminating their withdrawal or disruption of the other's resources or activities (Alinsky 1972; Gamson 1975; McAdam 1982).

11.   Those who deliberately plan and arrange for assembling processes for religious (Johnson et al. 1984), political (Bruno and Greenfield 1971) and sports gatherings (cf. McPhail and Miller 1973) go to great lengths: (1) to state and repeat assembling instructions—who will do what at the gathering, when, where, plus invitations to participate; (2) to schedule gatherings at a time that maximizes the availability of persons to whom the invitations are directed; and (3) where necessary or possible, to arrange for access to the gathering site (e.g., free or cut-rate transportation).

12.   I do not wish to imply a linear relationship between the number of participants and complexity of their collective actions. The collective work of surgical teams and of string quartets belies such implications. I regret that space limitations do not permit the examination of very complex sequences of purposive collective action by these and by other, somewhat larger, groups of persons, e.g., corps de ballet, synchronized swimming teams, offensive and defensive football units, and choral music groups.

Epilogue

I have attempted in the preceding pages to state and critically to evaluate the prevailing twentieth-century characterizations and explanations of crowds and collective behavior. I began by tracing the development of the transformation explanation of collective behavior from LeBon's late nineteenth-century theory of crowd mind, through Park's turn-of-the-century dissertation on rational and critical discussion in publics vs. psychic reciprocity in crowds, to Blumer's midcentury distinction between symbolic interaction in routine social life and circular reaction in collective behavior. I then reviewed the accumulated conceptual criticisms and empirical evidence against this transformation hypothesis. I concluded, as others have before me, that individuals are not driven mad by crowds; nor do they lose cognitive control!

But an even more significant problem with the transformation perspective is the lack of attention to the full range of social behaviors in which people engage in crowds, not to mention alternation between individual and social behaviors. This was the first instance of a much more general pattern in virtually all the theories I reviewed; namely, the failure to specify the phenomena to be explained before proceeding to develop an explanation for those phenomena. Theories of the crowd and crowd behavior should not be theories of rare events. They should be developed to describe and explain the full range of crowds and crowd behavior, the ordinary as well as the extraordinary. The prevailing theories in the twentieth century have all failed to do this. The particular irony for the transformation perspectives is that Herbert Blumer was perhaps the foremost advocate of field research—direct observation, description, and analysis—in twentieth-century sociology. Yet he too proceeded to develop an explanation without first establishing the range of phenomena to be explained.

In Chapter 2 I reviewed Allport's and then Miller and Dollard's predispositionist explanations of the crowd. If the transformation perspective is the oldest explanation of the crowd and collective behavior, the predisposition perspective probably has been the most pervasive and influential expla-nation of human behavior in the twentieth century. Whether by instinct, acquired personality, learned behavior repertoires, or acquired values, norms, or attitudes, the argument is that people do what they do because of the kinds of people they are, because of innate or learned tendencies to behave that, carried within themselves from place to place, predispose those people to behave in certain ways.

The application of the predisposition argument to crowds and collective behavior is quite simple and straightforward. People converge on a common location by virtue of predispositions—motives, attitudes, values and beliefs, or social, economic, and political deprivations, and frustrations—which they share in common; hence the phrase "birds of a feather flock together." Further, nothing new or different is added by the crowd. People behave the same inside as outside the crowd, and for the same reasons, namely, because of their similar tendencies to behave. The predispositions alleged to have brought them together are also alleged to produce collective behavior within the gathering. When the predispositions are triggered or stimulated, the result is collective behavior. Although the sights and sounds of others behav-ing the same are said to be responsible for augmenting, intensifying, *socially facilitating* both predispositions and behavior, "nothing new or different is added by the crowd. People behave the same as when alone, only more so" (Allport 1924:295).

Drawing upon a wide range of empirical evidence, I critically evaluated the predisposition perspective. I concluded, as have others before me, that individuals are not compelled to participate by some madness-in-common, nor by any other sovereign psychological motive, attribute, cognitive style, or predisposition that distinguishes them from nonparticipants. The crowd is no more composed of persons who share some distinguishing madness than it is a means of driving mad those persons who share nothing in common; hence, the myth of the madding crowd.

Perhaps more damning, in my judgment, is the inability of the predisposi-tion perspective to explain logically or conceptually the alternating and var-ied behaviors that occur within gatherings. Predispositions are constants; the behaviors to be explained within temporary gatherings are variable. It is difficult to sustain a coherent and compelling argument for, let alone to demonstrate empirically, the connection between an explanatory factor that is constant and phenomena to be explained that are variable.

The authors of the predisposition theoretical perspectives, like those of the transformation theorists who preceded them, rushed to develop explana-tions before familiarizing themselves with the phenomena to be explained. It is difficult to find a better example of this than Miller and Dollard's conten-tion that "generations of sociologists and psychologists have examined [crowd behavior] and have made available *a body of facts and principles.* The

most obvious and certain of these conclusions will be analyzed here"
(1941:218; emphasis added). What was to be explained may have been obvious and certain to Miller and Dollard from reading books, written by
others who had drawn similar conclusions from reading other books; the
phenomena to be explained might well have been different, and perhaps less
obvious and certain, if Miller and Dollard had constructed that problem
from their own direct observations rather than secondary and tertiary
accounts!

In Chapter 3, I turned to an examination of the emergent-norm perspective, a much more recent but very influential theory of crowds and collective
behavior and the twentieth century. I first examined Sherif's (1936) classic
autokinetic experiments and his subsequent work with O. J. Harvey (Sherif
and Harvey 1952) on the development of emergent norms in situations of
varying uncertainty. Turner and Killian (1957, 1972, 1987) placed those ideas
in a macro sociological framework of emergent problems in the community,
of ecological, political, and attitudinal conditions within which crowds might
develop, and of communication processes by which that development might
occur. They further attempted to translate the interaction processes Sherif
and Harvey studied in the laboratory into the interaction that takes place in a
milling crowd, as well as the development of an emergent norm that allows
the crowd to engage in collective behavior.

Most contemporary students of the crowd and collective behavior share
my sense of indebtedness to Turner and Killian's pioneering sociological
analysis of the crowd, this despite the several problems I noted with their
formulation. For example, there is a pervasive dependence on an archaic
predisposition model of individual actors in the interaction process. Comparatively little attention is given to the types or forms of actions within
gatherings that constitute the social interaction by which norms or definitions of the situation are developed and which may subsequently affect
sequences of collective behavior. Last but not least, Turner and Killian
provide no operational definition of collective behavior, nor does their theory address the range of collective action to be explained.

In Chapter 4, I reviewed some additional criticisms of and some alternatives to the transformation, predisposition, and emergent-norm explanations of crowd advanced by four sociologists who have studied contemporary
demonstrations and riots in the United States and in other countries and
centuries as well. These scholars offer diverse but important alternative
characterizations and explanations that must be taken into consideration by
any serious student of crowds and collective behavior.

Carl Couch's classic critique of stereotypical characterizations and explanations of collective behavior was surpassed only by his then radical proposal
to view crowds as elementary social phenomena rather than as individualistic
phenomena. He has continued to pursue the central sociological problem of

examining, describing, and explaining how two or more individuals merge their respective behaviors into sequences of collective actions, actions that differ from those taken by more complex social systems in degree more than in kind.

Richard Berk first observed and described a variety of sequences of collective action within crowds before offering an explanation for the rational organization of the behaviors composing those sequences. The phenomena he sought to explain demands more than his explanation can provide but he did seek to make sense of what he observed rather than what he read in the reports or claims of others.

Charles Tilly also treats collective action as rational efforts by human beings to promote or resist change. He has identified, documented, and described a wide range of repertoires of collective action forms in nineteenth- and twentieth-century France, Italy, Germany, England, and the United States. Perhaps to a greater extent than any other living scholar, Tilly's examination of accounts of thousands of political gatherings and demonstrations documents the claim that violence is a rare phenomenon; violence develops from routine actions that are not themselves violent; and the majority of violence will not likely be understood without an examination of the transition from routine to nonroutine that is effected by the rational claims of one group and the equally rational resistance of another group, each pursuing their respective interests. Thus, Tilly addresses at a macro level of analysis the related dimensions of rational interaction that Couch (and Berk) examine at the micro level of analysis.

Last but not least, John Lofland persistently reminds us that rational, collective actions also have an emotional dimension that should not be ignored. Equally important, Lofland reminds us that different students of collective action (e.g., Couch, Berk, and Tilly) often work with different units and at different levels of analysis, the relationships among which must be considered if we are fully to understand the context, the development, the organization, and the individual and social consequences of collective action. Although I find some limitations in the units and levels of analysis to which Lofland devotes most of his own extensive field observations and analysis, this is overshadowed by his call for more attention to the phenomena to be explained, for more work on the identification and description of the varied units and levels of collective action in which human beings engage. I applaud Lofland's position because it calls for a program of research not unlike that which my colleagues and I have pursued for a number of years.

Therefore, I devoted Chapter 5 to the presentation of some criteria and a taxonomic scheme for the study of collective behavior in temporary gatherings. The concepts of crowd and collective behavior have been used interchangeably in the sociological literature for more than a half-century. Neither has proven fruitful. The traditional concept of crowd has been useless because it has connoted too much. Traditional conceptions of collective behavior have been equally useless because they have denoted too little, more frequently implying an explanatory perspective than specifying, describing, and classifying a class of social phenomena to be explained.

The common denominator in most dictionary definitions of *crowd* is a compact gathering or collection of people. Unfortunately the additional suggestion or connotation ordinarily conveyed is one of the homogeneity of that collection of people or the unanimity of their behavior, or both. Neither popular nor scholarly usage has allowed for, let alone recognized, variation in behavior across the collection of people at any one point in time, let alone across successive points in time. In short, the concept of the crowd has prevented recognition of the alternation between and variation within sequences of individual and collective behaviors by the two or more persons who make up temporary gatherings. In failing to recognize this variation and alternation, students of the crowd (and of collective behavior) have proceeded to develop explanations for unanimous and homogeneous behavior, for phenomena that rarely occur and are short-lived, if and when they do occur.

People do behave collectively, but what they do together varies greatly in complexity, in duration, and in the proportion of the gathering that actually participates. In one sense, recognition of this variation would appear to make more difficult the task of the student of crowds and collective behavior. But in fact, the task is made more manageable and is therefore made a simpler one. Attempts to describe and explain the crowd have been an impossibly large task to date. By breaking that task into smaller components, the problem can be reduced to several tasks, each of more realistic proportions. I proposed several such steps.

First, in lieu of the crowd, I proposed the alternate concept of the temporary gathering, i.e., two or more persons in a common space and time frame who may behave collectively, although not necessarily so. I further argued that just as behaviors within gatherings vary across space and time, so does the gathering itself. I therefore proposed recasting temporary gatherings into a simple three-phase life cycle: the assembling or formation process, itself one form of people behaving collectively; the assembled gathering of people, within which a variety of sequences of individual and collective behavior may occur; and the dispersing process that ends the temporary gathering.

Second, I offered a working definition of collective behavior, of collective behavior-in-common, and of collective behavior-in-concert. I specified and briefly described 40 elementary forms of the former and 6 forms of the latter, illustrated by the work of sociologists and social psychologists who have systematically examined what people do collectively in temporary gatherings. I also discussed variation in the duration and complexity of these forms of elementary collective behavior, and in the proportion of the gathering participating.

If comparatively few sociologists have given attention to what people do collectively within gatherings, an increasing number have given attention to more inclusive units of analysis, at more macro levels of analysis, e.g., gatherings, events, and campaigns. The relationships between micro collective actions within gatherings and macro collective actions across gatherings, events, and campaigns are too important to ignore. They must be examined in relation to one another.

Third, to demonstrate some of those relationships, I first suggested a way of characterizing gatherings by scaling variation in their collective behavioral complexity. Thus, by establishing the phenomena to be explained—in effect, by decomposing or disaggregating the crowd into the varied and alternating elementary forms of collective behavior that occur within gatherings—I offered a way of specifying our ignorance about the composition of and variation across gatherings. I hope this will contribute to the systematic recharacterization and comparison of gatherings in terms of elementary forms of collective action like those I have proposed, or forms proposed by others.

I illustrated this analytic strategy with my own field research by aggregating sequences of political demonstration gatherings into political events, and then examining the relationships between these two units of analysis and the campaigns, and waves investigated by other sociological colleagues. This is but one small step toward an examination of the relationships among the various units and levels of analysis of collective human action, ranging from sequences of collective behavior, to gatherings, to events, to campaigns, and to waves and trends of those phenomena. My objective is to indicate the range of behaviors in which human beings collectively engage within and across temporary gatherings, and therefore the range of collective phenomena for which I believe explanations must be developed.

Finally, in Chapter 6, I sketched the elements of an explanation for many of the collective phenomena identified and described in Chapter 5. I first summarized Mead's purposive theories of the problem-solving self and of the individual act of problem solving. I then summarized Powers's cybernetic theory of purposive individual behavior. I returned to Mead's principle of organization—the role of significant symbols and taking the attitude of the other in coordinating the behaviors of two or more purposive individuals. I next recast Mead's analysis of social behavior in terms of Powers's cybernetic model and suggested three ways by which two or more purposive actors can generate a sequence of collective action. I offered some illustrative evidence for those arguments and discussed, all too briefly, the relationship between cooperation, competition, and conflict. I concluded with brief discussion of how this sociocybernetic model of collective action might be extended to macro levels and units of analysis on gatherings, events, campaigns, and waves. A longer discussion is forthcoming.

In *Acting Together: The Organization of Crowds* (in preparation) I examine in considerably greater detail the life cycle of temporary gatherings and the organization of individual and collective behaviors within those gatherings. In my judgment, *a primary set of problems* for the student of temporary gatherings involves *describing and explaining variations in the assembling processes* that produce such gatherings. Thus, I begin with an examination of periodic and nonperiodic assembling processes that develop over both macro and micro frames of space and time.

I then turn to *a second set of problems: describing and explaining the gatherings* yielded by those assembling processes and the sequences of individual and collective behavior of which those gatherings are composed. Drawing on my own fieldwork and that of others, I devote separate chapters to *prosaic gatherings* in public places (parks, plazas, beaches, quadrangles), to *religious gatherings*, to *sports gatherings*, and to *political gatherings*. In the first of those chapters, I describe and then examine the sources and consequences of some elementary forms of collective action (cluster, arcs, rings, queues) that appear in most gatherings. In the subsequent chapters, I describe and examine the more complex forms and combinations of forms of collective action (e.g., singing, chanting, marching blockading) that occur more frequently in religious demonstrations and ceremonial gatherings, events, and campaigns. I repeat that analysis with some sequences of individual and collective behaviors that make up sports and political demonstrations and ceremonial gatherings, events, and campaigns. I give particular attention to the role of organizations, specifically the role of third-party sources of objectives and directions for the behavioral adjustments to realize those objectives, which are required to generate the complex and often spectacular forms of human collective action of which the campaigns, events, and gatherings are frequently composed.

The penultimate chapter addresses *a third set of problems, variations in dispersing processes*. After brief attention to routine and nonproblematic dispersal, I examine the considerable disparity between popular stereotypes of panic and hysteria in emergency dispersal, and the abundant evidence to the contrary that documents rational, purposive individual and collective behavior in emergency dispersals.

I then examine the interaction of rational, purposive social-control agents, on the one hand, and rational, purposive, protesting civilians, on the other. I first examine the more frequent confrontations between control agents and civilians that end in the nonviolent exercise of the protesters' first amendment guarantees as well as the control agents' fulfillment of their obligations to maintain law and order. I attempt to contrast, analyze, and explain the differences between those nonviolent resolutions and the much less frequent violent resolutions that develop when social-control agents attempt to coerce dispersal, when demonstrators then resist, and when one or both parties subsequently escalate their use of force to resist or to overcome the coercion offered by the other. Resistance to force, on either side of the barricade, results in violence; that violence is sometimes tragic; and, regardless of degree, it is a serious problem that social and behavioral scientists must address in both old and new democratic societies.

In the United States and other nations with democratic traditions, civilians have long been guaranteed the freedom to assemble, to speak, to petition the state for the redress of grievances. The same democratic nations have generally sworn their agents of social control to protect the rights of those who assemble, speak, and petition as well as the property and person of those who are the targets of protest or merely onlookers and passersby. Thus, control agents are faced with the dilemma of solving two problems that are related but, for which no one solution will satisfy everyone involved. More frequently, even in nations with long established democratic traditions, the agents of social control are inclined to protect and preserve the status quo than the rights of those who challenge it.

Presently, democracy is spreading throughout central and eastern European countries where freedom of assembly, speech, and petition have not existed for 50 years, if ever at all. It remains to be seen if the agents of social control in these new democracies will be required to guarantee those freedoms, or will lapse more frequently into the preservation of the status quo. Democracy is easily preached; it is far more difficult to practice.

In the final chapter, I will review the problems the book has addressed as well as those which have emerged but have yet to be addressed. I will attempt to outline a program of research that is relevant to those problems.

References

Abudu, Margaret J. G., Walter J. Raine, Stephen L. Burbeck, and Keith K. Davison. 1972. "Black Ghetto Violence: A Case Study into the Spatial Pattern of Four Los Angeles Riot Event Types." *Social Problems* 19:408–26.

Aguirre, Benigno. 1984. "Conventionalization of Collective Behavior in Cuba." *American Journal of Sociology* 90:541–66.

Aguirre, Benigno and E. L. Quarantelli. 1983. "Methodological, Ideological and Conceptual-Theoretical Criticisms of the Field of Collective Behavior." *Sociological Focus* 16:195–216.

Aguirre, Benigno E. and Enrico L. Quarantelli. 1990. "Problems in Conceptualizing Crowd Behavior." Paper delivered at the XII World Congress of the International Sociological Association, Madrid, Spain.

Aguirre, Benigno, E. L. Quarantelli, and Jorge Mendoza. 1988. "The Collective Behavior of Fads: The Characteristics, Effects, and Career of Streaking." *American Sociological Review* 53:569–84.

Ajzen, Ivo and Martin Fishbein. 1977. "Attitude-Behavior Relationships: A Theoretical Analysis and a Review of Empirical Research." *Psychological Bulletin* 84:888–918.

Alexander, C. Norman, Lynn Zucker and Charles Brody. 1970. "Experimental Expectations and Autokinetic Experiences: Consistency Theories and Judgmental Convergence." *Sociometry* 33:108–22.

Alinsky, Saul. 1972. *Rules for Radicals.* New York: Random House.

Al-Khateeb, Mohammed J. n.d. *Teaching Prayers.* Beirut: Dar Al-Arabia.

Allport, Floyd H. 1920a. "The Influence of the Group upon Association and Thought." *Journal of Experimental Psychology* 3:159–82.

———. 1920b. "The Group Fallacy in Relation to Social Science." *Journal of Abnormal and Social Psychology* 19:60–73.

———. 1924. *Social Psychology.* Boston: Houghton Mifflin.

———. 1927a. "Group and Institution as Concepts in a Natural Science of Social Phenomena." *Publications of the American Sociological Society* 22:83–100.

———. 1927b. "The Psychological Nature of Political Structure." *American Political Science Review* 21:611–618.

———. 1961. "The Contemporary Appraisal of An Old Problem." *Contemporary Psychology* 6:195–96.

———. 1962. "A Structuronomic Concept of Behavior: Individual and Collective. I. Structural Theory and the Master Problem of Social Psychology." *Journal of Abnormal and Social Psychology* 64:3–30.

Allport, Gordon. 1954. "The Historical Background of Modern Social Psychology." Pp. 3–56 in *Handbook of Social Psychology,* edited by Gardner Lindzey. Reading, MA: Addison-Wesley.

Allport, Gordon and Leo Postman. 1945. "The Basic Psychology of Rumor." *Transactions of the New York Academy of Sciences* 8:61–81.

Altheide, D. L. and J. M. Johnson. 1977. "Counting Souls: A Study of Counseling at Evangelical Crusades." *Pacific Sociological Review* 20:323–48.

Amin, Mohamed. 1978, *Pilgrimage to Mecca*. London: Alan Hutchison.

Anderson, William. 1977. "The Social Organization and Social Control of a Fad: Streaking on a College Campus." *Urban Life* 6:221–240.

Anonymous. 1988. Review of a manuscript submitted by Clark McPhail to a sociological journal.

Applegate, Rex. 1969. *Riot Control*. Harrisburg, PA: Stackpole.

Aron, William. 1974. "Student Activism of the 1960s Revisited: A Multivariate Analysis Research Note." *Social Forces* 52:408–14.

Asch, Solomon. 1951. "Effects of Group Pressure Upon the Modification and Distortion of Judgment." Pp. 177–96 in *Groups, Leadership and Men*, edited by H. Guetzkow. Pittsburgh: Carnegie Press.

Atkinson, J. Maxwell. 1984a. *Our Masters' Voices: The Language and Body Language of Politics*. New York: Methuen.

———. 1984b. "Public Speaking and Audience Responses: Some Techniques for Inviting Applause." Pp. 370–410 in *Structures of Social Action: Studies in Conversation Analysis*, edited by J. Maxwell Atkinson and John Heritage. Cambridge: Cambridge University Press.

Aveni, Adrian. 1977. "The Not-So-Lonely Crowd: Friendship Groups in Collective Behavior." *Sociometry* 40:96–99.

———. 1985. "Analyzing Audience Sounds: Methodological and Theoretical Issues." Paper presented at the annual meeting of the Southern Sociological Society, Atlanta.

Azim, Syed Aftab. 1985. *Pilgrimage*. Karachi: Pakastani International Airlines.

Bakeman, Roger and Steve Beck. 1973. "The Size of Informal Groups in Public." *Man-Environment Systems* 3:51–2.

Bales, Robert, Frederick L. Strodtbeck, Theodore M. Mills, and M. E. Roseborough. 1951. "Channels of Communication in Small Groups." *American Sociological Review* 16:461–68.

Barber, Theodore X. 1969. *Hypnosis: A Scientific Approach*. New York: Van Nostrand.

———. 1972. "Suggested ('Hypnotic') Behavior: The Trance Paradigm vs. An Alternative Paradigm." Pp. 115–182 in *Hypnosis: Research Developments and Perspectives*, edited by Ericka Fromm and Ronald E. Short. Chicago: Aldine.

———. 1973. "Experimental Hypnosis." Pp. 942–63 in *Handbook of General Psychology*, edited by B. B. Wolman. Englewood Cliffs, NJ: Prentice-Hall.

Bass, Jack. 1969. "Charleston Hospital Workers Strike." *New South* 24:35–44.

Bayley, David H. 1976. *Forces of Order: Police Behavior in Japan and the United States*. Berkeley: University of California Press.

Becker, Howard and Harry Barnes. 1961. *Social Thought: From Lore to Science*. New York: Dover.

Bentley, M. 1916. "The Psychological Foundations of Social Aggregations." *Psychological Monographs* 21:6–24.

Berger, Seymour and S. W. Hadley. 1975. "Some Effects of a Model's Performance on an Observer's Electromyographic Activity." *American Journal of Psychology* 88:263–76.

Berk, Richard. 1972a. "The Controversy Surrounding Analyses of Collective Violence: Some Methodological Notes." Pp. 112–18 in *Collective Violence*, edited by James F. Short and Marvin Wolfgang. Chicago: Aldine.

———. 1972b. "The Emergence of Muted Violence in Crowd Behavior: A Case Study of an Almost Race Riot." Pp. 309–28 in *Collective Violence*, edited by James F. Short and Marvin Wolfgang. Chicago: Aldine.

———. 1974a. "A Gaming Approach to Crowd Behavior." *American Sociological Review* 39:355–73.

———. 1974b. *Collective Behavior*. Dubuque, IA: Wm. C. Brown.

Berk, Richard and Howard Aldrich. 1972. "Patterns of Vandalism During Civil Disorders as an Indicator of Selection of Targets." *American Sociological Review* 37:533–47.

Berkowitz, Leonard. 1965a. "The Concept of Aggressive Drive: Some Additional Considerations." Pp. 302–29 in *Advances in Experimental Social Psychology*, Volume 2, edited by Leonard Berkowitz. New York: Academic Press.

———. 1965b. "Some Aspects of Observed Aggression." *Journal of Personality and Social Psychology* 2:359–69.

———. 1969. *Roots of Aggression: A Re-examination of the Frustration Aggression Hypothesis*. New York: Atherton Press.

Berkowitz, William. 1971. "A Cross-National Comparison of Some Social Patterns of Urban Pedestrians." *Journal of Cross-Cultural Psychology* 2:129–144.

Bernard, Luther L. 1924. *Instinct: A Study in Social Psychology*. New York: Holt.

———. 1926. *An Introduction to Social Psychology*. New York: Holt. [Cited in Neal Miller and John Dollard, *Social Learning and Imitation*, (1941) New Haven, CT: Yale University Press.]

Blake, Judith and Kingsley Davis. 1964. "Norms, Values, and Sanctions." Pp. 456–84 in *Handbook of Modern Sociology*, edited by Robert E. L. Faris. Chicago: Rand-McNally.

Blumer, Herbert George. 1936. "Social Attitudes and Nonsymbolic Interaction." *Journal of Educational Sociology* 9:515–23.

———. 1937. "Social Psychology," Chapter IV, Pp. 144–98 in *Man and Society*, edited by Emerson P. Schmitt. Englewood-Cliffs, NJ: Prentice-Hall.

———. 1939. "Collective behavior." Pp. 219–88 in *Principles of Sociology*, edited by Robert E. Park. New York: Barnes & Noble. Pagination here from *Principles of Sociology*, second edition (1946), edited by Alfred. McClung Lee. New York: Barnes & Noble.

———. 1957. "Collective Behavior." Pp. 127–158 in *Review of Sociology*, edited by Joseph B. Gittler. New York: Wiley.

———. 1969. *Symbolic Interaction*. Englewood-Cliffs, NJ: Prentice-Hall.

———. 1978. "Social Unrest and Collective Protest." Pp. 1–54 in *Studies in Symbolic Interaction*, Volume 1, edited by Norman K. Denzin. Greenwich, CT: JAI Press.

Bogardus, Emory. 1924. "Golf Galleries as a Social Group." *Sociology and Social Research* 15:270–76.

Bourbon, Tom. 1989. "Modeling Voluntary Control by Individuals and Pairs." Pp. 235–254 in *Volitional Action*, edited by Wayne Hershberger. Amsterdam: Elsevier.

Bramson, Leon. 1961. *The Political Context of Sociology.* Princeton, NJ: Princeton University Press.

Branch, Taylor. 1988. *Parting the Waters: America in the King Years 1954–1963.* New York: Simon and Schuster.

Bray, Robert, Norbert Kerr, and Robert Akin. 1978. "Effects of Group Size, Problem Difficulty and Sex on Group Performance and Member Reactions." *Journal of Personality and Social Psychology* 36:1224–40.

Brewer, William. 1974. "There Is No Convincing Evidence for Classical or Operant Conditioning in Human Beings." Pp. 1–42 in *Cognition and the Symbolic Processes*, edited by W. B. Weimer and D. S. Palermo. Hillsdale, NJ: Erlbaum.

Bruner, Jerome. 1983. *Child's Talk: Learning to Use Language.* New York: Norton.

Bruno, Jerry and Jeff Greenfield. 1971. *The Advance Man.* New York: Bantam.

Bryan, John. 1981. "Implications for Codes and Behavior Models from the Analysis of Behavior Response Patterns in Fire Situations." College Park, MD: Department of Fire Protection Engineering, College of Engineering, University of Maryland.

———. 1982. "An Examination and Analysis of the Dynamics of Human Behavior in the MGM Grand Hotel Fire: Clark County, Nevada November 21, 1980." Washington, DC: National Fire Protection Association.

Burden, Hamilton. 1967. *The Nuremberg Party Rallies: 1923–1939.* New York: Praeger.

Burrage, Michael and David Corry. 1981. "Occupational Status in 14th-17th Century London." *American Sociological Review* 46:375–92.

Canetti, Elias. 1960. *Crowds and Power.* New York: Continuum.

Canter, David, ed. 1980. *Fires and Human Behaviour.* New York: Wiley.

Chomsky, Noam. 1959. "A Review of B. F. Skinner's *Verbal Behavior.*" *Language* 35:26–58.

Clark, H. 1916. "The Crowd." *Psychological Monographs* 21:26–36.

Clark, Terry. 1969. *Gabriel Tarde: On Communication and Social Influence.* Chicago: University of Chicago Press.

Clark, Walter Van Tilburg. 1940. *The Ox-Bow Incident.* New York: New American Library.

Clelland, Donald, Thomas Hood, C. M. Lipsey, and, Ronald Wimberly. 1974. "In the Company of the Converted: Characteristics of a Billy Graham Crusade Audience." *Sociological Analysis* 35:45–56.

Collins, Randall. 1981. "On the Microfoundations of Macrosociology." *American Journal of Sociology* 86:984–1014.

Cottrell, Leonard. 1971. "Covert Behavior in Interpersonal Interaction." *Proceedings of the American Philosophical Society* 115:462–69.

Couch, Carl J. 1968. "Collective Behavior: An Examination of Some Stereotypes." *Social Problems* 15:310–22.

———. 1970. "Dimensions of Association in Collective Behavior Episodes." *Sociometry* 33:457–71.

————. 1984. "Symbolic Interaction and Generic Sociological Principles." *Symbolic Interaction* 7:1–13.

Crawley, A. E. 1918. "Processions and Dances." *Encyclopedia of Religion and Ethics* 10:356–62.

Currie, Elliot and Jerome Skolnick. 1972. " A Critical Note on Conceptions of Collective Behavior." Pp. 60–71 in *Collective Violence*, edited by James F. Short Jr. and Marvin E. Wolfgang Chicago: Aldine.

Darley, John, A. Teger, and L. Lewis. 1973. "Do Groups Always Inhibit Individuals' Responses to Potential Emergencies?" *Journal of Personality and Social Psychology* 26:295–99.

Davis, Susan G. 1986. *Parades and Power.* Philadelphia: Temple University Press.

Denzin, Norman K. 1968. "Collective Behavior in Total Institutions: The Case of the Metal Hospital and Prison." *Social Problems* 15:535–65.

Dewey, John. 1896. "The Reflex Arc Concept in Psychology." *Psychological Review* 3:357–70.

Diener, Edward. 1977. "Deindividuation: Causes and Consequences." *Social Behavior and Personality* 5:143–55.

————. 1980. "Deindividuation: The Absence of Self-Awareness and Self-Regulation in Group Members." Pp. 209–44 in *Psychology of Group Influence*, edited by Paul B. Paulus. Hillsdale, NJ: Erlbaum.

Dollard, John, Leonard Doob, Neal Miller, Herbert Mowrer, and Robert Sears. 1939. *Frustration and Aggression.* New Haven, CT: Yale University Press.

Drabeck, Thomas. 1986. *Human System Responses to Disaster: An Inventory of Sociological Findings.* New York: Springer-Verlag.

Duncan, Starkey and Donald Fiske. 1977. *Face to Face Interaction.* New York: Halsted.

Durkheim, Emile. 1895. *The Rules of Sociological Method.* New York: Free Press.

————. 1912. *The Elementary Forms of Religious Life.* [English translation by Joseph Ward Swain, (1915).] New York: Macmillan.

Dynes, Russell R. and E. L. Quarantelli. 1968. "Group Behavior Under Stress: A Required Convergence of Organizational and Collective Behavior Perspectives." *Sociology and Social Research* 52:416–28.

Edgerton, Robert B. 1979. *Alone Together: Social Order on an Urban Beach.* Berkeley: University of California Press.

Edney, Julian J., and Nancy L. Jordan-Edney. 1974. "Territorial Spacing on a Beach." *Sociometry* 37:92–104.

Eisinger, Peter. 1973. "The Conditions of Protest Behavior in American Cities." *American Political Science Review.* 67:11–28.

Ekman, Paul. 1982. *Emotion in the Human Face*, second edition. Cambridge: University of Cambridge Press.

Elms, Alan C., and Stanley Milgram. 1966. "Personality Characteristics Associated with Obedience and Defiance Toward Authoritative Command." *Journal of Experimental Research on Personality* 2:282–89.

Elsner, Henry. 1972. "Introduction." Pp. vii–xxv in *Robert E. Park: The Crowd and The Public and Other Essays*, translated by Charlotte Elsner, edited by Henry Elsner. Chicago: The University of Chicago Press.

Erickson, P. E. and J. Flynn. 1980. "Police Control During a National Political Convention." *Qualitative Sociology* 3:272–98.

Evans, Robert. 1969. *Readings in Collective Behavior.* Chicago: Rand-McNally.

Evans, Robert and Jerry Miller. 1975. "Barely An End in Sight." Pp. 401–17 in *Readings in Collective Behavior,* second edition, edited by Robert Evans. Chicago: Rand-McNally.

Faris, Robert E. L. 1972. *Chicago Sociology: 1920–1932.* Chicago. University of Chicago Press.

Feinberg, William and Norris Johnson. 1988. "'Outside Agitators' and Crowds: Results from a Computer Simulation Model." *Social Forces* 67:398–423.

Festinger, Leon, Anthony Pepitone, and Theodore Newcomb. 1952. "Some Consequences of Deindividuation in a Group." *Journal of Abnormal and Social Psychology* 47:382–89.

Fine, Sidney. 1969. *Sit-In.* Ann Arbor: University of Michigan Press.

Fisher, Charles D. 1972. "Observing a Crowd: The Structure and Description of Protest Demonstrations." Pp. 187–211 in *Research on Deviance,* edited by Jack D. Douglas. New York: Random House.

Franzoni, Roberto. 1987. "The Press as a Source of SocioHistorical Data: Issues in the Methodology of Data Collection from Newspapers." *Historical Methods* 20(Winter):5–16.

Freud, Sigmund. 1921. *Group Psychology and Analysis of the Ego.* London: International Psychoanalytical Press.

Fritz, Charles E. and J. H. Mathewson. 1957. *Convergence Behavior in Disasters.* Washington: National Academy of Sciences-National Research Council, Publication 476.

Gambrell, Richard. 1979. "Displays of Arousal in Audience Settings." Paper presented at the annual meeting of the American Sociological Association, Boston.

Gamson, William. 1975. *The Strategy of Social Protest.* Homewood, IL: Dorsey.

Gamson, William, Bruce Fireman and Steven Rytina. 1982. *Encounters With Unjust Authority.* Homewood, IL: Dorsey.

Garrow, David J. 1978. *Protest at Selma.* New Haven: Yale University Press.

Geen, Russell and Leonard Berkowitz. 1967. "Some Conditions Facilitating the Occurrence of Aggression After the Observation of Violence." *Journal of Personality* 35:666–76.

Geen, Russell and Michael Quanty. 1977. "This Catharsis of Aggression: An Evaluation of a Hypothesis." Pp. 1–37 in *Advances in Experimental Social Psychology,* Volume 10, edited by L. Berkowitz. New York: Academic Press.

Geyer, R. Felix and Johannes van der Zouwen. (eds.) 1978. *Sociocybernetics.* Leiden: Martinus Niihoff.

Gibbs, Jack. 1965. "Norms: The Problem of Definition and Classification." *American Journal of Sociology* 70:586–94.

Goffman, Erving. 1963. *Behavior in Public Places.* New York: Free Press.

———. 1971. *Relations in Public.* New York: Basic Books.

———. 1983. "The Interaction Order." *American Sociological Review* 48:1–17.

Gould, Stephen Jay. 1990. "Taxonomy as Politics." *Dissent* 38 (Winter):73–78.

Gouldner, Alvin W. 1970. *The Coming Crisis of Western Sociology.* New York: Basic Books.

Granovetter, Mark. 1978. "Threshold Models of Collective Behavior." *American Journal of Sociology* 82:1420–43.

Graumann, Carl F. and Serge Moscovici. (eds.) 1986. *Changing Conceptions of the Crowd Mind*. New York: Springer-Verlag.

Gray, Thomas. 1750. "Elegy Written in a Country Churchyard." Pp. 331–35 in *The English Poets*, Volume II, edited by Thomas Humphry Ward (1892). London: MacMillian.

Greer, David. 1983. "Spectator Booing and the Home Advantage." *Social Psychology Quarterly* 46:252–61.

Griffith, C. R. 1921. "A Comment Upon the Psychology of the Audience." *Psychological Monographs* 30:36–47.

Gurr, Theodore. 1968. "Urban Disorder: Perspectives from the Comparative Study of Civil Strife." Pp. 51–67 in *Riots and Rebellion: Civil Violence in the Urban Community*, edited by Louis H. Masotti and Don R. Bowen. Beverly Hills: Sage Publications.

Guten, Sharon and Vernon L. Allen. 1972. "Likelihood of Escape, Likelihood of Danger, and Panic Behavior." *The Journal of Social Psychology* 87:29–36.

Hare, Paul. 1981. "Group size." *American Behavioral Scientist.* 24:696–708.

Harrison, Sally. 1984. "Drawing a Circle in Washington Square [Park]." *Studies in Visual Communication* 10:68–83.

Hastorf, Albert and Hadley Cantril. 1954. "They Saw a Game: A Case Study." *Journal of Abnormal and Social Psychology* 49:129–34.

Heritage, John and David Greatbatch. 1986. "Generating Applause: A Study of Rhetoric and Response at Party Political Conferences." *American Journal of Sociology* 92:110–57.

Hovland, Carl and Robert Sears. 1940. "Minor Studies of Aggression: VI. Correlation of Lynchings with Economic Indices." *Journal of Psychology* 9:301–10.

Hraba, Joseph. 1985. "Consumer Shortages in Poland: Looking Beyond the Queue into a World of Making Do." *The Sociological Quarterly* 26:387–404.

Huie, William Bradford. 1965. *Three Lives for Mississippi*. New York: WCC Publishing Company.

Jackman, Norman R. 1957. "Collective Protest in Relocation Centers." *American Journal of Sociology* 63:264–72.

Jacobsen, E. 1931. "Electrical Measurements of Neuromuscular states During Mental Activities." *American Journal of Physiology* 97:200–09.

———. 1973. "Electrophysiology of Mental Activities and Introduction to the Psychological Process of Thinking." Pp. 3–24 in *The Psychophysiology of Thinking*, edited by J. McGuigan and R. A. Schoonover. New York: Academic Press.

James, John. 1951. "A Preliminary Study of the Size Determinant in Small Group Interaction." *American Sociological Review* 16:474–7.

———. 1953. "The Distribution of Free-Forming Small Group Size." *American Sociological Review* 18:569–70.

Jenkins, J. Craig. 1983. "Resource Mobilization Theory and the Study of Social Movements." *Annual Review of Sociology* 9:527–553.

Johnson, Norris. 1987a. "Panic at 'The Who' Concert 'Stampede': An Empirical Assessment." *Social Problems* 34:362–73.

———. 1987b. "Panic and the Breakdown of Social Order: Popular Myth, Social

Theory, Empirical Evidence." *Sociological Focus* 20:171–83.

———. 1988. "Fire in a Crowded Theater." *International Journal of Mass Emergencies and Disasters* 6:7–26.

Johnson, Norris and William Feinberg. 1977. "A Computer Simulation of the Emergence of Consensus in Crowds." *American Sociological Review* 42:505–21.

———. 1989. "Crowd Structure and Process: Theoretical Framework and Computer Simulation Model." Pp. 49–86 in *Advances in Group Processes,* Volume 6, edited by Edward Lawler and Barry Markovsky. Greenwich, CT: JAI Press.

Johnson, Norris, David Choate and William Bunis. 1984. "Attendance at a Billy Graham Crusade: A Resource Mobilization Approach." *Sociological Analysis* 45:383–92.

Johnson, Weldon. 1971. "The religious crusade: revival or ritual?" *American Journal of Sociology* 76:873–90.

Kamal, Ahmad. 1961. *The Sacred Journey: Pilgrimage to Makkah.* New York: Duell, Sloan and Pearce.

Keating, John. 1982. "The Myth of Panic." *Fire Journal* 77:57–61, 147.

Kendon, Adam. 1982. "The Organization of Behavior in Face-to Face Interaction." Pp. 440–505 in *Handbook of Methods in Nonverbal Behavior Research,* edited by Klaus Scherer and Paul Ekman. Cambridge: Cambridge University Press.

King, Martin Luther Jr. 1958. *Stride Toward Freedom.* New York: Harper and Row.

Klapp, Orrin. 1972. *Currents of Unrest: Introduction to Collective Behavior.* New York: Holt, Rinehart and Winston.

Knowles, Eric and Rodney Bassett. 1976. "Groups and Crowds as Social Entities: Effects of Activity, Size, and Member Similarity on Non-Members." *Journal of Personality and Social Psychology* 38:837–45.

Kritzer, Herbert. 1977. "Political Protest and Political Violence." *Social Forces* 55:630–40.

Landsman, Gail. 1978. "The Ghost Dance and the Policy of Land Allotment." *American Sociological Review* 43:162–66.

Lane, Christel. 1976. *The Rites of Rulers.* Cambridge: Cambridge University Press.

Lang, Kurt and Gladys Engel Lang. 1960. "Decision for Christ: Billy Graham in New York City." Pp. 415–27 in *Identity and Anxiety,* edited by Maurice R. Stein, Arthur J. Vidich and David M. White. Glencoe, IL: Free Press.

Lang, Kurt and Gladys Engel Lang. 1961. *Collective Dynamics.* New York: Crowell.

Lang, Kurt and Gladys Engel Lang. 1968. "Collective Behavior." Pp. 556–64 in *International Encyclopedia of the Social Sciences,* second edition, edited by David Sills. New York: MacMillan.

Larson, Knud, Don Coleman, Jim Forbes and Robert Johnson. 1972. "Is the Subject's Personality or the Experimental Situation a Better Predictor of a Subject's Willingness to Administer Shock to a Victim?" *Journal of Personality and Social Psychology* 22:287–95.

Latane, Bibb and John Darley. 1970. *The Unresponsive Bystander.* New York: Appleton-Century-Crofts.

Latane, Bibb and Judith Rodin. 1969. "A Lady in Distress: Inhibiting Effects of Friends and Strangers on Bystander Intervention." *Journal of Experimental Social Psychology* 15:189–202.

Laurentin, Rene. 1977. *Catholic Pentacostalism* Garden City, NJ: Doubleday.

LeBon, Gustav. 1895. *Psychologie des Foules*. Paris: Alcan. [English translation (1896), *The Psychology of the Crowd*, London. Pagination here from the English edition, New York: Viking, (1960).]

Leibowitz, Martin. 1968. "Queues." *Scientific American* 219:96–103.

Levy, Sheldon and William Fenley. 1979. "Audience Size and Likelihood and Intensity of Response During Humorous Movie." *Bulletin of the Psychonomic Society* 13:409–12.

Lewis, Jerry. 1982. "Fan violence." Pp. 175–206 in *Research on Social Problems and Public Policy*, Volume 2, edited by Michael Lewis. Greenwich, CT: JAI Press.

Lieberson, Stanley and Arnold R. Silverman. 1965. "The Precipitants and Underlying Conditions of Race Riots." *American Sociological Review* 30:887–98.

Lofland, John. 1981. "Collective Behavior: The Elementary Forms." Pp. 411–46 in *Social Psychology*, edited by Morris Rosenberg and Ralph H. Turner. New York: Basic Books.

———. 1982a. *Crowd Lobbying*. Davis: University of California at Davis, Institute of Governmental Affairs.

———. 1982b. "Crowd Joys." *Urban Life* 10:355–81.

———. 1985. *Protest: Studies of Collective Behavior and Social Movements*. New Brunswick, NJ: Transaction Books.

Lofland, John and Michael Fink. 1982. *Symbolic Sit-Ins*. Washington: University Press of America.

Lohman, Joseph. 1947. *The Police and Minority Groups*. Chicago: Chicago Park District.

Long, David E. 1979. *The Hajj Today: A Survey of the Contemporary Makkah Pilgrimage*. Albany: SUNY-Albany Press.

Loy, John and D. S. Andrews. 1981. "They Also Saw a Game: A Replication of a Case Study." *Replications in Social Psychology* 1:45–49.

Lukes, Steven. 1975. "Political Ritual and Social Integration." *Sociology* 9:289–308.

MacAloon, John. 1984. "Olympic Games and the Theory of Spectacle." Pp. 241–80 in *Rite, Drama, Festival, Spectacle*, edited by John MacAloon. Philadelphia: Institute for the Study of Human Issues.

MacCannell, Dean. 1973. "Nonviolent Action as Theater," Nonviolent Action Research Project Monograph Series No. 10, Haverford College for the Century of Nonviolent Conflict Resolution, Haverford, PA.

Mackay, Charles. 1852. *Extraordinary Popular Delusions and the Madness of Crowds*. London: Office of the National Illustrated Library. [Re-issued (1980) by Farrar, Straus and Giroux, New York.]

Manchester, William. 1964. *Death of a President*. New York: Arbor House.

Mann, Leon. 1969. "Queue Culture: The Waiting Line as a Social System." *American Journal of Sociology* 75:340–54.

———. 1973. "Learning to Live With Lines." Pp. 42–61 in *The Psychology of Urban Survival*, edited by John Helmer and Neal Eddington. New York: Free Press.

———. 1977. "The Effect of Stimulus Queues on Queue-Joining Behavior." *Journal of Personality and Social Psychology* 12:95–103.

Mantell, David. 1971. "The Potential for Violence in Germany." *Journal of Social Issues* 27:101–12.

Marken, Richard. 1980. "The Cause of Control Movements in a Tracking Task." *Perceptual and Motor Skills.* 51:755–58.

———. 1986. "Perceptual Organization of Behavior: A Hierarchical Control Model of Coordinated Action." *Journal of Experimental Psychology: Human Perception and Performance.* 12:267–76.

———. 1988. "The Nature of Behavior: Control as Fact and Theory." *Behavioral Science* 33:196–206.

Mars, Florence. 1977. *Witness in Philadelphia.* Baton Rouge, LA: Louisiana State University Press.

Marsh, Peter. 1981. "Unpublished Study of Synchro-Clapping", cited in Desmond Morris, *The Soccer Tribe.* London: Jonathan Cape.

Martin, Everett Dean. 1920. *The Behavior of Crowds: A Psychological Study.* New York: Harper and Brothers.

Marx, Gary. 1980. "Conceptual Problems in the Field of Collective Behavior." Pp. 258–74 in *Sociological Theory and Research,* edited by Hubert M. Blalock. New York: Free Press.

Mayer, A. 1903. "Uber Einzel- and Gesamtleistung des Shulkindes." *Arch. ges. Psychol.* 1:276–416 [Cited in Floyd Allport, *Psychology,* (1924) Boston: Houghton-Mifflin.]

McAdam, Doug. 1982. *Political Process and the Development of Black Insurgency.* Chicago: University of Chicago Press.

———. 1983. "Tactical Innovation and the Pace of Insurgency." *American Sociological Review* 48:735–54.

McCarthy, John and Mayer Zald. 1973. *The Trend of Social Movements in America: Professionalism and Resource Mobilization.* Morristown, NJ: General Learning Press.

———. 1977. "Resource Mobilization and Social Movements: A Partial Theory." *American Journal of Sociology* 82:1212–41.

McDougall, William. 1908. *Introduction to Social Psychology.* London: Methuen.

McDowell, Jennifer. 1974. "Soviet Civil Ceremonies." *Journal for the Scientific Study of Religion* 13:265–79.

McGovern, James R. 1982. *Anatomy of a Lynching: The Killing of Claude Neal.* Baton Rouge: Louisiana State University Press.

McGuire, William. 1985. "Attitudes and Attitude-Change." Pp. 233–346 in *Handbook of Social Psychology,* Volume II, third edition, edited by Gardner Lindzey and Elliot Aranson. New York: Random-House, Third Edition.

McHugh, Peter. 1968. *Defining the Situation.* Indianapolis: Bobbs-Merrill.

McLoughlin, William G. 1959. *Modern Revivalism.* New York: Ronald.

McPhail, Clark. 1969. "Student Walkout: An Examination of Elementary Collective Behavior." *Social Problems* 16:441–55.

———. 1971. "Civil Disorder Participation." *American Sociological Review* 36:1058–72.

———. 1972. "Theoretical and Methodological Strategies for the Study of Individual and Collective Behavior Sequences." Paper presented at the annual meeting of the American Sociological Association, New Orleans.

———. 1978. "Toward a Theory of Collective Behavior." Paper presented at the annual meeting of the Society for the Study of Symbolic Interaction, University of South Carolina at Columbia.

———. 1983. "The Origins of Gatherings, Demonstrations and Riots." Paper presented at the annual meeting of the Midwest Sociological Society, Kansas City.

———. 1985. "The Social Organization of Demonstrations." Paper presented at the annual meeting of the American Sociological Association, Washington, DC.

———. 1986. "Toward a Meadean theory of Individual and Collective Behavior: The Cybernetic Extension." Paper presented at the annual meeting of the Midwest Sociological Society, Des Moines.

———. 1987. "Social behavior in Public Places: From Clusters to Arcs and Rings." Paper presented at the annual meeting of the American Sociological Association, Chicago.

———. 1988. "Micro-Macro Levels and Units of Analysis in the Study of Collective Behavior and Collective Action." Paper presented at the annual meeting of the American Sociological Association, Atlanta.

———. 1989a. "Meadian vs. Neo-Meadian Theories of Mind." *Symbolic Interaction* 12:43–51.

———. 1989b. "Blumer's Theory of Collective Behavior." *The Sociological Quarterly* 30:401–23.

McPhail, Clark and Jane Bailey. 1979. "The Assembling Process: A Procedure for and the Results of a Replication." Revision of a paper presented at the annual meeting of the Midwest Sociological Society, Minneapolis.

McPhail, Clark and David L. Miller. 1973. "The Assembling Process: a Theoretical and Empirical Examination." *American Sociological Review* 38:721–35.

McPhail, Clark and Robert Pickens. 1975. "The Explananda of Collective Behavior." Paper presented at the annual meeting of the American Sociological Association, Denver.

———. 1981. "Variation in Spectator Crowd Behavior: The Illusion of Unanimity." Paper presented at the annual meeting of the American Sociological Association, Toronto.

McPhail, Clark and Cynthia Rexroat. 1979. "Mead vrs. Blumer: The Divergent Methodological Perspectives of Social Behaviorism vs. Symbolic Interactionism." *American Sociological Review* 44:449–67.

———. 1980. "Ex Libris Mead or Ex Cathedra Blumer?" *American Sociological Review* 45:420–29.

McPhail, Clark and Charles W. Tucker. 1990. "Purposive Collective Action." *American Behavioral Scientist* 34:81–94.

McPhail, Clark and Ronald Wohlstein. 1982. "The Use of Film for Studying Pedestrian Behavior." *Social Methods and Research* 10:347–75.

———. 1983. "Individual and Collective Behavior Within Gatherings, Demonstrations, and Riots." *Annual Review of Sociology* 9:579–600.

———. 1986. "Collective Behavior as Collective Locomotion." *American Sociological Review* 51:447–63.

Mead, George Herbert. 1922. "A Behavioristic Account of the Significant Symbol." *Journal of Philosophy* 19:157–63.

———. 1924. "Genesis of the Self and Social Control." *International Journal of Ethics*, 35:251–77.

———. 1936. "The Problem of Society." Pp. 360–85 in *Movements of Thought in the Nineteenth Century*, edited by Merritt H. Moore. Chicago: University of Chicago Press.

————. 1938. *The Philosophy of the Act.* Chicago: University of Chicago Press.

Meeker, William B. and Theodore X. Barber. 1971. "Toward an Explanation of Stage Hypnosis." *Journal of Abnormal Psychology* 77:61–70.

Melbin, Murray. 1969. "Behavior Rhythms in Mental Hospitals." *American Journal of Sociology* 74:650–65.

Melucci, Alberto. 1990. *Nomads of the Present: Social Movements and Individual Needs in Modern Society.* Philadelphia: Temple University Press.

Merton, Robert K. 1987. "Three Fragments from a Sociologist's Notebooks: Establishing the Phenomenon, Specified Ignorance, and Strategic Research Materials." *Annual Review of Sociology* 13:1–28.

Meyer, Katherine and John Seidler. 1978. "The Structure of Gatherings." *Sociology and Social Research* 63:131–53.

Milgram, Stanley. 1961. "Nationality and Conformity." *Scientific American* 206:45–52.

————. 1963. "Behavioral Study of Obedience." *Journal of Abnormal and Social Psychology* 67:371–78.

————. 1964. "Group Pressure and Action Against a Person." *Journal of Abnormal and Social Psychology* 69:137–43.

————. 1965a. "Liberating Effects of Group Pressure." *Journal of Personality and Social Psychology* 2:127–34.

————. 1965b. "Some Conditions of Obedience and Disobedience to Authority." *Human Relations* 18:57–76.

————. 1974. *Obedience to Authority.* New York: Harper.

Milgram, Stanley and Hans Toch. 1969. "Collective Behavior: Crowds and Social Movements." Pp. 507–610 in *Handbook of Social Psychology,* Volume 4, second edition, edited by Gardner Lindzey and Elliot Aronson. Reading, MA: Addison-Wesley.

Milgram, Stanley, Leonard Bickman, and William Berkowitz. 1969. "Note on the Drawing Power of Crowds." *Journal of Personality and Social Psychology* 13:79–82.

Milgram, Stanley, H. J. Liberty, R. Toledo, and J. Wackenhut. 1986. "Response to Intrusion into Waiting Lines." *Journal of Personality and Social Psychology* 51:683–89.

Miller, Abraham, Louis Bolce, and Mark Halligan. 1977. "The J-Curve Theory and the Black Urban Riots." *The American Political Science Review.* 71:964–82.

Miller, Arthur G. 1986. *The Obedience Experiments: A Case Study of Controversy in Social Science.* New York: Praeger.

Miller, Dan. 1986. "Hypnosis as Asymmetric Interaction." In *Studies in Symbolic Interaction,* Volume 8, edited by Carl J. Couch. Greenwich, CT: JAI Press.

Miller, Dan, Robert Hintz, and Carl Couch. 1975. "The Structure of Openings." *The Sociological Quarterly* 16:479–99.

Miller, David L. 1973. *Assemblage Formation: An Empirical Study.* Columbia: University of South Carolina, unpublished M.A. thesis.

————. 1985. Introduction to Collective Behavior. Belmont, CA: Wadsworth Publishing Company.

Miller, George A., Eugene Galanter, and Karl H. Pribram. 1960. *Plans and the Structure of Behavior*. New York: Holt, Rinehart and Winston.

Miller, Neal and John Dollard. 1941. *Social Learning and Imitation*. New Haven: Yale University Press.

Mintz, Alexander. 1946. "A Re-Examination of Correlations Between Lynchings and Economic Indices." *Journal of Abnormal and Social Psychology* 41:154–60.

Mischel, Walter. 1968. *Personality and Assessment*. New York: John Wiley.

Mooney, James. 1965. *The Ghost Dance Religion and the Sioux Outbreak of 1890*. Chicago: University of Chicago Press. [First published 1896.]

Morris, Aldon. 1981. "The Black Southern Sit-in Movement: An Analysis of Internal Organization." *American Sociological Review* 46:744–67.

———. 1984. *The Origins of the Civil Rights Movement: Black Communities Organizing for Change*. New York: Free Press.

Morris, Aldon and Cedric Herring. 1984. "Theory and Research in Social Movements: A Critical Review." *Annual Review of Political Science* 2:137–198.

Morris, Desmond. 1981. *The Soccer Tribe*. London: Jonathan Cape.

———. 1985. *Body Watching*. New York: Crown Publishing.

Moscovici, Serge. 1981. *L'age des foules*. Paris: Fayard. [English translation by J. C. Whitehouse (1985), *The Age of the Crowd*, Cambridge: Cambridge University Press.]

Mullins, Nicholas C. 1973. *Theories and Theory Groups in Contemporary American Sociology*. New York: Harper and Row.

Newton, James and Leon Mann. 1980. "Crowd Size as a Factor in the Persuasion Process: A Study of Religious Crusade Meetings." *Journal of Personality and Social Psychology* 39:874–83.

Nye, Robert. 1975. *The Origins of Crowd Psychology*. Beverly Hills, CA: Sage.

Ofshe, Richard, Kenneth Christman and Robert Saltz. 1981. "Obedience to Authority: Re-Analyzed and Explained." Unpublished paper, Department of Sociology, University of California at Berkeley.

Ogburn, William F. and Meyer F. Nimkoff. 1940. *Sociology*. Boston: Houghton Mifflin Company. [Cited in Neal Miller and John Dollard, *Social Learning and Imitation*, (1941) New Haven, CT: Yale University Press.]

Oki, Morihiro. 1989. *India: Fairs and Festivals*. New York: Farrar, Straus & Giroux.

Oliver, Pamela. 1989. "Bringing the Crowd Back In." Pp. 1–30 in *Research in Social Movements, Conflict and Change*, Vol. 11, edited by Louis Kriesberg. Greenwich, CT: JAI Press.

Olzak, Susan. 1989. "Analysis of Events in the Study of Collective Action." *Annual Review of Sociology* 15:119–41.

Orum, Anthony and Amy Orum. 1968. "The Class and Status Bases of Negro Student Protests." *Social Science Quarterly* 49:521–33.

O'Toole, Richard and Robert Dubin. 1968. "Baby Feeding and Body Sway: An Experiment in G. H. Mead's 'Taking the Role of the Other.' " *Journal of Personality and Social Psychology* 10:59–65.

Park, Robert E. 1904. *Masse und Publikum*. Bern: Lack and Grunau. [English translation by Charlotte Elsner (1982), edited by Henry Elsner. *The Crowd and the Public*. Chicago: University of Chicago Press.]

Park, Robert E. 1930. "Collective Behavior." Pp. 631–33 in *Encyclopedia of the*

Social Sciences, Volume 3, edited by Edwin R. A. Seligman. New York: Mac-Millan.

Park, Robert E. and Ernest W. Burgess. 1921. *Introduction to the Science of Sociology.* Chicago: University of Chicago Press.

Pauls, Jake. 1977. "Movement of people in building evacuations." Pp. 281–92 in *Human Response to Tall buildings,* edited by D. J. Conway. Stroudsburg, PA: Dowden, Hutchinson & Ross, Inc.

———. 1980. "Building Evacuation: Research Findings and Recommendations." Pp. 251–76 in *Fires and Human Behaviour,* edited by David Canter. Chichester: John Wiley & Sons.

Perry, Joseph B. and Meredith D. Pugh. 1978. *Collective Behavior: Response to Social Stress.* St. Paul. MN: West Publishing Co.

Peterson, Richard E. and John A. Bilorusky. 1971. *May 1970: The Campus Aftermath of Cambodia and Kent State.* Berkeley: Carnegie Commission on Higher Education.

Peven, Dorothy E. 1968. "The Use of Religious Revival Techniques to Indoctrinate Personnel: The Home Party Sales Organization." *The Sociological Quarterly* 9:97–106.

Pickens, Robert G. 1975. "The Explananda of Collective Behavior." Unpublished Ph.D. dissertation. University of Illinois at Urbana-Champaign.

Pinard, Maurice, Jerome Kirk, and Donald von Eschen. 1969. "Processes of Recruitment in the Sit-in Movement." *Public Opinion Quarterly* 33:355–69.

Plooij, Francis. 1984. *The Behavioral Development of Free-Living Chimpanzee Babies and Infants.* Norwood, NJ: Ablex Publishing Corporation.

Pope, Liston. 1942. *Millhands and Preachers.* New Haven: Yale University Press.

Powers, William. 1973a. *Behavior: The Control of Perception.* Chicago: Aldine.

———. 1973b. "Feedback: Beyond Behaviorism." *Science* 179:351–56.

———. 1978. "Quantitative Analysis of Purposive Systems: Some Spadework at the Foundations of Scientific Psychology." *Psychological Review* 85:417–35.

———. 1979. "A Cybernetic Model for Research in Human Development." Pp. 11–66 in Mark Ozer (ed) *A Cybernetic Approach to the Assessment of Children.* Boulder: Westview Press.

———. 1988. "An Outline of Control Theory." Pp. 253–93 in *Living Control Systems: Selected Papers of William T. Powers.* Gravel Switch, KY: Control Systems Theory Group, Inc.

Quanty, Michael. 1976. "Aggression and Catharsis: Experimental Investigations and Implications." In *Perspectives on Aggression,* edited by Russell Geen and E. C. O'Neal. New York: Academic Press.

Quarantelli, E. L. 1954. "The Nature and Conditions of Panic." *American Journal of Sociology* 60:267–75.

———. 1957. "The Behavior of Panic Participants." *Sociology and Social Research* 41:187–94.

———. 1960. "Images of Withdrawal Behavior in Disasters." *Social Problems* 8:68–79.

———. 1981. "Panic Behavior in Fire Situations." Pp. 405–28 in *Proceedings of the Japan Panel on Fire Research and Safety.* Tokyo: Ministry of Construction.

Quarantelli, E. L. and Russell Dynes. 1968. "Looting In Civil Disorders: An Index of

Social Change." Pp. 131–41 in *Riots and Rebellion*, edited by Louis Masotti and Don R. Bowen. Beverly Hills, CA: Sage.

———. 1970. "Property Norms and Looting." *Phylon* 31:168–82.

Quarantelli, E. L. and James Hundley. 1969. "A Test of Some Propositions About Crowd Formation and Behavior." Pp. 538–54 in *Readings in Collective Behavior*, edited by Robert Evans. Chicago: Rand-McNally.

Quarantelli, Enrico L. and Jack M. Weller. 1974. "The Structural Problems of a Sociological Specialty: Collective Behavior's Lack of a Critical Mass." *Social Problems* 8:68–79.

Rai, Raghu. 1986. "Kumbh Mela: Nectar of the Gods." *India Today* (May 15):74–84.

Raiffa, Howard. 1970. *Decision Analysis*. Reading, MA: Addison-Wesley.

Raines, Howell. 1977. *My Soul is Rested*. New York: Bantam.

Raper, Arthur. 1933. *The Tragedy of Lynching*. Chapel Hill, NC: University of North Carolina Press.

Reed, John Shelton. 1969. "A Note on the Control of Lynching." *Public Opinion Quarterly* 33:268–71.

Reicher, S. D. 1984. "The St. Pauls' Riot: An Explanation of the Limits of Crowd Action in Terms of a Social Identity Model." *European Journal of Social Psychology* 14:1-21.

Rigney, Ernest G. 1972. "A Behavioral Examination of Compliance." Unpublished M.A. thesis. Department of Sociology, Columbia: University of South Carolina.

———. 1982. "The Production of Nonconformity within an Experimental Setting." Unpublished Ph.D. dissertation. Department of Sociology, University of Illinois at Urbana-Champaign.

Rosen, George. 1968. *Madness in Society.* New York: Harper.

Rosenberg, Bruce. 1970. *The Art of the American Folk Preacher*. New York: Oxford University Press.

Rosnow, Ralph L. and Gary Alan Fine. 1976. *Rumor and Gossip: The Social Psychology of Hearsay.* New York: Elsevier.

Ross, E.A. 1908. *Social Psychology.* New York: MacMillan.

Rossi, Pasquale. 1904. *Sociologica e psicologia collettiva*. [Cited in Howard Becker and Harry Barnes, *Social Thought From Lore to Science*, (1961). New York: Dover.]

Rude, George. 1964. *The Crowd in History, 1730-1848*. New York: Wiley.

Samarin, William J. 1972. *Tongues of Men and Angels: The Religious Language of Pentacostalism*. New York: MacMillan.

Sampson, Samuel Frank. 1968a. "Crisis in the Cloisters: A Sociological Analysis." Unpublished Ph.D. dissertation. Department of Sociology, Cornell University, Ithica, New York.

———. 1986b. "The Effects of Selected Social Relationships on the Resolution and Maintenance of Dissensus in the Autokinetic Situation." Paper presented at the annual meeting of the American Sociological Association, Boston.

Sarbin, Theodore. 1950. "Contributions to Role-Taking Theory: I. Hypnotic Behavior." *Psychological Review* 57:255–70.

Schegloff, Emanuel A. 1968. "Sequencing of Conversational Openings." *American Anthropologist* 70:1075–95.

Seidler, John, Katherine Meyer, and Lois MacGillivray. 1977. "Collecting Data on Crowds and Rallies: A New Method of Stationary Sampling." *Social Forces* 55:507–18.

Sharp, Gene. 1973. *The Politics of Non-Violent Action. II. The Methods*. Boston: Porter-Sargent.

Sherif, Muzafer. 1936. *The Psychology of Social Norms*. New York: Harper.

———. 1966. *In Common Predicament: Social Psychology of Intergroup Conflict and Cooperation*. Boston: Houghton-Mifflin.

Sherif, Muzafer and O. J. Harvey. 1952. "A Study in Ego Functioning: The Elimination of Stable Anchorages in Individual and Group Situations." *Sociometry* 15:272–305.

Sherif, Muzafer and Carolyn Sherif. 1953. *Groups in Harmony and Tension*. New York: Harper and Row.

Shibutani, Tamotsu. 1966. *Improvised News: A Sociological Study of Rumor*. Indianapolis, IN: Bobbs-Merrill.

———. 1968. "A Cybernetic Theory of Motivation." Pp. 330–36 in *Modern Systems Research for the Behavioral Scientist*, edited by Walter Buckley. Chicago: Aldine.

Shils, Edward. 1980. "Tradition, Ecology and Institution in the History of Sociology." Pp. 165–258 in *The Calling of Sociology*, edited by Edward Shils. Chicago: University of Chicago Press.

Sighele, Scipio. 1891. *Psychologie des Sectes*. Paris: Giard et Briere. [Cited in Howard Becker and Harry Barnes, *Social Thought: From Lore to Science*, (1961). New York: Dover.]

———. 1894. *La Foule Criminelle*. Paris: Alcan. Cited in Howard Becker and Harry Barnes, [*Social Thought: From Lore to Science*. (1961). New York: Dover.]

Silva, J. M. and J. A. Andrew. 1987. "Analysis of Game Location and Basketball Performance in the Atlantic Coast Conference." International Journal of Sport Psychology 18:188–204.

Sime, Jonathan D. 1980. "The Concept of Panic." Pp. 63–82 in *Fires and Human Behavior*, edited by David Canter. New York: Wiley.

Simmel, E. C., R. A. Hoppe, and G. A. Milton. 1968. *Social Facilitation and Imitative Behavior*. Boston: Allyn and Bacon.

Singer, Benjamin. 1970. "Mass Media and Communication Processes in the Detroit Riot of 1967." *Public Opinion Quarterly* 34:236–45.

Skolnick, Jerome. 1969. *The Politics of Protest: A Report Submitted to the National Commission on the Causes and Prevention of Violence*. Washington, D.C.: U.S. Government Printing Office.

Smead, Howard. 1986. *Blood Justice: The Lynching of Mack Charles Parker*. New York: Oxford University Press.

Smelser, Neil. 1963. *Theory of Collective Behavior*. New York: Free Press.

———. 1964. "Theoretical Issues of Scope and Problems." *The Sociological Quarterly* 5:116–21.

Smith, Don. 1976. "Primary Group Interaction in Panic Behavior: A Test of Theories." Paper presented at the annual meeting of the Southern Sociological Society, Miami Beach.

Smith, Herman. 1981. "Territorial Spacing on a Beach Revisited: A Cross-National Exploration." *Social Psychology Quarterly* 44:132–7.

Smith, Michael. 1983. *Violence and Sport*. Toronto: Butterworth.

Smith, Richard L. 1971. "Reflexive Behavior: An Experimental Examination of G. H. Mead's Treatment of Vocal Gestures." Unpublished M.A. thesis, University of South Carolina, Columbia.

Smith, Richard L., Clark McPhail and Robert G. Pickens. 1975. "Reactivity to Systematic Observation with Film: A Field Experiment." *Sociometry* 38:536–50.

Snow, David, Louis Zurcher and Robert Peters. 1981. "Victory Celebrations as Theater: A Dramaturgical Approach to Crowd Behavior." *Symbolic Interaction* 4:21–42.

Snyder, David. 1979. "Collective Violence Processes: Implications for Disaggregated Theory and Research." Pp. 35–61 in *Research in Social Movements, Conflicts and Change*, Volume 2, edited by Louis Kriesberg. Greenwich, CT: JAI Press.

Snyder, David and Charles Tilly. 1972. "Hardship and Collective Violence in France, 1830–1960." *American Sociological Review* 37:520–32.

Spanos, Nicholas P. 1982. "A Social Psychological Approach to Hypnotic Behavior." Pp. 231–271 in *Integrations of Clinical and Social Psychology*, edited by Gifford Weary and Herbert L. Mirels. New York: Oxford University Press.

Spanos, Nicholas P. and Theodore X. Barber. 1974. "Toward a Convergence in Hypnosis Research." *American Psychologist* 29 (July):500–11.

Spanos, Nicholas P., Martin W. Ham, and Theodore X. Barber. 1973. "Suggested ('Hypnotic') Visual Hallucinations: Experimental and Phenomenological Data." *Journal of Abnormal Psychology* 81:96–106.

Spilerman, Seymour. 1970. "The Causes of Racial Disturbances: A Comparison of Alternative Explanations." *American Sociological Review* 35:627–49.

———. 1976. "Structural Characteristics of Cities and the Severity of Racial Disorders." *American Sociological Review*. 41:771–93.

Stark, Rodney. 1972. *Police Riots*. Belmont, CA: Wadsworth.

Stewart, Robert L. 1981a. "What George Herbert Mead Should Have Said: Exploration of a Problem of Interpretation." *Symbolic Interaction* 4:157–66.

———. 1981b. "Meadian Motion: Toward a Behavioral Behavior Science." Paper presented at the annual meeting of the Midwest Sociological Society, Minneapolis.

Stewart, Robert L. and Charles W. Tucker. 1983. "Research for What? Notes on Mead's Pragmatic Theory of Truth." Revision of a (1979) Paper Presented at the Third Conference on Social Behaviorism, Notre Dame University.

Swanson, G. E. 1953. "A Preliminary Laboratory Study of the Acting Crowd" *American Sociological Review* 18:522–33.

Taft, Philip and Philip Ross. 1968. "American labor violence: causes, character, and outcome." Pp. 270–376 in *Violence in America*, edited by Hugh D. Graham and Ted R. Gurr. New York: New American Library.

Tarde, Gabriel. 1890. *The Laws of Imitation*. New York: Henry Holt. [English translation by Elsie Clews Parson, (1903).]

———. 1892. "The Crimes of Crowds" [Cited in *Gabriel Tarde: On Communication and Social Influence*, edited by Terry Clark. (1969). Chicago: University of Chicago Press.]

_____. 1893. "Crowds and Sects from the Point of View of the Criminal." *Revue des Deux Mondes* [Cited in *Gabriel Tarde: On Communication and Social Influence*, edited by Terry Clark. (1969). Chicago: University of Chicago Press.]

_____. 1898. "The Public and the Crowd." *La Revue de Paris* 4:287. [Cited in *Gabriel Tarde: On Communication and Social Influence*, edited by Terry Clark. (1969). Chicago: University of Chicago Press.]

_____. 1901. *Opinion and the Crowd*. Selected English translations by Terry Clark (1969), in *Gabriel Tarde: On Communication and Social Influence*, edited by Terry Clark. Chicago: University of Chicago Press.

Tarrow, Sidney. 1983. "Struggling to Reform: Social Movements and Policy Change During Cycles of Protest." Cornell University Center for International Studies Occasional paper No. 15, Ithaca, New York.

Tarrow, Sidney. 1989. *Democracy and Disorder: Protest and Politics in Italy 1965–1975*. New York: Oxford University Press.

Thornton, Robert. 1971. "The Kidotai: The Mobile [Riot] Task Forces of Japan." *The Police Chief* 18:65–73.

Tierney, Kathleen. 1980. "Emergent Norm Theory as 'Theory': An Analysis and Critique of Turner's Formulation." Pp. 42–53 in *Collective Behavior: A Source Book*, edited by Meredith Pugh. St. Paul, MN: West Publishing Co.

Tilly, Charles. 1975. "Major Forms of Collective Action in Western Europe." University of Michigan Center for Research on Social Organization. Working Paper Number 123, Ann Arbor.

_____. 1978. *From Mobilization to Revolution*. Reading, MA: Addison-Wesley.

_____. 1979. "Repertoires of Contention in American and Britain: 1750–1820." Pp. 126–55 in *The Dynamics of Social Movements*, edited by Mayer Zald and John McCarthy. Cambridge, MA: Winthrop.

_____. 1981. *As Sociology Meets History*. New York: Academic Press.

Tilly, Charles, Louise Tilly, and Richard Tilly. 1975. *The Rebellious Century: 1830–1930*. Cambridge, MA: Harvard University Press.

Tomlinson, Graham. 1981. "The Comedic Performance: An Interactive Analysis." Unpublished Ph.D. dissertation, University of Indiana, Bloomington.

Triplett, Norman. 1898. "The Dynamogenic Factors in Pacemaking and Competition." *American Journal of Psychology* 9:507–33.

Tucker, Charles W. and Robert L. Stewart. 1989. "Science, Self and Symbolic interaction." Pp. 45–60 in *Studies in Symbolic Interaction*, Volume 10, edited by Norman K. Denzin. Greenwich, CT: JAI Press.

Turner, Ralph. 1964a. "Collective Behavior." Pp. 382–425 in *Handbook of Modern Sociology*, edited by Robert E. L. Faris. Chicago: Rand-McNally.

_____. 1964b. "New Theoretical Frameworks." *The Sociological Quarterly* 5:122–132.

_____. 1967. "Introduction," Pp. ix-xl *Robert E. Park: On Social Control and Collective Behavior*, edited by Ralph Turner. Chicago: University of Chicago Press.

Turner, Ralph and Lewis Killian. 1957. *Collective Behavior*. Englewood-Cliffs, NJ:Prentice-Hall.

_____. 1972. *Collective Behavior*, second edition. Englewood-Cliffs, NJ: Prentice-Hall.

_____. 1987. *Collective Behavior,* third edition. Englewood-Cliffs, NJ: Prentice-Hall.

Vandall, Frank. 1973. "Riot Prevention: Police Training for the Street Gathering." *Journal of Urban Law* 51:49–68.

Van Gennep, Arnold. 1909. *The Rites of Passage.* Chicago: University of Chicago Press, (1960 English translation).

Wallace, Walter. 1969. *Sociological Theory.* Chicago: Aldine.

_____. 1983. *Principles of Scientific Sociology.* New York: Aldine.

Wanderer, Jules. 1968. "1967 Riots: A Test of the Congruity of Events." *Social Problems* 16:191–98.

_____. 1969. "An Index of Riot Severity and Some Correlates." *American Journal of Sociology* 74:500–505.

Wechsberg, Joseph. 1945. "My Life in the Claque." Pp. 70–80 in *Looking for a Bluebird,* by Joseph Wechsberg. Boston: Houghton.

Weller, Jack and E. L. Quarantelli. 1973. "Neglected Characteristics of Collective Behavior." *American Journal of Sociology* 79:665–85.

Wenger, Dennis E., James D. Dykes, Thomas D. Sebok, and Joan L. Neff. 1975. "It's a Matter of Myths: An Empirical Examination of Individual Insight into Disaster Response." *Mass Emergencies* 1:33–46.

Wheeler, Ladd. 1966. "Toward a Theory of Behavioral Contagion." *Psychological Review* 73:179–92.

Wheeler, Ladd and John Arrowood. 1966. "Restraints Against Imitation and their Reduction." *Journal of Experimental Social Psychology* 2:288–300.

Wheeler, Ladd and Anthony Caggiula. 1966. "The Contagion of Aggression." *Journal of Experimental Social Psychology* 2:1–10.

Wheeler, Ladd and Seward Smith. 1967. "Censure of the Model in the Contagion of Aggression." *Journal of Personality and Social Psychology* 6:93–98.

Whitam, Frederick L. 1968. "Revivalism As Institutionalized Behavior: An Analysis of the Social Base of a Billy Graham Crusade." *Social Science Quarterly* 49:115–127.

Whitfield, Steven. 1988. *A Death in the Delta: The Story of Emmett Till.* New York: Free Press.

Whyte, William Hollingswood. 1980. *The Social Life of Small Urban Spaces.* Washington, DC: The Conservation Foundation.

Wicker, Alan. 1969. "Attitudes vs. Action." *Journal of Social Issues* 25:41–78.

Wiener, Norbert. 1948. *Cybernetics.* Cambridge, MA: MIT Press.

_____. 1954. *The Human Use of Human Beings: Cybernetics and Society.* Garden City, NY: Doubleday Anchor.

Williams, Daniel T. 1970. "The Lynching Records [1882–1969] at Tuskegee Institute." Number 7, 39 pages, in *Eight Negro Bibliographies,* edited by Daniel T. Williams. New York: Kraus Reprint Company.

Wilson, Kenneth and Anthony Orum. 1976. "Mobilizing People for Collective Political Action." *Journal of Political and Military Sociology* 4:187–202.

Wimberly, Ronald, Thomas Hood, C. M. Lipsey, Donald Clelland, and Marguerite Hay. 1975. "Conversion in a Billy Graham Crusade: Spontaneous Event or Ritual Performance." *The Sociological Quarterly* 16:162–70.

Woelfel, Joseph, John Woelfel, James Gillham and Thomas McPhail. 1974. "Political Radicalization as a Communication Process." *Communications Research* 1:243–63.

Wohlstein, Ronald T. 1977a. "The Theoretical and Methodological Specification and Description of Collective Locomotion." Unpublished Ph.D. dissertation, University of Illinois at Urbana-Champaign.

———. 1977b. "Filming Collective Behavior and the Problem of Foreshortened Perspective: A Corrective Method." *Studies in Visual Communication* 4:81–5.

Wohlstein, Ronald T. and Clark McPhail. 1979. "Judging the Presence and Extent of Collective Behavior from Film Records." *Social Psychology Quarterly* 42:76–81.

Woolbert, C. H. 1916. "The Audience." *Psychological Monographs* 21:36–54.

Wright, Sam. 1978. *Crowds and Riots: A Study in Social Organization*. Beverly Hills, CA: Sage Publications.

Young, Frank. 1966. "A Proposal for Cooperative Cross-Cultural Research on Intervillage Systems." *Human Organization* 25:46–50.

Young, Kimball. 1927. *Source Book for Social Psychology*. New York: F. S. Crofts and Co. [Cited in Neal Miller and John Dollard, *Social Learning and Imitation*, (1941) New Haven, CT: Yale University Press.]

Zajonc, Robert. 1965. "Social Facilitation." *Science* 149:269–74.

Zillman, Dolph, Jennings Bryant and Barry Sapolsky. 1979. "The Enjoyment of Watching Sports Contests." Pp. 297–335 in *Sports, Games, and Play*, edited by Jeffrey Goldstein. Hillsdale, NJ: Erlbaum.

Zimbardo, Phillip. 1969. "Individuation, Reason and Order vs. Deindividuation, Impulse, and Chaos." In *Nebraska Symposium on Motivation*, Volume 17, edited by W. J. Arnold and D. Levine. Lincoln: University of Nebraska Press.

Author Index

Subject Index